Fusion

Integrated Reading and Writing

Book 2

KEMPER / MEYER / VAN RYS / SEBRANEK   Second Edition

Dave Kemper

Verne Meyer
Dordt College

John Van Rys
Redeemer University College

Pat Sebranek

CENGAGE
Learning·

Australia • Brazil • Mexico • Singapore • United Kingdom • United States

W9-BCI-731

CENGAGE
Learning®

Fusion: Integrated Reading and Writing,
Book 2, Second Edition
Dave Kemper, Verne Meyer,
John Van Rys, and Pat Sebranek

Vice President, General Manager,
Developmental Studies: Liz Covello

Senior Product Manager: Shani Fisher

Senior Content Developer:
Marita Sermolins

Associate Content Developer:
Elizabeth Rice

Associate Content Developer:
Kathryn Jorawsky

Media Developer: Elizabeth Neustaetter

Marketing Manager: Necco McKinley

Senior Content Project Manager:
Rosemary Winfield

Senior Art Director: Linda May

Manufacturing Planner: Betsy Donaghey

IP Analyst: Ann Hoffman

IP Project Manager: Farah Fard

Compositor: Sebranek, Inc.

Production & Managing Editor: Tim Kemper
(Sebranek, Inc.)

Designer: Mark Lalumondier
(Sebranek, Inc.)

Cover Image: Leigh Prather, 2014 / Used
under license from Shutterstock.com

Library of Congress Control Number: 2014952470

ISBN-13: 978-1-305-10370-2

ISBN-10: 1-305-10370-X

Cengage Learning
20 Channel Center Street
Boston, MA 02210
USA

Cengage Learning is a leading provider of customized learning solutions
with office locations around the globe, including Singapore, the United
Kingdom, Australia, Mexico, Brazil, and Japan. Locate your local office at
www.cengage.com/global.

Cengage Learning products are represented in Canada by Nelson
Education, Ltd.

For your course and learning solutions, visit **www.cengage.com**.

Purchase any of our products at your local college store or at our preferred online store **www.cengagebrain.com**.

Printed in the United States of America
Print number: 01   Print year: 2014

Fusion 2 Brief Contents

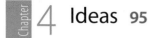

Chapter **5** **Organization** **145**

bopav, 2014 / Used under license from Shutterstock.com

Part 3: Types of Reading and Writing 249

Chapter 8 Reading and Writing Narrative Texts 251

Erlo Brown, 2014 / Used under license from Shutterstock.com

Part 4: Research 343

Chapter 11 Understanding Research 345

pisaphotography, 2014 / Used under license from Shutterstock.com

Chapter 12 **Research Report** 361

wavebreakmedia, 2014 / Used under license from Shutterstock.com

Part 5: Sentence Workshops 383

Chapter 13 Sentence Basics 385

hxdbzxy, 2014 / Used under license from Shutterstock.com

Chapter 14 Simple, Compound, and Complex Sentences 401

Robsonphoto, 2014 / Used under license from Shutterstock.com

18 Pronoun 463

FiledIMAGE, 2014 / Used under license from Shutterstock.com

19 Verb 473

Kristina Vackova, 2014 / Used under license from Shutterstock.com

20 Adjective and Adverb 491

CHAINFOTO24, 2014 / Used under license from Shutterstock.com

zeljkodan, 2014 / Used under license from Shutterstock.com

Preface

Fusion reflects the way instructors want to teach the integrated developmental reading and writing course. We know because we asked.

Informed by instructors from across the country, *Fusion: Integrated Reading and Writing, Book 2*, connects the reading and writing processes so that students learn to use the processes hand-in-hand. High-interest readings encourage students to participate in discussions and think critically. Students can then generate thoughtful writing that combines what they have learned with their own thinking about their topics. Strategies for analyzing readings and producing writing prepare students for their future college courses.

> *Fusion* combines an integrated approach to teaching both curriculums, focusing on the integration of reading and writing. The strength of the text is the integrated approach throughout the text, educating students on how and why teaching the curriculum in an integrated approach helps them be successful in all other course work. The authors of the textbook are longtime educators in the field of developmental reading and writing, and their expertise is evident throughout the content. This approach allows other educators to create a rich, pedagogically sound curriculum for their own students."
>
> Ulanda Forbess, North Lake College

> *Fusion* does not allow students or instructors to separate reading and/from writing. It shows the relationship between the two and helps students understand how one impacts the other. For an undertaking that was quite intimidating (teaching reading and writing together), this text has certainly helped lessen the load and demonstrates how such a blended approach is possible."
>
> Jenny Beaver, Rowan-Cabarrus Community College

> With feedback from students, I have taken the best ways I teach writing and the best ways I teach reading and integrated them together to create a completely new course that focuses on skill proficiency and critical thinking. *Fusion* helps me to accomplish this by reinforcing concepts I teach in the classroom and providing students with ample opportunities to study examples of content and apply these newly learned skills in their reading/writing assignments."
>
> Kina Lara, San Jacinto College South

> *Fusion* is as much a process for teaching reading and writing as it is a textbook. It shows students the clear connection between reading and writing while also demonstrating that the critical thinking, reading, and writing skills they learn are transferable to other academic areas. Its logical organization is what makes the process of teaching reading and writing a bit easier."
>
> Kim Davis, Oakland Community

Presenting a More Integrated Approach to Reading and Writing

Integrated reading and writing courses are challenging to teach because of the breadth of material to be covered in the time allotted, but with *Fusion* students are provided with the instruction needed to understand how reading and writing are interconnected. The Table of Contents has been restructured based on feedback from instructors across the country to better model the close relationship between reading and writing.

■ **Parallel reading and writing strategies are introduced in Chapter 1: "The Reading-Writing Connection."** Students are introduced to the five shared features of reading and writing assignments: *subject*, *purpose*, *audience*, *type* and *role*.

Similarly, students learn how to apply the traits of writing to their critical reading and writing: *ideas*, *organization*, *voice*, *word choice*, *sentence fluency*, and *conventions*.

■ **NEW Chapter 2: "Approaches to Reading and Writing" sets the stage for the integrated reading and writing in *Fusion*.** Students are introduced to the reading and writing processes and important strategies such as annotating, note taking, and summarizing that students need to apply to their reading and writing projects.

■ **NEW Part 2: "Reading and Writing Essays" brings new emphasis to the integration of reading and writing.** Chapters 4 through 7 introduce students to important traits common to reading and writing—ideas, organization, coherence, and voice—and offer strategies for reading for these traits and for applying them in writing.

Providing Skills Needed for Future Coursework

When students complete their work in *Fusion*, they will have acquired the necessary reading and writing competencies needed for future coursework.

■ **NEW Summarizing skills coverage and reinforcement.** Chapter 2 addresses the importance of summarizing reading material. With guidelines, models, and multiple opportunities to practice summarizing with the Enrichment readings, students gain a strategy to apply to any challenging reading they will encounter in the future.

■ **NEW Part 3: "Types of Reading and Writing" focuses on the kinds of reading and writing assignments students are likely to encounter in their future college courses.** Students are given strategies for reading and writing narratives, expository texts, and arguments. Relevant grammar instruction is provided within the context of the students' own writing. Additional grammar instruction and practice appears in the Workshops in Parts 5 through 7.

“ [This edition is] a more integrated approach to reading and writing. Teaching the interconnectedness of the content will help students understand from the very beginning of the course how these two subject matters are related."

Ulanda Forbess, North Lake College

Integrating Key Reading and Writing Course Objectives

Common Course Objectives	Where This Is Covered in *Fusion*
■ Use reading and writing strategies to draw conclusions and clearly articulate an analysis.	See the Enrichment feature at the end of all chapters, Part 3: "Types of Reading and Writing," and Part 8: "Readings for Writers." All provide prompts for thinking and writing critically.
■ Critically read and respond to a variety of texts, demonstrating the ability to draw inferences and analyze information.	See Chapter 3: "Critical Thinking and Viewing." Students learn to consider basic thinking patterns, ask critical questions, and use analysis and evaluation strategies. See Chapter 4: "Ideas," where drawing inferences is covered.
■ Understand and use appropriate vocabulary in conjunction with clear and logical development of ideas to demonstrate reading comprehension.	See Chapter 2: "Approaches to Reading and Writing" for detailed instruction for writing summaries, as well as Part 2: "Reading and Writing Essays," where students learn how to apply important traits to their reading and writing. Vocabulary practice is reinforced with every reading.
■ Select and apply the appropriate rhetorical strategies in both reading and writing.	See Part 3: "Types of Reading and Writing," where students learn how to apply strategies to read and write narratives, explanatory texts, and arguments.
■ Identify audience and purpose; employ effective brainstorming strategies, gather relevant information, and integrate the ideas and words of other writers.	See Chapters 1 and 7, where identifying audience and purpose are discussed. In Part 4: "Reading and Writing Research" students learn how to find, evaluate, and incorporate sources of information into their writing.
■ Utilize revision strategies to ensure college-level work.	Part 3: "Types of Reading and Writing" features revising and editing instruction in context for narrative, expository, and argumentative writing. Part 5: "Sentence Workshops," Part 6: "Word Workshops," and Part 7: "Punctuation and Mechanics Workshops" provide additional grammar practice.
■ Read a wide variety of reading selections.	Part 8: "Readings for Writers" features selections demonstrating a variety of topics, voices, and patterns of organization. Each reading is accompanied by pre- and post-reading questions that emphasize reading and writing strategies.

Fostering Engagement and Critical Thinking

Fusion provides a selection of readings designed to capture students' attention and inspire higher levels of thinking. Each reading is supported by new critical thinking prompts to help students shape their own thoughtful responses to the text. In addition, the selections enrich college-ready vocabulary skills and serve as models of the types of reading and writing expected of them in their college courses.

- **Many NEW readings in the Enrichment sections** cover topics such as:

    Political Science: "America Through Foreign Eyes: Hyperpower or Hapless Power?" (page 87)

    Current Events: "Stop Panicking About Bullies" (page 175)

    History: "Remarks at the Brandenburg Gate" (page 318)

- **NEW Part 8: "Readings for Writers" offers an anthology of readings that can be used to foster critical thinking, discussion, and writing opportunities.** The readings vary in length, demonstrate different patterns of organization, and offer unique perspectives on timely topics. High-interest topics include:

    Ecology: "American Campuses Get Greener than Ever" (page 563)

    Immigration: "Undocumented Students Walk the 'Trail of Dreams'" (page 580)

    Health: "The Homeless Brother I Cannot Save" (page 559)

- **Chapter 3: "Critical Thinking and Viewing" outlines the skills needed to become critical readers and writers.** Students are introduced to deductive and inductive thinking, as well as more advanced analytical and evaluative thinking. Students also learn to ask critical questions and view visuals critically.

- **NEW Summarizing and Critical Thinking prompts.** Summarizing prompts have been included after the Enrichment readings so that students can practice this skill often. Also included are critical thinking prompts to challenge students to formulate their own thoughts about the readings.

- **A focus on vocabulary practice builds an academic vocabulary for future coursework.** While challenging words are defined, integrated vocabulary prompts encourage students to practice defining words. Chapter 2: "Approaches to Reading and Writing" provides guidelines and practice for using a dictionary, context clues, and word parts.

> ❝ I love this textbook! And so do the students. It works as a confidence builder and resource all in one. A great refresher for the returning student who has been out of academia for a number of years as well as a tutorial and reference for ELLs. Plus there are interesting readings that demonstrate the principles being studied and practiced. I wish we had more time to spend with the textbook (class is seven weeks)."
>
> Marcia Hines-Colvin, Saint Mary's University Minnesota

Promoting Skills Development and Tracking Learning Outcomes

The integrated reading and writing course is often a new environment for instructors, and *Fusion* provides the perfect resource and guide for such a course.

- **NEW MindTap is a fully online, highly personalized learning experience built upon** *Fusion: Integrated Reading and Writing, Book 2.* MindTap combines student learning tools—an interactive ebook, instructive animations, additional readings, video instruction, pre-built flashcards, practice activities, and assessments—into a singular Learning Path that guides students through their course. Instructors personalize the experience by customizing authoritative Cengage Learning content and learning tools with their own content in the Learning Path via apps that integrate into the MindTap framework. Engaging assignments powered by **Aplia**™ reinforce key concepts and provide students with the practice they need to build fundamental reading, writing, and grammar skills.

    - **Teaches and promotes study skills in students**—highlighting and note taking—a skill often needing attention in this course, but usually little time left to devote to it
    - **Addresses students' busy lives**—students can listen to chapters via the ReadSpeaker app while on-the-go, and watch course videos in the small bursts of time that they have
    - **Allows students to prepare for class ahead of class time** so that class time can be spent working together through reading and writing strategies

    ❝ Having the forward notice of what will be addressed in the next class is most beneficial to students. Students have that time to preview, complete a reading quiz, and come into the next class ready to 'flesh' it out with other students and the instructor."

    Sarah Bruton, Fayetteville Technical Community College

- **Aplia™ for *Fusion*.** Through diagnostic tests, succinct instruction, and engaging assignments, Aplia™ for *Fusion: Integrated Reading and Writing* reinforces key concepts and provides students with the practice they need to build fundamental reading, writing, and grammar skills:

    - Diagnostic tests provide an overall picture of a class's performance, allowing instructors to instantly see where students are succeeding and where they need additional help.
    - Assignments include immediate and constructive feedback, reinforcing key concepts and motivating students to improve their reading and writing skills.
    - Grades are automatically recorded in the Aplia grade book, keeping students accountable while minimizing time spent grading.

- **The Individualized Study Path (ISP).** An ISP course generates a personalized list of assignments for each student that is tailored to his or her specific strengths and weaknesses. ISP assignments are randomized, auto-graded problems that correspond to skills and concepts for a specific topic. Students get as much help and practice as they require on topics where they are weak. Conversely, if there are topics they understand well, no remediation is necessary and no additional assignments will be present.

- **Instructor Manual and Test Bank.** The Instructor Manual and Test Bank is located on the Instructor Companion Site in a convenient printable format. This supplement features a wealth of resources for course enrichment, including
    - test bank material: chapter quizzes, a midterm exam, and a final exam;
    - detailed sample syllabi, including syllabi mapped to North Carolina, Texas, and Virginia state objectives;
    - a variety of writing prompts to be used in class or as homework assignments;
    - a success story about how Aplia and *Fusion* can be used together in the classroom; and
    - a guide to teaching ESL learners using *Fusion*.

- **Cognero®.** Cengage Learning testing powered by Cognero® is a flexible, online system that allows you to author, edit, and manage test-bank content from multiple Cengage Learning solutions, including the quizzes and exams available on *Fusion*'s Instructor Companion Site. Multiple test versions can be created in an instant, and tests can be delivered from your LMS or your classroom.

- **Instructor Companion Site.** Access the Instructor's Manual and Test Bank, and PowerPoint slides organized around topics covered in the book with a high-level chapter overview, as well as an opening and closing activity.

- **Write Experience 2.0.** Students need to learn how to write well in order to communicate effectively and think critically. Cengage Learning's Write Experience provides students with additional writing practice without adding to your workload. Utilizing artificial intelligence to score student writing instantly and accurately, it also provides students with detailed revision goals and feedback on their writing to help them improve. Write Experience is powered by e-Write IntelliMetric Within—the gold standard for automated scoring of writing—used to score the Graduate Management Admissions Test (GMAT) analytical writing assessment. Visit www.cengage.com/writeexperience to learn more.

- **Course Redesign for Developmental Education.** Course Redesign is one of the latest trends impacting the landscape of higher education and developmental studies. Cengage Learning's trained consultants, instructional designers, subject matter experts, and educational researchers offer a variety of services to guide you through the process of redesigning your curriculum. Combining that with a wealth of powerful digital and print offerings allows us to personalize solutions to your state or institution's needs. Contact your Learning Consultant to learn more about these services or visit www.cengage.com/services.

Customizing *Fusion* to Tailor Your Course Materials

As the integrated reading and writing course continues to evolve, Cengage Learning can address your unique course needs. It's possible to align your course materials with custom solutions that deliver the content you want in your preferred style and format. Maximize learner engagement by:

- adding, rearranging, and/or removing content.
- combining content from multiple sources.
- integrating supplements.
- simplifying access to digital resources.

Cengage Learning offers a variety of products, both online and in print, to expand the reading selections to be used with *Fusion*. For more information about these options, consult your Cengage Learning sales representative.

- **CourseReader.** CourseReader leverages Cengage Learning's Gale databases, including its authoritative reference content and full-text magazine and newspaper articles. The product offers instructors thousands of articles and historical documents, including both primary and secondary sources specific to their discipline, all in one location. Instructors select a series of materials from these databases for their courses, which are then compiled into an online collection for their students to access.

- **Compose.** Drawing from a vast library of educational materials including readings, cases, and labs, a custom reader is just a few clicks away with the intuitive search engine and a Custom Service and Sales team who specializes in the development of effective customized learning solutions. After selection or organizing course materials, instructors can immediately review and then publish a printed custom reading collection.

- **National Geographic Learning Readers.** *Environment: Our Impact on the Earth* and *Diversity of America* are part of a ground-breaking new National Geographic Learning series that brings learning to life by featuring compelling images, media, and text from National Geographic. Pre- and post-reading pedagogy developed especially for developmental reading and writing students accompanies each article to reinforce reading skills and comprehension. The National Geographic Learning Reading Series connects current topics with reading and writing skills and can be used in conjunction with any standard texts or online material available for your courses.

> ❝ *Fusion* is a customizable package that reaches well beyond the minimum standards of the state, emphasizing the very objectives our content instructors complain about regarding students' ability to critically analyze. With the focus on "summary" and "critical thinking," I believe our students will be much better prepared to meet the challenges that content teachers are assigning."
>
> Brian Longacre, Asheville Buncombe Technical Community College

What's New in *Fusion: Integrated Reading and Writing,* Book 2?

Global Revisions

- The Table of Contents has been restructured to better model the reciprocal relationship between reading and writing, based on feedback from instructors who are teaching integrated reading and writing courses.
- A new Part 8, "Readings for Writers," offers an anthology of readings that can be used to foster critical thinking, discussion, and various writing opportunities. Designed to engage students' interest in a variety of topics, the anthology provides flexibility to assign more reading and writing practice.
- Throughout the text, exercises have been expanded and revised to emphasize critical thinking and put critical reading and writing skills to work.
- Summary skills are introduced in Chapter 2 and reinforced with the addition of summarizing activities to the end-of-chapter Enrichment readings.

Chapter Revisions

Part I: "Reading and Writing for Success"

Chapter 1: "The Reading-Writing Connection"

- **NEW** "Reading and Writing to Learn" lays the foundation for the integration of reading and writing skills.
- **NEW** "Changing Your Attitude" emphasizes bringing a positive attitude to the classroom.
- **NEW** "Writing to Share Learning" explores writing to demonstrate learning paragraphs and essays.
- **NEW** Enrichment reading (previously in Chapter 11), "The ABC Daily To-Do List"

Chapter 2: "Approaches to Reading and Writing"

- **NEW** "Understanding the Writing Process" now follows "Understanding the Reading Process."
- **REVISED** "Using Reading and Writing Strategies" (formally "Using Basic Reading Strategies") increases the emphasis on writing as a reading tool and includes instruction on annotating, note taking, and summarizing.
- **NEW** reading, "Democracy Does Not Always Allow for Quick Solutions," to demonstrate annotating
- **REVISED** "Improving Vocabulary" has been expanded to cover dictionaries, context clues, and word parts.
- **NEW** Enrichment reading, "What the Frack? Natural Gas from Subterranean Shale Promises U.S. Energy Independence—With Environmental Costs"

Chapter 3: "Critical Thinking and Viewing"

- **NEW CHAPTER** that includes basic patterns of thinking; accessing deeper thinking; asking critical questions; evaluating for credibility, relevance, and quality (with **NEW** reading, "West Antarctic Glacier Loss Appears Unstoppable"); and viewing visuals critically.

- **NEW** Enrichment reading, "America Through Foreign Eyes: Hyperpower or Hapless Power?"

NEW Part 2: "Reading and Writing Essays"

- **Chapter 4: "Ideas"** builds the skills necessary for identifying and developing topics, reading for and developing main ideas in writing, and reading for and writing with strong supporting details.
- **Chapter 5: "Organization"** highlights the three-part structure and emphasizes the importance of organized, clear writing. The basic patterns of organization are also covered.
- **Chapter 6: "Coherence"** first addresses recognizing transitions in readings and using them in writing. The second part of the chapter addresses additional techniques for establishing coherency.
- **Chapter 7: "Voice"** addresses reading for voice and utilizing voice most effectively in writing. Types of voice are covered as well as effective word choice and sentence style.

Part 3: "Types of Reading and Writing"

Chapter 8: "Reading and Writing Narrative Texts"

- **NEW** "Forms of Narrative Writing" introduces students to a wide variety of narrative forms: personal narrative, personal essay, memoir, and anecdote.
- **REVISED** "Planning a Personal Narrative" now better integrates the writing process.
- **NEW** Enrichment reading, "Lipstick Jihad"

Chapter 9: "Reading and Writing Expository Texts"

- **NEW** chapter reviews the basic forms of exposition: illustration, definition, process, classification, cause-effect, and comparison.
- It provides a **NEW** Reading and Reacting to a Professional Exposition reading, "The Power and Glory of the Maya Queens."
- **NEW** Enrichment reading, "Hypnosis–Look into My Eyes"

Chapter 10: "Reading and Writing Arguments"

- **NEW** "Essays Related to Argumentation" reviews basic forms of argumentation: editorial, personal commentary, problem-solution essay, and position paper.
- **NEW** "Analyzing Arguments" and "Analyzing Logic" encourage students to think critically about the structure of arguments.
- **REVISED** "Common Logical Fallacies" provides more in-depth explanations of the logical fallacies that students are most likely to encounter.
- **NEW** Reading and Reacting to a Professional Argument reading, "Remarks at the Brandenburg Gate"

- REVISED "Planning an Argument Essay" covers the elements of an argument in more detail.
- NEW Enrichment reading, "The George W. Bush Presidency"

Part 5: "Word Workshops," Part 6: "Word Workshops," and Part 7: "Punctuation and Mechanics Workshops"

- REVISED and expanded exercises provide additional practice.

NEW Part 8: "Readings for Writers"

- **Chapter 27: "Anthology"** includes selections covering a wide variety of topics, modes, and patterns of organization. Readings are drawn from magazines, textbooks, newspapers, presidential remarks, and other sources so that students have the opportunity to engage with multiple sources. Each reading is accompanied by pre- and post-reading questions designed to utilize reading strategies and prompt students to think critically about their reading.

    " I am excited that summarizing activities have been worked into more areas of the textbook. I especially like that summarizing and critical thinking activities accompany all readings. I like that the Part 5 and Part 7 sections have been revised and expanded. I also like the new Part 8, which includes more reading selections and has pre-and post-reading questions. . . . Overall, I'm excited to see all of the changes."
Tiffany Daniel, Oconee Fall Line Technical College

Acknowledgements

Second Edition

A special thanks to the *Fusion* Advisory Board for all the feedback they provided related to how they teach their integrated reading and writing courses and how *Fusion* can support their students.

Jenny Beaver, Rowan-Cabarrus Community College
Sarah Bruton, Fayetteville Technical Community College
Tiffany Daniel, Oconee Fall Line Technical College
Kim Davis, Oakland Community College
Ulanda Forbess, North Lake College

Marcia Hines-Colvin, Saint Mary's University Minnesota
Kimberly Koledoye, Houston Community College
Kina Lara, San Jacinto College South
Brian Longacre, Asheville Buncombe Technical Community College

Special thanks also to the many reviewers who have helped to shape *Fusion* into the text you have before you:

Sandra Blystone, University of Texas at El Paso; Wendy Crader, Northeast Lakeview College; Kathleen Cuyler, Coastal Bend College; Leona Fisher ,Chaffey College; Marsi Franceschini, Central Piedmont Community College; Kris Giere, Ivy Tech Community College of Indiana; Scarlett Hill, Brookhaven College; Alice Kimara, Baltimore County Community College; Karen LaPanna, Collin College; Glenda Lowery, Rappahannock Community College; Irma Luna, San Antonio College; Gail Malone, South Plains College; Beth McCall, Gaston College; Annette Mewborn, Tidewater Community College; Marti Miles-Rosenfield, Collin College; Lana Myers, Lone Star College – Montgomery; Sonya Prince, San Jacinto College; Nancy Risch, Caldwell Community College and Technical Institute; Jennifer Riske, Northeast Lakeview College; Linda Robinett, Oklahoma City Community College; Robert Sandhaas, San Jacinto College South; Vanessa Sekinger, Germanna Community College; Tanya Stanley, San Jacinto College Central; Ra Shaunda Sterling, San Jacinto College; Claudia Swicegood, Rowan-Cabarrus Community College; Kelly Terzaken, Coastal Carolina Community College; Tondalaya VanLear, Dabney S. Lancaster Community College; Shari Waldrop, Navarro College; Charles Warnberg, Brookhaven College; Tina Willhoite, San Jacinto College

Previous Editions

Brenda Ashcraft, Virginia Western Community College; Teena Boone, Rowan-Cabarrus Community College; Mike Coulehan, El Paso Commuity College; Kris DeAngelis, Central Piedmont Community College; Meribeth Fields, Central Florida Community College; Cynthia Gomez, Hodges University; Eric Hibbison, J. Sargeant Reynolds Community College; Marcia Hines, Saint Mary's University of Minnesota; Alice Kimara, Baltimore City Community College; Kimberly Koledoye, Houston Community College; Kina Lara, San Jacinto College South; Alice Leonhardt, Blue Ridge Community College; Glenda Lowery, Rappahannock Community College; Breanna Lutterbie, Germanna Community College; Gail Malone, South Plains College; Deborah Maness, Wake Technical Community College; Abigail Montgomery, Blue Ridge Community College; Miriam Moore, Lord Fairfax Community College; Lana Myers, Lone Star College-Montgomery; Elizabeth Powell, Forsyth Technical Community College; Tony Procell, El Paso Community College; Robert Sandhaas, San Jacinto College South Campus; Melissa Shafner, Mitchell College; Deborah Spradlin, Tyler Jr. College; Claudia Swicegood, Rowan-Cabarrus Community College; Gene Voss, Houston Community College; Shari Waldrop, Navarro College; Dawn White, Davidson County Community College; Lori Witkowich, College of Central Florida; Wes Anthony, Cleveland Community College; Joe Antinarella, Tidewater Community College; Stacey Ariel, Santa Rosa Junior College; Margaret Bartelt, Owens Community College; Jon Bell, Pima College; Christina Blount, Lewis and Clark Community College; Mary Boudreaux, San Jacinto College; Kimberly Bovee, Tidewater Community College; Janice Brantley, University of Arkansas at Pine Bluff; Robyn Browder, Davenport University; Doris Bryant, Thomas Nelson Community College; Jennifer Call, Cape Fear Community College; Jana Carter, Montana State University Great Falls; Roberta Cohen, Union County College; Annette Dammer, Fayetteville Technical Community College; Melissa DuBrowa, Berkeley College; Arlene Edmundson, United Tribes Technical College; Mary Etter, Davenport University; Shannon Fernandes, Yakima Valley Community College; JoAnn Foriest, Prairie State College; Marty Frailey, Pima Community College; Johnanna Grimes, Tennessee State University; David Harper, Chesapeake College; Gina Henderson, Tallahassee Community College; Eric Hibbison, J. Sargeant Reynolds Community College; Donna Hill, College of the Ouachitas; Brent Kendrick, Lord Fairfax Community College; Shayna Kessel, Los Angeles City College; Sara Kuhn, Chattanooga State Community College; Glenda Lowery, Rappahannock Community College; Deborah Maness, Wake Technical Community College; Katherine McEwen, Cape Fear Community College; Carolyn Miller, Chattanooga State Community College; Miriam Moore, Lord Fairfax Community College; Ann Moser, Virginia Western Community College; Ray Orkwis, Northern Virginia Community College; Jay Peterson, Atlantic Cape Community College; Laura Powell, Danville Community College; Pam Price, Greenville Technical College; Carole Quine, Baltimore City Community College; Janet Rico Everett, Southern Arkansas University Tech; David Robinson, College of Southern Maryland; Mary S. Leonard, Wytheville Community College; Brenda Sickles, Tidewater Community College; Virginia Smith, Carteret Community College; Suba Subbarao, Oakland Community College; Claudia Swicegood, Rowan-Cabarrus Community College; Jennifer Taylor Feller, Northern Virginia Community College-Woodbridge; Nicole Tong, Northern Virginia Community College; Patricia Tymon, Virginia Highlands Community College; Kathy Tyndall, Wake Technical Community College; Julie Voss, Front Range Community College; Michelle Zollars, Patrick Henry Community College

PART 1:

Reading and Writing for Success

Part 1: Reading and Writing for Success

Tyler Olson, 2014 / Used under license from Shutterstock.com

Chapter

1

> "Meaning doesn't reside ready-made in the text or in the reader; it happens during the transaction between reader and text."
>
> —Louise Rosenblatt

The Reading-Writing Connection

If there is one profession that has always appreciated the special connection between reading and writing, it is that of the professional writer. "Read, read, read. Read everything," stated twentieth-century author William Faulkner. "There's nothing so exciting to me than to read books," states present-day novelist Toni Morrison. Writers know that reading helps them write and that their writing prompts them to read more.

As a student, you need to make your own special connection between reading and writing. You will be reading texts by experts in their fields. In order to make sense of this new information, to make it part of your own thinking, you will need to write about it. This chapter explores the reading-writing connection.

Learning Outcomes

LO1 Read and write to learn.

LO2 Write to share learning.

LO3 Understand reading and writing assignments.

LO4 Use the traits for reading and writing.

LO5 Use graphic organizers for reading and writing.

What do you think?

In the quotation, Louise Rosenblatt says that when reading, meaning happens during a "transaction between reader and text." What do you think she means by a "transaction"? And how can writing be part of that transaction?

> "The discipline of real learning consists of The Self and The Others flowing into each other."
>
> —Ken Macrorie

L01   Reading and Writing to Learn

For humans, making contact is an important aspect of communication. You make contact when you acknowledge someone with a smile, a handshake, or a hug. You make contact when you text someone or tune into a favorite television show. The list could go on and on. But to be specific to reading and writing, consider these actions.

- By focusing on reading material, you make contact with the ideas and concepts developing on the page.
- By putting fingers to the keyboard (or pen to paper), you automatically make contact with your own ideas.

What's important for you to understand is the reciprocal relationship between reading and writing. As a student, you can expect to do a great deal of reading, which means you will come in contact with many new ideas. It's unlikely that everything you read will make sense to you right away. This is where writing can truly assist you. Writing allows you to respond to a text on a personal level—to make sense of it, to agree or disagree with it, to connect it with other texts—using your own thoughts and words.

Changing Your Attitude

If you think of reading as just another assignment to complete, you will never discover it as a resource of valuable information. Likewise, if you think of writing as just another paragraph or essay to complete, you will never discover the true value of putting your thoughts on paper. Reading and writing work best when you think of them as learning tools. Reading assignments provide the important content; writing can help you engage with the content to learn from it. In fact, you can't effectively complete an academic reading assignment without employing some form of writing, even if that writing consists of nothing more than a list of ideas or a brief free writing. It's important to note that there are different reasons to write. When you write for yourself, you are writing to help yourself learn. When you write for an instructor, you are writing to show what you have learned.

Practice ▸ Write freely for five minutes, exploring how you typically carry out academic reading assignments. Think about the strategies you employ and frustrations you encounter. Then explore your feelings about writing. Consider your strengths and weaknesses as a writer and whether or not you have used writing as a learning tool.

Keeping a Class Notebook

Keeping a class notebook or journal is important if you are going to make writing an important part of your learning routine. Certainly you can take notes in this notebook, but you can also use it to explore your thoughts about your reading and about other aspects of your coursework by employing a variety of writing-to-learn strategies.

Writing-to-Learn Strategies

- **Note Taking** As you read, take notes to help you keep track of key ideas and details in the reading.

- **First Thoughts** Freely explore your first thoughts soon after you start reading. This writing gives you a point of reference for the rest of your reading and responding.

- **Status Check** Explore your thoughts during your reading. These writings help you check your understanding of the text as it develops.

- **Listing** Freely list ideas about your reading. Listing can be useful as a quick review or progress check.

- **Written Dialogues** Write an imaginary dialogue or conversation about your reading between two individuals. (You may be one of the speakers. The other speaker may be a character from the reading.) This strategy can help you sort out your thoughts about your reading.

- **Nutshelling** "Nutshell," or summarize, the importance of a reading in one sentence. Doing so clarifies your thinking about a text.

- **Pointed Questions** To help you review a text, ask yourself and answer a series of *Why?* questions.

- **Final Thoughts** Sum up your thoughts and feelings about the text. Consider what you have learned and what questions you still have about the topic.

Practice In one sentence, "nutshell" the essential message in this chapter so far.

Effective Academic Reading

Reading and learning go hand in hand. You read to learn about new concepts and ideas; you read to learn how to do something; and you read to understand the past, the present, and the future. To maximize how much you learn from your reading, follow these guidelines.

1   **Find a quiet place.** You'll need space to read and write without distractions. Quiet background music is okay if it helps you stay on task.

2   **Gather your materials.** Have on hand a notebook or laptop, related handouts, Web access, and a pen and/or highlighter if you are annotating the text.

3   **Divide the assignment into parts.** It's difficult to maintain the proper level of concentration over extended periods of time. Instead, try to read for 15-30 minutes at a time; then rest for a brief period. Use a timer to help you manage your reading.

4   **Approach your reading as a process.** Academic reading requires that you do a number of things—prereading, reading, rereading, reflecting—in a certain order.

5   **Use proven reading strategies.** For example, taking notes and annotating a text gets you actively involved in your reading and helps you learn.

6   **Identify the features of the reading.** For example, recognizing the intended audience and purpose will help you more fully appreciate the text. Use the **STRAP** strategy to do this. (See later in this chapter.)

7   **Know what to look for.** In order to understand a reading, you need to identify the main idea or thesis of the text, plus the key points and details that support it.

8   **Summarize what you have learned.** Writing a summary helps you gauge your understanding of the reading.

9   **Note questions about the text.** And more importantly, find answers to these questions as soon as you can.

10   **Review the reading and your notes.** Doing this from time to time will help you internalize the information and connect it to new concepts you are studying.

Practice Compare these ten reading guidelines to the method of reading that you normally follow. Which of these guidelines do you typically follow? Which of them do you need to employ?

LO2 Writing to Share Learning

Writing to learn is one function of writing; writing to share what you have learned is another important function. When you write to learn, you are your only audience. But when you write to share learning, your audience expands to include your instructor, your classmates, and others. When you develop assigned paragraphs, essays, and research papers, you are writing to share learning.

Understanding the Learning Connection

There is a direct link between clear thinking and developing strong writing. Writing to learn involves exploring and forming your thoughts, and writing to share involves clarifying and fine-tuning them. Figure 1.1 shows the connection between thinking and the two functions of writing.

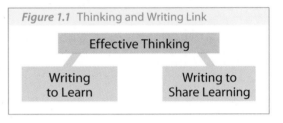

Figure 1.1 Thinking and Writing Link

Effective Thinking

Writing to Learn

Writing to Share Learning

All assigned writing projects begin with writing to learn as you read and collect your thoughts about the topic; but once you develop a first draft, your attention turns to making the writing clear, complete, and ready to share with others. Of course, writing to share learning demands more time and effort because it will be read and reviewed by your instructors and peers.

Reviewing the Range of Writing

The range of forms of writing is wide and varied, as you can see in Figure 1.2. Your college writing will likely cover the complete spectrum, with a focus on the more formal forms, such as essays and research papers.

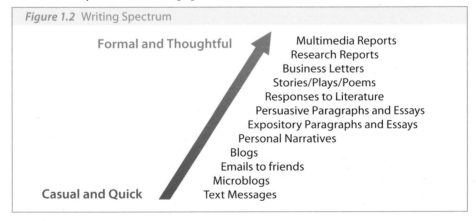

Figure 1.2 Writing Spectrum

Formal and Thoughtful

Multimedia Reports
Research Reports
Business Letters
Stories/Plays/Poems
Responses to Literature
Persuasive Paragraphs and Essays
Expository Paragraphs and Essays
Personal Narratives
Blogs
Emails to friends
Microblogs
Text Messages

Casual and Quick

Practice What forms of writing from Figure 1.2 do you most often engage in? How does your approach to writing change at different points along the spectrum?

"Easy writing makes hard reading, but hard writing makes easy reading."

—Florence King

Effective Academic Writing

When your instructors give writing assignments, they will expect you to submit finished products that are clear, complete, and correct. Following these guidelines will help you meet their expectations.

1 **Find a quiet place to work.** Writing is essentially thinking on paper. You cannot think effectively if you are distracted. Quiet background music is okay if it helps you focus on your writing.

2 **Gather your materials.** Have on hand all of your notes from your reading, the assignment guidelines, related handouts, and whatever supplies you need to write.

3 **Identify the features of the assignment.** For example, knowing the purpose of the writing and the intended audience will help you develop your work. Use the **STRAP** strategy to do this. (See later in this chapter.)

4 **Understand the dynamics of the assignment.** Know what is expected of you: when the final copy is due and how the paper will be assessed.

5 **Approach your writing as a process.** Developing academic writing requires that you do a number of things—prewriting (planning), drafting, revising, editing—before it will be ready to share. Approaching your writing one step at a time helps you do your best work.

6 **Know the basics of writing.** Your writing should form a unified whole with strongly developed beginning, middle, and ending parts. And it should be built around a thoughtful thesis statement supported with plenty of details.

7 **Collaborate.** At different points during your writing, get feedback from your classmates, writing tutors, and/or instructor. Their insights and advice will help you keep on track and produce your best work.

Practice ▸ Compare these guidelines to the method of writing that you normally follow: Which of these guidelines do you typically follow? Which of them do you need to employ?

L03 Understanding Reading and Writing Assignments

Being prepared is an important part of making good choices. For example, you would want to know the basics about a job or an internship before you applied for it. The same holds true for your college reading and writing assignments. Before you get started on your work, you should identify the main parts, including subject, purpose, audience, type (form), and the role of the writer. These two assignments will be considered for a discussion of each part:

> **Reading Assignment:** Read "Squeezing New Evidence into Old Beliefs" in your biology textbook. In this selection, the authors trace nineteenth-century theories of evolution, leading up to Charles Darwin's groundbreaking discovery. Be prepared to explain each naturalist's theory.
>
> ———————————————————————————————
>
> **Writing Assignment:** In a posting on the class blog, reflect on the importance of a specific school-related experience. Consider who was involved, what happened, and why it was significant.

Subject

The **subject** is the person, idea, event, or object being discussed or described. The terms *subject* and *topic* are often used interchangeably. Simply stated, you must identify the subject of your reading assignments; and for writing assignments, you must understand what type of subject you are expected to write about. You really can't begin either type of assignment without this information.

The subject for the reading assignment—nineteenth-century theories of evolution—is clearly identified. If that were not the case, you could identify the subject by skimming the title of the reading, the first few paragraphs, and, if needed, the first lines of other paragraphs. The subject for the writing assignment—a specific school-related experience—is clearly stated as well. If, for some reason, the subject of the writing is not clear to you, consult with your instructor before you get started.

Purpose

Purpose is the specific reason for the reading or writing. Generally, the reason for reading and writing assignments is either to inform, persuade, or share. The general purpose of a textbook, for example, is to inform the reader about a general subject. More specifically, however, the purpose may be to compare, analyze, evaluate, trace, or reflect upon.

In the reading assignment under discussion, the general purpose is to inform, but more specifically the reading is intended to trace the development of the different theories. For argumentative texts, the purpose is generally to persuade, but more specifically it may be to evaluate or review. For personal narratives and essays, the general purpose may be either to inform or to entertain, or perhaps a little bit of both, but more specifically to reflect or to analyze.

For the writing assignment under discussion, the general purpose is to inform, but more specifically, the writer must reflect upon (consider the importance) of the event. Usually, a key word in an assignment reveals the specific purpose of the writing: *Summarize* the article on vertical farming. *Explain* the results of your experiment. *Describe* your meeting with the career counselor.

Purpose Words

- **Analyze:** To examine the parts of a topic, noting any interrelationships
- **Argue:** To give reasons for or against something
- **Compare:** To point out the similarities and differences, perhaps with greater emphasis on similarities
- **Contrast:** To point out differences
- **Define:** To provide a concise or extended meaning of a topic
- **Describe:** To depict the appearance of a person, place, or thing; to give an account of; to convey an impression
- **Discuss:** To examine a topic from all sides

- **Evaluate:** To judge the value or condition of a topic in a thoughtful and careful way
- **Explain:** To make clear or easy to understand; show cause-effect relationships or a step-by-step process
- **Prove:** To give evidence to support a point
- **Review:** To re-examine the key characteristics or key points of a topic
- **Reflect:** To express carefully considered thoughts
- **Summarize:** To present the main points in a condensed, shortened form
- **Trace:** To present in sequence a series of steps or occurrences

Audience

Audience, in this case, is the intended readership for printed matter that you read or write yourself. For example, if the reading comes from a biology textbook, then, of course, biology students are the intended audience. Your instructors may also assign readings in which students may not be the primary audience—say, perhaps an article from a professional journal in which professionals in the field are the intended audience. With this information in mind, you would need to take extra care with your reading.

Since the writing assignment under discussion will be posted on the class blog, fellow students and the instructor are the intended audience. On the other hand, if you are writing in response to an exam prompt or you are developing an end-of-term research report, your instructor is the intended audience. Understanding the intended audience helps you shape your writing. When you are sharing a personal experience on a class blog, you may speak in a more relaxed style than you would when you are writing for an instructor or someone else in a position of authority.

Type

Type refers to the form of a reading selection or piece of writing to be produced. The primary type of informational readings will be textbook chapters, as is the case with the biology assignment. Textbook chapters are well organized and contain headings, subheadings, labels, glossaries, graphics, and summaries to make the information as accessible as possible. Other common forms of informational reading, such as essays, articles, and professional reports, may not be as accessible as textbook chapters because students are generally not their intended audience.

The typical types of academic writing include essays, reports, summaries, narratives, personal responses, and blog postings. Before you begin a writing project, be sure that you understand the key features of the form being assigned. For example, if your instructor assigns a blog posting, you would want to know the requirements for that type of writing.

Role **Role** refers to what position the writer assumes. For textbook reading assignments, the authors assume the role of experts in their fields. Likewise, the authors of essays or articles in respected publications assume the role as individuals knowledgeable about their topics. The qualifications of authors are provided at the beginning or the end of the textbook and respected publications. Writers in some fringe publications or questionable Web sites often try to assume positions of expertise but do not possess the qualifications to do so.

For academic writing assignments, you assume the role of a student producing essays and reports sharing what you have learned. To meet this expectation, you must approach your writing as a process requiring multiple drafts before it is ready to share. The same approach applies to any important informational writing that you produce in the workplace or community.

Using the STRAP Strategy

The first letters of the five parts of a reading or writing assignment can be arranged to spell out **STRAP**. Thinking of this word will help you remember the five parts that you should identify. Here are the main parts for the reading assignment from the biology textbook using the **STRAP** strategy.

Subject:	Nineteenth-century theories of evolution
Type:	Biology textbook selection
Role:	Authors of biology textbook
Audience:	Students
Purpose:	To inform readers about landmark work leading up to Darwin's theory

Here are the main parts for the writing assignment about the class blog posting.

Subject:	School-related experience
Type:	Class blog posting
Role:	Student in the class
Audience:	Peers and instructor
Purpose:	To inform; to reflect upon the significance of the experience

Practice Identify the main parts of the following reading assignment by answering the STRAP questions for it.

Assignment: Read "The ABC Daily To-Do List" provided in the Review and Enrichment section of this chapter. Note how the author explains a method for creating and using to-do lists. The reading comes from a textbook called *Becoming a Master Student*.

Subject: What specific topic does the reading address?

_____

Type: What form (*essay, narrative, textbook chapter*) does the reading take?

_____

Role: What position (*expert, observer, participant*) does the writer assume?

_____

Audience: Who is the intended audience?

_____

Purpose: What is the goal of the text (*to inform, to persuade, to share*)?

_____

Practice Identify the main parts of the following writing assignment by answering the STRAP questions for it.

Assignment: The ability to work in groups is important in school and in the workplace. Write an essay to share with the class in which you explain three or four group skills that students should learn and practice.

Subject: What specific topic does the writing assignment address?

_____

Type: What form (*essay, report, blog posting*) should my writing take?

_____

Role: What position (*student, citizen, family member*) should I assume?

_____

Audience: Who is the intended audience?

_____

Purpose: What is the goal of my writing (*to inform, to persuade, to share*)?

_____

L04 Using the Traits for Reading and Writing

Using the traits of writing can help you gain a full understanding of reading assignments, and they can help you develop your own paragraphs and essays. The traits identify the key elements of written language, including ideas, organization, voice, word choice, sentence fluency, and conventions.

Ideas
Informational texts are built upon a foundation of ideas. There is nothing more essential for you to remember.

When you read for ideas, you identify . . .	When you write for ideas, you develop . . .
■ the topic. ■ the thesis (main idea). ■ the key supporting details.	■ a thesis or focus. ■ your thoughts on the topic. ■ effective supporting details.

Organization
To create meaning, ideas need to be organized. Readers expect that a reading will follow a sensible pattern of organization.

When you read for organization, you identify . . .	When you write for organization, you develop . . .
■ the beginning, middle, and ending parts. ■ the organization of the supporting details.	■ an effective beginning, middle, and ending. ■ a logical presentation of supporting details.

Voice
A text also has voice, or tone, which refers to the special way the writer speaks to his or her readers. Voice reflects on the writer's attitude about the topic and text.

When you read for voice, you identify . . .	When you write for voice, you develop . . .
■ the level of the writer's interest in and knowledge about the topic.	■ a voice that sounds interesting, honest, and knowledgeable.

Word Choice
Academic texts are characterized by specific terminology related to the subject. Personal texts are characterized by more informal, casual words.

When you read for word choice, you identify . . .	When you write for word choice, you develop . . .
■ the quality of the words. (Are they interesting and clear?)	■ words that are specific, clear, and fitting for the assignment.

Sentence Fluency

Sentence Fluency The sentences carry the ideas. In order to be effective, they must flow smoothly and clearly communicate the information.

When you read for sentence fluency, you identify . . .	When you write for sentence fluency, you develop . . .
▪ the effectiveness of the sentences. (Do they flow smoothly? Are they clear?)	▪ smooth-reading, clear, and accurate sentences.

Conventions

Conventions The conventions are the rules for grammar, usage, and mechanics that produce clear and correct texts.

When you read for conventions, you identify . . .	When you write for conventions, you develop . . .
▪ to what degree the writing follows conventions (and why or why not).	▪ paragraphs or essays that follow the conventions.

Practice For a first attempt with using the traits for reading, answer the following questions for "The ABC Daily To-Do List" from the Review and Enrichment section of this chapter.

Questions to Answer for Reading

Ideas: What is the topic of this essay?
What main point is made about the topic? (Look for a thesis statement.)
What details stand out? Name two.

Organization: How does it start? What happens in the middle? How does it end?

Voice: Does the writer seem interested in and knowledgeable about the topic? Why or why not?

Practice For a first attempt with using the traits for writing, answer the following questions for this assignment:

▪ In a posting on the class blog, reflect on the importance of a specific school-related experience. Consider who was involved, what happened, and why it is significant.

Questions to Answer for Writing

Ideas: What topic will you write about?
What main point about the topic could you focus on?
What types of details could you include (explanations, examples, descriptions, personal thoughts, conversations, etc.)? Name two.

Organization: How might you start your writing? What happens in the middle? How might you end your writing?

Voice: What kind of writing voice and language will best fit this assignment?

L05 Using Graphic Organizers for Reading and Writing

Graphic organizers help you map out your thinking for writing and reading assignments. You can, for example, use a Venn diagram or a T-chart to arrange your thoughts for a comparison essay assignment or to take notes about an essay you have just read. Other common graphics help you organize your thinking for problem-solution, cause-effect, and narrative writing and reading assignments. See **Figures 1.3 through 1.11**.

Charting a Reading Selection

A time line is a basic graphic organizer used to list the key actions in a reading selection that is organized chronologically, such as a personal narrative or a historical account. A time line will not include many details or explanations. Here is a sample time line for a narrative from *Gifted Hands*, the autobiography of Ben Carson, a renowned neurosurgeon.

Figure 1.3 Narrative Time Line

Awards Day

— Carson receives an award for best student at an all-school assembly.

— The teacher who presents the award then lectures the student body.

— Her remarks imply that a black person shouldn't be number one.

— Carson sits quietly, holding in his anger and hurt.

— Several students look at him, rolling their eyes at the teacher's remarks.

Practice Use a time line to list the main actions for a narrative reading selection in *Fusion 2*.

Practice Use a time line to list the main actions for a personal essay about an important school-related experience.

Sample Graphic Organizers

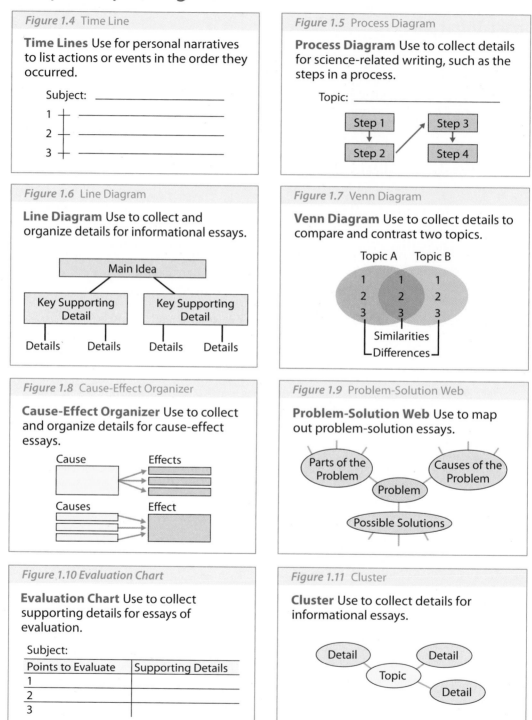

Figure 1.4 Time Line

Time Lines Use for personal narratives to list actions or events in the order they occurred.

Subject: _____

1
2
3

Figure 1.5 Process Diagram

Process Diagram Use to collect details for science-related writing, such as the steps in a process.

Topic: _____

Step 1 → Step 3
Step 2 → Step 4

Figure 1.6 Line Diagram

Line Diagram Use to collect and organize details for informational essays.

Main Idea

Key Supporting Detail

Key Supporting Detail

Details   Details   Details   Details

Figure 1.7 Venn Diagram

Venn Diagram Use to collect details to compare and contrast two topics.

Topic A   Topic B

1   1   1
2   2   2
3   3   3

Similarities
Differences

Figure 1.8 Cause-Effect Organizer

Cause-Effect Organizer Use to collect and organize details for cause-effect essays.

Cause   Effects

Causes   Effect

Figure 1.9 Problem-Solution Web

Problem-Solution Web Use to map out problem-solution essays.

Parts of the Problem   Causes of the Problem

Problem

Possible Solutions

Figure 1.10 Evaluation Chart

Evaluation Chart Use to collect supporting details for essays of evaluation.

Subject:

Points to Evaluate	Supporting Details
1	
2	
3	

Figure 1.11 Cluster

Cluster Use to collect details for informational essays.

Detail   Detail

Topic

Detail

☑ Review **and** Enrichment

Reviewing the Chapter

Read and Write to Learn

1. Why can reading and writing be considered learning tools?

2. What are pointed questions, and how can they help you learn?

Write to Share Learning

3. How is writing to share learning different from writing to learn?

4. What are two formal forms of writing?

Understand Reading and Writing Assignments

5. What is the **STRAP** strategy?

6. What does each letter in **STRAP** stand for?

Use the Traits for Reading and Writing

7. What traits of writing should you address in reading and writing assignments?

8. Which trait deals with the main idea of writing?

Use Graphic Organizers for Reading and Writing

9. How can graphic organizers help you with your reading and writing assignments?

"Education is not a product: mark, diploma, job, money—in that order; it is a process, a never-ending one."

—Bel Kaufman

Reading for Enrichment

You will be reading a selection from *Becoming a Master Student* that provides directions for creating and using "to-do" lists to help you manage daily tasks. Use the guidelines for "Effective Academic Reading" to help you carry out your reading.

About the Author

Dave Ellis is an author, an educator, a workshop leader, and a lecturer. His book *Becoming a Master Student* is a best seller in its 15th edition, and it is used by students in the United States and in several other countries. He has coauthored other books on subjects such as human effectiveness and career planning.

Consider the Traits

As you read this selection, consider the **ideas**: What process is he explaining, and does he provide plenty of details? Also note the **organization** of the text: Does the design and structure help you follow the process? Finally, note the author's **voice**: Does he sound interested in helping you, or is he simply presenting information?

Prereading

People in all walks of life establish processes to complete tasks. Chefs determine the best sequence to incorporate ingredients into their signature dishes; coaches break down fundamental skills into teachable steps; software developers provide step-by-step directions for downloading their newest products. List two other examples of processes established in different professions. Then list two processes that you have established for yourself.

On-the-job processes:

_____

_____

Personal processes:

_____

_____

What do you think?

Novelist Bel Kaufman says that education is a process. How is that so? And how is it never-ending?

Before you read, answer the **STRAP** questions to identify the main features of the assignment.

Subject: What specific topic does the reading address?

Type: What form (*essay, narrative, textbook selection*) does the reading take?

Role: What position (*concerned individual, observer, participant, educator*) does the writer assume?

Audience: Who is the intended audience?

Purpose: What is the general goal of the reading (*to inform, to persuade, to entertain*)?

Reading and Rereading

As you read, make it your goal to (1) identify the topic, (2) confirm the purpose and audience, and (3) pay careful attention to the steps in the process. Consider taking notes to help you remember important points. Reread as needed to confirm your understanding of the text and to analyze its ideas and organization.

The Reading Process

Prereading   Rereading

Reading   Reflecting

The ABC Daily To-Do List

One advantage of keeping a daily to-do list is that you don't have 1 to remember what to do next. It's on the list. A typical day in the life of a student is full of separate, often unrelated tasks—reading, attending lectures, reviewing notes, working at a job, writing papers, researching special projects, running errands. It's easy to forget an important task on a busy day. When that task is written down, you don't have to rely on your memory.

The following steps present one method for creating and using 2 to-do lists. This method involves ranking each item on your list according to three levels of importance—A, B, and C. Experiment with these steps, modify them as you see fit, and invent new techniques that work for you.

Step 1: Brainstorm tasks

To get started, list all of the tasks you want to get done 3 tomorrow. Each task will become an item on a to-do list. Don't worry about putting the entries in order or scheduling them yet. Just list everything you want to accomplish on a sheet of paper or planning calendar or in a special notebook. You can also use 3x5 cards, writing one task on each card. Cards work well because you can slip them into your pocket or rearrange them, and you never have to copy to-do items from one list to another.

Step 2: Estimate time

For each task you wrote down in Step 1, estimate how long it   4
will take you to complete it. This can be tricky. If you allow too little time, you end up feeling rushed. If you allow too much time, you become less productive. For now, give it your best guess. If you are unsure, overestimate rather than underestimate how long it will take you for each task. Overestimating has two benefits: (1) It avoids a schedule that is too tight, missed deadlines, and the resulting feelings of frustration and failure; and (2) it allows time for the unexpected things that come up every day—the spontaneous to-dos. Now pull out your calendar or Time Monitor/Time Plan. You've probably scheduled some hours for activities such as classes or work. This leaves the unscheduled hours for tackling your to-do lists.

Add up the time needed to complete all your to-do items. Also   5
add up the number of unscheduled hours in your day. Then compare the two totals. The power of this step is that you can spot overload in advance. If you have eight hours' worth of to-do items but only four unscheduled hours, that's a potential problem. To solve it, proceed to Step 3.

Step 3: Rate each task by priority

To prevent over-scheduling, decide which to-do items are the   6
most important, given the time you have available. One suggestion for making this decision comes from the book *How to Get Control of Your Time and Your Life* by Alan Lakein: Simply label each task A, B, or C.

The A's on your list are those things that are the most critical.   7
They include assignments that are coming due or jobs that need to be done immediately. Also included are activities that lead directly to your short-term goals.

The B's on your list are important, but less so than the A's. B's   8
might someday become A's. For the present, these tasks are not as urgent as A's. They can be postponed, if necessary, for another day.

The C's do not require immediate attention. C priorities include 9 activities such as "shop for a new blender" and "research genealogy on the Internet." C's are often small, easy jobs with no set time line. They, too, can be postponed.

Once you've labeled the items on your to-do list, schedule time 10 for all of the A's. The B's and C's can be done randomly during the day when you are in between tasks and are not yet ready to start the next A.

Step 4: Cross off tasks

Keep your to-do list with you at all times. Cross off activities 11 when you finish them, and add new ones when you think of them. If you're using 3x5 note cards, you can toss away or recycle the cards with completed items. Crossing off tasks and releasing cards can be fun—a visible reward for your diligence. This step fosters a sense of accomplishment.

When using the ABC priority method, you might experience 12 an ailment common to students: C fever. Symptoms include the uncontrollable urge to drop the A task and begin crossing C's off your to-do list. If your history paper is due tomorrow, you might feel compelled to vacuum the rug, call your third cousin in Tulsa, and make a trip to the store for shoelaces. The reason C fever is so common is that A tasks are usually more difficult or time-consuming to achieve, with a higher risk of failure.

If you notice symptoms of C fever, ask yourself, "Does this job 13 really need to be done now? Do I really need to alphabetize my CD collection, or might I better use this time to study for tomorrow's data-processing exam?" Use your to-do list to keep yourself on task, working on your A's. But don't panic or berate yourself when you realize that in the last six hours, you have completed eleven C's and not a single A. Just calmly return to the A's.

Step 5: Evaluate

At the end of the day, evaluate your performance. Look for A 14 priorities you didn't complete. Look for items that repeatedly turn up as B's or C's on your list and never seem to get done. Consider changing them to A's or dropping them altogether. Similarly, you might consider changing an A that didn't get done to a B or C priority. When you're done evaluating, start on tomorrow's to-do list. Be willing to admit mistakes. You might at first rank some items as

A's only to realize later that they are actually C's. And some of the C's that lurk at the bottom of your list day after day might really be A's. When you keep a daily to-do list, you can adjust these priorities before they become problems.

The ABC system is not the only way to rank items on your to-do list. Some people prefer the 80-20 system. This method is based on the idea that 80 percent of the value of any to-do list comes from only 20 percent of the tasks on that list. So on a to-do list of ten items, find the two that will contribute most to your life, and complete those tasks without fail. *15*

Another option is to rank items as "yes," "no," or "maybe." Do all of the tasks marked "yes." Ignore those marked "no." And put all of the "maybes" on the shelf for later. You can come back to the "maybes" at a future point and rank them as "yes" or "no." *16*

Or you can develop your own style for to-do lists. You might find that grouping items by categories such as "errands" or "reading assignments" works best. Be creative. *17*

Keep in mind the power of planning a whole week or even two weeks in advance. Planning in this way can make it easier to put activities in context and see how your daily goals relate to your long-term goals. Weekly planning can also free you from feeling that you have to polish off your whole to-do list in one day. Instead, you can spread tasks out over the whole week. *18*

In any case, make starting your own to-do list an A priority. *19*

From Ellis, *Becoming a Master Student,* 13E. © 2011 Cengage Learning.

Oleg Golovnev, 2014 / Used under license from Shutterstock.com

Writing to Learn

Create a dialogue between you and another person (real or imagined) in which y[...]
discuss the reading selection. Consider what you learned, what questions remain unanswere[...]
how this approach matches up with your own learning style, and so on.

Keep the conversation going as long as you can. Set up your dialogue like this:

> **Your first name:** So what do you think of making to-do lists?
> **Other person's first name:** Well, . . .

Reflecting

1. What is the subject of this selection?

   Creating a to-do list

2. What headings are used to identify each part of the process?

   Brainstorm, Estimate time, Rate each tasks cross off tasks, Evaluate

3. What graphic organizer would work well to list the key points in the text?

4. How would you characterize the writer's voice—knowledgeable but distant, knowledgeable and helpful, uncertain and questioning?

   Knowlegcable and helpful

5. What one piece of advice seems most important to you and why?

   Estimating time because there's a lot to do and time is limited. Therefore, it may push other stuff back.

Vocabulary

Define the following words by studying how each is used in the sentence and using your understanding of word parts as aids. (See Appendix D for a glossary of word parts.)

1. **productive**
   (paragraph 4)

2. **priority**
   (paragraph 6)

3. **diligence**
   (paragraph 11)

Critical Thinking

- What assumption or belief has the writer made about the readers of his advice?
- How do you feel about turning tasks into processes?

Writing

What follows are possible writing activities to complete in response to the reading.

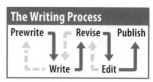

Prewriting

Choose one of the following writing ideas, or decide upon an idea of your own related to the reading.

1. In a personal blog, illustrate whether or not you are a "process" person. Some people, of course, rely on directions and manuals, and others do not. (To *illustrate* means "to show with examples.")

2. Compare your process personality with that of a peer, workmate, or family member.

3. Explain in detail one of the on-the-job processes you identified in the Prereading section. Assume you are preparing your paper for someone new to the job. Consider using headings as is done in "The ABC Daily To-Do List."

4. Explain in detail one of the personal processes that you identified earlier in the Prereading section. Provide necessary background information and at least one example of the process in action.

5. Describe the most frustrating set of directions that you have ever tried to follow.

When planning . . .
- Complete the STRAP strategy for your writing.
- Gather plenty of details about your topic—including a complete listing of the steps in the process if you are responding to prompt 4 or 5.
- Establish a main idea (thesis) to serve as a focus for your writing. For example, a process may be very complicated, or your impulsiveness may lead you to dislike directions.
- Arrange your notes accordingly for writing.

When writing . . .
- Develop effective beginning, middle, and ending parts in your writing.
- Present your main idea in the beginning part.
- Support and explain the main idea in the middle part.
- Close your essay with final thoughts about your topic.

When revising and editing . . .
- Carefully review your first draft. Make sure that you have included enough detail to explain the process. Illustrate your experiences with directions.
- Ask at least one peer to review your writing as well.
- Improve the content as needed.
- Then edit your revised writing for smoothness and correctness.

Chapter

2

"Write. Rewrite. When not writing or rewriting, read.
I know of no shortcuts."

—Larry King

Approaches to Reading and Writing

You can't expect to gain a full appreciation of a text with one quick read through it. Likewise, you can't expect to produce a quality piece of writing by simply producing one quick draft. Effective reading and writing are never the product of a single, quick step. You can't hurry either one. Instead, academic reading and writing are best approached as processes, each with a series of steps helping you carry out your task.

This chapter will describe the steps in the reading and writing processes and show you how the steps in each process work together. There can be a lot of forward and backward movement between the steps. You'll also be introduced to other reading and writing strategies that you can use in all of your academic classes.

Learning Outcomes

LO1 Understand the reading process.
LO2 Understand the writing process.
LO3 Use reading and writing strategies.
LO4 Improve vocabulary skills.
LO5 Understand the structure of textbooks.

What do you think?

How do you approach reading and writing? Do you follow a personal reading process? How about a writing process? What are the steps that you follow?

L01 Understanding the Reading Process

Reading an entertainment or fashion magazine can be easy because you are reading for enjoyment. Reading an academic text is entirely different because you are reading to gain information. To ensure that you read academic texts carefully, follow the steps in an effective process. By doing so, you will gain a full appreciation of a text.

> **Insight** The reading process helps you prepare for, carry out, and reflect on your reading.

The reading process helps you pace yourself and read actively. Active reading is close, thoughtful reading. It keeps you engaged with the text with annotating, note taking, and/or summarizing, and it helps you understand all the key parts.

Process	Activities
Prereading	First become familiar with the text and establish a starting point for reading.
Reading	Read the assignment once to get a basic understanding of the text. Use reading strategies such as annotating, outlining, and summarizing.
Rereading	Reread the text and analyze its parts as many times as needed until you have a clear understanding of the text's key topic and ideas.
Reflecting	Reflect on your reading experience: *How would you summarize the text? What have you learned? What questions do you have about the material? How has this reading changed or expanded what you know about the topic?*

Figure 2.1 presents the reading process in action. The arrows show how you may move back and forth between the steps. For example, after beginning your reading, you may refer back to something in your prereading.

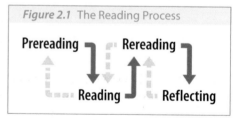

Figure 2.1 The Reading Process

Prereading   Rereading

Reading   Reflecting

Practice What observations can you make about the reading process after reviewing this information? For instance, one observation might be, "Academic reading cannot be done quickly." List three or four additional observations on your own paper.

"To learn to read is to light a fire; every syllable that is spelled out is a spark."

—Victor Hugo

Prereading

Prereading addresses what you should do *before* your actual reading. A cook reviews a recipe in order to have everything in place before starting; prereading serves a similar purpose. Here are the basic prereading tasks.

- **Review the title.** Many readers give the title very little thought. Bad move. The title often identifies the topic of the reading and helps you understand the author's attitude or feeling about it.

- **Learn about the author.** Read the brief biography about the author if it is provided with the text. Otherwise, check online for information about the writer. This information may help you appreciate the author's approach or point of view taken in the text.

- **Preview the text.** To do so, complete the following actions: Read the first paragraph or two to get a general idea about the topic, the level of language used, and the writer's tone. Next, skim the text for headings, bold words, and graphics. Then read the final paragraph or two to see how the text ends. Finally, consider the author's purpose and audience: Why was the text written, and who was intended to read it?

- **Establish a starting point for reading.** Once you have done all of these things, write down your first thoughts about the text. Consider what you already know about the topic, what questions you have, and what you expect to learn.

- **Ask questions.** Forming a set of prereading questions helps you stay on task as you read. A common practice is to base your questions on information that you've collected while previewing the text's title, objectives, headings, subheadings, first sentences in paragraphs, bold-faced terms, and so on. Here are three possible prereading questions.

The learning objective "Explain when searches can be made without a warrant" can be turned into this question:	The heading "The Fourth Amendment" can be turned into this question:	The bold-faced term "probable cause" can be turned into this question:
When can searches be made without a warrant?	How does the Fourth Amendment protect the rights of the people?	What is meant by probable cause?

Reading

Reading a text requires your undivided attention. These are your goals during your first reading.

- **Confirm the author's purpose and audience.** Is the material intended to explain, describe, or persuade? And does it address general readers, college students, professionals, or some other audience?
- **Annotate the text.** Annotating involves underlining key passages, writing questions about what you're reading, and marking and defining new terms.
- **Identify the thesis or the main idea** of the text. The main idea is the special feature, part, or feeling about the topic that the author wants to emphasize. The main idea of an essay or longer piece of writing is stated in a thesis.
- **Locate the evidence**—the facts and details that support the main idea.
- **Consider the conclusion**—the closing thoughts of the writer.
- **Answer the questions** you posed during prereading.

Rereading

Rereading a text helps you to better understand its main points. These are your goals during your rereading.

- **Confirm your basic understanding of the text.** Are you still sure about the thesis and support? If not, adjust your thinking as needed.
- **Analyze the development of the ideas.** Is the topic timely or important? Does the thesis seem reasonable? What types of support are provided—facts, statistics, or examples? Does the conclusion seem logical?
- **Consider the organization of the material.** How does the writer organize the details?
- **Check the voice and style of the writing.** Does the writer seem knowledgeable about the topic and interested in it? Are the ideas easy to follow?
- **Check for answers to your annotations,** and make further annotations as needed.

Reflecting

Reflecting helps you fine-tune your thinking about the material. Writing about your reading is the best way to reflect on it. These are your goals during this step.

- **Summarize what you have learned.** What new information have you gained?
- **Explore your feelings about the reading.** Did the reading surprise you? Did it disappoint you? Did it answer your questions? How will you use what you learned? Does this new information change your thinking in any way? Explain.
- **Identify what questions you still have.** Then try to answer them.

You will practice the skills related to the reading process at the end of the chapter in the Enrichment section.

"The books that help you the most are those [that]
make you think the most."

—Theodore Parker

Other Reading Processes

Two other reading processes—KWL and SQ3R—are variations on the prereading, reading, rereading, and reflecting process.

KWL

KWL stands for what I *know*, what I *want to know*, and what I *learned*. Identifying what you know (K) and want to know (W) occurs during prereading. Identifying what you learned (L) occurs after your reading, rereading, and reflecting. See Figure 2.2.

1. Write the topic of your reading at the top of your paper. Then divide the paper into three columns and label them **K**, **W**, and **L**.
2. In the **K** column, identify what you already know.
3. In the **W** column, identify the questions you want answered.
4. In the **L** column, note what you have learned.

Figure 2.2 KWL Chart

Topic: _____

K	W	L
Identify what you **KNOW**.	Identify what you **WANT** to know.	List what you **LEARNED**.

SQ3R

SQ3R is a thorough reading process, very similar to prereading, reading, rereading, and reflecting. The letters SQ3R stand for *survey*, *question*, *read*, *recite*, and *review*.

Survey: When you survey, you skim the title, headings, graphics, and first and last paragraphs to get a general idea about the text.

Question: During this step, you ask questions that you hope the text will answer about the topic.

Read: While you do the reading, you take careful notes and reread challenging parts.

Recite: At the end of each page, section, or chapter, you should state out loud what you have learned. (This could involve answering the 5 W's and H—*who? what? when? where? why?* and *how?*) Reread as necessary.

Review: After reading, you study your notes, answer questions about the reading, and summarize the text.

L02 Understanding the Writing Process

When facing an extended writing assignment, a common question often comes to mind: How will I ever get this done? Even professional writers sometimes labor for the right answer. But have no fear. A writing project is much less imposing when you approach it as a process rather than as an end product. This section introduces you to the steps in the writing process.

You cannot change a flat tire with one simple action. It takes a number of steps to get the job done right. The same goes for writing. If you expect to complete a paper in one general attempt, you (and your instructor) will be disappointed in the results. On the other hand, if you follow the writing process, you'll complete the job in the right way—one step at a time.

Process	Activities
Prewriting	Start the process by ■ selecting a topic to write about, ■ collecting details about it, and ■ finding a focus or thesis to direct your writing.
Writing	Then write your first draft, using your prewriting plan as a general guide. Writing a first draft allows you to connect your thoughts about a topic.
Revising	Carefully review your first draft and have a classmate read it as well. Change any parts that need to be clearer, and add missing information.
Editing	Edit your revised writing by checking for style, grammar, punctuation, and spelling errors.
Publishing	During the final step, prepare your writing to share with your instructor, your peers, or another audience.

Reasons to Write

Always use the writing process when you are writing to share learning and when you are writing certain personal forms. You don't need to use it when you are simply writing to learn, such as note taking and freewriting.

Reason	Forms	Purpose
Writing to share learning	Summaries, informational essays	To show your understanding of subjects you are studying
Personal writing	Personal essays, blog postings, short stories, plays	To share your personal thoughts, feelings, and creativity with others

Practice ▶ Explain how the writing process turns writing into a meaningful project rather than just another assignment.

"A writer is not so much someone who has something to say as he is someone who has found a process that will bring about new things he would not have thought of if he had not started to say them."

—William Stafford

Like the reading process, there can be forward and backward movement between the steps in the writing process (see **Figure 2.3**). For example, after writing a first draft, you may decide to collect more details about your topic, which is actually a prewriting activity. When using the writing process, you need to understand the following points.

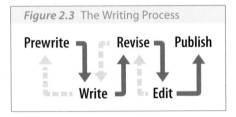

Figure 2.3 The Writing Process

- **All the steps require some type of writing.** Prewriting (planning), revising, and editing are as much writing activities as composing the first draft is.

- **It is unlikely that the process will work the same for any two writing assignments.** For one assignment, you may struggle with gathering details. For another, you may have trouble starting the first draft. For still another, you may move from step to step with little difficulty.

- **No two writers develop their writing in the same way.** Some writers need to talk about their writing early on, while others would rather keep their ideas to themselves. Some writers need to step away from their writing at times to let their thoughts percolate. Other writers can't stop until they produce a first draft. Your own writing personality will develop as you gain more writing experience.

- **All the information about the writing process won't make you a better writer unless you make a sincere effort to use it**. You wouldn't expect to play the piano just by reading about it—you must follow the instructions and practice. The same holds true for writing.

When you respond to a writing prompt on a test, use an abbreviated form of the writing process. Spend a few minutes gathering and organizing your ideas; then write your response. Afterward, read what you have produced and quickly revise and edit it.

Practice Study the reading and writing processes in **Figures 2.1** and **2.3**. Then list four or five ways in which the two processes are similar.

Prewriting

Prewriting is the first step in the writing process. In many ways, it is the most important step because it involves all of the decisions and planning that come before writing a first draft. If you plan well, you will be well prepared to work through the rest of the process. These are the basic prewriting tasks.

- **Identify a meaningful writing idea.** Pick a topic that meets the requirements of the assignment and that truly interests you. Otherwise, you will have a hard time writing about it. Begin your topic search by writing freely about the assignment or by simply listing your ideas.

- **Collect plenty of details.** Explore your own thoughts and feelings about the topic. Then gather additional information, either through firsthand experience (observations, interviews) or by reading about the topic in books, in magazines, and on the Internet. You will need these details to support the focus of your writing.

- **Establish a focus.** Just as a skilled photographer focuses or centers the subject before taking a photograph, you must identify a special part or feeling about the topic before writing your first draft. This focus, or emphasis, is usually expressed in a thesis statement.

- **Choose a pattern of arrangement.** Once you have established a focus, decide what details to include in your writing and how to organize them. You can arrange your details chronologically (by time), logically, by order of importance, or in other ways.

- **Organize your information.** With a pattern of arrangement in mind, you can organize your details in one of three basic ways:

  - **Make a quick list of main points and support.**
  - **Create a topic or sentence outline**—a more formal arrangement of main points and subpoints.
  - **Fill in a graphic organizer**—arranging main points and details in a chart or diagram. See **Figure 2.4.**

Figure 2.4 Graphic Organizers

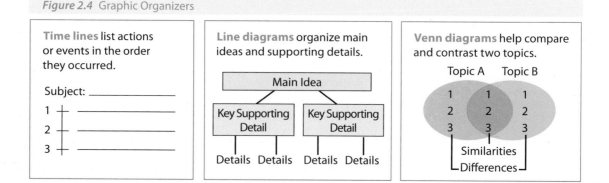

> "The first draft is a skeleton . . . just bare bones. The rest of the story comes later with revising."
>
> —Judy Blume

Drafting

Drafting is the next step in the writing process. You have one important task during this step—to connect your thoughts and ideas about your topic. Just put these thoughts on paper so you have something to work with. They do not have to be perfectly worded. Here is a basic guide to drafting.

- **Strike while you're hot.** Write your first draft while your planning is still fresh in your mind.

- **Refer to your prewriting.** Use all of your planning and organizing as a basic writing guide. But also be open to new ideas as they come to mind.

- **Write as much as you can.** Keep writing until you get all of your ideas on paper or until you come to a natural stopping point. Concentrate on forming your ideas rather than on making everything correct.

- **Form a meaningful whole.** A meaningful whole for a paragraph means a topic sentence, multiple body sentences, and a closing sentence. For an essay, it means an opening paragraph (with a thesis statement), multiple middle paragraphs, and a closing paragraph.

Paragraph	Essay
Topic sentence ⟶	Opening paragraph (with thesis statement)
Body sentences ⟶	Middle paragraphs
Closing sentence ⟶	Closing paragraph

- **Pay special attention to each part.** All three parts—the opening, the middle, and the closing—play important roles in your writing. Give each part special attention.

  - The opening gets the reader's interest and states your thesis.
  - The middle supports your thesis.
  - The closing offers important final thoughts about the topic.

- **Look back to move forward.** Sometimes it helps to stop and reread what you have written to help you add new ideas.

- **Write naturally and honestly.** "Talk" to your readers, as if a group of classmates were gathered around you.

- **Remember, it's a draft.** A first draft is your first look at a developing writing idea. You will have plenty of opportunities to improve upon it later in the process.

> "The first draft reveals the art; revision reveals the artist."
>
> —Michael Lee

Revising

Revising is the third step in the process. During this step, you shape and improve the ideas, organization, and voice in your first draft. You would never expect a musician to record a song after putting lyrics and music together for the first time. The same holds true with your writing. You still have a lot of work ahead of you. Here is a basic guide to revising.

- **Step away from your draft.** Your time away will help you see your first draft more clearly and with a fresh outlook.

- **Revisit your purpose.** Are you writing to explain, to persuade, to describe, or to share?

- **Read your draft many times.** Read it silently and out loud to get an overall impression of your work.

- **Have peers read it.** Their comments and questions will help you decide what changes to make. This chapter contains additional information about peer revising.

- **Check your overall focus.** Decide if your thesis still works and if you have provided enough support for it.

- **Review each part.** Be sure that the opening sets the proper tone for your writing, the middle part supports your thesis, and the closing provides worthy final thoughts about the topic.

- **Know your basic moves.** There are four basic ways to make changes—adding, cutting, rewriting, or reordering information. Each change or improvement that you make will bring you closer to a strong finished paper.

Add information to . . .
- make a main point more convincing.
- complete an explanation.
- improve the flow of your writing.

Cut information if it . . .
- doesn't support the thesis.
- seems repetitious.

Rewrite information if it . . .
- seems confusing or unclear.
- appears too complicated.
- lacks the proper voice.

Reorder information if it . . .
- seems out of order.
- would make more sense in another spot.

- **Plan a revising strategy.** Decide what you need to do first, second, and third, and then make the necessary changes.

- **Follow a similar process for each remaining draft.** The best writing results from more than one revision.

Peer Revising

Sharing your writing with peers can help you gain valuable feedback during the revision process. Peer revision offers a fresh perspective on your writing, revealing strengths and weaknesses in your draft. To get the best feedback, writers and reviewers need to have a clear understanding of their roles and responsibilities.

Role of the Writer

The writer is responsible for creating an open environment that encourages reviewers to feel comfortable giving honest feedback. Here are steps you should follow when sharing your writing for review.

- Introduce your writing and any requirements of the assignment.
- Describe your goals and objectives for the writing.
- Share your concerns or areas of focus. For example, if you are concerned with the organization of the piece, ask the reviewer to pay special attention to it.
- Provide reviewers with a peer review sheet for the feedback. See Figure 2.5.
- Step away and give the reviewer plenty of time to read and respond to your work.

Role of the Reviewer

The reviewer is responsible for giving honest and constructive feedback in a positive manner. If a writer asks you to review her or his work, be prepared to give clear, specific, and complete advice. You can do so by following the **OAQS Method: Observe, Appreciate, Question,** and **Suggest**.

1. **Observe** means to focus on what the writer's work is designed to do or say and judge how well the writing accomplishes its purpose. For example, you may say, "Your writing shows a clear cause-effect relationship between tropical deforestation and endangered species."

2. **Appreciate** means to highlight the strengths of the writing. This is meant to boost the writer's confidence and to show what is working well. You may say, "The evidence you've outlined is clear and convincing" or "I especially like . . ."

3. **Question** means to ask about what confuses you or what you still need to know after reading the essay. You might ask for more information or for clarification on a certain point. You may say, "You glossed over the link between deforestation and increased river levels. Could you provide more information about that?"

4. **Suggest** means to give helpful advice about possible changes. Keep your suggestions honest and courteous as well as specific. Don't say, "The ending was boring." Instead you may say, "Your beginning really pulled me in, and the middle explained the main idea strongly, but the ending felt a bit flat. Here are some ideas I have to help you bring the end of the essay all together . . ."

Using a Peer Review Sheet

Provide the reviewer with a peer review sheet to make comments about your writing. Refer back to the sheet as you revise your writing.

Figure 2.5 Peer Review Sheet

Peer Review Sheet

Title: _____

Writer: _____

Reviewer: _____

1. Which part of the draft works best—opening, middle, or closing? Why?

   _____

   _____

   _____

2. Which part of the draft needs work—opening, middle, or closing? Why?

   _____

   _____

   _____

3. What details do you like best? What details need clarification?

   _____

   _____

   _____

4. What questions do you still have about the topic ?

   _____

   _____

   _____

5. What changes do you suggest making to the draft? Explain.

   _____

   _____

   _____

   _____

Editing

Editing is the fourth step, when you check your revised writing for style and correctness. Editing becomes important *after* you have revised the content of your writing. Editing is like buffing out the smudges and scratches on a newly painted car. The buffing is important, but only after the main work—the actual painting—is complete. Here is a basic guide to editing.

- **Start with a clean copy.** Do your editing on a clean copy of your revised writing.
- **Check first for style.** Make sure that you have used the best words, such as specific nouns and verbs and smooth-reading sentences.
- **Then check for correctness.** Check your spelling first; then check the punctuation and mechanics.
- **For spelling, read from the last word to the first.** This strategy forces you to look at each word. A spell checker will not catch every error.
- **Circle punctuation.** This strategy will force you to look at each mark.
- **Refer to an editing checklist.** The Workshops in Parts V, VI, and VII in *Fusion* explain sentence, grammar, punctuation, and mechanics rules.

> **Editing Checklist**
> ____ 1. Have I used specific nouns and verbs?
> ____ 2. Have I used more action verbs than "be" verbs?
> ____ 3. Have I avoided improper shifts in sentences?
> ____ 4. Have I avoided fragments and run-ons?
> ____ 5. Do my subjects and verbs agree (*she speaks,* not *she speak*)?
> ____ 6. Have I used the right words (*their, there, they're*)?
> ____ 7. Have I capitalized first words and proper nouns and adjectives?
> ____ 8. Have I used commas after long introductory word groups and to separate items in a series?
> ____ 9. Have I used commas correctly in compound sentences?
> ____ 10. Have I used apostrophes correctly?

- **Get help.** Ask a trusted classmate to check for errors.

Publishing

Publishing is the final step in the writing process. During this step, you prepare your writing before submitting or sharing it.

- **Prepare a final copy.** Incorporate all of your editing changes.
- **Follow design requirements.** Format your final copy according to the requirements established by your instructor.
- **Proofread the text.** Check your writing one last time for errors.

L03 Using Reading and Writing Strategies

Writing about your reading assignments is one of the best ways to understand them. The physical act of writing—recording one word after another—brings your thoughts into focus. So when you write about your reading, you are bringing the ideas in the text into focus.

It is no surprise then that three of most essential reading strategies involve writing: **annotating, note taking,** and **summarizing.** Each of these strategies builds upon the other, with annotating and note taking providing the support for writing a summary.

Annotating a Text

To annotate means "to add comments or make notes in a text." Annotating a text allows you to interact with the ideas in a reading selection. Here are some suggestions:

- Write questions in the margins.
- Underline or highlight important points.
- Define new terms.
- Make connections to other parts.

SPECIAL NOTE: Annotate the material only if you own the text or if you are reading a photocopy.

Why is this so?

Democracy Does Not Always Allow for Quick Solutions

Democracy is government by the people through elected officials and representatives. In a ⟨constitutional⟩

The USA is this.

⟨democracy,⟩ a constitution (a document recording the rights of citizens and the laws by which a government functions) provides the basis of government authority and, in most cases, limits government power by mandating free elections and guaranteeing the right of free speech.

1st reason for slow solutions

Political institutions in most constitutional democracies are designed to allow gradual change that ensures economic and political stability. In the United States, for example, rapid and destabilizing change is

What are some other examples?

curbed by ⟨a system of checks and balances⟩ that distributes power among three branches of government—*legislative, executive,* and *judicial*—and among federal, state, and local governments.

In passing laws, developing budgets, and formulating

2nd reason for slow solutions

regulations, elected and appointed government officials must deal with pressure from many competing special-interest groups. Each of these groups advocates passing laws, providing subsidies or tax breaks, or establishing regulations favorable to its cause while attempting to weaken or repeal laws, subsidies, tax breaks, and regulations unfavorable to its position. Some special-interest groups such as corporations are profit-making organizations. Others are nongovernmental organizations (NGOs), most of which are nonprofit, such as labor unions and environmental organizations.

Find out more about these.

Key point

The design for stability and gradual change in democracies is highly desirable. But several features of democratic governments hinder their ability to deal with environmental problems. For example, problems such as climate change and biodiversity loss are complex and difficult to understand. Such problems also have long-lasting effects, are interrelated, and require integrated, long-term solutions that emphasize prevention. But because local, state, and national elections are held as often as every two years, most politicians spend much of their time seeking re-election and tend to focus on short-term, isolated issues rather than on long-term, complex, and time-consuming problems.

Need to define this term.

First time the writer directly addresses reader.

One of our greatest challenges is to place more emphasis on long-term thinking and policies and to educate political leaders and the public about the need for long-range thinking and actions. Another problem is that many political leaders, with hundreds of issues to deal with, have too little understanding of how the earth's natural systems work and how those systems support all life, economies, and societies. Again, there is an urgent need to educate politicians and voters about these vital matters.

The tone in this paragraph seems different.

Call to action

From Miller, *Living in the Environment,* 17E. © 2012 Cengage Learning.

Taking Effective Notes

Taking notes helps you to focus on reading material and understand it more fully. Notes change information you have read about to information that you are working with. Of course, taking effective notes makes summarizing texts and studying for exams much easier because note taking helps you internalize information. When taking notes, follow these tips.

- Use your own words as much as possible.
- Record only key points and details rather than long passages.
- Consider **boldfaced** or *italicized* words, graphics, and captions as well as the main text.
- Employ abbreviations and symbols to save time (vs., #, &, etc.).
- Decide on a system to organize or arrange your notes so they are easy to follow.

Using Two-Column Notes

To make your note taking more active, use a two-column system called the Cornell Method. One column (two-thirds of the page) is for your main notes, and the other column (one-third of the page) is for questions and key terms. Fill in this column after you're done with your main notes. To review your work, cover the main notes and answer the questions in the left column.

**Democracy Does Not Always Allow for
Quick Solutions
by G. Tyler Miller**

March 3

Questions and key terms	Main notes
How does democracy make quick solutions more difficult?	- Reason 1: Democracy is designed for gradual change - Reason 2: Government must deal with competing special-interest groups.
special interest groups—groups who influence policy through money and lobbying	
How do election cycles impact legislation for environmental problems?	- Elections happen every two-four years. - Politicians prefer short-term solutions that will help them win elections. - Climate change requires complicated, long-term solutions. - Voters might not recognize the impact of long-term solutions.

SPECIAL NOTE: Save space at the bottom of the page to summarize the notes after class.

Using an Outline

An outline shows how ideas fit together. The ideas in a **topic outline** are expressed in words and phrases. The ideas in a **sentence outline** are expressed in sentences. In a traditional outline, each new division represents another level of detail. As is demonstrated, if you have a "I," you should have at least a "II." If you have an "A," you should at least have a "B," and so on.

Topic Outline

Here's the start of a topic outline for "Democracy Does Not Always Allow for Quick Solutions."

Text subject: Democracy and Change
  I. Constitutional democracies
     A. Designed for gradual change
        1. Checks and balances
        2. Lobbying
     B. Ruled by election cycles that encourage short-term solutions
  II. Environmental problems—climate change and biodiversity
     A. Complex problems
     B. Long-term solutions

SPECIAL NOTE: Unless your instructor says otherwise, adapt your outline to meet your needs rather than worry whether or not you've followed all of the rules.

Sentence Outline

Here is a portion of a sentence outline for the same article.

  I. A constitutional democracy is government ruled by elected officials and a governing document.
     A. This type of government does not always allow for quick solutions.
        1. Checks and balances are designed for gradual, sensible change.
        2. Lobbying from competing special-interests groups makes it hard for elected officials to enact long-term, meaningful solutions.
     B. Election cycles have a major impact on what gets done.
        1. Politicians prefer short-term solutions that voters will recognize.

Practice Outline a sample reading from this text or an academic reading from one of your other classes.

Using Clusters or Webs

Clustering or webbing is a more graphic way to collect and organize the key points in a reading assignment. Begin a cluster with a nucleus word or idea—most often, the main idea in the reading. Then cluster key points and supporting details around the nucleus concept. Circle each point or detail and connect it to the closest related word. The end result should be a structure that graphically shows you all the important information in a reading selection at a glance.

Figure 2.6 is a cluster that presents the key facts and details in the essay "Democracy Does Not Allow for Quick Solutions." Study the cluster to see how it shows how the important information fits together.

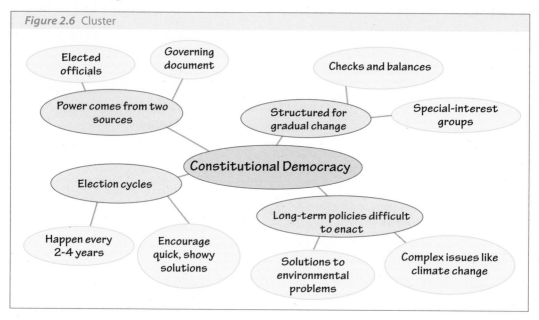

Figure 2.6 Cluster

SPECIAL NOTE: Suppose you want to explore your thoughts and feelings about a text. You can do so in a cluster or—as it is sometimes called—a **mind map**. Simply start with an appropriate nucleus word (perhaps the title of the selection) and record and connect your ideas. Clustering in this way may help you gain a firmer understanding of the text.

Practice > Read an essay in *Fusion*. (Or read another selection recommended by your instructor.) Then use a cluster to gather and connect the important information in the text. Afterward, compare your cluster with a classmate's to see if your cluster includes the same information. Discuss any differences in information.

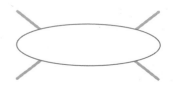

Using a Table Diagram

Part of the challenge when reading an informative text is keeping track of the main idea and key supporting details. Filling in a table diagram works well for this purpose. In this graphic organizer, you identify the thesis, or main idea, of the reading at the top of the table and list the key supporting details underneath. You can refer back to this information as you write a summary of the text or study for a test.

Figure 2.7 is a table diagram that presents the thesis and key supporting points in the essay "Democracy Does Not Allow for Quick Solutions."

Figure 2.7 Table Diagram

New environmental policies are difficult to achieve in constitutional democracies.			
Democracies encourage gradual change through checks and balances.	Lobbying delays the process of making policies.	Short election cycles encourage quick changes.	Climate change and biodiversity require long-term policies.

Practice Read an essay or article from a respected news source. Create a table diagram that identifies the thesis and key supporting details. Use your own words rather than copying directly from the text. **Note:** Not all texts will include four supporting points. Adapt your table diagram, adding or removing columns as needed.

Thesis or main idea			
supporting points	supporting points	supporting points	supporting points

Summarizing a Text

Summarizing a reading assignment is an especially effective form of writing to learn. It is the process of identifying and explaining the most important ideas in the text. Along with annotating and taking notes, summarizing is an excellent way of becoming actively involved in your reading.

Writing a summary will tell you how well you understand the information. When summarizing a text, you should present the main points in a clear, concise form using your own words. Generally speaking, a summary should be about one-third as long as the original. Here are some other summarizing tips.

- Start by clearly stating the main point of the text.
- Share only the essential supporting facts and details (names, dates, times, and places) in the next sentences.
- Present your ideas in a logical order.
- Tie all of your points together in a closing sentence.

This paragraph summarizes a G. Tyler Miller's "Democracy Does Not Allow for Quick Solutions."

The opening identifies the main idea (underlined).

In "Democracy Does Not Allow for Quick Solutions," G. Tyler Miller explains that a constitutional democracy is a challenging system for enacting environmental policies. To start, democracy encourages

The middle describes essential supporting details.

gradual changes through a series of checks and balances. Policies must pass through each check and balance before going into effect. Legislators must also contend with special-interest groups, who lobby in favor of competing positions. Short election cycles pose yet another challenge. With elections every two to four years, politicians often focus on simple, short-term solutions to attract voters. Conversely, environmental problems like climate change require complex, long-term prevention policies.

The closing sentence restates the thesis.

For these policies to become reality, politicians must have the patience and environmental awareness to clear the hurdles of today's democratic process.

Planning Your Summary

Most of your prewriting and planning will occur when you read and react to the text. During your planning . . .

- Annotate and take notes as needed.
- Name the thesis or main idea of the text.
- Identify the key points that support the thesis. Remember that in academic texts, each middle paragraph often addresses one key supporting point. This point is usually stated in the topic sentence.

Drafting Your Summary

Remember that you are writing a paragraph, starting with a topic sentence and following with supporting ideas. As you write your first draft . . .

- Use your own words as much as possible.
- Start with a topic sentence, naming the title, author, and topic of the text.
- Continue with the key points that explain the thesis. Focus on big ideas, rather than specific details.
- Arrange your ideas in the most logical order.
- Add a closing sentence if one seems necessary.

Revising and Editing Your Summary

Remember that your summary should address the essential information from the original text. As you review your first draft . . .

- Determine if it identifies the main idea of the text.
- Decide if you've limited yourself to key supporting details.
- Check if your summary reads smoothly and logically.
- Determine if you've used your own words, except for key ideas. For example, you may find it necessary to include a few exact ideas or specialized words from the original text. When this type of information is taken directly from the text, enclose it within quotation marks.

   Exact idea: The author describes himself as "soaring with a lightness I'd never known before" after the ceremony.

   Specialized word: One teacher recognized as a master teacher serves as a "standard-bearer" for all great teachers.

- Check your summary for proper usage and grammar.
- Fix any spelling, capitalization, and punctuation errors.

Practice Summarize one of the professional essays in this book or an essay provided by your instructor. Use these tips as a guide.

Forming Personal Responses

While summaries show how well you understood what you've read, personal responses reveal your personal feelings about a reading. Personal responses help you think critically about what you've read—to agree with it, to question it, to make connections with it. This level of analysis is something college instructors will expect from you for almost everything you read.

Reserve part of your class notebook or create an online blog or document for personal responses. The length and form of your personal response doesn't matter so much as your level of thinking. Your goal is to take an informed stance on the text. The following guidelines will help you do this:

- **Write several times,** perhaps once before you read, two or three times during the reading, and one time afterward.
- **Write freely and honestly** to make genuine connections with the text. Don't stop writing to worry about grammar, punctuation, or mechanics. These errors can be quickly cleaned up before you share or submit your response.
- **Respond to points of view** that you like or agree with, information that confuses you, connections that you can make with other material, and ideas that seem significant.
- **Label and date your responses.** You can use these entries to prepare for exams or complete other assignments.
- **Share your discoveries.** Your entries can provide conversation starters in discussions with classmates.

Types of Personal Responses

Here are some specific ways to respond to a text:

Discuss	Carry on a conversation with the author or a character to get to know her or him and yourself a little better.
Illustrate	Create graphics or draw pictures to help you figure out parts of the text.
Imitate	Continue the article or story line, trying to write like the author.
Express	Share your feelings about the text, perhaps in a poem.

Practice Follow the guidelines to write a personal response for one of your next reading assignments.

L04 Improving Vocabulary Skills

In the process of reading you may come across an unfamiliar word. Academic readings, in particular, contain high-level words and technical terms related to a specific field of study. Instead of glossing over these words, you can employ a variety of tools to discover their meaning.

Using a Dictionary

The most basic way to understand a new word is to look up its meaning in a dictionary. Dictionaries are available in print and online formats, but you should make sure the one you choose is published by a reliable institution. Besides providing the spelling and definition of words, dictionaries include other features that can help you better understand the word and make it a permanent part of your memory (see Figure 2.8).

- **Pronunciation guides** break up words into parts and use symbols to explain how each part sounds. Accents show which syllables to stress. In addition, online dictionaries may include audio pronunciations.
- **Parts-of-speech abbreviations** tell how the word can be used in a sentence (*n.* for noun, *v.* for verb). Some words can be used as more than one part of speech.
- **Etymology** describes the history and language origins of a word.
- **Examples** show how the word is used in a sentence.
- **Inflected forms** show other forms of the word. For example, an inflected form of the word *spy* is *spies*, which is the plural form of the word.

Figure 2.8 Sample Dictionary Entry

augur (AW-gur)

n.   1. One of a group of ancient Roman religious officials who foretold events by observing and interpreting signs and omens.
    2. A seer or prophet; a soothsayer

An *augur* predicted a bountiful harvest season.

v.   1. To foretell something or to predict the future
    2. To give a promise of

The closing of the community center seemed to *augur* the downturn of the neighborhood.

["Augur" comes from Latin and is related to the Latin verb "augēre," which means "to increase" and is the source of "augment," "auction," and "author."]

SPECIAL NOTE: Find a trustworthy print or online dictionary. Keep it handy when you are completing a reading assignment.

Using Context

Instead of skipping new words in your reading, try to figure out what they mean in context—or by looking for clues in the other words and ideas around them. In some cases, the context clues can be very easy to identify. In the following passage, the word "affiliates" is defined right after the word is mentioned (underlined).

> Broadcast networks can have as many *affiliates* as they want. Affiliates are stations that use network programming but are owned by companies other than the networks. No network, however, can have two affiliates in the same geographic broadcast area.

In other cases, you must study a text more carefully for context clues. In this passage, an antonym (opposite) suggested in the first part of a sentence (underlined) helps you understand the word "exemptions" in the second part.

> The French peasants slowly became aware of the contrasts between the taxes they had to bear and the *exemptions* enjoyed by the clergy and the nobility. When that discontent was later joined by the resentment [anger] of the middle-class townspeople, the potential for revolution would exist.

Types of Context Clues

- **Cause-effect relationships**
  Suggesting the use of seat belts didn't work, so the state officials made seat-belt use *mandatory*.
- **Definitions built into the text**
  Dr. Williams is an *anthropologist*, a person who scientifically studies the physical, social, and cultural development of humans.
- **Comparisons and contrasts**
  Lynn Dery lives in New York, so she is used to a fast-paced life; Mandy Williams lives in the country, so she is used to a more *serene* lifestyle.
- **Words in a series**
  Spaghetti, lasagna, and *ziti* all have their own special shape.
- **Synonyms (words with the same meaning)**
  Hector's essay contains too many *banal*, overused phrases.
- **Antonyms (words with the opposite meaning)**
  Mrs. Wolfe still seemed strong and energetic after the storm, but Mr. Wolfe looked *haggard*.
- **The tone of the text**
  The street was filled with *bellicose* protesters who pushed and shoved their way through the crowd. The scene was no longer peaceful and calm, as the marchers promised it would be.

Practice ▶ Define the italicized word or term in each passage that follows. Also indicate the type of context clue that helped you understand the word.

1.   In 2001 the Federal Bureau of Investigation recorded 9,730 *hate crimes,* or criminal incidents motivated by a person's race, religion, or ethnicity. Each incident may involve multiple offenses, such as assault and property damage.

   From Brym/Lie, *Sociology,* 2E. © 2007 Cengage Learning.

Definition: _____

Type of context clue: _____

2.   To prevent future frostbite incidents, the administration intends to convert several of the existing sidewalks to protected walkways so that students can go from any building on campus to any other building without being exposed to *inclement* weather.   From Parks et al., *A Mathematical View of Our World,* 1E © 2007 Cengage Learning.

Definition: _____

Type of context clue: _____

3.   The president is the *ultimate* decision maker in military matters and, as such, has the final authority to launch a nuclear strike using missiles or bombs. Everywhere the president goes, so too goes the "Football"—a briefcase filled with all the codes necessary to order a nuclear attack.

   From Schmidt et al., *American Government and Politics Today,* 2013-2014 Edition, 16E. © 2014 Cengage Learning.

Definition: _____

Type of context clue: _____

4.   The Blackfoot River flows among beautiful mountain ranges in the west-central part of the U.S. state of Montana. This large *watershed* is home to more than 600 species of plants, 21 species of waterfowl, bald eagles, peregrine falcons, grizzly bears, and rare species of trout. Some species, such as the Howell's gumweed and the bull trout, are threatened with extinction. In other words, this watershed is a precious jewel of biodiversity.

   From Miller, *Living in the Environment,* 17E. © 2012 Cengage Learning.

Definition: _____

Type of context clue: _____

Understanding Word Parts

Roots, prefixes, and **suffixes** are different word parts. Many words in our language are made up of combinations of these parts. (See Appendix D for a glossary of common prefixes, suffixes, and roots.)

- **Roots** like *liber* (as in liberate) or *rupt* (as in interrupt) are the starting points for most words.
- **Prefixes** like *anti* (as in antibiotic) or *un* (as in unreal) are word parts that come before roots to form new words.
- **Suffixes** like *dom* (as in boredom) or *ly* (as in hourly) are word parts that come after roots to form new words.

Transportation combines . . .

- the prefix *trans* meaning "across" or "beyond,"
- the root *port* meaning "carry," and
- the suffix *tion* meaning "act of."

So, *transportation* means "the act of carrying across or beyond."

Biographic combines . . .

- the root *bio* meaning "life,"
- the root *graph* meaning "write," and
- the suffix *ic* meaning "nature of" or "relating to."

So, *biographic* means "relating to writing about real life."

Note the word *rearmament* in the following passage. You may already know the meaning of this word. If not, studying its parts can help you unlock its meaning.

> The huge road construction and public works programs he [Hitler] began in 1934 absorbed a large portion of the pool of unemployed. With *rearmament*, the military was greatly enlarged, and munitions factories and their suppliers received government orders.

Word parts:

- *Re* is a prefix meaning "again."
- *Arm* is a root or base word meaning "equip or supply with weapons."
- The suffix *ment* basically means "act of."

Definition/explanation of *rearmament*:

- *Rearmament*, then, means "the act of arming again."

Practice Using the examples above as a guide, analyze and define the following words.

- mediate (*medi* + *ate*)
- portable (*port* + *able*)
- interrupt (*inter* + *rupt*)
- retrospective (*retro* + *spec* + *tive*)

L04 Understanding the Structure of Textbooks

In many of your college courses, you will be assigned a textbook, and your instructor will regularly ask you to read particular chapters as background for class lectures and discussions. Since reading textbooks plays such an important role in your coursework, it is important that you first recognize and understand the main parts they usually include.

Parts of a Textbook

- The **title page** is usually the first printed page in a book. It provides the full title of the book, the authors' names, the publisher's name, and the place of publication.

- The **copyright page** comes right after the title page. This page gives the year in which a copyright was issued, which is usually the same year the book was published. The copyright gives an author or publisher the legal right to the production, publication, and use of the text.

- The **table of contents** shows the major divisions (units, parts, chapters, and topics) in the textbook. It contains page numbers to locate the different divisions. (Many textbooks precede the full table of contents with a table of contents in brief used as a quick guide to the text.)

- A **preface, foreword,** and/or **introduction** often follows the table of contents and introduces the reader to the book.

- The **body** is the main part of the book, containing the actual text.

- Following the body, an **appendix** is sometimes included. This section gives extra information, often in the form of charts, tables, letters, or copies of official documents.

- If included, the **glossary** follows the appendix and serves as the dictionary portion of the book. It is an alphabetical listing of key terms, with an explanation or definition for each one.

- Some textbooks then provide a **reference** section identifying the books or articles the author used during the development of the text.

- The **index** at the end of a textbook lists alphabetically the important topics, terms, and names appearing in the book and the page location for each one.

Practice ▸ Locate the different parts of each of your textbooks, including this one. Do any of your textbooks not contain all of these parts, and do any of them contain other parts?

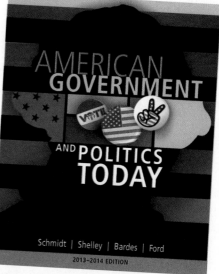

From Schmidt/Shelley/Bardes/Ford, American Government and Politics Today, 2013-2014 Edition, 16E. © 2014 Cengage

Parts of a Textbook Chapter

As you approach each textbook reading assignment, be aware that most chapters share common features. These features are designed to help you carry out your reading, so it's important that you know what they are and that you use them.

Key features in a chapter from *American Government and Politics Today* are identified and explained. Each one is an important part of the text.

- The **chapter title** identifies the topic of the chapter.
- **Learning outcomes** identify the different things that you can expect to learn from that chapter.
- Many chapters provide **special opening text** to prompt you to think about the chapter.
- **Key terms** are often highlighted and defined.
- **Main headings** are the largest headings and announce each main part of the topic to be discussed.
- **Subheadings** are similar headings and help direct the reading of each main part. (There can be different levels of subheadings. As they get more detailed, they are reduced in size.)
- **Graphics** provide visual representations of important facts and figures.
- **Photographs** and **captions** enhance the discussion in the main text.
- **Side notes** can have a variety of uses, depending on the textbook. They can define key terms, identify learning outcomes, or provide interesting facts or ideas, among other things.
- **Summaries** at the end of chapters review the main ideas and details covered in the reading.
- **Resources** to additional reading or viewing may also be provided at the end of a chapter.

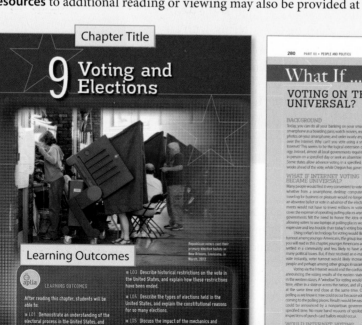

Chapter Title

9 Voting and Elections

Learning Outcomes

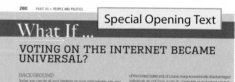

Special Opening Text

280 PART III • PEOPLE AND POLITICS

What If ...

VOTING ON THE INTERNET BECAME UNIVERSAL?

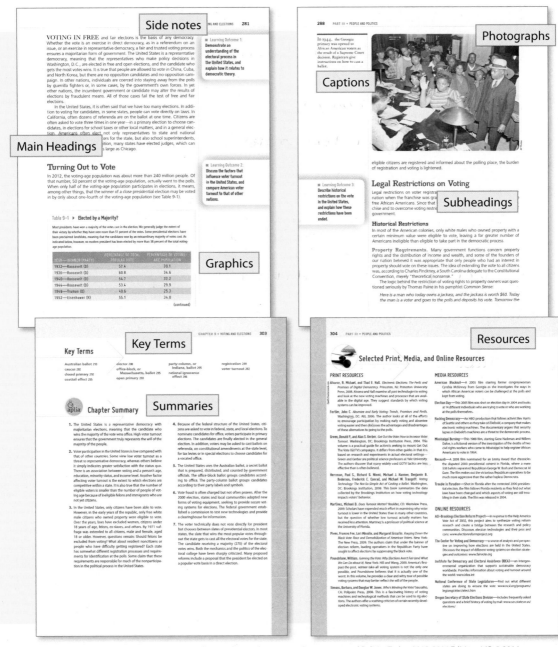

From Schmidt/Shelley/Bardes/Ford, American Government and Politics Today, 2013-2014 Edition, 16E. © 2014 Cengage Learning.

Practice Review the parts of one chapter from one of your textbooks as well as this one. How are they similar or different from the parts you just learned about? Be prepared to discuss the makeup of one textbook chapter with your classmates.

☑ Review and Enrichment

Reviewing the Chapter

Understand the Reading Process

1. Identify two things that you should do during prereading.

   Skim over the text, titles & subtitles

Understand the Writing Process

2. What are the steps in the writing process?

   Pre-writing, Drafting, Revising, Editing

3. Explain the forward and backward movement of this process.

   Revision & editing

Use Reading and Writing Strategies

4. What does annotating a text involve?

   Taking notes

5. What does it mean to summarize a text?

   Identifying and explaining the main points in your own words.

6. What is one benefit of writing a personal response to a reading?

   A better understanding

Improve Vocabulary Skills

7. What are two types of context clues that can help you understand the meaning of a new word?

8. How can word parts help you figure out the meaning of an unfamiliar word?

Understand the Structure of Textbooks

9. What role do headings serve in academic textbooks?

   The topic

> "Reading furnishes the mind only with materials of knowledge;
> it is thinking that makes what we read ours."
>
> —John Locke

Reading for Enrichment

You will be reading about hydraulic fracturing, a process of natural gas extraction that has caused much environmental debate. Be sure to follow the steps in the reading process to help you gain a full understanding of the text.

About the Author

David Biello is an award-winning environmental journalist. In addition to working as the environment and energy editor for *Scientific American* magazine, Biello hosts the *60-Second Earth* podcast, contributes to the *Instant Egghead* video series, and is a regular guest on a variety of radio shows. His writing has appeared in *Scientific American*, *LA Review of Books*, and *Yale Environment 360*.

Prereading

Before you begin reading, create a KWL chart like the one that follows. Fill out the first two columns of the chart to reflect on what you know and what you want to learn about hydraulic fracturing. Complete the third column when you've finished reading.

Hydraulic Fracturing:

K	W	L
Identify what you **know**.	Identify what you **want** to know.	List what you **learned**.

What do you think?

How would you explain John Locke's quotation? What reading strategies from this chapter help you think about what you read?

Before you read, answer these questions:

1. What do the title, the first two paragraphs, and the headings tell you about the text?

   Environmental changes

2. What are your first thoughts about the author's purpose and audience?

   The entire economy

Reading and Rereading

As you read, make it your goal to (1) identify the topic and thesis, (2) confirm the purpose and audience, (3) note the level of support provided, and (4) answer the questions you posed during prereading. Consider annotating the text and/or taking notes to help you keep track of important information during your reading. Follow these annotating tips:

- Underline or highlight important points. Comment on the ideas in the margin.
- Write questions in the margin.
- Circle words that you are unsure of. Then define or explain these words.

Reread as needed to confirm your understanding of the text and to analyze the development of the ideas.

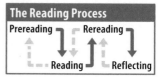

What the Frack? Natural Gas from Subterranean Shale Promises U.S. Energy Independence—With Environmental Costs

A satellite broadcasting company bought the rights to rename this town a few years ago in exchange for a decade of free television, but it is another industry that dominates the 200 or so residents: natural gas. Five facilities perched on the north Texas town's outskirts compress the gas newly flowing to the surface from the cracked Barnett Shale more than two kilometers beneath the surface, collectively contributing a brew of toxic chemicals to the air.   1

It is because of places like DISH (formerly known as Clark) and similar sites from Colorado to Wyoming that the U.S. Environmental Protection Agency (EPA) has launched a new review of the practice known as hydraulic fracturing, or "fracking." From compressor stations emitting known human **carcinogens** such as benzene to the poor lining of wells after drilling that has led some water taps to literally spout flames, the full set of activities needed to produce natural gas gives rise to a **panoply** of potential problems. The EPA   2 study may examine everything from site selection to the ultimate disposal of the fluids used in fracking.

The picture from DISH is not pretty. A set of seven samples collected throughout the town analyzed for a variety of air pollutants in August 2009 found that benzene was present at levels as much as 55 times higher than allowed by the Texas Commission on Environmental Quality (TCEQ). Similarly, xylene and carbon disulfide (neurotoxicants), along with naphthalene (a blood poison) and pyridines (potential carcinogens) all exceeded legal limits, as much as 384 times levels deemed safe. "They're trying to get the pipelines in the ground so fast that they're not doing them properly," says Calvin Tillman, DISH's mayor. "Then you've got nobody looking, so nobody knows if it's going in the ground properly…. You just have an opportunity for disaster here." *3*

DISH sits at the heart of a pipeline network now tuned to exploit a gas drilling boom in the Fort Worth region. The Barnett Shale, a geologic formation more than two kilometers deep and more than 13,000 square kilometers in extent, holds as much as 735 billion cubic meters of natural gas—and the city of Fort Worth alone boasts hundreds of wells, according to Ed Ireland, executive director of the Barnett Shale Energy Education Council, an industry group. "It's urban drilling, so you literally have drilling rigs that are located next door to subdivisions or shopping malls." *4*

Although the first well was drilled in 1982, it took until 2002 for the boom to really get started. Now there are more than 14,000 wells in the Barnett Shale, thanks to a combination of being able to drill horizontally and fracking—pumping water at high pressure deep beneath the ground to literally crack the rock and release natural gas. *5*

"They pump a mixture of water and sand—and half a percent of that is some chemicals, like lubricants," Ireland explains. "They pump that into the formation at a very high pressure. Cracks it just like a windshield. And the cracks go out a couple hundred feet on either side, and that forms the pathway for the natural gas to migrate to the well bore and up to the surface." *6*

All that natural gas may prove a **boon** to a U.S. bid for energy independence. Plus, burning natural gas to produce electricity releases roughly 40 percent less of the greenhouse gas carbon dioxide than burning coal. So the question is: Can extracting that natural gas be done safely? *7*

Water pollution

As Ireland notes: "There's never been a documented case of contaminated water supply." That is technically true, but residents of Dimock, Pa., may disagree. That town sits atop the Marcellus Shale—a giant natural gas–laden rock formation that stretches from Tennessee to New York State—and the kind of extraction now going on in Texas is just getting started there. In Dimock, leaks from badly cased wells contaminated drinking water wells—and one even exploded. *8*

It all comes down to the fact that fracking involves a lot of water. There's the at least 11.5 million liters involved in fracking a well in the first place. There's the **brine** and other fluids that can come to the surface with the natural gas. And there's the problem of what to do with all that waste fluid at the end of the day. *9*

In Dimock's case, Houston-based Cabot Oil and Gas has spilled fracturing fluid, diesel, and other fluids, according to Pennsylvania's Department of Environmental Protection. And elsewhere in the state, fracturing fluid contamination has been detected in the Monongahela River, which is a source of drinking water. In a more common practice, companies dump used fracking fluid back beneath the surface, usually injecting it into other formations beneath the shale. For example, in the case of the Barnett Shale, disposal wells send that water into the deeper Ellenburger Formation. *10*

But there's also the problem of what's actually in the fracking fluid. EPA tests in Wyoming have found suspected fracking fluid chemicals in drinking water wells, and a study by the New York State Department of Environmental Conservation identified 260 chemicals used in the process—a review undertaken as the state decides whether to allow such drilling on lands comprising the watershed providing New York City with its drinking water. And Dow Chemical notes that it sells biocides—antimicrobial poisons—to be included in the mix. But companies **zealously** guard the secret of what exactly makes up their individual "special sauce." It is one of the ways the companies distinguish themselves. *11*

Air pollution

In places where required by law, natural gas companies also distinguish themselves by how they filter out air pollutants. "There's [a vapor recovery unit] that they can put in place to cut out 95 percent of the emissions from a site," Tillman says. "In states where *12* it's been mandated they do it, and they do it willingly—and they do presentations that show how they're going to comply and how their vapor recovery unit is better than the next guy's vapor recovery unit."

That obviously does not happen in DISH, and a big part of such negligence is a lack of appropriate oversight. For example, after it received complaints, the TCEQ sent an SUV with a gas detection unit to drive around Dish for a couple of hours. Despite widespread complaints of odor, the commission found "no leaks that would be detectable to the human nose," Tillman says. "So obviously they're trying to deceive us; they're treating us like we're blooming idiots." *13*

As a result, DISH conducted its own air quality test—at a cost of 15 percent of the town's annual budget of $70,000—that revealed the toxic mix of air pollution. Subsequently, the town petitioned and won the right to install one of seven permanent air monitors in the entire state of Texas. "It's not just writing regulations," Tillman notes. "Somebody has to go out and make sure they're following regulations. And when they're not following regulations, the punishments need to be swift and harsh. . . . " *14*

Climate savior?

Nevertheless, a 2004 study by the EPA found hydraulic fracturing harmless, and the oil industry has been using a roughly similar extraction method since the 1940s. If shale gas can be extracted safely, it might go a long way to cutting back on U.S. emissions of greenhouse gases, as acknowledged at the U.N. Copenhagen climate conference this past December by environmentalists such as Christopher Flavin of the Washington, D.C.–based World Resources Institute. "Compared with coal, natural gas allows a 50 to 70 percent reduction in greenhouse gas emissions," he said. "It's a good complement to the wind and solar generators that will be the backbones of a low-carbon electricity system." *15*

Already, the U.S. produces nearly 600 billion cubic meters of natural gas **annually**, according to the U.S. Department of Energy (DoE), and it estimates proved reserves of natural gas of at least 6.7 trillion cubic meters. The Marcellus Shale alone may have at least 10 trillion cubic meters. *16*

A host of companies have moved in to exploit this resource, and a "few hundred" wildcatters operate in the Barnett Shale alone, according to Ireland. "The wildcatters are the small companies; they *17* have a low overhead, and they can afford to go out and take some risks," he says. "That's been the history of the business, and I think that will continue." But major companies have also taken an interest; ExxonMobil hopes to buy natural gas producer XTO Energy pending regulatory approval.

That's because natural gas is becoming more and more the fuel [18] of choice for generating electricity; the DoE expects 21 percent of U.S. electricity to be derived from natural gas by 2035, and by 2034 power plant builder and consulting firm Black & Veatch expects almost half of all U.S. electricity to come from burning natural gas. "I don't see gas shales having an insurmountable environmental problem that is expensive to fix," says Mark Griffith, head of Black & Veatch's power market analysis.

And the gaseous fossil fuel is used for everything from home [19] heating to making plastics and fertilizer. "It's good that we've discovered all this natural gas, because we're going to need it to generate electricity," Ireland says. "Twenty years from now, we're still going to need all the natural gas we can get."

Some, such as Texas oil and gas millionaire T. Boone Pickens, [20] have even suggested using this new **surfeit** of natural gas to help wean the U.S. off foreign oil, turning it into vehicle fuel. Of course, compressed natural gas is already the fuel of choice for many metropolitan area bus fleets.

Ultimately, however, shale gas extraction—and the hydraulic [21] fracturing that goes with it—will have to be done right. "If something comes out that you're poisoning the population, it's going to be a very bad thing," Ireland notes.

The EPA anticipates finishing its latest study of the practice by [22] 2012. "Six months ago, nobody knew that facilities like this would be spewing benzene," Tillman notes. "Someone could come in here and look at us and say, 'You know what? They've sacrificed you. You've been sacrificed for the good of the shale.'"

---

carcinogens
toxins that can cause cancer

panoply
many, or a wide variety of

boon
a blessing

brine
mixture of fluids

zealously
bringing great action or attention to something

annually
something that happens yearly

surfeit
an excess

Outlining

■ Create a topic outline that shows the key ideas discussed in this reading. See the guidelines discussed in this chapter for help. Use the headings from the reading as your first level of details (I, II, III, IV).

Summarizing

■ Write a summary paragraph of the article using the guidelines from this chapter as a guide. Remember to use your own words and to focus only on the key ideas in the text.

Reflecting

1. What is the most important thing you learned about the topic?

   Fracking is a way to consume natural gas

2. Did any details from the reading surprise you? Which ones?

   How natural gas can be consumed because it can cause other environmental issues

3. What questions do you still have about the topic?

   Why proceed with fracking when we all know it can harm other species?

Vocabulary

Create vocabulary entries for these words. For each word, identify the pronunciation and helpful word parts, give a primary definition, and use the word in a sentence. (See Appendix D for a glossary of common word parts.)

1. **fracking** (paragraph 5)

2. **negligence** (paragraph 13)

Critical Thinking

■ Does the author describe both sides of shale gas extraction? How so? Is the treatment fair and balanced?

■ Would you classify the supporting details as reliable or unreliable? Explain.

■ How does this selection illustrate the delicate balance between environmental protection and energy production?

Writing for Enrichment

What follows are possible writing activities to complete in response to the reading.

Prewriting

Choose one of the following writing ideas, or decide upon an idea of your own related to the reading.

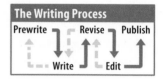

The Writing Process
Prewrite — Revise — Publish
Write — Edit

1. Explain in a personal blog your own relationship with the environment.

2. Read another article about hydraulic fracturing, and write a summary of the article.

3. Compare and contrast oil, coal, and natural gas as providers of energy. Which option is cheaper? Cleaner? More effective?

4. Take a stand on hydraulic fracturing. Write an essay in which you argue for or against the procedure.

5. Explain why this juxtaposition matters in the debate over energy: *Earth's natural resources are both bountiful and finite.*

When planning . . .

- Research your topic as needed, taking thorough notes as you go along.
- Establish a main idea about the topic to emphasize.
- Review your notes for key ideas to support your main idea.
- Decide on the details that you will use to develop it.

When writing . . .

- Include a beginning, middle, and ending in your essay.
- Present your main idea in the beginning part.
- Support it in the middle paragraphs.
- Close your essay with final thoughts about your topic.

When revising and editing. . .

- Carefully review your first draft.
- Ask at least one peer to review your writing as well.
- Improve the content as needed.
- Then edit your revised writing for style and correctness.

Shots Studio, 2014 / Used under license from Shutterstock.com

Shots Studio, 2014 / Used under license from Shutterstock.com

"The eye sees only what the mind is prepared to comprehend."

—Henri Bergson

Chapter 3

Critical Thinking and Viewing

Have you ever heard the expression "going through the motions"? It refers to doing just enough to get something done but without much thought or effort. Going through the motions is perfectly okay for some activities, such as preparing a snack or getting ready for your day. At other times, it has a negative effect, such as when an athlete fails to put forth effort and loses the trust of his or her teammates, or when a student rushes through an assignment just to get it done.

This chapter will help you avoid going through the motions in your academic work. You will learn strategies that will help you think critically when reading, writing, and viewing. Doing so will not only help you connect more deeply with your course work but also improve your learning.

Learning Outcomes

LO1 Consider basic thinking patterns.
LO2 Access deeper thinking.
LO3 Ask critical questions.
LO4 Analyze visuals.

What do you think?

How would you describe the meaning of Henri Bergson's quotation? In what ways can you prepare your mind to comprehend?

L01 Considering Basic Thinking Patterns

Nearly all texts communicate ideas using one of two basic patterns of thinking. **Deductive thinking** begins with a general idea or principle (usually stated in a topic sentence or a thesis) and follows with specific details. It is the most common pattern of thinking that you will read and use. Conversely, **inductive thinking** moves from specific facts and details to a general conclusion. Figure 3.1 shows how the two patterns of thinking move in different directions.

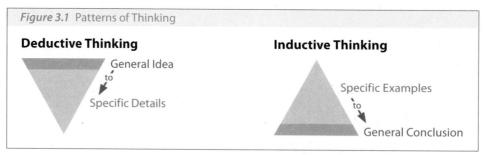

Figure 3.1 Patterns of Thinking

Recognizing whether an academic selection is written deductively or inductively helps you analyze and evaluate the text for two reasons.

1. It helps you locate the main idea of the paragraph or essay.
2. It helps you trace the author's logic or way of supporting the main idea.

Deductive Thinking

The following paragraph is arranged deductively. The main idea (underlined) is followed by specific details. As you can see, when a text is arranged deductively, the main idea appears at the beginning of the text.

> It's hard to say how humpback whales find their way. They may rely on their excellent sense of hearing to pick up low-frequency sound waves that bounce off common ocean features such as rock and coral. Scientists also believe that they may look for familiar landforms. Two researchers recently detected a small amount of magnetic material in humpbacks, which may allow them to migrate by sensing the earth's magnetic field. This may explain why whales get stranded. Some researchers think it's because they are drawn to coasts with low magnetic forces, thinking these coasts are clear waterways. This would also explain how they could follow such precise migration paths.

These questions can help you check for deductive thinking. If you can answer "yes" to the questions, the text follows deductive logic.

- Does the text start with a topic sentence or thesis (main idea or claim)?
- Do the details logically support or follow from the thesis?
- Does the conclusion restate or summarize the main idea?

Inductive Thinking

The following paragraph is arranged inductively. It begins with specific examples leading to a general conclusion (underlined). With this pattern of thinking, the main idea comes at the end of the text.

> Arctic air masses dipped repeatedly across the nation's midsection. The results were reported on the nightly news. In the Texas panhandle, pipes burst as cloudless skies brought a rare hard freeze. In Tennessee, some 200 cars piled up in a dense fog, and many lives were lost. Many people were injured and one was killed in New York City as a short circuit caused by melting snow led to an underground train derailment. In California, old-timers couldn't remember a colder spell than the one that this year ruined nearly 85 percent of the citrus crop and most of the avocados, the strawberries, and the broccoli. The winter of 2000-01 will be remembered as a costly one.

These questions can help you check for inductive thinking. If you can answer "yes" to the questions, the text follows inductive logic.

- Does the text start with a series of facts, examples, and explanations?
- Do they logically lead up to the general conclusion?
- Does the general conclusion make sense in terms of the preceding evidence?

Practice Read the paragraphs closely. Then apply the deductive and inductive questions to identify the pattern of thinking demonstrated in the paragraph.

1. A good indicator of the influence and extent of globalization is the spread of English. In 1600, English was the mother tongue of between 4 and 7 million people. Not even all people in England spoke it. Today, about 1.5 billion people worldwide speak English, more than half as a second language. English is the most widespread language on earth. Most of the world's technical and scientific periodicals are written in English. English is the official language of the Olympics, of navigation in the air and on the seas, and of the World Council of Churches.

What pattern of thinking is used? _____

2. Mounds of paperwork, cluttered office desks, long lines of complaining citizens, and indifferent clerks who quietly shuffle papers—this image of bureaucracy can be found in all modern and postmodern societies. Few people are without a story or two of frustrating struggles against one bureaucracy or another. Most movies depict bureaucracy as perpetually mired in red tape and as an impersonal, soulless machine. *Ikiru*, directed by the Japanese filmmaker Akira Kurosawa, is a profound portrait of the individual versus bureaucracy.

What pattern of thinking is used? _____

Writing Deductively and Inductively

In most academic writing, you will use deductive thinking, moving from a general thesis to specific supporting details. Deduction is effective for exploring and expanding on ideas that are generally agreed upon. Therefore, deduction is popular in explanatory writing. The following writing prompts call for a deductive response.

- Explain why World War II helped create conditions for an economic boom in 1950s America.

- Plunging readership and advertising rates have forced massive staff layoffs at newspapers across the country. Analyze the causes and effects of the decline in the newspaper industry.

Conversely, inductive thinking uses a series of details or events to draw a general conclusion. Inductive conclusions are often based on observations and experiences. Therefore, induction is a common feature in personal essays and narratives, where a writer may draw from personal experiences to come to a general conclusion.

When you write inductively, your goal is to provide enough evidence to improve the probability of your general conclusion. The following writing prompts could elicit an inductive response.

- How did the conditions in which you grew up influence the person you have become?

- Describe how a character in a novel reacts to a moral dilemma. Consider how you would react to the same dilemma. Use the character's experiences as well as your own to decide the best way to handle the situation.

Some academic writing will use a mix of inductive and deductive thinking. While the main thesis may be supported deductively, a supporting idea within an essay may be organized inductively.

Practice Analyze the following writing prompts. Decide whether you would use deductive or inductive thinking to respond to the prompt. Explain your choice.

1. Write about your own observations or experiences that helped you learn about the true meaning of courage.

2. Explain the role of social media in the 2011 Arab Spring demonstrations in the Middle East.

3. Describe the impact of legalized marijuana in Colorado. Use this information to decide whether or not other states should adopt similar laws.

4. Define "redlining," and describe its impact on the civil rights movement.

L02 Accessing Deeper Thinking

Critical thinking involves deep thinking, particularly when you analyze and evaluate. To *analyze* means to break down a subject into its essential parts, examine the parts, and recognize the ways they work together. To *evaluate* means to judge the value of a text, idea, or visual and consider its strengths and weaknesses.

An educational psychologist named Benjamin Bloom classified thinking skills in a list, moving from simple, surface thinking to deeper levels of thinking. The thinking skills in Table 3.1 become more focused as you move down the list. You'll find *analyzing* and *evaluating* near the bottom of the list.

Table 3.1 Bloom's Revised Taxonomy of Thinking Skills

	Reading	Writing
Remember	Collect basic information, identify key terms, and remember main points.	Recall basic information about a topic (facts, ideas, examples, definitions).
Understand	Draw inferences and conclusions about the topic based on what you know about it.	Explain what you have learned, give examples, and restate information.
Apply	Identify the main idea and crucial details; model or show understanding.	State a thesis about the topic and outline key supporting points.
Analyze	Carefully examine the topic and organization, classify the key points, show cause-effect relationships, and make comparisons.	Carefully examine all parts of the topic, recognize relationships between the parts, and choose an appropriate approach.
Evaluate	Judge the value of information and identify a text's strengths and weaknesses.	Judge the value and logic of other people's ideas as well as your own ideas, organization, and voice.
Create	Develop something new from what you have learned.	Develop new ideas and create a draft that draws from your learning, understanding, and analysis of the topic.

Analyzing

When you analyze a text, you study all of its parts separately and consider how they fit together. To analyze a text, first identify the essential parts. Then examine each part separately.

Recognizing the Three Basic Parts

All paragraphs and essays consist of three basic parts: a beginning, a middle, and an ending. Each of these parts functions similarly in paragraphs and essays. See **Figure 3.2**.

Figure 3.2 Basic Three-Part Structure

	Paragraphs	Essays
Beginning	The topic sentence introduces the topic and states the focus of the paragraph.	The first paragraph (or paragraphs) introduces the topic, explains why the topic is important, and states the focus of the essay in a thesis statement.
Middle	The middle sentences provide details about the topic and focus.	The middle paragraphs support the thesis statement with details and evidence. Each middle paragraph focuses on a different supporting idea and includes its own beginning, middle, and ending parts.
Ending	The last sentence provides a concluding point or summarizes the information that came before it.	The ending paragraph restates the thesis and sums up why it is important.

Using Graphics to Analyze the Parts

Once you recognize the basic parts of a text, focus on the details in each part. One way to do so is to create a graphic representation of the details. Figure 3.3 shows how one reader created a line diagram to analyze a paragraph about white blood cells. The diagram allows the writer to study details individually and as a part of the whole.

As the human body's primary protector against infections, viruses, and bacteria, white blood cells come in five different types. Neutrophils are the most numerous white blood cells in the circulatory system. They fight bacteria in infections. Eosinophils account for only between 2 and 5 percent of white blood cells but increase in number when needed to ward off intestinal worms. Basophils also come in low quantities but increase during infectious periods. Lymphocytes capture and fight cellular bacteria by creating antibodies. Finally, the biggest of the white blood cells, monocytes, attack and ward off germs and other dead cells.

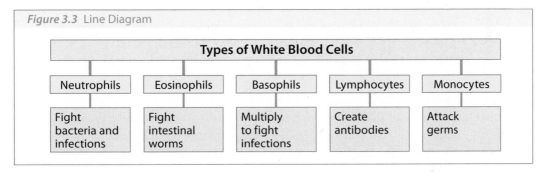

Figure 3.3 Line Diagram

Practice Read the text and then create a line diagram to analyze its details.

John Hagan usefully classifies various types of deviance and crime along three dimensions. The first dimension is the *severity of the social response*. At one extreme, homicide and other very serious forms of deviance result in the most severe negative reactions, such as life imprisonment or capital punishment. At the other end of the spectrum, slight deviations from a norm, such as wearing a nose ring, will cause people to do little more than express mild disapproval.   1

The second dimension of deviance and crime is *perceived harmfulness* of the deviant or criminal act. Some deviant acts, such as rape, are generally seen as very harmful, whereas others, such as tattooing, are commonly regarded as being of little consequence. Note that actual harmfulness is not the only issue here. Perceived harmfulness is . . .   2

The third characteristic of deviance is the *degree of public agreement* about whether an act should be considered deviant. For example, people disagree whether smoking marijuana should be considered a crime. . . . In contrast, virtually everyone agrees that murder is seriously deviant.   3

From BRYM/LIE, Sociology, 2E. © 2007 Cengage Learning.

Evaluating

When you evaluate a text, you judge its strengths and weaknesses. You may judge a text on a variety of factors, including credibility, relevance, and quality.

Considering Credibility

Credibility refers to the trustworthiness of a text's ideas and information. To evaluate a text's credibility, ask questions about key factors.

- **Authorship:** A piece written by an established writer or subject-matter expert enhances its credibility. Beware of texts authored by organizations for commercial purposes and authors writing something simply for personal gain.

  Authorship questions: Is the author an expert on the topic? What are her or his credentials? Does she or he have an established reputation?

- **Source:** In general, scholarly and peer-reviewed books and journals provide more credible information than basic Web resources. Likewise, information in newspaper articles is considered more credible than social media posts.

  Source questions: What person or organization published the text? Is the source scholarly? Is the text published in print or on the Web?

- **Balance:** A balanced text improves credibility by presenting information neutrally, meaning it covers all sides of an issue equally and is free of bias. Biased information is one sided—it presents information in a manner that is partial to one point of view. Some signs of bias include overly emotional language, obvious partiality, or gaps in information.

  Balance questions: Does the text cover different sides of the issue? Are different voices and perspectives represented? Do I detect any bias? Does the author seem overly emotional about the topic? Does the author ignore or misrepresent a certain viewpoint?

- **Accuracy:** The information should be correct, and sources should be cited within the text. If any facts or details seem suspicious, search for other sources that either confirm or contradict the details.

  Accuracy questions: Is the information true and accurate? Are sources cited within the text? Does any information seem suspicious?

- **Purpose**: Texts written to educate generally present information neutrally and let the reader decide what to do with it. Informative texts are typically more credible than those that are meant to entertain or persuade. Texts written to persuade readers to do something or feel a certain way should be read with a particularly critical eye.

  Purpose questions: What is the purpose of the text? To inform? To persuade? To entertain? Is the text trying to sell me something, either a product or an idea?

Checking for Relevance

Relevance refers to how well a text fulfills your reading purpose. If you're reading to learn something new, a relevant text may simply be one that contains accurate and timely information about an interesting topic. If you're reading for a research project, a relevant source will contain accurate information related to your topic of study. Consider these factors when evaluating a text for relevancy.

- **Timeliness**: The information is current and up-to-date. No new information exists that is essential for understanding the topic.
- **Applicability**: The information fulfills your needs as a reader.
- **Accuracy**: The information is correct, and sources are cited within the text.
- **Completeness**: The coverage of the topic is thorough, meaning information that is needed to understand the topic is not missing.

If the text fails to meet any of these factors, you may need to find a different text with information more relevant to your reading purpose.

SPECIAL NOTE: *Timeliness* alone does not always make a text relevant. An older text may be more relevant than a new one. For example, a three-year-old study on vaccinations may be outdated, while a 50-year-old biography may still contain valid information.

Assessing Quality

Quality refers to the overall excellence of a text's information, readability, and design. To help you assess quality, ask and answer critical questions about those important factors.

- **Information:** A quality text contains accurate, balanced, and complete information.
  Information questions: Is the information accurate, up-to-date, and rich in details? Is the information comprehensive and complete? Is the information free of bias, and does it address all sides of the issue? Does the writing clearly credit sources of information through in-text citations, Web links, or a works-cited section?

- **Readability:** A quality text is easy to read and free of writing errors.
  Readability questions: Do the sentences flow smoothly, making the writing easier to read? Is the writing free of obvious errors in spelling, grammar, punctuation, and usage?

- **Design:** A quality text looks clean and professional and is easy to navigate.
  Design questions: Does the design look clean and professional? Do design features like headings and subheadings make the writing easy to navigate? Do the font (type style) and type size improve the text's readability?

Read the news release from NASA. Then read how one student evaluated the text for credibility, relevance, and quality.

West Antarctic Glacier Loss Appears Unstoppable

By Carol Rasmussen, *NASA Earth Science News Team*

A new study by researchers at NASA and the University of California, Irvine, finds a rapidly melting section of the West Antarctic Ice Sheet appears to be in an irreversible state of decline, with nothing to stop the glaciers in this area from melting into the sea.   1

The study presents multiple lines of evidence, incorporating 40 years of observations that indicate the glaciers in the Amundsen Sea sector of West Antarctica "have passed the point of no return," according to glaciologist and lead author Eric Rignot of UC Irvine and NASA's Jet Propulsion Laboratory in Pasadena, California. The new study has been accepted for publication in the journal *Geophysical Research Letters*.   2

These glaciers already contribute significantly to sea-level rise, releasing almost as much ice into the ocean annually as the entire Greenland Ice Sheet. They contain enough ice to raise global sea level by four feet (1.2 meters) and are melting faster than most scientists had expected. Rignot said these findings will require an upward revision to current predictions of sea level rise.   3

"This sector will be a major contributor to sea-level rise in the decades and centuries to come," Rignot said. "A conservative estimate is it could take several centuries for all of the ice to flow into the sea."   4

Three major lines of evidence point to the glaciers' eventual demise: the changes in their flow speeds, how much of each glacier floats on seawater, and the slope of the terrain they are flowing over and its depth below sea level. In a paper in April, Rignot's research group discussed the steadily increasing flow speeds of these glaciers over the past 40 years. This new study examines the other two lines of evidence.   5

The glaciers flow out from land to the ocean, with their leading edges afloat on the seawater. The point on a glacier where it first loses contact with land is called the grounding line. Nearly all glacier melt occurs on the underside of the glacier beyond the grounding line, on the section floating on seawater.   6

Just as a grounded boat can float again on shallow water if it is made lighter, a glacier can float over an area where it used to be grounded if it becomes lighter, which it does by melting or by the thinning effects of the glacier stretching out. The Antarctic glaciers studied by Rignot's group have thinned so much they are now floating above places where they used to sit solidly on land, which means their grounding lines are retreating inland.   From Nasa.gov.   7

Consider Credibility: Is the reading credible? What factors prove its credibility or lack thereof?

The text is written by Carol Rasmussen, who is a writer for NASA. NASA is a government agency with a respected reputation in the science community. The source is a news release from the NASA Web site. It contains information about a study that was accepted for publication in a peer-reviewed journal, so the study itself must be credible. However, since the news release was written by a NASA employee on behalf of a NASA study, some bias may occur in the writing. Likewise, not many alternative perspectives are presented in the release. In general, the information seems accurate and well supported by sources and expert testimony. Overall, I find the reading credible, but I will need to do additional research to find alternative perspectives about the study.

Checking for Relevance: Is the reading timely, accurate, applicable, and complete?

The article displays all of the characteristics of relevancy. It describes a recent study of glaciers. It provides accurate and detailed information that relates to my research project on rising sea levels. The article does not describe the complete details of the study, but it answers all of my basic questions about it. It also contains Web links to related resources at the bottom of the article [not pictured].

Assessing for Quality: Does the reading contain quality information, readability, and design?

This is a quality text. The information is accurate, complete, and up-to-date. It contains a lot of details and clearly credits the sources of information. Though some bias may have crept into the release, the information seems well supported with accurate details. The article is easy to read, and the writing is free of errors. Lastly, the design looks clean and professional, though additional headings could make it easier to navigate.

L03 Asking Critical Questions

When you apply critical thinking to reading and writing, you are, in effect, asking and answering thoughtful questions about a text. Critical questioning happens at all stages of the reading and writing processes.

Critical Reading Questions

During prereading . . . ask critical questions about the topic, title, author, audience, and purpose.

1. **Purpose:** What is the purpose of the reading (to inform, to entertain, to persuade)?
2. **Audience:** Who is intended to read this? General readers? Students? Professionals?
3. **Author:** Who is the author? Is any biographical background information provided? What qualifies this person to write about the topic? Have I read anything else by this person, and if so, what was my opinion of it?
4. **Title/headings**: Turn the title and headings into a series of journalistic questions (*who? what? when? why? where?* and *how?*). Study how one student transformed the title "Mars Rover Finds 'Paving Stone'" into prereading questions:

   - *What* is the Mars rover, and who controls it?
   - *What* is a "paving stone"?
   - *Where* on Mars was the paving stone found?
   - *When* did the Mars rover find the paving stone?
   - *How* did the Mars rover find the paving stone?
   - *Why* is the discovery important?

5. **Prior knowledge:** What do I already know about the topic? What more do I want learn about it?

During reading and rereading . . . search for answers to your prereading questions and ask questions about key ideas and terms.

6. **Content/information:** What big idea is the author trying to convey? What details help me come to this conclusion?

During reflecting . . . question what you've learned, what you still need to learn, and your own personal connections to the reading.

7. **Information gained:** What did I learn about the topic? How can I use this information? Did the text fulfill my reading purpose?
8. **Information gaps:** What do I still want to know about the topic? What information does the author leave out?
9. **Personal connection:** How did the reading challenge me? How has my understanding of the topic changed after reading this? Does the reading call into question any of my values or beliefs?

Practice Pretend you need to give an oral presentation to your class on the topic of neural implants. Imagine you've found the following article on the topic and want to know if it provides sufficient information to make a presentation. Ask and answer the critical prereading questions that apply to the article. Then read the article. Afterward, apply the critical reflecting questions. Based on your critical questioning, decide whether or not the article provides enough information to make a presentation on the neural implants. Write a paragraph summarizing how your critical questioning helped you come to your decision.

Neural Implants Offer Hope for Medical Disabilities

By Dr. Fabian Krutz, *Neural Surgeon*

It sounds like science fiction, but neural prosthetics are a reality, with the potential to change the lives of individuals with a range of medical disabilities including epilepsy, Alzheimer's disease, and spinal cord injuries. 1

Neural prosthetics are miniature bioengineered devices that are implanted in the brain. The prosthetics serve as replacements for damaged nerves, just as a prosthetic arm or leg replaces an amputated one or a cochlear implant simulates the auditory nerve in a deaf ear. 2

The ongoing research and development of neural prosthetics is a multidisciplinary effort involving neurologists, orthopedic surgeons, materials scientists, and mechanical engineers. 3

Many engineers today are receiving funding from the National Institutes of Health to design neural prosthetics. One key engineering challenge is to create an electronic device that will work for a long time within the unique and dynamic environment of the human body. But the engineers are up for the challenge. Notably, Sarah Felix, research engineer at Lawrence Livermore National Laboratory and a member of the American Society of Mechanical Engineers, has made significant progress with thin-film flexible polymer materials. These materials are designed to allow devices to conform to the live tissue in which they are implanted. 4

Other engineers and researchers at Lawrence Livermore are working on neural implants that can restore hearing, assist in speech therapy, and help manage depression and epilepsy. Additional programs on the horizon include using deep brain and spinal cord stimulation to take neural prosthetics to the next level. 5

Stay tuned: Scientists and engineers at major research centers throughout the United States will expand the use of neural prosthetics to improve an increasing range of medical conditions in the years to come. Copyright NewsUSA 6

Critical Writing Questions

During prewriting . . . ask critical questions about the topic, focus, audience, and purpose.

1. **Purpose:** Am I writing this to inform? To entertain? To persuade? What do I want to accomplish with this writing?

2. **Audience:** Who is my intended audience? General readers? An instructor? Peers? A special-interest group? What does my audience know about the topic? What do they need to know about it?

3. **Topic:** What do I know about the topic? What further research do I need to complete? What are some alternative or opposing perspectives about it?

4. **Focus/thesis:** What will be the focus, or thesis, of my writing? Will my audience feel supportive, neutral, or resistent to my focus? If they are resistant, what information do I need to include to gain their support? Has my research changed or altered my feelings toward the topic? If so, does my focus need to be refined?

During writing . . . ask "big-picture" questions that won't interrupt your writing flow.

5. **Purpose:** Am I writing in a way that fulfills my purpose?

6. **Audience:** Am I keeping my audience in mind? Am I answering their questions and meeting their basic needs?

7. **Organization:** Is my draft following a basic structure? Have I attempted to create beginning, middle, and ending parts?

During revising and editing . . . ask thoughtful questions about the first draft.

8. **Ideas:** Is my focus (thesis or topic sentence) clear? Do I support the focus with convincing details ? Are there any weak supporting points, and if so, how could I strengthen them? Have I answered all of the questions my audience will have about the topic?

9. **Organization:** Does my writing have clear beginning, middle, and ending parts? Does any information need to be rearranged to make my main point clearer?

10. **Coherence:** Do the sentences flow well, making the writing easy to read? Can I replace any general words with more specific ones?

11. **Voice:** Do I sound knowledgbable about the topic? Is my writing voice, or tone, appropriate for my topic, audience, and purpose?

12. **Correctness:** Are all names and facts accurate? Is the writing free of grammatical errors?

13. **Design:** Does the writing look clean and professional? Could I add any headings to make it easier for my audience to navigate? Is the font and type size easy to read?

Practice ▸ Apply the critical prewriting questions to the following writing prompt:

- Clothing is a form of self-expression for many people. Evaluate the clothing choices that you or someone else (famous or not) makes, and explain what these fashion choices express about the person.

L04 Analyzing Visuals

In many of your college texts, a significant portion of the information will be given in charts, graphs, figures, illustrations, diagrams, photographs, and drawings. Knowing how to read these types of visuals and how to create visuals of your own is important to your success as a college student.

Visuals such as photographs can be compelling storytelling devices. Often they convey emotion, actions, and events better than words can. Sometimes visuals accompany a reading. Other times they convey a story all by themselves. To derive meaning from visuals, follow this critical-viewing process.

1. **Scan** the whole visual. What catches your eye? This is the focal point of a photo and often the most important part. What else catches your attention? How does it make you feel?

2. **Analyze** the visual by dividing it into smaller sections and studying each section closely. Small clues may hint at a larger meaning.

3. **Ask** critical questions about the visual.
   - **Creator:** Who created the visual? Why did the person create it?
   - **Message:** What does the visual show? What is the subject?
   - **Medium:** Where did the visual appear? When did it first appear there?
   - **Viewer:** Who was supposed to see this visual? Why am I viewing it?
   - **Context:** What is this visual meant to do? How is it supposed to make viewers feel? Why does it appear in this specific medium?

4. **Associate** the visual to its title, caption, or surrounding text. Also consider associations between the visual and your own knowledge and experiences.

5. **Interpret** what the visual means. Use what you learned in steps 1–4 to help you come to a decision. Most visuals are open to multiple interpretations.

Review the sample analysis of Figure 3.5.

Denotative Meaning: What meaning can I interpret from the symbol's physical features?

The Olympic symbol (Figure 3.5) features five interlocking rings, representing the five continents, or regions, of the world. They are interlocked to show unity. The rings' individual colors—blue, yellow, black, green, and red—represent the colors found on all national flags.

Figure 3.5 Olympic Rings

Connotative Meaning: What feelings, associations, or connections does the symbol bring to mind?

I associate the symbols with great athletic feats. It also brings to mind mixed feelings about the unity of the world. On one hand, it makes me think about those glamorous opening and closing ceremonies, where everyone celebrates each other's cultures and applauds each other's flags. On the other hand, the Olympic rings make me disappointed that that goodwill doesn't endure in everyday life. The rings also have the negative connotation associated with some of the tragedies of the Olympics, specifically the events in Munich when 11 Israeli athletes were taken hostage by terrorists. The symbol makes me feel hopeful about the world, but sometimes it feels like false hope.

Practice Analyze the denotative and connotative meaning of one of the symbols in Figure 3.6.

- **Denotative Meaning:** What meaning can I interpret from the symbol's physical features?
- **Connotative Meaning:** What feelings, associations, or connections does the symbol bring to mind?

Figure 3.6 Well-Known Symbols

Reading Graphics

Graphics are visual representations of data. They can add value to writing because they communicate statistical trends and visual information better than words can. As critical thinkers, you should know how to "read" graphics and create ones of your own. To understand and evaluate a graphic, you need to study its parts closely.

- **Scan the graphic.** Consider it as a whole to get an overall idea about its message. Note its type (bar graph, pie graph, diagram, line graph, map, or illustration), its topic, labels, features, and level of complexity.

- **Study the specific parts.** Start with the main heading or title. Next, note any additional labels or guides (such as the horizontal and vertical guides on a bar graph). Then focus on the actual information displayed in the graphic.

- **Question the graphic.** Does it address an important topic? What is its purpose (to make a comparison, to show a change)? What is the source of the information? Is the graphic out of date or biased in any way?

- **Reflect on its effectiveness.** Explain in your own words the main message of the graphic. Then consider its effectiveness, how it relates to the surrounding text, and how it matches up to your previous knowledge of the topic.

Scan the bar graph in **Figure 3.7**. Then read the discussion to learn how all of the parts work together.

- **Study:** This bar graph compares the labor force in 2001 to the labor force in 2013 for five specific age groups. The heading identifies the subject or topic of the graphic. The horizontal line identifies the different age groups, and the vertical line identifies the percentage of the labor force for each group. The key in the upper right-hand corner of the graphic explains the color-coded bars.

- **Question:** The graphic addresses a relevant topic—labor force by age group. Its purpose is to show the changes in the ages of the labor force through time. The data comes from the Bureau of Labor Statistics. The information is not completely up-to-date since it ends in 2013.

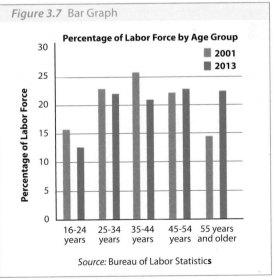

Figure 3.7 Bar Graph

- **Reflect:** The graphic reads quite clearly—and many interesting comparisons can be made. The most noteworthy comparison is that many more people over the age of 55 remained in the workforce in 2013 as compared to 2001.

Practice Read the graphic in Figure 3.8 and answer the analysis questions about it.

Figure 3.8 Pictograph

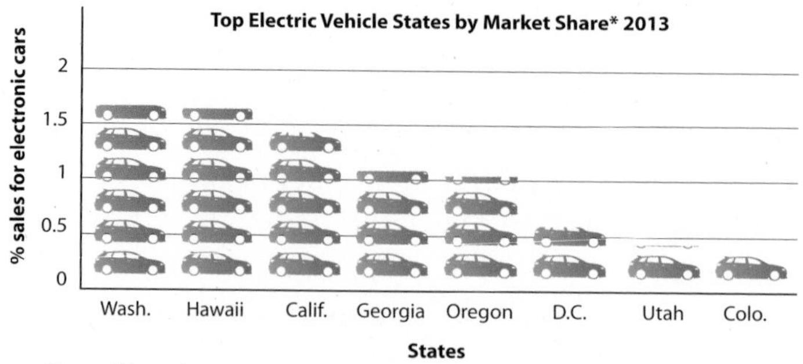

Top Electric Vehicle States by Market Share* 2013

% sales for electronic cars

Wash.   Hawaii   Calif.   Georgia   Oregon   D.C.   Utah   Colo.

States

Source: Edmunds.com

1. Figure 3.8 is called a pictograph rather than a bar graph. What makes it a "pictograph"?

_____

2. What is the topic of Figure 3.8?

_____

3. What information is provided on the horizontal line? On the vertical line?

_____

4. What is the purpose of the graphic?

_____

5. Is the information up-to-date?

_____

6. What comparisons can you make from the graphic?

_____

_____

7. Do you think the graphic is effective? Why or why not?

_____

_____

Using Graphics in Writing

Graphics tell the story of numbers and figures and can add value to your academic writing. With today's technology, creating effective graphics is easier than ever before. To get started, gather your data and choose an appropriate form.

- **Identify a purpose.** What idea do you want the graphic to express? Ideally, it should emphasize or complement an idea from the text.

- **Check your data.** A graphic is meaningless without clear and accurate data. Make sure the source of the numbers is accurate and credible. Figure 3.9 shows how one writer found a data set for an essay on hydraulic fracturing of shale (natural) gas. The data will help support an idea in the writer's essay.

Figure 3.9 Planning a Graphic

Purpose: To show the relationship between the "hydraulic fracturing boom" and natural gas production in the United States

Data: The data set comes from the U.S. Energy Information Administration.

Total Natural Gas Production

Year	Production (billion cubic feet)
2007	19266
2008	20159
2009	20624
2010	21316
2011	22902
2012	24057
2013	24281

Shale Gas Production

Year	Production (billion cubic feet)
2007	1293
2008	2116
2009	3110
2010	5336
2011	7994
2012	10371
2013	11371

- **Understand your options.** Different types of graphics serve different purposes.

Line graphs show changes in amounts over time. (See Figure 3.10.) A scatter plot serves a similar purpose, but it doesn't connect its data points with a line, like a line graph does.

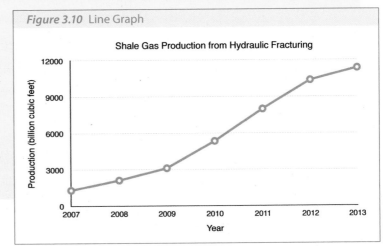

Figure 3.10 Line Graph

Shale Gas Production from Hydraulic Fracturing

Bar graphs show comparisons between amounts of something or the number of times something occurs (see Figure 3.11). A stacked bar graph shows comparisons of multiple data sets (see Figure 3.14).

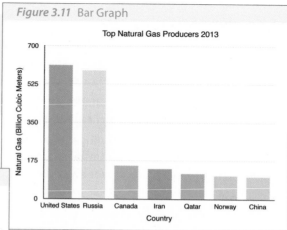

Figure 3.11 Bar Graph

Pie charts show how something is divided up. The whole pie represents the whole sample, while the wedges represent the different parts (see Figure 3.12).

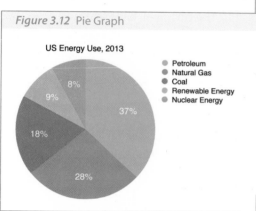

Figure 3.12 Pie Graph

Information maps use colors and symbols to show relationships between geographic data (see Figure 3.13).

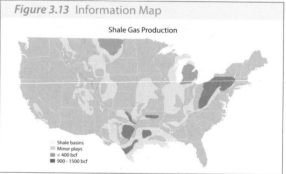

Figure 3.13 Information Map

- **Check your focus.** Your graphic should focus on one main idea.
- **Create a title and label the axes.** The title should summarize what the graphic shows. Label the x and y axes and any important data points. If necessary, add a separate legend to identify icon sets, colors, or data bars (see Figure 3.14).
- **Choose reader-friendly design features**, including colors, type size and font, and graphics. Use white space wisely and avoid clutter.

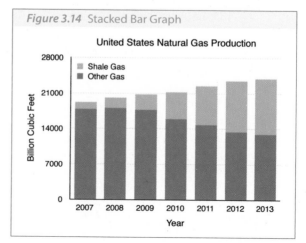

Figure 3.14 Stacked Bar Graph

☑ Review and Enrichment

Reviewing the Chapter

Consider Basic Thinking Patterns

1. Which type of thinking starts with a series of facts, observations, or details that lead to a general conclusion?

2. Where is the main idea usually located in a deductive text? Where is it located in an inductive text?

Access Deeper Thinking

3. According to Benjamin Bloom, what three thinking skills require the deepest level of thought?

4. What is the difference between *analyzing* and *evaluating* a text?

5. How does graphing details help you analyze a reading?

6. What factors should you consider when you evaluate a text's credibility?

Ask Critical Questions

7. What critical questions should you ask about your audience during prewriting?

8. Turn the following title into a series of journalistic questions: The New Hope Antipoverty Program

Analyze Visuals

9. What five steps can you follow to critically view an image or photograph?

10. What role do graphics serve in academic writing?

"Read not to contradict and confute; nor to believe and take for granted; nor to find talk and discourse; but to weigh and consider."

—Francis Bacon

Reading for Enrichment

The following reading selection is from *The American Pageant*, a textbook on the history of the American people. Be sure to follow the steps in the reading process to help you gain a full understanding of the text.

About the Authors

David M. Kennedy is an accomplished historian, professor, and author. His 1999 book *Freedom from Fear: The American People in Depression and War, 1929–1945* won the 2000 Pulitzer Prize for history writing. **Lizabeth Cohen** is a professor of American Studies at Harvard University, where she once served as chair of the History Department. Her 1990 book *Making a New Deal* won the annual Bancroft Prize for American history writing.

Prereading

1. What do the title, the first paragraph, and the first lines of other paragraphs tell you about the topic?

2. What do the photograph and graphic tell you about the topic?

3. What do you already know about the topic? What do you want to know about it?

4. What makes the authors qualified to write about this topic?

5. Turn the title into a series of journalist questions that you can search for answers for while you read.

What do you think?

Reread Francis Bacon's quotation. How can you carefully weigh and consider a reading text? Can you use a similar process to evaluate your writing?

Reading and Rereading

As you read, make it your goal to analyze and evaluate the text. Consider annotating the text and/or taking notes to help you keep track of the information during your reading.

Also think carefully about how the United States' foreign policies shape the way people think of the country. Consider how someone from outside the U.S. might view some of this country's actions abroad. Then weigh the outsider's perspective with your own.

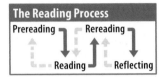

America Through Foreign Eyes: Hyperpower or Hapless Power?

When the Soviet Union disintegrated in 1991, the Cold War concluded at last. So did an era in the history of American foreign policy and in the history of the international order. For nearly half a century following World War II, the confrontation with the Soviets had deeply shaped Americans' conception of themselves—their national identity—as well as their role and reputation in the wider world. In the long twilight struggle against Soviet communism, they had accumulated unprecedented economic, military, and cultural might and had taken **virtuous** pride in themselves as the global champions of democracy, justice, and human rights. Now, as the sole surviving "superpower," they faced no counterbalancing regime, and apparently, no check on their national ambitions. The United States seemed to wield all but limitless power to mold the international environment as it wished. Not since the days of ancient Rome did any people **bestride** the world so unopposed.

Not everyone welcomed the emergence of this international **colossus.** Australians grumbled that the United States was a "tall poppy" that needed to be cut down to size. French foreign minister Hubert Védrine coined a new term when he described the United States in 1999 not merely as a "hyper power," one that is dominant or predominant in all categories, including not only the traditional

1

2

domains of politics, economics, and the military, but even including "attitudes, concepts, languages, and modes of life." He called upon Europeans to create an alternative to the American "steamroller," to "work in favor of real multilateralism against unilateralism, for balanced multipolarism, for cultural diversity against uniformity." In the **parlance** of international relations, Védrine was promoting a "balancing" strategy to cope with U.S. power, rather than the "bandwagon" strategy of simply submitting to American **hegemony** and making the most of it. Notably, he was not proposing outright opposition.

As the last days of the twentieth century slipped through the hourglass, American power surely looked formidable. The United States was the world's third most populous nation (after China and India), enjoyed the world's largest economy (more than three times larger than second-ranked Japan), was the acknowledged global leader in high-tech information and biomedical innovations, and spent more on its armed forces than the rest of the world *combined*. Yet the realities of American power were somewhat less imposing. Uncle Sam struggled to find solid footing in the post-Cold War international arena. Washington in the 1990s badly botched a peacekeeping mission to lawless Somalia; stood by helplessly as genocidal militias murdered nearly a million Rwandans; **dithered** over how to stabilize chaotic Haiti; fumbled indecisively as nationalist and **sectarian** violence convulsed the former Balkan nation of Yugoslavia; found no effective response to terrorist attacks on New York City's World Trade Center, the destroyer USS *Cole*, and American embassies in Kenya and Tanzania; and notoriously failed to bring any conclusion to the decades-old confrontation between Israelis and Palestinians, who erupted in a bloody intifada (rebellion) against the Jewish state in 2000.

The **barbarous** Al Qaeda assault that finally toppled the twin towers of the World Trade Center on September 11, 2001, momentarily brought an outpouring of sympathy from an astonished and outraged world—and also brought a dramatic shift in American foreign policy. Even *Le Monde*, France's leading newspaper, declared that in this dangerous hour "Nous sommes tous Américains" (We are all Americans). For the first time in history, the North Atlantic Treaty Organization (NATO) invoked the treaty's Article Five, confirming that an attack on one member is an attack on all members.

But such sentiments proved short-lived. When President George 5 W. Bush in 2002 asserted a new right of preemptive war and then proceeded to invade Iraq for what looked to many observers like the most **dubious** of reasons, anti-American sentiment swelled the world over. In February 2002 some 10 million people in 60 countries demonstrated against the impending U.S. invasion of Iraq. Exacerbated by Washington's rejection of the Kyoto Treaty dealing with global warming and by several American states' continuing embrace of the death penalty (which had largely disappeared in Europe and elsewhere), America's standing deteriorated even among its traditional allies and sank to rock-bottom lows in Islamic countries. Simmering resentment over the detention of hundreds of captured Afghans at the U.S. military base in Guantánamo, Cuba; revelations about human rights abuses inflicted by American troops on Iraqi prisoners at Baghdad's Abu Ghraib prison; and "rendition" by American agents of suspected terrorists to the notoriously cruel security services of other countries further drained the depleted reservoirs of America's moral and political capital. The election of Barack Obama in 2008 briefly **burnished**

Figure 3.15 Prisoner at Abu Ghraib

Photo from Associated Press

the American image once more, but in the eyes of many global citizens, America was no longer a "City on a Hill" to be admired and emulated.

Once a moral beacon and political inspiration to a suffering world, the United States in the early twenty-first century had come to be regarded by millions of people the world over as a moral **scourge** and a political and military danger (see Figure 3.16). Recapturing its stature as a legitimate world leader, rebuilding its alliances, restructuring the myriad multilateral institutions it had worked so hard to build in the Cold War era, and recapturing a sense of itself as a just and humane society were tasks that urgently confronted the Republic as the new century advanced.

6

From Kennedy and Cohen. *The American Pageant*, 15th Edition. Copyright 2014. Cengage Learning.

Figure 3.16 World Opinion Bar Graph

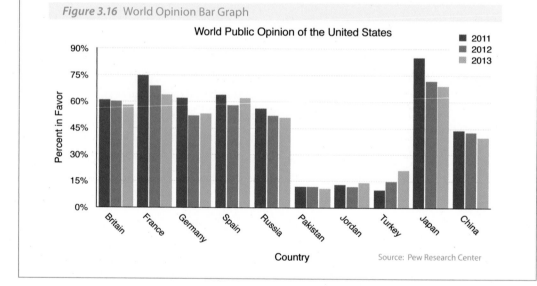

World Public Opinion of the United States

bestride
to possess great power

virtuous
moral goodness

colossus
gigantic size and power

parlance
a way of speaking

hegemony
rule of one nation over another

dithered
to act uncertainly or indecisively

sectarian
characterized by small or isolated groups

barbarous
wild and savagely

dubious
causing doubt or uncertainty

burnished
brightened

scourge
a cause of harm or ill will

Summarizing

Write a summary of "America Through Foreign Eyes: Hyperpower or Hapless Power?" Remember that a summary presents the main points in a clear, concise form using your own words.

Reflecting

1. Overall, is the essay organized deductively or inductively? Explain.

2. Explain what Figure 3.16 shows by closely studying its parts.

3. Did you notice any gaps of information in the reading? Is there anything you still want to know about the topic?

4. Did your understanding of the topic change after reading this? If so, how did it change?

Vocabulary Practice

Create vocabulary entries for the following words. For each word, identify the pronunciation and helpful word parts, give a primary definition, and use the word in a sentence.

1. **formidable** (paragraph 3)
2. **exacerbated** (paragraph 5)

Critical Thinking

- Did you find the reading credible? Why or why not?
- How would you assess the quality of the reading?
- Did the authors present the topic in a balanced manner? That is, did they present all sides of the topic equally? Or did they focus on one part more than the other?
- In what way did the reading call into question your own values or beliefs?
- What factors do you think shape a person's perception of the United States?
- What interpretations can you make by closely viewing the photograph in Figure 3.15? What about the photograph influenced you to make those interpretations?

Writing for Enrichment

Prewriting

Choose one of the following writing ideas, or decide upon an idea of your own related to the reading.

The Writing Process
Prewrite → Revise → Publish
↑ ↓ ↑ ↓ ↑
Write   Edit

1. Read a news story about the United States' role in a foreign affair. Evaluate the reading by analyzing its relevance, credibility, and quality.

2. Critically read an editorial or opinion text about current U.S. foreign policy. Write about how the author develops an argument and whether he or she does so logically.

3. Browse images of American life on the front page of a newspaper or major news site online. Choose one image that catches your eye. Write an analysis of it based on your critical viewing and your reading of the essay "America Through Foreign Eyes: Hyperpower or Hapless Power?"

4. Find an important symbol in American history. Analyze its connotative and denotative meaning.

When planning . . .

- Research your topic as needed to learn about your topic, taking thorough notes as you go along.
- Establish a thesis for your essay.
- Review your notes for key ideas to support your thesis.
- Decide on the details that you will use to develop these ideas.

When writing . . .

- Include a beginning, middle, and ending in your essay.
- Present your thesis in the beginning part.
- Support the thesis in the middle paragraphs.
- If possible, add a graphic to support your thesis or a key idea.
- Close your essay with final thoughts about your thesis.

When revising and editing . . .

- Carefully review your first draft.
- Ask at least one peer to review your writing as well.
- Improve the content as needed.
- Then edit your revised writing for style and correctness.

PART 2:

Reading and Writing Essays

Part 2: Reading and Writing Essays

Chapter 4

"A man's mind is stretched by a new idea or sensation and never shrinks back to its original dimensions."

—Oliver Wendell Holmes Sr.

Ideas

Ideas are the essential element behind every selection that you read and write. That is, a text needs a topic, a main idea that puts the topic into focus, and details that support the topic and main idea. Other elements such as organization, tone, and word choice depend on the ideas. A text without ideas would be like a recipe without any ingredients or a building plan without any building materials—there would be nothing to work with.

In this chapter, you will closely examine the development of ideas in academic reading and writing. First, you will learn about identifying topics and main ideas in reading selections and for your own writing. Then you will learn about reading for supporting details and using different types of details in your writing.

Learning Outcomes

LO1 Read for topics.

LO2 Select a topic for writing.

LO3 Read for main ideas.

LO4 Establish a main idea for writing.

LO5 Read for supporting details.

LO6 Draw inferences.

LO7 Choose supporting details in writing.

What do you think?

How would you explain the quotation by Holmes? How can a mind be stretched by a new idea or sensation? And what does it mean that a mind will "never shrink back to its original dimensions"?

L01 Reading for Topics

Any piece of writing has to be about something, and that something is called the topic. A **topic** can be a person *(Hillary Clinton)*, a place *(the Lorraine Motel)*, an object *(vinyl records)*, an idea *(trust)*, or an animal *(dogs)*. Identifying the topic is naturally the important first step when carrying out a reading assignment. You need to know what the text is about. Luckily, this task is seldom complicated. In almost all texts, the topic is identified in the title, in the first few sentences, or in the first few paragraphs.

Topic Stated in a Heading and First Sentence:

Harm

For most crimes to occur, some harm must have been done to a person or to a property. A certain number of crimes are actually categorized depending on the harm done to the victim, regardless of the intent behind the criminal act. Take two offenses, both of which involve one person hitting another in the back of the head with a tire iron. In the first instance, the victim dies, and the offender is charged with murder. In the second, the victim is only knocked unconscious, and the offender is charged with battery. Because the harm in the second instance was less severe, so was the crime with which the offender was charged.

From Gaines/Miller, *Cengage Advantage Books: Criminal Justice in Action*, 6E. © 2011 Cengage Learning.

Topic Stated in the First Sentence:

Every language has a logical structure. When people encounter an unfamiliar language for the first time, they are confused and disoriented, but after becoming familiar with the language, they eventually discover its rules and how the various parts are interrelated. All languages have rules and principles governing what sounds are to be used and how those sounds are to be combined to convey meaning. . . .

From Ferraro/Andreatta, *Cultural Anthropology*, 9E. © 2012 Cengage Learning.

Topic Stated at the End of the First Paragraph in an Essay:

Imagine a room containing a large group of people all working hard toward the same goal. Each person knows his or her job, does it carefully, and cooperates with other group members. Together, they function efficiently and smoothly—like a well-oiled machine. Then one worker stops his work and steps into someone else's workstation, using those materials to make little reproductions of himself. Soon the reproductions spill into other workstations, get in the way, and continue to multiply. A human body is like this room, and the body's cells are like these workers. If the body is healthy, each cell has a necessary job and does it correctly. When a cell begins to function abnormally, it can initiate a process that results in cancer.

Delayed Identification of a Topic:

In two days Kamal would have been four years old, but his wasted body now   *1*
lies under a pile of rocks behind his family's hut.

Why did Kamal die? The too-easy answer is malnutrition. A lack of vitamins   *2*
and protein opened him to intestinal infection and diarrhea. He could have been
saved with a simple solution of boiled water, salts, and sugar, which the UNICEF
distributes in a free kit called "oral rehydration therapy" (ORT). But Kamal's
mother, forced to work 18-hour days at home and in the fields, had missed the
rural health-care worker's demonstration in the village.

Why was Kamal malnourished in the first place? He and his six brothers and   *3*
sisters had known hunger all their lives. His father and mother scraped at five dry
acres of government land, earning no more than $500.00 (U.S.) even in a good
year. For the past seven years, an unrelenting drought had dried up the wells and
withered the crops.

Around the world, according to Roy Prosterman (*The Hunger Project Papers*),   *4*
18 children like Kamal die of hunger every 60 seconds. In the two minutes it may
have taken you to read these words, another 36 children died. Of all of today's
global problems, none can be more tragic than childhood deaths by starvation
and disease.

Practice Circle the topic in the following texts. Then write where the topic is first stated.

1.

Ethnicity

Ethnicity can be a powerful draw in terms of customer loyalty and community development. Restaurants identified as purveyors of ethnic foods may appeal to members of a cuisine's ethnic group as well as others who are interested in enjoying foods from different cultures. Ethnically based food service offers comfort and familiarity by providing foods that are considered to be part of a culture.   From Chon/Maier, *Welcome to Hospitality*, 3E. © 2010 Cengage Learning.

2.

We Have Been Here Before

Columbus, an Italian, arrived in the New World with a crew of more than   *1*
100 composed of Spaniards, Portuguese, some Jews who had been expelled from Spain, some convicts, and an Arab brought along to translate anticipated conversations with Chinese and Japanese—remember where Columbus thought he was going. Now, about this new American thing, "diversity."

Concerning which, Michael Barone says, "We have been here before." As   *2*
when Benjamin Franklin, a worrywart, doubted that the Germans who were 40 percent of Pennsylvanians could be assimilated [made similar]. It is generally wise to believe Barone, the author every two years of "The Almanac of American Politics" and now of a new book, *The New Americans: How the Melting Pot Can Work Again*. To those who say that traditionally white-bread America has suddenly become multigrain, Barone says: Fiddlesticks.

America, he says, has always been multigrain. . . .   *3*

From "We Have Been Here Before" by George Will, *Newsweek*, June 11, 2001.

3.   Bridewealth is the compensation given upon marriage by the family of the groom to the family of the bride. According to Murdock's "Ethnographic Atlas" (reported in Stephens 1963: 211), approximately 46 percent of all societies give substantial bridewealth payment as a normal part of the marriage process. Although bridewealth is practiced in most regions of the world, it is perhaps most widely found in Africa. . . .

From Ferraro/Andreatta, *Cultural Anthropology*, 9E. © 2012 Cengage Learning.

---

4.   From *The Big Burn*

On one of the last days of Teddy Roosevelt's time in the White House, the   1
president called in his handpicked successor to talk about plans to run the nation in the second decade of the American century. Despite his girth, William H. Taft was always the smaller man when in Roosevelt's presence, or so he felt. Roosevelt was the human volcano; Taft was a putting green. Roosevelt sucked the air out of a room; Taft tried to be invisible. Roosevelt barked; Taft had a low monotone, punctuated by a random and annoying chuckle. Roosevelt burned two thousand calories before noon and drank his coffee with seven lumps of sugar; Taft was the picture of sloth: multiple chins, a zest for five-course meals and long baths. Sleeping Beauty was the nickname his wife, Nellie, gave him, and oh, how he loved to nap. But to the question of how and where to lead the country, they did not differ, the president believed.

Taft had spent the past three years observing Roosevelt's likes and dislikes,   2
his private quirks and public persona. He took it all in carefully and then projected it back to him, hitting the right notes as Roosevelt probed him on his political beliefs. As such, he seemed to be the perfect successor. . . . More than any guiding principle, Will Taft simply was driven by the desire to please the man he considered his closest friend. And so when Roosevelt asked him to the White House in late 1908, after a campaign in which Taft won with the full backing and expert advice of the still-young Roosevelt, the incoming president again said all the right things. Taft had won in a landslide, crushing the perennial Democratic populist William Jennings Bryan.

From Egan, Timothy. *The Big Burn*. Boston: Houghton Mifflin Harcourt., 2010. Print.

LO2 Selecting a Topic for Writing

Ideas are the fuel that powers your writing. Without a strong topic, you are running on vapors, meaning that you won't get very far.

"Find a subject you care about and which you in your heart feel others should care about."

—Kurt Vonnegut

Choosing a Topic

The late personal essayist Andy Rooney of *60 Minutes* fame stated, "I don't pick subjects so much as they pick me." As a college student, your writing is tied to the specific subjects you are studying. But like Rooney, you will have an opportunity to take ownership of almost any topic you develop in your writing.

Some assignments will tell you specifically what you should write about, but in most cases, they will identify a general subject area that serves as a starting point for a topic search. Always try to select a topic within the subject area that interests you; otherwise, you will find it difficult to do your best work. **Figure 4.1** shows how the selecting process should work from the general subject area to a specific topic.

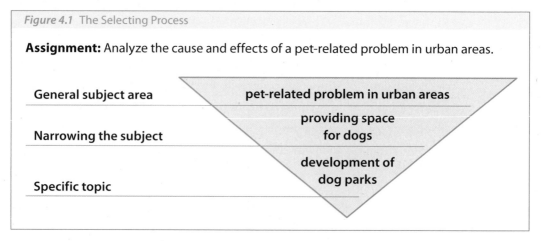

Figure 4.1 The Selecting Process

Assignment: Analyze the cause and effects of a pet-related problem in urban areas.

General subject area — **pet-related problem in urban areas**

Narrowing the subject — **providing space for dogs**

Specific topic — **development of dog parks**

Practice Identify a specific topic for the following assignment. (Use **Figure 4.1** as a guide.)

Assignment: In a persuasive essay, argue for or against a new or proposed mode of transportation.

1. General subject area
2. Narrow the subject
3. Specific topic

Searching Strategies

If you are having trouble selecting a specific topic, review your class notes or search the Internet for topics. The following strategies may also help you identify possible topics.

- **Clustering:** Begin a cluster with the general subject area or a narrowed subject. Cluster related words around it. Write about one of these ideas. See Figure 4.2.

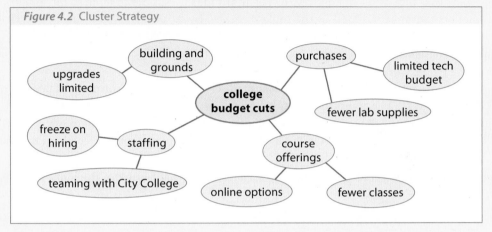

Figure 4.2 Cluster Strategy

- **Freewriting:** Write nonstop for 5–10 minutes about your assignment to discover possible topics. Begin by writing down a particular thought about the assignment. Then record whatever comes to mind without stopping to judge, edit, or correct your writing.
- **Developing a Dialogue:** Create a conversation between yourself and another person to see if a possible topic unfolds.

Practice Create a dialogue for the following writing assignment. Afterward, circle any possible writing ideas. (Use your own paper to continue the conversation.)

Assignment: Write a brief personal essay in which you reflect on this quote from William Shakespeare: "This above all: to thine own self be true."

You: _So what does it mean to be true to yourself?_____

Other person: _____

You: _____

Other person: _____

L03 Reading for Main Ideas

Writers don't expect to say everything about a topic in their writing. If they did, their writing could go on and on. Instead, they focus their attention on a main idea—a special feature, part, or feeling about the topic that they want to emphasize. The **main idea** in most paragraphs is stated in the topic sentence. In most essays and articles, the main idea is stated in a **thesis statement**, which is usually located in one of the opening paragraphs.

Insight An essay without a clear focus is like a glass of spilled water because the contents seem to run in every direction. Reading an unfocused text can be a challenge.

There are times, however, when the main idea is expressed in a summary statement near the end of a text. The main idea in some essays may be implied or suggested rather than directly stated, and some longer, more complex essays may have more than one main idea. The main idea can tell you a lot about a piece of writing. Consider the following examples:

- In an **informational essay,** the main idea tells you what feature of the topic will be addressed.

  > For the first time in history, an entire city can choose to become the urban equivalent of a natural ecosystem.

  Or it may indicate that a particular pattern of organization (*process, cause-effect,* etc.) will be used to discuss the main idea.

  > Sociological research is a cyclical process that involves six steps.

- In an **essay of argumentation,** the main idea identifies the claim about a topic that the writer will argue for.

  > The city of Chicago should build barriers between canals flowing to and from Lake Michigan to prevent invasive fish from invading the Great Lakes.

- In a **narrative,** the main idea may tell you how the writer feels about the topic, which will be an experience or event.

  > This is the tale of two sisters from Calcutta, who have lived in the United States for some 35 years but who find themselves on different sides in the current debate over the status of immigrants.

SPECIAL NOTE: The wording of a statement may signal it as the main idea: "This is a tale of two sisters who . . . ," "Study after study has shown that . . . ," or "Surprisingly, both sides discovered that . . ."

The following steps can help you identify the main idea or thesis in an essay, an article, or a chapter. In paragraphs, you usually need to look no further than the first sentence or the last sentence.

1 Review the title, any headings, and the first and last paragraphs of the text.

2 Then read the opening part, perhaps the first few paragraphs, to gain a general understanding of the topic.

3 Next, look for a sentence or two in one of the opening paragraphs that seems to direct the writing. (Often, this sentence comes at the end of one of these paragraphs.)

4 Underline this sentence, highlight it, or write it down. If you can't find such a sentence, try to state the main idea in your own words.

5 Then continue your initial reading to see if this statement makes sense as the main idea (or at least one of them). Each new paragraph should support or develop it with facts, statistics, and examples.

6 If your thinking changes, identify or write down what you now consider to be the main idea.

Topic Sentences and Thesis Statement

A topic sentence or thesis statement usually has two working parts: (1) a specific topic plus (2) a special feature, part, or feeling (opinion) about the topic.

"Dogs are diverse (*topic*) because of artificial rather than natural selection (*feature*)."

"Fatherlessness (*topic*) is the most harmful demographic trend of this generation (*opinion*)."

Study the following paragraph in which the writer describes the sense of taste.

All the flavors that a person can taste are made up of a few taste sensations. In the Western world, people are used to thinking about four tastes: salty, sweet, sour, and bitter. The salty taste comes from substances that include sodium, such as snacks like potato chips or pretzels. The sweet sensation comes from sugars, whether in processed foods like sweetened cereals or naturally occurring in fruit or honey. Sour tastes come from acidic foods such as lemons and grapefruits, and bitter tastes come from alkaline foods such as coffee or dark chocolate. But in the Eastern world, two other taste sensations are recognized. A savory taste comes from amino acids, which are a basic part of meats and proteins. And a spicy taste comes from substances like the capsaicin in hot peppers. Given the savory and spicy nature of Indian, Thai, Chinese, and other Eastern foods, it's no wonder that these tastes are recognized. With all the sensations to appeal to, chefs can make every dish a unique and tasty work of art.

A paragraph, by definition, is a group of sentences sharing details about a main idea, which is usually stated in the topic sentence. The topic sentence in the above paragraph is underlined. The sentences in the body of the paragraph explain the topic.

Study the title and opening part of the following article in which the author explores emotional intelligence.

What Is Emotional Intelligence?

Many experts believe that intelligence takes many forms. Rather than a narrow definition of intelligence, they believe in Multiple Intelligences: Linguistic, Logical-Mathematical, Spatial, Kinesthetic, Musical, Interpersonal, Intrapersonal, and Naturalistic. Emotional intelligence may well be a combination, at least in part, of **intrapersonal** and **interpersonal** intelligences.

Emotional intelligence is a set of skills that determines how well you cope with the demands and pressures you face every day. How well do you understand yourself, **empathize** with others, draw on your inner resources, and encourage the same qualities in people you care about? Emotional intelligence involves having people skills, a positive outlook, and the capacity to adapt to change. Emotional intelligence can propel you through difficult situations.

The bottom line? New research links emotional intelligence to college success, and learning about the impact of EI in the first year of college helps students stay in school.

As you read about the five scales of emotional intelligence, begin thinking about yourself in these areas. As each scale is introduced, ask yourself whether you agree or disagree with the sample statement from a well-known emotional intelligence instrument as it pertains to you.

From Staley/Staley, FOCUS on College and Career Success, 1E. © 2012 Cengage Learning.

---

intrapersonal
having to do with a person's inner thoughts and feelings

interpersonal
having to do with the relationships between people

empathize
imagine what another person feels

The underlined statement in the second paragraph answers the question in the title— which suggests that it is the main idea, or thesis. The third and fourth paragraphs indicate that the underlined idea will be explored further.

Practice Identify the main idea or thesis in each essay that follows. Remember that the thesis can appear anywhere in the opening part, and it may be more than one sentence. If you can't find such a statement, state it in your own words. Then explain each of your choices.

1.   Ancient Times

In primitive times, the common belief was that disease and illness were   *1*
caused by evil spirits and demons. Treatment was directed toward eliminating the evil spirits. As civilizations developed, changes occurred as people began to study the human body and make observations about how it functions.

Religion played an important role in health care. A common belief was   *2*
that illness and disease were punishments from the gods. Religious rites and ceremonies were frequently used to eliminate evil spirits and restore health. Exploring the structure of the human body was limited because most religions did not allow dissection, or cutting apart of the body. For this reason, animals were frequently dissected to learn about different body parts.

The ancient Egyptians were the first people to record health records. It is   *3*
important to remember that many people could not read; therefore, knowledge was limited to an educated few. Most of the records were recorded on stone and were created by priests, who also acted as physicians. . . .

From Simmers, *Diversified Health Occupations*, 7E. © 2009 Cengage Learning.

Main idea: _____

_____

_____

_____

Explain your choice: _____

_____

_____

2.

One-of-a-Kind Character(s)

Mystery books are hugely popular. In fact, they are so popular that a reader   *1*
can find a mystery set in just about any time and place. There are mysteries that
seem very real, and others that are more imaginative. What all mysteries have
in common is a main detective or investigator who leads the reader through the
mystery. The most famous mysteries have a one-of-a-kind main character leading
the investigation.

Many mystery experts feel that Arthur Conan Doyle created the most famous   *2*
detective of all, Sherlock Holmes. The mysterious Holmes hides out in his flat on
Baker Street in London where he conducts experiments, reads, and occasionally
goes into a funk (and smokes opium). His only friend and companion is the
understanding Dr. Watson. Holmes is a very serious man with dark hair and
piercing eyes, and he uses his great powers of observation and deduction to solve
each mystery.

Another British writer, Agatha Christie, invented the famous amateur   *3*
detective Jane Marple in the 1920s. Miss Marple is an elderly woman residing in
a small village in England with the personality of a sweet aunt or grandmother.
Miss Marple is a loner like Holmes, but she is very personable and understanding
in social situations. While Holmes busies himself in his laboratory, Miss Marple
works in her garden. Christie develops each mystery so Miss Marple just happens
to appear at the site of crime. She snoops around, listens, asks questions, and
eventually solves each crime.

These examples show that the most popular mysteries begin and end with   *4*
a special investigator. Each new mystery allows this individual to put his or her
special talents into action to solve a crime that no one else can figure out. Readers
enjoy each new opportunity to see how their favorite investigator does the job.

Main idea: _____

_____

_____

Explain your choice: _____

_____

_____

3.   Thinking Like Breathing

Which is more important for a successful career, *1* critical thinking or creative thinking? It's a trick question. I may as well ask which is more important, breathing out or breathing in? "Whichever one I need to do right now" is one good answer to this last question. Another is "Neither is more important since I need both to stay alive." It's the same with critical and creative thinking.

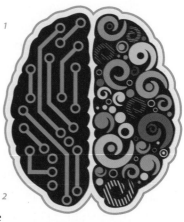

Creative and critical thinking are two halves of *2* a cycle: inspiration and expiration. And the interchange between the two is the key to success.

Creative thinking draws in possibilities. It is an expansive process, filling you *3* with new ideas from the outside. Creativity reaches beyond what is known and into the unknown . . . to discover something new. Creativity is not necessarily discerning. You don't separate nitrogen from oxygen before you breathe it in. Your chest simply expands, and in it comes. Creative thinking floods you with new possibilities.

Critical thinking, on the other hand, sorts through the possibilities to *4* do something practical. Critical thinking analyzes, applies, and evaluates. It categorizes, compares, contrasts, and traces causes and effects. It's like separating oxygen from the air to enrich your cells, or extracting the carbon dioxide from your blood to get rid of the waste.

Main idea: _____

_____

_____

Explain your choice: _____

_____

_____

Implied Main Ideas

There are times when the main idea is implied, or not directly stated. You will know that this is the case if no one sentence seems to direct the writing. When this occurs, follow these steps:

1 Identify the topic.

2 Pay close attention to each set of details.

3 Write down the important idea that covers all of the details.

4 Read the text again to make sure that this idea accurately covers the details. Revise the statement as needed.

This paragraph is about an eating disorder, but the main idea about this topic is not stated. Read this text and then see below how the implied main idea is identified.

> Every fiber and cell of my body was obsessed with the numbers on the scale and how much fat I could pinch on my thigh. I fought my sisters for control of the TV to do my exercise programs. The cupboards were stacked with cans of diet mixes, the refrigerator full of diet drinks. Hidden in my underwear drawer were stacks of diet pills that I popped along with my vitamins. At my worst, I would quietly excuse myself from family activities to turn on the bathroom faucet full blast and vomit into the toilet. Every day I stood in front of the mirror, a ritual not unlike brushing my teeth, and studied my body. I was never, ever small enough.

Topic: _Eating disorder (anorexia)_

Key details: _Weight a worry, insistent about exercise, using diet products_

Idea that covers the details: _The person suffered from a serious eating disorder._

Implied main idea: _I became a victim of anorexia._

Here is a multi-paragraph text about physical activity. While the topic is easy to identify, the main idea isn't directly stated. Read this text and then see how the implied main idea is identified.

To Work Out or Not to Work Out

The Greek philosopher Plato once said, "Lack of activity destroys the good condition of every human being." The American comedian Phyllis Diller once joked, "My idea of exercise is a good brisk sit."   *1*

Diller's attitude aligns with someone living a sedentary lifestyle. A person with a sedentary lifestyle exercises fewer than three times per week. This type of lifestyle is linked to weight gain and an increased risk of developing diseases such as type 2 diabetes.   *2*

A second level of physical activity is known simply as "lifestyle active." This level describes a person who performs everyday lifestyle activities such as walking to and from the grocery store, doing yard work, or playing pick-up basketball. Engaging in regular lifestyle activities can help control cholesterol levels and reduce body fat.   *3*

Someone who follows a cardiorespiratory exercise program for 20 to 60 minutes, three to five days per week, lives a moderate physical lifestyle, a third level of physical activity. This type of person might be a regular runner, weight lifter, or power walker. A moderate physical lifestyle helps a person become physically fit while reducing the risk of chronic diseases.   *4*

Finally, the highest level of physical activity is a vigorous physical lifestyle. People on this level exercise 20 to 60 minutes most days of the week and follow a routine of aerobic exercises, strength training, and stretching exercises. A vigorous physical lifestyle achieves the same benefits of moderate physical activities while also promoting a greater level of fitness.   *5*

Many factors contribute to a person's level of physical activity—work environment, family obligations, and other personal responsibilities. Depending on the time of year, a person may live a moderate physical lifestyle one week and a sedentary lifestyle the next week. What's important, of course, is to live a healthy lifestyle.   *6*

Topic: _Physical activity practiced by people_

Key details: _Explanations of sedentary lifestyle, "lifestyle active," moderate physical lifestyle, and vigorous physical lifestyle_

Idea that covers the details: _There are different levels of physical activity._

Implied main idea: _Different people pursue different levels of activity._

Practice ▸ Carefully read the following excerpts. Then identify the implied main idea by filling in the information that follows each excerpt.

1. The most frequently thrown pitch is a fastball. As its name suggests, fastballs travel at the highest velocity of any pitch. Generally speaking, a fastball travels on a straight line. A second type of pitch, a changeup, is used to trick hitters into thinking it is a fastball. However, a changeup is thrown much slower and tails slightly downward. The curveball is a third pitch. It is hard to hit because it travels with topspin that it causes it to break sharply both laterally and downward. A curveball is slower than a fastball but faster than a changeup. Another common pitch called the slider breaks laterally and downward. However, its break is shorter than a curve, and it is faster. A skilled pitcher will master at least two of these pitches.

Topic: _____

Key details: _____

Idea that covers the details: _____

Implied main idea: _____

2. The word *ethics* derives from the Greek word *ethos*, meaning the guiding spirit or traditions that govern a culture. Part of America's culture is the unique protection offered to journalists by the First Amendment of the U.S. Constitution, so any discussion of ethics and the American media acknowledges the cultural belief that the First Amendment privilege carries with it special obligations. Among these obligations are professional ethics, the rules or standards governing the conduct of the members of a profession. . . . When journalists make the wrong ethical choices, the consequences can be very damaging and very public. "It may well be that if journalism loses touch with ethical choices, it will then cease to be of use to society and cease to have any real reason for being," writes media ethics scholar John Hulteng. "But that, for the sake of all of us, must never be allowed to happen." Journalists sometimes make poor ethical judgments because they work quickly, and their actions can be haphazard because the lust to be first with a story can override the desire to be right. . . .

From Biagi. *Media Impact: An Introduction to Mass Media*, 10E © 2011 Cengage Learning.

Topic: _____

Key details: _____

Idea that covers the details: _____

Implied main idea: _____

Practice Use the numbers before each sentence to identify the pattern of major and minor details used in the following passages. The first one is done for you.

> [1] There are other, perhaps more significant differences that distinguish male and female brains. [2] Male brains are wired to move information quickly within each side—or hemisphere—of the brain. [3] This gives them better spatial abilities. [4] They can see an object in space, and react quickly. [5] In women's brains, areas of the cerebral cortex—linked to language, judgment, and memory—are more densely packed with nerve cells than men's brains are. [6] This allows them to process that information more effectively.
>
> From "The Brain Game"—an ABC NEWS special reported by Nancy Snyderman

Pattern of Major and Minor Details

1. main idea	2. major detail	3. minor detail	4. minor detail
5. major detail	6. minor detail		

1.
> [1] Desert ecosystems are fragile. [2] Their soils take from decades to hundreds of years to recover from disturbances such as off-road vehicle traffic. [3] This is because deserts have slow growth, low species diversity, slow nutrient cycling, and very little water. [4] Also, off-road vehicle traffic in deserts can destroy the habitats for a variety of animals that live underground in this biome.
>
> From Miller, *Living in the Environment*, 17E. © 2012 Cengage Learning.

Pattern of Major and Minor Details

_____

_____

2.
> [1] Every vegetarian has unique reasons for eating what he or she eats. [2] Many vegetarians see animals as creatures with intelligence and feelings. [3] So they don't like the idea of killing animals for food, especially not in the overcrowded and inhumane factory farms of today. [4] Other vegetarians reject modern American eating habits, with too much meat and too few vegetables. [5] The U.S. Department of Agriculture recommends that people "go lean on protein" and eat even less fat. [6] Still other vegetarians simply seek a better diet and a more sustainable lifestyle. [7] And for some, it's just a mater of personal preference. [8] They just would rather have a salad.

Pattern of Major and Minor Details

_____

_____

3. [1] Today, conservatism is often considered to have two quite different dimensions. [2] Some self-identified conservatives are "economic conservatives." [3] [They] believe in less government, support for capitalism and private property, and allowing individuals to pursue their own route to achievement with little government interference. [4] Recent presidential campaigns have seen great efforts to motivate those individuals who might be called "social conservatives" to support Republican candidates. [5] Social conservatives are much less interested in economic issues than in supporting particular social values, including opposition to abortion, support for the death penalty or the right to own firearms, and opposition to gay marriage.   From *American Government and Politics Today* 16E. © 2014 Cengage Learning.

Pattern of Major and Minor Details

_____

_____

4. [1] If poverty tends to criminalize people, it is also true that criminalization inexorably impoverishes them. [2] Scott Lovell, another homeless man I interviewed in Washington, earned his record by committing a significant crime—by participating in the armed robbery of a steakhouse when he was 15. [3] Although Mr. Lovell dresses and speaks more like a summer tourist from Ohio than a felon, his criminal record has made it extremely difficult for him to find a job.

[4] For Al Szekely, the arrest for trespassing meant a further descent down the circles of hell. [5] While in jail, he lost his slot in the shelter and now sleeps outside the Verizon Center sports arena, where the big problem, in addition to the security guards, is mosquitoes. [6] His stick-thin arms are covered with pink, crusty sores, which he treats with a regimen of frantic scratching.

Pattern of Major and Minor Details

_____

_____

Recognizing Types of Support

Consider the following types of details often included in writing. The examples come from the article "Yes, Accidents Happen. But Why?" by Robert Strauss. A text may contain any number and combination of these types of details.

- **Facts and statistics** provide numbers and data to support something about the main idea. This type of information usually comes from research that has been completed.

  > Drivers ages 18 to 20 were up to four times more likely to have an inattention-related accident than older drivers.

- **Anecdotes** provide a brief personal story to illustrate a key point.

  > When Fred Mannering takes his vintage MG sports car out for a spin, he always leaves plenty of room between the car in front of him and the MG. He brakes slowly and deliberately. He rarely speeds, and if he were to go fast, it would be only on a superhighway with little traffic.

- **Quotations** share the specific thoughts of people knowledgeable about the main idea. When used effectively, quotations offer an effective level of support.

  > "My other car is newer, with good antilock brakes and air bags, so I don't take nearly as much care," said Dr. Mannering, a Purdue University professor of civil engineering who studies the causes and results of traffic accidents.

- **References** to experts or studies provide authoritative support in the development of a thesis.

  > Dr. Mannering's study of accidents in Washington State from 1992 to 1997, a period during which air bags and antilock brakes became prevalent, showed that . . .

- **Analysis** shows the author's critical thinking about the topic or main idea.

  > In that way, he may reflect the behavior of the average driver, governed by hard-to-quantify influences.

■ **Explanations** discuss, clarify, demonstrate, interpret, or expound upon a key point.

> Insurance companies, carmakers, inventors, safety advocates and clearly drivers themselves all have an interest in learning about what might reduce the number of accidents.

■ **Examples** demonstrate or show something.

> For example, a driver is unlikely to tell an officer that he was using a cell phone, especially if he thinks it will increase his liability.

■ **Definitions** explain complex terms.

> The one thing you might conclude—it's called an offset hypothesis—is that people have an acceptance of a level of safety. If they felt safer because of the air bags and brakes, then maybe they drove faster. . . .

■ **Reasons** answer the question "Why?" about something.

> Drinking alcohol certainly causes crashes, but to what extent? That has been difficult determine. (*Why?*) Part of the problem stems from the limitations of researchers' information.

■ **Reflections** offer the writer's personal thoughts or feelings about the topic or main idea.

> Now the technology is available to separate out things like alcohol and different kinds of distractions. (*Reflection*) It is a long time coming, but soon we'll know what really does cause car accidents.

■ **Descriptions** provide details about how something or someone appears.

> Her orange track pants are worn and faded, her T-shirt is far too big, and her powder blue sweatshirt is tied around her waist. Her face and teeth are stained, hair greasy and unkempt.

Practice For each excerpt, identify the type of supporting detail that is underlined. The first one is done for you.

Slavery in the United States is the granting of that power by which one man exercises and enforces a right of property in the body and soul of another. The condition of a slave is simply that of the brute beast. . . .

—Frederick Douglass

Definition

1. All vegetarians are unique, with unique reasons for eating what they eat. For example, many see animals as more than meat—as creatures with intelligence and feelings.

   —Rob King

2. But the sun's rays do not present an unmitigated threat. As it falls on the skin, sunshine converts a fatty substance in the epidermis into vitamin D. The blood carries vitamin D from the skin to the intestines, where it plays a vital role in the absorption of calcium. . . .

   —Marvin Harris

3. Nearly 2,000 Pakistanis have lost their lives to terrorism in this year alone, including 1,400 civilians and 600 security personnel ranging in rank from ordinary soldier to three-star general.

4. Plants can't run away from a threat, but they can stand their ground. "They are very good at avoiding getting eaten," said Linda Walling of the University of California, Riverside. . . .

   —Natalie Angier

5. In short, [Rosa Parks] didn't make a spur-of-the-moment decision. She was part of a movement for change at a time when success was far from certain. There is no way to diminish her historical importance, but it reminds us that this powerful act might never have taken place without the humble, frustrating work that preceded it.

Details Working Together

The number and types of details used by writers will vary from text to text, depending on the purpose of the writing and the nature of the topic. However, some types of details logically work together. For instance, specific examples often follow an explanation, an analysis often follows key statistics, and an explanation or analysis generally follows a quotation. The passages that follow illustrate this working relationship. (The main idea is underlined in each one.)

<u>Although some roles (jobs) are played by both women and men throughout the world, many others are associated with one gender or the other.</u> Women generally tend crops, gather wild foods, care for children, prepare food, clean house, fetch water, and collect cooking fuel. Men, on the other hand, hunt, build houses, clear land for cultivation, herd large animals, fish, trap animals, and serve as political functionaries. There are exceptions to these broad generalizations about what constitutes men's and women's

Explanations

work, however. In some parts of traditional Africa, for example, women carry much heavier loads than men, work long hours in the fields, build houses, and even serve as warriors. And among the Northwest Coast peoples, such as the Tlingit, it is the women who collect shellfish, thereby attaching a stigma to the task. In Tlingit culture a man who collects shellfish is considered lazy because it is believed that men should be out hunting or fishing and not taking the easy way out by collecting shellfish.   From *Cultural Anthropology*, 9E. © 2012 Cengage Learning.

Examples for final explanation

<u>The main source of drug data is the National Survey on Drug Use and Health, conducted annually by the National Institute on Drug Abuse.</u> According to the survey, only about 9 percent of those questioned had used an illegal drug in the past month. Even so, this means that a significant number of Americans—nearly 23 million—are regularly using illegal drugs, and the figure mushrooms when users of legal substances such as alcohol (131 million users) and tobacco (70 million users) are included. Drug abuse often leads to further criminal behavior in adolescents. And in general, the growing market for illegal drugs causes significant damage both in the United States and in countries such as Mexico that supply America with its "fix."

Statistics

Analysis

From *Criminal Justice in Action*, 6E. © 2011 Cengage Learning.

<u>Earth-focused philosophers say that to be rooted, each of us needs to find a sense of place—a stream, a mountain, a yard, a neighborhood lot—any place of the earth with which we feel as one.</u> According to biologist Stephen Jay Gould, "We will not fight to save what we do not love." When we become part of a place, it becomes a part of us. Then we are driven to defend it from harm and to help heal its wounds.   From *Living in the Environment*, 17E. © 2012 Cengage Learning.

Quotation

Explanation

Practice Carefully read each of the following passages. Then circle the types of details used to support the main idea. Some of the passages will contain two types of details working together; other passages will contain only one type.

1.   One troublesome aspect of capital punishment is that a black defendant is much more likely to be sentenced to death for killing a white victim than a white defendant is for killing a black victim. Indeed, looking at the general statistics, a bleak picture of minority incarceration emerges. Even though African Americans make up only 13 percent of the general population in the United States, the number of black men in state and federal prisons (561,000) is significantly larger than the number of white men (452,000). In federal prisons, one in every three inmates is Hispanic, a ratio that has increased dramatically over the past decade as law enforcement has focused on immigration law violations.

From GAINES/MILLER, *Cengage Advantage Books: Criminal Justice in Action*, 6E. © 2011 Cengage Learning.

a. definition   c. statistics   e. an anecdote
b. quotations   d. reflections   f. description

2.   Reports show that many Burmese pythons have been imported into the United States, some of which end up in homes of irresponsible pet owners. "All of the Burmese pythons that we see in the park are a product of the international pet trade," said Skip Snow, a biologist at Everglades National Park. The problem is many pet owners don't fully understand the responsibility of caring for a python. Often the python, which grows to between 10 and 20 feet, becomes too big and too expensive to be kept in a home, and the owner releases the pet into the wild.

a. reflection   c. definition   e. explanation
b. quotation   d. example   f. reasons

3.   Throughout its long history, Islam has witnessed periodic episodes of **revivalism**. Sometimes, especially during times when Islam was in crisis, these developments took a decidedly fundamentalist and violent form. At other times, as was the case in the late 1800s, they assumed the character of movements of reform and **accommodation**. A modern example of the former violent reaction was Wahhabism, a militant reform begun in the late 1700s when a desert **shaykh**, Muhammed ibn Abd al-Wahhab, joined forces with a tribal leader, Muhammed ibn Saud. Together they fought a jihad to purge Islam of Sufis, Shi'ites, and all others whom they accused of introducing innovations.

From Adler/Pouwels, *World Civilizations*, 6E. © 2012 Cengage Learning.

a. reflection   c. definition   e. explanation
b. quotation   d. example   f. reasons

---

revivalism   accommodation   shaykh
a desire to make strong again settle or resolve   head of an Arab family or village

Evaluating Details

You can trust the details in your textbooks and other assigned readings because the authors are, for the most part, experts in their respective fields, and their writing has been carefully reviewed by other experts to assure that the details are accurate and trustworthy. Dr. Dickson Despommier is the author of *The Vertical Farm*. Dr. Despommier has spent 38 years as a professor of microbiology and public health in environmental health sciences at Columbia University, so when he discusses the value of vertical farming, you can assume that he knows what he is talking about. Therefore, when you read this paragraph from his book, you can trust that the supporting details are accurate and authentic.

> As populations grew and urban life became the norm, our habit for producing mountains of waste began to take its toll. Garbage provided sustenance for a wide variety of **peri-domestic** diseases that emerged and then became **endemic**. For example, in the twelfth century, trash of all kinds, strewn carelessly across the European landscape by returning crusaders from the Middle East, attracted hordes of rats. These vermin harbored the plague bacillus, a flea-borne infection. As the rats died, the fleas soon found human hosts to feed on, igniting the first outbreak of the Black Death in Europe. It killed more than one-third of all those living there. **Cholera** came to Europe in 1836 by way of trading vessels from the Bay of Bengal, first to London, England. Because of the high nutrient content of the Thames River, due mostly to garbage dumping, cholera became endemic, killing thousands of Londoners every year until John Snow figured out its **modus operandi**.

---

peri-domestic
living in or around humans

endemic
common to one area

cholera
disease of the small intestines

modus operandi
how something acts or works

But what if Despommier had been trained in sociology or psychology? You wouldn't (or shouldn't) feel as confident in his information about vertical farming. Likewise, you wouldn't feel confident in the text if Despommier discussed urban waste using vague details like these:

> As cities grew, waste became more of a problem. And the accumulation of garbage brought on all sorts of diseases. For example, there was the Black Death that nearly wiped out European cities during Medieval times. Then later cholera caused by dumped garbage did that same kind of thing, starting in England.

While the details in your textbooks and assigned readings will be reliable, the same might not be true in some other texts. For example, the details on some Web sites may be questionable; the same may hold true for information in some popular magazines or in books that may, for example, be out of date or written by people promoting a particular agenda.

The details in a reading text are most likely trustworthy if the text meets these criteria:

1. The source is a textbook, a book from a respected publisher, an essay in a respected periodical, or a Web article with a reliable domain such as *.edu, .org,* or *.gov.*

2. An author is identified and writing in his or her field of expertise. In addition, the text is in line with material written by other experts in the field.

3. The topic is covered in depth. The information seems balanced and timely, and it is easy to follow and logical. Plus, it is in line with other texts covering the same topic.

Read the extended definition of the term *utopia* and the evaluation of the supporting details that follows it.

Looking for Utopia

Everyone wishes to find a perfect place—a utopia that has no crime and no disease, where everyone is happy, healthy, wealthy, and wise. In fact, the word "utopia" would seem to mean "good place," coming from the Greek "eu" (good) and "topos" (place). However, the prefix in Greek is not "eu" but "ou," which means "not" or "no." That's right; "utopia" means "no place." Sir Thomas More coined the term in 1516, writing a book about a perfect place that didn't exist. His book was a satire, trying to show that a utopia wasn't possible. That didn't stop a number of utopian movements from springing up. In fact, one utopian community established in New Harmony, Indiana, proudly announced that it was based on ideas commended by Sir Thomas More. This 2,000-person communal city banned money but quickly dissolved due to quarreling. Nathaniel Hawthorne tells in *The Scarlet Letter* why such utopians are bound to fail: "The founders of any new colony, whatever Utopia of human virtues and happiness they originally project, have invariably recognized it among their earliest practical necessities to allot a portion of the virgin soil as a cemetery, and another portion as the site of a prison." In other words, no utopia can exist as long as any humans are in it.

1. What is the main idea of the reading? <u>Everyone wishes to find a perfect place.</u>

2. What types of details support it? <u>The initial support is a definition. Next, a reference to an expert (Sir Thomas More) is offered. An example utopian community follows. Then a quotation from Nathaniel Hawthorne adds further support and authority.</u>

3. Do the details seem reliable and trustworthy? Explain. <u>Yes, the information appears reliable and trustworthy. Facts and definitions can be checked.</u>

4. What questions do you still have about the main idea? <u>Have other attempts at utopia been made? What caused disharmony within the experimental groups?</u>

Practice Evaluate the supporting details in the following passage about the use of wind farms. To get started, carefully read the text; then answer the evaluation questions.

Support Wind Farm Energy

To counteract its dependence on fossil fuels, the United States must invest in wind farms for its energy needs. A wind farm is made up of a group of large wind turbines, which convert wind into energy. The benefits of wind farms are numerous. First, wind is a free and renewable source of energy. In comparison, fossil fuels like oil and coal are limited in supply and cost money to extract from the earth. Second, wind farms are a clean energy source. Unlike power plants, which emit dangerous pollutants, wind farms release no pollution into the air or water, meaning less smog, less acid rain, and fewer greenhouse emissions. And then there's this: The American Wind Energy Association reports that running a single wind turbine has the potential to displace 2,000 tons of carbon dioxide, or the equivalent of one square mile of forest trees. But despite being the fastest growing energy source in the U.S., wind energy accounts for only 1.5 percent of power supplied in the country. If the United States wants to limit carbon emissions and lessen its dependence on fossil fuels, it must act now and invest more money in wind farms. The answer is in the air.

1. What is the main idea of the reading?

   _____

2. What types of details support the main idea?

   _____

   _____

3. Do the details seem reliable and trustworthy? Explain.

   _____

   _____

4. What questions do you still have about the main idea?

   _____

   _____

L06   Drawing Inferences

An **inference** is a logical conclusion that you make about something that is not actually said or stated. A thoughtful inference results from a careful reading of a text. To make thoughtful inferences, follow these steps:

1. **Carefully read and reread the text**, using the reading process.
2. **Identify the main idea and supporting details.**
3. **Then ask yourself:** *What other conclusions can I draw from the reading?*

The following passage comes from the Bureau of Labor Statistics Web site. Among other things, this government body provides economic news releases summarizing regional and state unemployment and employment figures. Note the inferences that were drawn after a careful reading of the passage.

> Regional and state unemployment rates were little changed in February.   *1*
> Twenty-two states had unemployment rate decreases, 12 states had increases, and
> 16 states and the District of Columbia had no change, the U.S. Bureau of Labor
> Statistics reported today. Thirty-seven states and the District of Columbia had
> unemployment rate decreases from a year earlier, 10 states had increases, and
> three states had no change. The national jobless rate, 7.7 percent, edged down
> from January and was 0.6 percentage point lower than in February 2012.
>
> In February, the West continued to have the highest regional unemployment   *2*
> rate, 8.5 percent, while the South had the lowest rate, 7.3 percent. No region had a
> statistically significant over-the-month unemployment rate change.

"Regional and State Employment and Unemployment—February 2013" Bureau of Labor Statistics, 29 Mar. 2013.
Web. 31 Mar. 2013.

1. What is the main idea in the passage? <u>Regional and state unemployment did
   not change much in February 2013.</u>

2. What details support the main idea? <u>(1) While 22 states had lower
   unemployment, 12 states had increases and 16 states plus DC had no
   change. (2) There was only a 0.6 percentage decrease in February compared
   to January.</u>

3. What inferences can you draw from the passage? <u>(1) The recovery from a major
   recession is a slow process. (2) All parts of the country, to some degree, are
   feeling the effects of unemployment due to the recession.</u>

Practice ▶ To practice drawing inferences, carefully read each passage. Then answer the questions following each passage.

1.   In the early 1980s, very few Americans had ever heard of acquired immune deficiency syndrome (AIDS). By 2000, however, AIDS had become the leading infectious cause of death in the world. More than 60 million people worldwide have been infected with human immunodeficiency virus (HIV), the virus that causes AIDS. Since 1981 AIDS has claimed 25 million lives, or more than 890,000 people each year. That is about half as many deaths as in all of World War II, and it is not over. Today there are 33 million people in the world living with HIV. Tragically, 95 percent of all new AIDS cases are in the poorest countries that are least equipped to handle the epidemic.   From Ferraro/Andreatta, *Cultural Anthropology, 9E.* © 2012 Cengage Learning.

■ What is the main idea in the passage?

■ What inferences (conclusions) can you draw from the passage?

2.   The report documents for the first time an emerging "app gap" in which affluent children are likely to use mobile educational games, while those in low-income families are the most likely to have televisions in their bedrooms.

      The study, by Common Sense Media, a San Francisco nonprofit group, is the first of its kind since apps became widespread and the first to look at screen time from birth. It found that almost half the families with incomes above $75,000 had downloaded apps specifically for their young children, compared with one in eight of the families earning less than $30,000. More than a third of those low-income parents said they did not know what an "app"—short for application—was.   From Biagi. *Media Impact: An Introduction to Mass Media,* 10E © 2011 Cengage Learning.

■ What is the main idea in this passage? (Hint: Focus on the first paragraph.)

■ What details support this idea? Underline two.

■ What inferences (conclusions) can you draw from this passage? Name two.

L07 Choosing Supporting Details for Writing

When planning a piece of writing, you are making decisions about the ideas you will develop. First, you select a topic; next, you gather details about the topic, taking careful notes as you go along. After reviewing your notes, you form a thesis or focus for your writing. Then you are ready to decide how best to use the details you have collected. Suppose a student is planning an essay about the technology-driven sharing economy, and his focus is its simplicity of use.

- **Topic:** sharing economy
- **Focus:** simplicity leads to growth
- **Thesis:** The sharing economy *(topic)* thrives because users value its simplicity *(focus)*.

Here are the writer's notes about his topic. The annotations (in red type) reflect his thoughts as he reviews his notes.

Notes About the Sharing Economy

"The People Who Share" Web site
"What is the sharing economy?" by Benita Matofska

First off, I should define "sharing economy."

- "a socio-economic system built around the sharing of human and physical assets"
- includes shared production, distribution, trade, and consumption of goods by different people and organizations
- includes swapping, exchanging, purchasing, collaborative consumption, re-distribution, renting
- sharing economy supported by 10 building blocks
  1. people at the heart
  2. people and communities produce goods and services
  3. a hybrid economy—with a variety of forms of exchange
  4. distribution is equitable
  5. people and planet at heart of economy
  6. empowers citizens
  7. communication: shared, open, and accessible
  8. shared law: law-making democratic
  9. culture: wider community and greater good considered
  10. future—built for the long term

Forbes **Web site – 7/30/2013**

"What Is the New Sharing Economy?" by James Gardner

Then I will stress the simplicity and ease of use.

- possible because of advances in technology
- human need—strive for simplicity
- ease of use—access resources when we need

Airbnb

- started in San Fran in 2008 by 2 people with a spare bed and inability to meet the rent
- now operating in 192 countries
- make spare room or spare house available to rent
- 10 million nights booked in 5 years

I'll follow with some popular examples.

ZipCar

- gives people access to a car when they need it and for as long as they need it
- book car online, select one nearby, unlock it with mobile, and drive away
- can have car for as little as one hour

TaskRabbit

- formed by Leah Busque in 2008
- people for hire pick up laundry, do the shopping, etc.
- post job online and TaskRabbit will bid for work

Time **Web site**

"Today's Smart Choice: Don't Own—Share" by Bryan Walsh, 3/17/11

- sharing replacing ownership society
- "ownership" just about ruined the economy
- has a green element
- Rachel Botsman, co-author of *What's Mine Is Yours: The Rise of Collaborative Consumption*: "It works because people can trust each other."

New York News & Politics **Web site**

I'll consider its future at the end.

"The Sharing Economy Isn't About Trust; It's About Desperation" by Kevin Roose

- shared economy succeeds because digital tools enable and encourage trust; also because economy is struggling
- Sarah Kessler (Fast Company): "Hard to make it in the sharing economy."

After reviewing these notes, the student decided on these key points to support the thesis about the sharing economy.

1. **Define the sharing economy** (to make sure readers understand what it is).
2. **Explain its simplicity and ease of use** (to segue into the focus of the essay).
3. **Provide examples** (to illustrate the simplicity).
4. **Consider its future** (to conclude the essay).

Next, he identified the details that support each point. He would also note if he needed to gather additional details to support any of these idea.

1. Define the sharing economy.

from "People Who Share" Web site

- "a socio-economic system built around the sharing of human and physical assets"
- includes shared production, distribution, trade, and consumption of goods by different people and organizations

from SearchCIO Web Site TechTarget

- also known as collaborative consumption

2. Explain its simplicity and ease of use.

from "The People Who Share" Web site

- sharing economy supported by nine building blocks

from *Forbes* Web site – 7/30/2013

- possible because of advances in technology
- human need—strive for simplicity
- ease of use—access resources when we need them

from *Time* Web site

- sharing replacing ownership society
- "ownership" just about ruined the economy

3. Provide examples.

from *Forbes* Web site – 7/30/2013

Airbnb

- started in San Fran in 2008 by 2 people with a spare bed and needing cash
- now operating in 192 countries; 10 million nights booked in 5 years

ZipCar

- gives people access to a car when they need it and for as long as they need it
- book car online, select one nearby, unlock it with mobile, and drive away
- can have car for as little as one hour

TaskRabbit

- formed by Leah Busque in 2008
- people for hire pick up laundry, do the shopping, etc.
- post job online and TaskRabbit will bid for work

4. Consider its future.

from "The People Who Share" Web site

- future—built for the long term

from *Time* Web site

- one of 10 ideas that will change the world according to *Time*
- young leading to different forms of consumption
- has a green element

from *New York News & Politics* Web site

- Sarah Kessler (Fast Company): "Hard to make it in the sharing economy."
- no benefits, little money

Practice Collect details from at least three or four sources that address the thesis statement that you wrote in this chapter. Take notes as you go along. Then decide on two or three two key points that support your thesis and list details that you could use to develop each one.

☑ Review and Enrichment

Reviewing the Chapter

Read and Write for Topics

1. Where should you look in a reading selection to find the topic?

_____

Read and Write for Main Ideas

2. What is the main idea in a reading?

_____

3. What is an implied main idea?

_____

4. Why is it important to decide on a main idea or focus for your writing?

_____

Read for Supporting Details

5. What is the difference between major and minor details?

_____

6. What are common types of supporting details? Name at least four.

_____

Draw Inferences

7. What is an inference?

_____

Choose Supporting Details in Writing

8. Why is it important to include plenty of details in your writing?

_____

"Technology has to be invented or adopted."

—Jared Diamond

Reading for Enrichment

You will be reading the story behind the evolution of a backward Native American tribe living in the dry and arid southwest part of North America. Be sure to follow the steps in the reading process to help you gain a full understanding of the text.

About the Author

S.C. Gwynne is an award-winning journalist writing for *The Dallas Morning News*. He also has served as a correspondent and editor for *Time* and as executive editor for *Texas Monthly*. His book *Empire of the Summer Moon* was a finalist for the Pulitzer Prize and the National Book Critics Circle Award.

Prereading

Early in the essay, S.C. Gwynne states that more than 250 years ago the Comanche tribe experienced a "transformative technology"—or a technology that significantly affected their lives, just as steam and electricity affected the rest of the world. What might this technology be, especially when considering that the Comanches were a backward people? List a few ideas here; then list three technologies that have significantly transformed your life.

Consider the Elements

As you read this selection, first identify the **topic** and **thesis** (main idea) of the essay. Then pay careful attention to the details that support the thesis. Notice the different types of **details** used and in what combinations.

■ Possible life-changing technologies for the Comanches:

_____

_____

■ Life-changing technologies in your life:

_____

_____

What do you think?

How would you paraphrase Jared Diamond's quotation? What relationship would you assume that the Comanche people had with technology?

Before you read, answer these four questions:

1. What do the title, the opening two paragraphs, and the first lines of the other paragraphs tell you about the topic and main idea?

   _____

2. What are your first thoughts about the author's purpose and audience?

   _____

3. What do you already know about this topic?

   _____

4. What questions would you like answered in your reading?

   _____

Reading and Rereading

As you read, make it your goal to (1) identify the topic and thesis, (2) confirm the purpose and audience, (3) note the level of support provided, and (4) answer the questions you posed during prereading. Consider annotating the text and/or taking notes to help you keep track of important information during your reading.

Be sure to reread as needed to confirm your understanding of the text and to analyze the development of the ideas. Consider the topic's interest or timeliness, the effectiveness of the thesis, and the types of supporting details that are provided.

The Reading Process

Prereading → Rereading
↕   ↓   ↑   ↓
Reading   Reflecting

Incredible Transformation

What happened to the Comanche between roughly 1625 and   1
1750 was one of the great social and military transformations in
history. Few nations have ever progressed with such breathtaking
speed from the status of skulking **pariah** to dominant power. The
change was total and irrevocable, and it was accompanied by a
complete reordering of the balance of power on the American
plains. The Nermernuh (Comanche) were like the small boy who is
bullied in junior high school and then grows into a large, strong, and
vengeful high schooler. Vengeance they were good at, and they had

extremely long memories for evils done to them.

The agent of this astonishing change was the horse. Or, more   *2*
precisely, what this backward tribe of Stone Age hunters did with the
horse, an astonishing piece of transformative technology that had as
much of an effect on the Great Plains as steam and electricity had on
the rest of civilization.

The story of the Comanches' implausible ascent begins with the   *3*
arrival of the first conquistadors in Mexico in the early sixteenth
century. The invaders brought horses with them from Spain. The
animals terrified the natives, provided obvious military superiority,
and gave the Spaniards a sort of easy mobility never before seen by
the inhabitants of the New World. The Spaniards' horses were also,
by the purest of accidents, brilliantly suited to the arid and semiarid
plains and mesas of Mexico and the American West. The Iberian
mustang was a far different creature from its larger grain-fed cousin
from farther north in Europe. It was a desert horse, one whose
remote ancestors had thrived on the level, dry steppes of central
Asia. Down the ages, the breed had migrated to North Africa by way
of the Middle East, mixing blood with other desert hybrids along
the way. The Moorish invasions brought it to Spain. By that time it
had become, more or less, the horse that found its way to America:
light, small, and sturdy, barely fourteen hands high, with a concave
Arabian face and tapering muzzle. This horse didn't look like much,
but it was smart, fast, trainable, bred to live off the grasses of the
hot Spanish plains and to go long distances between watering holes.
Possessed of great endurance, the animal could forage for food even
in winter. . . .

No one knows exactly how or when the Comanche bands   *4*
in eastern Wyoming first encountered the horse, but that event
probably happened somewhere near the midpoint of the seventeenth
century. Since the Pawnees, who lived in the area we now call

Nebraska, were known to be mounted by 1680, the Comanches almost certainly had horses by that time. There were no witnesses to this great coming together of Stone Age hunters and horses, nothing to record what happened when they met or what there was in the soul of the Comanches that understood the horse so much better than everyone else did. Whatever it was, whatever sort of accidental brilliance, whatever the particular, subliminal bond between warrior and horse, it must have thrilled these dark-skinned pariahs from the Wind River country.

The Comanches adapted to the horse earlier and more completely than any other plains tribe. They are considered, without much debate, the prototype horse tribe in North America. No one could outride them or outshoot them from the back of a horse. Among other horse tribes, only the Kiowas fought entirely mounted, as the Comanches did. Pawnees, Crows, even the Dakotas used the horse primarily for transport. They would ride to the battle, then dismount and fight. No tribe other than the Comanches ever learned to breed horses—an intensely demanding, knowledge-based skill that helped create enormous wealth for the tribe. They were always careful in the castration of the herd; almost all riding horses were **geldings**. Few other tribes bothered with this. It was not uncommon for a Comanche warrior to have one hundred to two hundred mounts, or for a chief to have fifteen hundred. (A Sioux chief might have forty horses, by comparison.) They were not only the richest of all tribes in sheer horseflesh, their horses were also the main medium through which the rest of the tribes became mounted.

The first Europeans and Americans to see Comanche horsemanship did not fail to notice this. Athanas de Mezieres, a Spanish Indian agent of French descent, described them thus:

> They are a people so numerous and haughty that when asked their number, they make no difficulty of comparing it to that of

the stars. They are so skillful in horsemanship that they have no equal; so daring that they never ask for or grant truces; and in the possession of such territory that, finding in it an abundance of pasturage for their horses and an incredible number of [buffalo] which furnish them all the **raiment**, food, and shelter, they only just fall short of possessing all the conveniences of the earth.

Other observers said the same thing. Colonel Richard Dodge, whose expedition made early contact with Comanches, believed them to be the finest light cavalry in the world, superior to any mounted soldiers in Europe or America. [George] Catlin also saw them as incomparable horseman. As he described it, the American soldiers were dumbfounded at what they saw. "On their feet they are one of the most unattractive and slovenly looking races of Indians I have ever seen, but the moment they mount their horses, they seem at once metamorphosed," wrote Catlin. "I am ready, without hesitation, to pronounce the Comanches the most extraordinary horsemen I have seen yet in all my travels." He went on to write: 8

Amongst their feats of riding there is one that has astonished me more than anything of the kind I have ever seen or expect to see, in my life—a strategem of war, learned and practiced by every young man in the tribe; by which he is able to drop his body on the side of his horse at the instant he is passing, effectively screened from his enemies' weapons, as he lay in a horizontal position behind the body of the horse, with his heel handing over the horse's back. . . . In this wonderful condition, he will hang whilst his horse is at fullest speed, carrying with him his bow and shield and also his long lance 14 feet in length. 9

Thus positioned, a Comanche warrior could loose twenty arrows in the time it took a soldier to load and fire one round from his musket; each of those arrows could kill a man at thirty yards. 10

Other observers were amazed at the Comanche technique 11
of breaking horses. A Comanche would lasso a wild horse, then
tighten the noose, choking the horse and driving it to the ground.
When it seemed as if the horse was nearly dead, the choking lariat
was slacked. The horse finally rose, trembling and in a full lather.
Its captor gently stroked its nose, ears, and forehead, and then put
his mouth over the horse's nostrils and blew air into its nose. The
Indian would then throw a thong around the now-gentled horse's
lower jaw, mount up, and ride away. The Comanches, as it turned
out, were geniuses at anything to do with horses: breeding, breaking,
selling, and riding. They even excelled at stealing horses. Colonel
Dodge wrote that a Comanche could enter "a bivouac where a dozen
men were sleeping, each with a horse tied to his wrist by the lariat,
cut a rope within six feet of the sleeper, and get away with the horse
without waking a soul."

Children were given their own horses at four or five. Soon 12
the boys were expected to learn tricks, which included picking
up objects on the ground at a gallop. The young rider would start
with light objects and move to progressively heavier objects until
finally, without assistance and at a full gallop, he could pick up a
man. Rescuing a fallen comrade was seen as one of the most basic
obligations of a Comanche warrior. They all learned the leather
thong trick as young men. Women could often ride as well as men.
One observer watched two Comanche women set out at full speed
with lassoes and each rope a bounding antelope on the first throw.
Women had their own mounts, as well as mules and gentle horses for
packing.

When they were not stealing horses or breeding them, they 13
were capturing them in the wild. General Thomas James told a
story of how he had witnessed this in 1832, when he had visited the
Comanches as a horse buyer. He watched as many riders headed
bands of wild horses into a deep ravine where a hundred men waited

on horseback with coiled lariats. When the "terrified wild horses reached the ambush," there was a good deal of dust and confusion as the riders lassoed them by the neck or forefeet. But every rider got an animal. Only one horse got away. The Comanches pursued him, and in two hours he came back "tamed and gentle." Within twenty-four hours one hundred or more wild horses had been captured "amid the wildest excitement" and appeared to be "as subject to their masters as farm horses." They would chase a herd of mustangs for several days until the animals were exhausted, making them easy to capture. Comanches waited by water holes for parched horses to gorge themselves so they could barely run, then captured them. While the Comanches had a limited vocabulary to describe most things—a trait common to primitive peoples—their **equine** lexicon was large and minutely descriptive. For color alone, there were distinct Comanche words for brown, light bay, reddish brown, black, white, blue, dun, sorrel, roan, red, yellow, yellow-horse-with-a-black mane-and-tail; red, sorrel, and black pintos. There were even words to describe horses with red, yellow, and black ears.

Comanche horsemanship also played a leading role in another [14] Comanche pastime: gambling. Stories of Comanche horse hustles are **legion**. One the most famous came from the Texas frontier. A small band of Comanches showed up at Fort Chadbourne, where the army officers challenged them to a race. The chief seemed indifferent to the idea, but the officers were so insistent that he agreed to it anyway. A race was arranged over a distance of four hundred yards. Soon a large, portly brave appeared on a long-haired "miserable sheep of a pony." He carried a heavy club, with which he hit the horse. Unimpressed, the officers trotted out their third-best horse and bet the Comanches flour, sugar, and coffee against buffalo robes. Swinging the club "ostentatiously," the Indian won. For the next race, the soldiers brought out their second-best horse. They lost this race, too. Now they insisted on a third race and finally trotted out their number-one horse, a magnificent Kentucky mare. Bets were doubled, tripled. The Comanches took everything the soldiers would wager. At the starting signal, the Comanche warrior whooped, threw away his club, and "went away like the wind." Fifty yards from the finish, the Comanche rider turned full around in his saddle, and with "hideous grimaces" beckoned the other rider to catch up. The losers later learned that the same shaggy horse had just been used to take six hundred horses away from the Kickapoo Indians.

In the late 1600s, Comanche mastery of the horse had led them   15 to migrate southward out of the harsh, cold lands of the Wind River and into more temperate climates. The meaning of the migration was simple: They were challenging other tribes for supremacy over the single richest hunting prize on the continent, the buffalo herds of the southern plains.

In 1706, they rode, for the first time, into recorded history. In   16 July of that year a Spanish sergeant major named Juan De Ulibarri, on his way to gather Pueblo Indians for conversion in northern New Mexico, reported that Comanches, in the company of the Utes, were preparing to attack Taos pueblo. He later heard of actual Comanche attacks. This was the first the Spanish or any white men had heard of these Indians who had many names. One name in particular, given to them by the Utes, was Koh-mats, sometimes given as Komantcia, and meant "anyone who is against me all the time." The authorities in New Mexico translated this various ways (Cumanche, Commanche) but eventually as "Comanche." It would take the Spaniards years to figure out exactly who these new invaders were.

pariah
a person rejected by others

geldings
castrated male horse

raiment
clothes, apparel

equine
of or relating to horses

legion
a great number of people or things; a multitude

Summarizing

Write a summary of "Incredible Transformation." Remember that a summary presents the key points in a clear, concise form using your own words.

Reflecting

1. What is the topic of the selection? The thesis or main idea?

   _____

   _____

2. What is the primary type of detail used in paragraph 3—*statistics, definitions,* or *explanations*? (Circle the correct one.)

3. In paragraph 5, what is one example of a major detail and a clarifying minor detail?

   _____

   _____

4. How would you characterize the quality of the details in this selection? Do they seem reliable?

   _____

5. What inferences can you draw about the impact that explorers and adventurers play in the development of an area?

   _____

Vocabulary

Create vocabulary entries for these words. For each word, identify the pronunciation, and helpful word parts, give a primary definition, and use the word in a sentence.

1. **irrevocable** (paragraph 1)
2. **prototype** (paragraph 5)

Critical Thinking

- How does the author make the story of the Comanches so compelling?
- How does this selection illustrate the connectedness of people and places in history?
- How do animals impact different aspects of society today? Is there one animal that is the most influential? How so?
- For the Comanches, the horse was a transformative transportation technology. How does the availability of transportation technology and infrastructure (interstate systems, rail lines, airports) impact the distribution of military and political power in today's world?

Writing for Enrichment

Choose one of the following writing ideas, or decide upon an idea of your own related to the reading. Be sure to follow the steps in the writing process to develop your work.

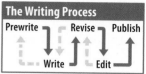

1. Explain how the horse was considered a "transformative technology" for the Comanche in the same way that steam and electricity were transformative for other civilizations of the time.

2. Explain the Comanche lifestyle before and after the tribe's introduction to the horse.

3. Write a brief biography of one of the most famous Comanche warriors, Quanah Parker.

4. Describe how the Comanche story evolves after they became skilled horsemen.

5. Analyze the transformative impact of a particular technology in your own life.

When prewriting and planning . . .

- Research your topic as needed, taking thorough notes as you go along.
- Establish a thesis for your essay.
- Review your notes for key ideas to support your thesis.
- Decide on the details that you will use to develop these ideas.

When writing . . .

- Include a beginning, middle, and ending in your essay.
- Present your thesis in the beginning part.
- Support the thesis in the middle paragraphs with plenty of major and minor details.
- Close your essay with final thoughts about your thesis.

When revising and editing. . .

- Carefully review your first draft, making sure that you develop each key point with sufficient details.
- Ask at least one peer to review your writing as well.
- Improve the content as needed.
- Then edit your revised writing for style and correctness. See Appendix B for an editing checklist.

bopav, 2014 / Used under license from Shutterstock.com

bopav, 2014 / Used under license from Shutterstock.com

Chapter

5

"An idea can only become a reality once it is broken down into organized, actionable elements."

—Scott Belsky

Organization

Ideas and organization work together to create a text. For example, the directions in manuals are organized chronologically so they can be followed, just as the explanations in textbooks are organized logically so they can be understood. It would be almost impossible to understand any piece of writing if the ideas weren't thoughtfully organized. Ideas need form and structure to make meaning.

In terms of basic organization, a text needs a clearly developed beginning, middle, and ending to form a meaningful whole. Within the body of a text, the ideas and details must be arranged according to an appropriate pattern of organization such as cause-effect or time order. In this chapter, you will learn how to recognize and appreciate the organization in reading selections and how to effectively organize the ideas in your own essays.

Learning Outcomes

LO1 Understand the three-part structure.
LO2 Read the beginning part.
LO3 Write the beginning part of an essay.
LO4 Read the middle part.
LO5 Develop the middle part of an essay.
LO6 Read the ending part.
LO7 Write the ending part of an essay.

What do you think?

How would you explain Scott Belsky's quotation? What does it say about the relationship between ideas and organization?

L01 Understanding the Three-Part Structure

Figure 5.1 identifies the basic structure of paragraphs and essays (and other multi-paragraph informational texts). When you are reading and writing academic texts, keep this three-part structure in mind.

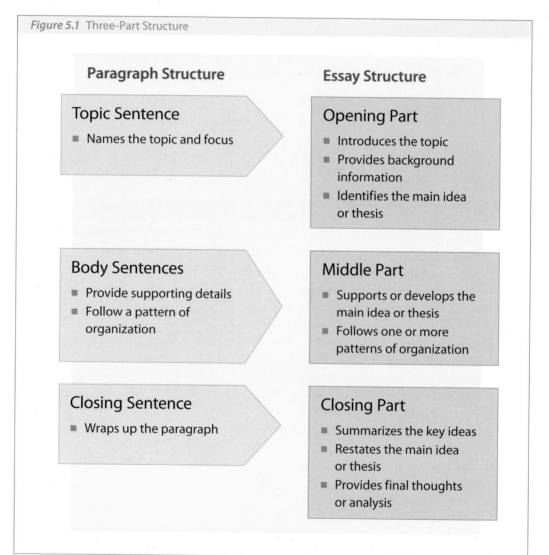

Figure 5.1 Three-Part Structure

Paragraph Structure

Topic Sentence
- Names the topic and focus

Body Sentences
- Provide supporting details
- Follow a pattern of organization

Closing Sentence
- Wraps up the paragraph

Essay Structure

Opening Part
- Introduces the topic
- Provides background information
- Identifies the main idea or thesis

Middle Part
- Supports or develops the main idea or thesis
- Follows one or more patterns of organization

Closing Part
- Summarizes the key ideas
- Restates the main idea or thesis
- Provides final thoughts or analysis

L02 Reading the Beginning Part

Generally speaking, the beginning part of an informational reading introduces the topic and provides background information that leads up to the thesis statement. The thesis statement usually completes the beginning part of an essay. Reading an academic text can be challenging when the beginning part does not lead up to the thesis. Here is the beginning of an essay entitled "Shrouded in Contradiction" by Gelareh Asayesh, who grew up in Iran before moving to Florida.

I grew up wearing the miniskirt to school, the veil to the mosque. In the Tehran of my childhood, women in bright sundresses shared the sidewalk with women swathed in black. The tension between the two ways of life was palpable. As a schoolgirl, I often cringed when my bare legs got leering or contemptuous glances. Yet, at times, I long for the days when I could walk the streets of my country with the wind in my hair. When clothes were clothes. In today's Iran, whatever I wear sends a message. If it's chador, it embarrasses my Westernized relatives. If it's a skimpy scarf, I risk being accused of stepping on the blood of the martyrs who died in the war with Iraq. Each time I return to Tehran, I wait until the last possible moment, when my plane lands on the tarmac, to don the scarf and long jacket that many Iranian women wear in lieu of a veil. To wear hijab— Islamic covering—is to invite contradictions.

- **Topic:** A young woman's clothing when returning to Tehran, Iran.
- **Background information:** The writer first describes how she dressed as a girl in Tehran. Then she describes how she must dress now upon returning there for visits.
- **Thesis:** "To wear hijab—Islamic covering—*(topic)* is to invite contradictions *(feature).*"

3.   For several years a picture of Warren Spahn of the Milwaukee Braves (now   *1*
the Atlanta Braves) hung on my closet door, one leg poised in midair before he
delivered a smoking fastball. Time passed and Spahn's picture gave way to others:
Elvis, John F. Kennedy, **Carl Jung**, **Joseph Campbell**, **Ben Hogan**. These heroic
images have reflected back to me what I hoped to become: a man with good
moves, a sex symbol, an electrifying orator, a plumber of depths, a teller of tales,
a graceful golfer. Like serpents, we keep shedding the skins of our heroes as we
move toward new phases in our lives.

Like many of my generation, I have a weakness for hero worship. At some   *2*
point, however, we all begin to question our heroes and our need for them. This
leads us to ask: What is a hero? Despite immense differences in cultures, heroes
around the world generally share a number of traits that instruct and inspire
people.   From *Is a Hero Really Nothing but a Sandwich?* by Ted Tollefson

Carl Jung	Joseph Campbell	Ben Hogan
Swiss psychologist, founded analytical psychology	a collector of myths who was influenced by Jung	a great golfer

Topic: _____

Background Information: _____

_____

Thesis: _____

_____

_____

"Start with something interesting and promising; wind up with something the reader will remember."

—Rudolf Flesch

LO3 Writing the Beginning Part of an Essay

The beginning part of an essay, usually consisting of one or two paragraphs, should (1) introduce the topic in an interesting and/or important way; (2) provide background information, if needed, leading up to the thesis; and (3) state the thesis.

Strategies for Introducing a Topic

First impressions are important—say, for instance, when you're interviewing for a job or introducing yourself to a roommate or a work supervisor. First impressions are important in writing as well, because the first few sentences should introduce the topic in an interesting and/or important way and set the tone and direction for the rest of the piece. Here are strategies to fulfill this function.

Surprising or Little-Known Facts

To gain your reader's attention, you can open with a surprising or little-known fact about your topic. This strategy works well if readers are unfamiliar or perhaps uninterested in a topic. In an essay about fetal alcohol syndrome, the writer provides this surprising opening idea.

> Thousands of babies are born each year with alcohol-related defects, making fetal alcohol syndrome one of the leading causes of mental retardation.

Important or Challenging Questions

Asking an important or challenging question will naturally lead the reader into the text, because he or she will expect an answer to follow. In an essay about homeless people, the writer poses this thought-provoking question.

> What exactly do the signs held up by homeless people tell us?

Quotation from an Expert

A revealing quotation from an expert can also be used to provide an immediate level of authority to an essay. In an essay about the sharing economy, a writer uses a telling quotation about his topic.

> Thomas Friedman is a prize-winning journalist who, among other things, is interested in trends shaping the global economy. He states, "The sharing economy is producing both new entrepreneurs and a new concept of ownership."

Brief, Dramatic Stories

Readers are naturally attracted to interesting stories, even if they are very brief, so sharing a story can be an effective way to introduce a topic. In a family history piece, the writer shares a dramatic story about his great-grandmother's city of birth.

> It was May 1945; World War II had just ended, and Yugoslavia had been overtaken. The town of Vrhnika, Yugoslavia, was no longer safe for my great-grandmother and her family. Russian troops were breaking into houses, taking what they wanted, and even killing.

Bold Statements

A bold statement can effectively gain a reader's interest about a topic. In the problem-solution essay, the writer introduces her topic, childhood malnourishment, with this dramatic statement.

> Dry weather may be to blame for the unrelenting drought in parts of Africa. But cruel government politics have created a devastating famine.

Identifying the Main Idea

At times, the best way to begin may be to state the main idea and get on with the rest of the text, especially if the topic really doesn't need an introduction. In a descriptive essay about kayaking, the writer simply stated his main idea.

> On most summer mornings, I kayak on Castle Rock Lake for exercise and enjoyment.

Practice ⟩ Introduce each of these essay topics using the prescribed strategy.

1. **Topic:** A community or neighborhood problem

   Strategy: Ask one or more important questions.

   _____

   _____

2. **Topic:** An appealing career choice

   Strategy: Provide either a surprising fact or one or more bold statements.

   _____

   _____

Completing the Beginning Part

Suppose you are writing an informational essay about Legg-Calve-Perthes (pronounced leg-cal-VAY-PER-theez), a rare, degenerative bone disease. You could share *a brief, dramatic story* to introduce your topic and then state the thesis (underlined).

> Allie Mason acted like a typical coed. She was bubbly, energetic, and friendly. She was also a conscientious student, belonging to the Honors Art Club in high school. What set Allie apart was a debilitating physical condition that caused one of her legs to be noticeably shorter that the other one. As a result, she had to endure endless medical procedures and missed out on physical activities such as running and dancing. She also has had to endure more than her share of cruel remarks. She remembers one girl complaining to the gym teacher, "Hey, it's not fair that Allie doesn't have to run the mile and we do." The insensitivity of comments like this one obviously hurt. The reason for Allie's suffering has been Legg-Calve-Perthes, a painful, degenerative bone disease that truly challenges the sufferer.

If you were explaining the process of water purification, you could introduce your topic with *surprising facts* and *statistics* before stating your thesis (underlined).

> One of the most overlooked luxuries of living in the United States is access to clean drinking water. Statistics show roughly one-eighth of the world's population lack access to safe water supplies, while as many as 2.5 billion people live without sanitized water. Untreated water is full of dangerous chemicals and contaminants that, if consumed, lead to debilitating and sometimes fatal diseases, including dysentery and diarrhea. What is needed worldwide are dependable purification systems that remove harmful impurities to make water safe to drink.

If you were writing about the sharing economy, you might introduce your topic with a *revealing quotation* and then expand on the quotation to lead up to the thesis (underlined).

> Thomas Friedman is a Pulitzer prize-winning author who, among other things, is interested in trends shaping the global economy. He states, "The sharing economy is producing both new entrepreneurs and a new concept of ownership." Brian Chesky and Nathan Blecharczyk, who created Airbnb, and Leah Busque, who created TaskRabbit, are three such entrepreneurs who are changing the way we conduct business. These businesses, with the help of advances in technology, connect people directly and promote sharing rather than buying. The sharing economy is thriving because users value its simplicity.

Practice Complete an opening paragraph for one of the topics that you introduced in the previous activity.

L04 Reading the Middle Part

The details that support the thesis of an essay often follow one main pattern of organization. For example, an essay explaining a process will almost always follow the chronological pattern. Within such an essay, however, other patterns of organization may be employed as well, but in a secondary role. For example, a process essay may contain a comparison and/or a detailed description. Knowing how the patterns of organization work will help you follow the supporting details in a reading selection.

Chronological Order

Narratives that recall experiences and essays that explain how something works or how to do something follow chronological, or time, order. This paragraph explains the process for making cheese. The highlighted words show that chronological order is used.

Cheese Making

Cheese making starts by heating the milk to kill off any unsafe bacteria. Once the milk is heated, a starter culture is added to curdle it. The culture contains different enzymes and bacteria that give cheese its unique flavor. Next, the cheese sits for a day, until the milk has curdled into solids. The solids are called *curds*, while the leftover liquid is called *whey*. After the cheese maker separates the curds from the whey, the process continues by reheating the curds, letting them settle, and stirring away as much liquid as possible. This step is repeated until the cheese maker believes the cheese is sufficiently solid. When the cheese solidifies, it is poured into molds of different shapes and sizes. Finally, the cheese is placed in cooler temperatures so that it can ripen.

Cause-Effect

Texts commonly explain the relationship between causes and effects. For example, a science text may explain the causes and effects of suburban expansion on the environment, or a history text may discuss the causes and effects of an important event. The following paragraph discusses the causes and effects of hypothermia. The highlighted words show that cause-effect organization is followed. A secondary pattern is used as well because there is a process involved in the effects of the condition.

Hypothermia

Even a slight drop in the normal human body temperature of 98.6 degrees Fahrenheit causes hypothermia. Often produced by accidental or prolonged exposure to cold, the condition forces all bodily functions to slow down. The heart rate and blood pressure decrease. Breathing becomes slower and shallower. As the body temperature drops, these effects become even more dramatic until it reaches somewhere between 88 and 82 degrees Fahrenheit and the person lapses into unconsciousness. When the temperature reaches between 65 and 59 degrees Fahrenheit, heart action, blood flow, and electrical brain activity stop. Normally such a condition would be fatal. However, as the body cools down, the need for oxygen also slows down. A person can survive in a deep hypothermic state for an hour or longer and be revived without serious complications.

Logical

Texts that simply present information in a sensible order are organized logically. The supporting details essentially follow one another in a reasonable way to create a coherent text. One idea or detail logically leads to the next one. This passage logically discusses the skill of listening.

Listen Hard!

It's estimated that college students spend 10 hours per week listening to lectures.   1

Instructors can speak 2,500-5,000 words during a 50 minute lecture. That's a   2 lot of words flying by at breakneck speed, so it's important to listen correctly. But what does that mean?

Think about the various situations in which you find yourself listening. You   3 often listen to empty chit-chat on your way to class. "Hey, how's it going?" when you spot your best friend in the hallway is an example, right? Listening in this situation doesn't require a lot of brainpower.

You also listen in challenging situations, some that are emotionally charged;   4 for example, a friend needs to vent, relieve stress, or verbalize her anxieties. Most people who are blowing off steam aren't looking for you to fix their problems. They just want to be heard and hear you say something like "I understand" or "That's too bad."

Listening to chit-chat and listening in emotionally charged situations   5 require what are called soft listening skills. You must be accepting, sensitive, and nonjudgmental. You don't have to assess, analyze, or conclude. You just have to be   *5*

there for someone else.

When you're listening to new information, as you do in your college classes,   *6*
you have to pay close attention, think critically, and ultimately make decisions
about what you're hearing. When you're listening to a person trying to inform
you or to persuade you, you need hard listening skills. In situations like these you
must evaluate, analyze, and decide.   From *FOCUS on College and Career Success*, 1E. © 2012 Cengage Learning

Comparison

Texts that show the similarities and differences between two topics follow one of
the comparison patterns of organization. One
text may make a topic-by-topic comparison,
discussing one topic completely and then the
other topic. Another text may discuss all of
the similarities between the two topics and
then their differences. Still another text may
make a point-by-point comparison of the
two topics. This paragraph makes a topic-
by-topic comparison of the two main legal
representatives in the British legal system.

Solicitors and Barristers

In the British legal system, both solicitors and barristers serve the public, but
they do so in different ways. Someone in Great Britain seeking legal help contacts
a solicitor, who will usually be part of a law firm. A solicitor then serves as a
client's legal representative, providing legal guidance and advice. When a client
needs specialized legal help before the high court, a solicitor will contact his legal
counterpart, a barrister. Unlike a solicitor, a barrister has no attachment to any
firm but instead is a member of chambers, a group of barristers that share legal
aides and office help. A barrister's main responsibility is to argue a client's case
before a judge and jury. This legal division of power has served the British public
well for ages, even though the solicitors are now gaining more responsibility
before the courts.

Problem-Solution

Texts that explore a particular problem often follow the problem-solution pattern of
organization. Usually, the parts of the problem are identified and analyzed, followed by a

discussion of possible solutions. Sometimes the best solution is addressed in detail. Cause-effect is a common secondary pattern of organization when problems are discussed. This passage follows the problem-solution pattern regarding lead poisoning, a serious health problem in the young.

Lead Poisoning

(*Problem*) Lead poisoning is a serious health problem for young children. According to the Alliance for Healthy Homes, the problem is especially acute for inner-city children living in homes still containing lead-based paints, the major source of the problem. Young children may ingest peeling paint or breath in the dust from the paint; both are potentially harmful. Lead poisoning can lead to headaches and nausea, as well as more deep-seated problems such as learning disabilities and behavioral problems.

(*Solutions*) Tragically, there are no complete cures to lead poisoning. The best immediate solution is for home dwellers to carry out daily house cleanings and to regularly wash their hands. For the long term, walls covered in lead paint should be repainted with a safer paint, but without any sanding beforehand. In addition, the Mayo Clinic Web site on lead poisoning reminds renters that they have rights protecting their health and safety. Landlords by law are required to find and address sources of lead.

Practice Identify the main pattern of organization used in the following texts: *chronological, logical, cause-effect, comparison,* or *problem-solution.*

1.   Each year, more and more homeless people roam the largest cities in the United States. Many experts point to the shortage of affordable housing as the reason for this. According to Peter Marcuse in a recent *Nation* article, the 2 percent vacancy rate of affordable housing in the U.S. is not great enough to fill the need. Experimental voucher programs and the rent-control systems are intended to provide housing for low-income families that need shelter. Despite the good intensions behind these varied programs, none of them has provided sufficient help because they operate under different governing bodies. So what is the solution? First of all, the federal government, not state or local governments, must accept responsibility for sheltering the homeless and immediately increase production of affordable housing. And secondly, the federal government must ensure that the proper housing is made available. This would include temporary emergency shelters as well as transitional shelters and affordable permanent

housing. With the proper housing, homelessness could become a matter of choice rather than necessity.

Pattern of organization: _____

2.   Every vegetarian is unique, with unique causes or reasons for eating what he   *1*
or she eats. Many see animals as more than meat—creatures with intelligence and feelings. These vegetarians don't like the idea of killing animals for food, especially not in the overcrowded and inhumane factory farms of today. Other vegetarians reject modern American eating habits, with too much meat and too few vegetables. The U.S. Department of Agriculture recommends that people "go lean on protein" and eat even less fat. However, the average American eats 16 percent of calories in proteins and 44 percent in fat. Vegetarians seek a better diet and a more sustainable lifestyle. And for some, it's just a matter of personal preference.

For most vegetarians, their choice has very positive effects. Vegetarians have   *2*
to think about what they eat and where it comes from, and therefore they tend to eat better-quality food and less of it. As a result, vegetarians are often slimmer than omnivores and less prone to arteriosclerosis and colon cancer—caused by fatty red meats. And vegetarians feel that they live a more sustainable lifestyle with less impact on the natural world.

Pattern of organization: _____

3.   The brain divides its work in interesting ways. Roughly 95 percent of us   *1*
use our left brain for language (speaking, writing, and understanding). In addition, the left hemisphere is superior in math, judging time and rhythm, and coordinating the order of complex movements, such as those needed for speech.

In contrast, the right hemisphere can produce only the simplest language   *2*
and numbers. Working with the right brain is like talking to a child who can say only a dozen words or so. To answer questions, the right hemisphere must use nonverbal responses, such as pointing at objects.

Although it is poor at producing language, the right brain is especially good   *3*
at perceptual skills, such as recognizing patterns, faces, and melodies, putting together a puzzle, or drawing a picture. It also helps us express emotions and detect the emotions that other people are feeling (Borod et al., 2002; Castro-Schilo & Kee, 2010).   From Coon/Mitterer. *Psychology*, 12E. © 2012 Cengage Learning

Pattern of organization: _____

4.

Born in 1533, [Elizabeth I] was only three years old when her mother was executed. She was declared illegitimate by order of the disappointed Henry, who had wished for a son. But after her father's death, Parliament established her as third in line to the throne behind her half-brother, Edward, and her Catholic half-sister, Mary. During Mary's reign (1553-1558), Elizabeth was imprisoned for a time, but she was careful to stay clear of the hectic Protestant-Catholic struggles of the day. By doing so, she managed to stay alive until she could become ruler in her own right.

1

Her rule began amid many internal dangers. The Catholic party in England opposed her as a suspected Protestant. The **Calvinists** opposed her as being too much like her father, Henry, who never accepted Protestant **theology**. The Scots were becoming rabid Calvinists who despised the English's halfway measures in religious affairs. On top of this, the government was deeply in debt.

2

Elizabeth showed great insight in selecting her officials and maintained good relations with Parliament. She conducted **diplomatic** affairs with farsightedness and found she could use her status as an unmarried queen to definite advantage. . . .

3

In 1588, after long negotiations failed, Philip of Spain sent the Spanish Armada to punish England for aiding the rebellious Dutch Calvinists across the Channel. The queen rallied her sailors in a stirring visit before the battle. The resulting defeat of the Armada not only signaled England's rise to naval equality with Spain but also made Elizabeth the most popular monarch England had ever seen.   From Adler/Pouwels, *World Civilizations*, 6E. © 2012 Cengage Learning.

4

Calvinists
religious doctrine of John Calvin, maintains salvation comes through faith and that God has already chosen who will believe and be saved

theology
study of religion

diplomatic
showing skill in dealing with people

Main pattern of organization: _____

Second pattern: _____

Using a Graphic Organizer

Once you identify the pattern of organization, consider using an appropriate graphic organizer to help you keep track of the important details during your reading. You can customize any of these organizers to meet your needs for a particular text.

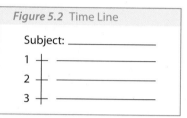

Figure 5.2 Time Line

Subject: _____

1 _____
2 _____
3 _____

Chronological: Use a time line to identify the steps in a narrative or process. See Figure 5.2 Time Line.

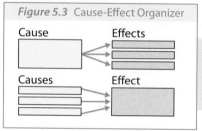

Figure 5.3 Cause-Effect Organizer

Cause   Effects

Causes   Effect

Cause-Effect: Use a cause-effect organizer to identify the key details following this pattern of organization. See Figure 5.3 Cause-Effect Organizer.

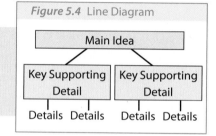

Figure 5.4 Line Diagram

Main Idea

Key Supporting Detail   Key Supporting Detail

Details Details   Details Details

Logical: Use a line diagram to identify the main points and supporting details for some texts following the logical pattern of organization. See Figure 5.4 Line Diagram.

Figure 5.5 Venn Diagram

A   B

1   1   1
2   2   2
3   3   3

A and B
Differences

Figure 5.6 T Chart

Topic A	Topic B

Comparison: Use a Venn diagram to identify the similarities and differences in a comparison text. See Figure 5.5 Venn Diagram. Or use a simple T chart if only similarities or differences are provided. See Figure 5.6 T Chart.

Problem-Solution: Use a problem-solution web to identify the main points in a text following this pattern of organization. See Figure 5.7 Problem-Solution Web.

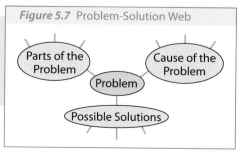

Figure 5.7 Problem-Solution Web

Parts of the Problem   Cause of the Problem

Problem

Possible Solutions

LO5 Developing the Middle Part of an Essay

After identifying your thesis, you need to determine how to organize the details that support it. Usually, the thesis will suggest a pattern of organization to follow. For example, the thesis statement "I am Korean, but I am American, too" suggests that the writer will compare the two cultures. The thesis statement "The boardwalk makes Coney Island unique among other New York neighborhoods" suggests that the writer will describe the boardwalk, perhaps organizing the details spatially—from left to right, top to bottom, or near to far. The thesis statement "The sharing economy thrives because users value its simplicity" suggests that the writer will present the support logically, moving sensibly and coherently from one key point to the next.

Here are three ways to arrange the supporting information when writing the main part of your essay after identifying an appropriate pattern of organization:

- **Make a quick list** of key points.
- **Create an outline**—an organized arrangement of key points and supporting details.
- **Fill in a graphic organizer**, arranging key points and details in a chart or diagram.

Making a Quick List

A **quick list** (see **Figure 5.8**) works well for shorter essays or when your planning time is limited. For an essay organized chronologically, simply list the key supporting details according to time. For an essay organized spatially, list the key details from left to right, top to bottom, or near to far. For an essay organized logically, decide which supporting details go together; then determine what key point they make. Here is a quick list for an essay about the sharing economy, following logical order.

> **Figure 5.8** Quick List
>
> **Thesis statement:** The sharing economy thrives because users value its simplicity.
>
> 1. Define the sharing economy.
> 2. Explain its simplicity and ease of use.
> 3. Provide examples.
> 4. Consider its future.

Practice Write a thesis statement and a quick list for an essay explaining why a certain television show is one of your favorites.

Using an Outline

An **outline** carefully arranges ideas for your writing. The ideas in a topic outline are expressed in words and phrases; the ideas in a sentence outline are expressed in sentences. In a traditional outline, if you have a "I," you should have at least a "II." If you have an "A," you should have at least a "B," and so on. Each new division represents another level of detail. You also know that you change or simplify the form to meet your writing needs. Figure 5.9 is the first part of a simplified outline that includes key points in complete sentences and supporting details in phrases.

Figure 5.9 Simplified Outline

Thesis statement: Charlotte Perkins Gilman rejected common beliefs about male dominance.

1. Gilman's beliefs did little to prepare her for married life.
   - in 1884, married Charles W. Stetson
   - gave birth to a daughter
   - visited CA shortly after to mentally and emotionally heal
   - wrote a book about a pregnant woman locked in a room

2. During the next stage in her life, Gilman became a leading feminist.
   - delivered speeches on women's rights
   - edited *Impress* for Women's Press Associate
   - from 1895-1900, continued lecturing
   - in 1896, a delegate to the National Socialist and Labor Congress in London

---

Practice Develop the first part of a simplified outline for an essay about television viewing. A thesis statement and two key points are provided. Put the key points in a logical order and make up two supporting details for each one.

Thesis statement: Unregulated television viewing has harmful effects on young viewers.

Main points: Television is passive, requiring almost no skill or thinking. Television viewing takes away from study and reading time.

1. _____

   – _____

   – _____

2. _____

   – _____

   – _____

Using a Graphic Organizer

A **graphic organizer** helps you map out your writing using a chart, table, or diagram. For example, you can use a line diagram to organize information for an essay that identifies three examples of the topic. **Figure 5.10** shows an example.

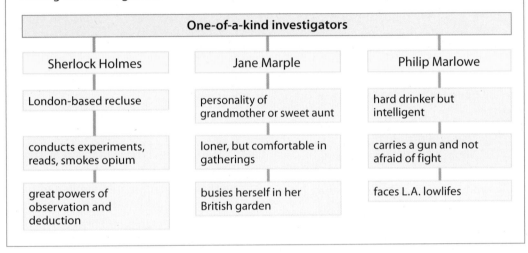

Figure 5.10 Sample Line Diagram

Thesis statement: The most famous mysteries have a one-of-a-kind main character leading the investigation.

One-of-a-kind investigators

Sherlock Holmes	Jane Marple	Philip Marlowe
London-based recluse	personality of grandmother or sweet aunt	hard drinker but intelligent
conducts experiments, reads, smokes opium	loner, but comfortable in gatherings	carries a gun and not afraid of fight
great powers of observation and deduction	busies herself in her British garden	faces L.A. lowlifes

Practice Fill in the following graphic organizer, a Venn diagram, with details for an essay comparing two similar television shows (two comedies, two detective shows, two reality shows, etc.).

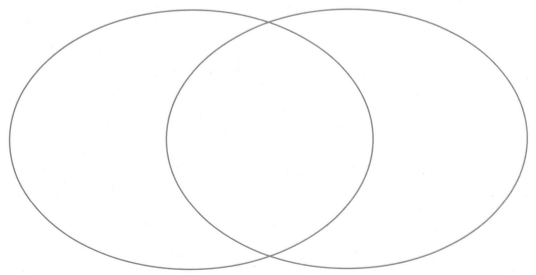

Writing the Middle Part

In the middle paragraphs, you develop the key points that support your thesis statement. Use your quick list, outline, or graphic organizer as a general guide; also, consider these writing tips:

- **Keep your thesis statement in mind** as you write. All of your key points should support or explain this statement.
- **Develop each key point in a separate paragraph** (or two). State the key point in the form of a topic sentence, and follow with details that support it.
- **Fully explain each point.**
- **Use your own words,** except on those few occasions when you use the exact words from one of your sources.
- **Be open to new ideas** as they occur to you as you write.

The paragraphs in the middle part of your essay should, among other things, *define, explain, describe, show,* and *analyze* your topic and thesis. In an informational essay about the degenerative bone disease Legg-Calve-Perthes, the writer developed one middle paragraph using this part of his outline.

> 1. Legg-Calve-Perthes is both rare and mysterious
>   – affects 5 out of 100,000 children (5 to 12)
>   – boys affected more frequently, 4 to 1
>   – believed not to be genetic
>   – factor—lessening blood flow to hip joint
>   – distorts femur fitting into hip (Allie's doubled in size)

Legg-Calve-Perthes is both rare and mysterious. The disease affects only five of every 100,000 children, usually when they are between the ages of five and twelve. While boys suffer from the disease far more frequently than girls do by a ratio of 4 to 1, when girls do develop Legg-Calve-Perthes, they tend to suffer more severely from it. At this point, researchers are not really sure of the cause of the disease. They are, however, fairly certain that it is not genetic. They also know that a reduction of blood flow at the hip joint contributes to the disease and causes the bone tissue to collapse or react in other strange ways. Usually, the rounded part of the femur bone that fits into the hip joint becomes deformed. In Allie's case, the top of her femur bone grew to double its normal size, a condition that produced extreme pain when she tried to walk. It's hard to imagine how Allie or anyone else is able to deal with this condition during the active childhood years.

Practice ▸ Write a middle paragraph (or two) based on the details that you have included in your planning for a thesis statement in this chapter or in the previous chapter.

L06 Reading the Ending Part

The ending, of course, brings an informational text to a close. In this part, a writer may restate the thesis, summarize the main supporting details, and/or offer a final thought to keep the reader thinking about the topic. The ending of an essay is usually the final paragraph, but it may consist of the final few paragraphs. It may even begin with a transitional phrase such as *in summary, in conclusion,* or *as I have just shown.*

Think of the ending as the ribbon that secures and wraps up the reading. It should reinforce, enhance, or broaden what you have learned in the main part of the writing. The ending sentence in the following paragraph broadens the discussion of the topic.

> The bush honeysuckle is one of the most common invasive plants in central Indiana. Bush honeysuckle was originally planted for food for wildlife and erosion control, but it does not function well as either. Birds flock to the berries on these bushes, and the berries are high in fat and sugar, leading Dr. Rebecca Dolan, director of the Friesener Herbarium at Butler University, to call the berries "bird candy." As such, they do not provide migrating birds with effective fuel for long-distance flying. Bush honeysuckle can easily take over its environment. These plants produce vast quantities of seeds, which berry-eating birds spread. In addition, they contaminate the ground with toxic chemicals, and they leaf out so quickly that native plants have no chance to grow. And without native plants, erosion control suffers. Unfortunately, eliminating bush honeysuckle is incredibly work intensive and time consuming.

The ending paragraph in this brief essay reinforces the thesis (underlined) and adds additional information.

> As much as puppies or pandas or even children, dolphins are universally beloved. They seem to cavort and frolic at the least provocation. Their mouths are fixed in what looks like a state of perpetual merriment, and their behavior and enormous brain suggests an intelligence approaching that of humans—even, some might argue, surpassing it.
>
> Dolphins are turning out to be exceedingly clever, but not in the loving, **utopian-socialist** manner that sentimental Flipperophiles may have hoped. Researchers who spent thousands of hours observing the behavior of bottle-nosed dolphins off the coast of Australia have discovered that the males from social alliances are far more sophisticated and devious than seen in any animals other than human beings. In these sleek submarine partnerships, one team of dolphins

1

2

will recruit the help of another band of males to gang up against a third group, a sort of multi-tiered battle plan that requires considerable mental calculus.

The purpose of these complex **alliances** is not exactly sportive. Males collide with their peers in order to steal fertile females from competing bands. And after they succeed in spiriting a female away, the males remain in their tight-knit group and perform a series of feats, at once spectacular and threatening, to guarantee that the female stays in line. Two or three males will surround her, leaping and bellyflopping, swiveling and somersaulting, all in perfect **synchrony**. Should the female be so unimpressed by the choreography as to attempt to flee, the males will chase after her, bite her, slap her with their fins, or slam into her with their bodies. The scientists call this effort to control females "herding," but they acknowledge that the word does not convey the aggressiveness of the act. As the herding proceeds, the sounds of fin swatting and body bashing rumble the waters, and sometimes the female emerges with deep tooth rakes on her side.

Although biologists have long been impressed with the intelligence and social complexity of bottle-nose dolphins—the type of porpoise often enlisted for marine mammal shows because they are so responsive to trainers—they were nonetheless surprised by the **Machiavellian** flavor of the males' stratagems. Equally impressive, the multipart alliances among dolphins seemed flexible, shifting from day to day depending on the dolphins' needs, whether one group owed a favor to another, and the dolphins' perceptions of what they could get away with. The creatures seem to be highly opportunistic, which meant that each animal was always computing who was friend and who was foe.

From "The Beauty and the Beastly", by Natalie Angier, Houghton Mifflin, 1995. Found in *The Riverside Reader*.)

utopian-socialist
peaceful means to harmony and well-being

alliances
unions or agreements

synchrony
things occurring at the same time

Machiavellian
selfish, secretive, without moral principles

eva_mask, 2014 / Used under license from Shutterstock.com

Practice ▷ Read each essay that follows; then answer the questions that follow each one.

1.

A Penny for Your World-Saving Thoughts

Most people in the developed world think of technology as the newest $300   *1*
cell phone or the best $50,000 hybrid vehicle or one of our many $40,000,000
predator drones. In the developing world, however, a whole different breed of
entrepreneurs is working on technologies that cost very little and use materials as
simple as corncobs and discarded two-liter bottles. These inventors don't care so
much about the future as about the present, in which more than a billion people
live without access to safe drinking water (World). With a rare combination of
ingenuity and compassion, a generation of inventors is fixing the world's worst
problems with the simplest solutions.

For example, Amy Smith, an instructor at MIT, works in the Peruvian Andes   *2*
to turn corncobs into charcoal. Like 800 million others in the world, the locals of
El Valle Sagrado de los Incas currently heat their homes with agricultural waste
products such as dung, straw, and corncobs. These fuels produce a great deal of
smoke, which causes respiratory infections, the leading cause of death for those
under five in such homes. By turning corncobs into charcoal, Smith converts a
high-smoke fuel to a low-smoke one, not only heating homes but saving lives. Her
process involves corncobs, matches, a 55-gallon drum with a lid, and patience. She
jokingly calls her creations "carbon macro-tubes" (Ward).

While Smith works in Peru to bring clean heat to family homes, a man called   *3*
"Solar Demi" is working to bring light to the slums of Manila, Philippines. In
these tight-packed quarters, electricity is scarce, and most people live in total
darkness. Demi takes discarded two-liter bottles, strips off their labels, cleans
them, and fills them with a mixture of distilled water and bleach. He then cuts a
hole in the roof of a home and fits the bottle in place with a watertight flange. This
simple arrangement costs $1 per installation and produces 55 watts of free solar
lighting. The Liter of Light Project aims to bring solar bottle lighting into one
million homes in the Philippines (Ambani).

In South Africa, the problem is not lack of light but lack of water. 4
Traditionally in many tribes, women and girls carry water in containers on their
heads, a technique that requires numerous trips (keeping girls out of school) and
causes stress injuries to necks. To solve this problem, architect Hans Hendrikse
and his brother Piet have developed a wheel-shaped plastic drum that can hold up
to 50 liters and is durable enough to roll across the ground behind a person. Four
trips for water turn into one, and backbreaking loads turn into an easy stroll with
a sloshing drum behind. By working with global partners, the Hendrikses are
providing the Q-drum cheaply to those who need it most (Hendrikse).

Throughout the developing world, unsafe drinking water is a huge problem. It 5
causes diarrhea, which kills 1.5 million children every year—more than AIDS and
malaria combined. The company Vestergaard Frandsen wants to put a stop to it,
so it has developed the LifeStraw—a compact filtering device that is about the size
of a fat ballpoint pen. Children can carry this straw with them and drink surface
water without fear of getting waterborne diseases. The straw costs about $20 in
the developed world, but Vestergaard Frandsen is working with international
partners to provide the straw affordably to those elsewhere who do not have safe
supplies of water ("LifeStraw").

It's become fashionable to talk about how the future belongs to the 6
innovators, and people who say such things are often thinking about space
elevators and the like. But the present also belongs to the innovators—those who
make corncob coal and soda-bottle lights and drums and straws that deliver
water. All of these inventions are simple, elegant solutions to the world's oldest
problems. With thinking like this, not only is our future bright, but our present
can be as well.

1. What sentences restate the thesis statement?

_____

2. What additional information is shared?

_____

2.

Hawaiian Children

A basic premise of educational **anthropology** is that the cultural patterns students bring with them into the classroom must be taken into account if these students are to be successfully integrated into the culture of the school. This is precisely the objective that educational anthropologist Cathie Jordan brought to her work with the Kamehameha Elementary Education Program (KEEP), a privately funded educational research effort designed to develop more effective methods for teaching Hawaiian children in the public schools.

For decades children of Hawaiian ancestry, particularly those from low-income families, have been chronic underachievers in the public school system. Classroom teachers often describe these children as lazy, uncooperative, uninvolved, and disinterested in school. Differences do exist between their dialect, known as Hawaiian Creole English, and the Standard English used by teachers, but the linguistic differences are minimal. Thus Jordan and her colleagues at KEEP needed to look beyond linguistic differences to find an explanation for why Hawaiian children were not succeeding in school. Accordingly, KEEP focuses on the wider Hawaiian culture—particularly interaction patterns within the family—in order to discover learning skills the children had developed at home that could be used and built upon in the classroom.

When dealing with parents and siblings at home, Hawaiian children behave very differently than when interacting with teachers and classmates. From a very early age, Hawaiian children contribute significantly to the everyday work of the household. Tasks that all children are expected to perform regularly include cleaning, cooking, laundry, yard work, caring for younger siblings, and (for male children) earning cash from outside employment. Working together in cooperative sibling groups, brothers and sisters organize their own household work routines with only minimal supervision from parents. Young children learn to perform their household tasks by observing their older siblings and adults. And, according to Jordan and her colleagues, these chores are performed willingly within a "context of strong values of helping, cooperation, and contributing to the family."

The **paradox** facing KEEP was: How could children be so cooperative and responsible at home and yet so disengaged and lazy in school? A comparison of the home and school cultures revealed some major structural differences. When a mother wants her children to do a job around the house, she makes that known and then allows the children to organize how it will be done. In other words, she gives responsibility for the job to the children. In contrast, the classroom is almost totally teacher dominated. The teacher makes the assignment, sets the rules, and manages the resources in the classroom. Children are controlled by the classroom rather than being responsible for it. Once these cultural differences between home and school were revealed, the educational anthropologist was able to suggest some changes for improving student involvement in their own education. The solution was fairly straightforward. Have teachers run their classrooms in much the same way as Hawaiian mothers run their households.

Here, then, is an example of how educational anthropologists can apply their findings to improve the learning environment for Hawaiian children. Interestingly, this case of applied anthropology did not follow the traditional solution to problems of minority education, which involves trying to change the child's family culture to make it conform to the culture of the classroom. Rather Jordan and her colleagues at KEEP solved the problem by modifying the culture of the classroom to conform to the skills, abilities, and behaviors that Hawaiian students brought with them from their family culture.

From Ferraro/Andreatta, *Cultural Anthropology*, 9E. © 2012 Cengage Learning

---

anthropology
study of human races, societies, and cultures

paradox
the idea of two opposite things that seem impossible but is actually true or possible

1. What sentence restates the thesis statement?

_____

_____

2. What additional information is shared?

_____

_____

_____

L07 Writing the Ending Part of an Essay

While the opening part of your writing offers important first impressions, the closing part offers important final impressions. More specifically, the closing helps the reader better understand and appreciate the importance of the topic and thesis.

Consider these strategies when writing your closing. In most cases, you will want to use more than one of these strategies, but whatever you choose to do, the ending must flow smoothly from your last middle paragraph.

- **Remind the reader of the thesis.**

  > Legg-Calve-Perthes is like a cancer in how it affects an individual and her family.

- **Summarize the main points** or highlight one or two of them.

  > By removing dirt and sludge through pretreatment and coagulation, then filtering the lingering particles, and finally disinfecting with chlorine and other chemicals, water purification plants make certain that the water our bodies desperately need to survive will do the job.

- **Reflect on the explanation or argument** you've presented in the main part of your essay.

  > Many factors contribute to a person's level of physical activity. Depending on the time of year, a person may live a moderate physical lifestyle one week and a sedentary lifestyle the next week. What's most important, though, is to live a healthy lifestyle, and a healthy lifestyle requires some form of exercise.

- **Offer a final idea** to keep the reader thinking about the topic.

  > Trust is the foundation of a source-reporter relationship. Journalists Williams and Fainaru-Wada knew this. They decided against revealing their source and would have served jail time if the source had not confessed. But the next journalist might not be so lucky. It's time to pass a federal shield law.

In this essay about choosing a vegetarian diet, the writer reminds the reader about the thesis and reflects on the explanation presented in the main part.

> The vegetarian lifestyle offers numerous physical and spiritual benefits to a person who chooses it. But the lifestyle isn't for everyone. People with poor impulse control will have a hard time resisting society's penchant for eating meat. Besides that, growing children and adolescents must be careful to get enough of the proteins and fats they need to keep growing. The vegetarian lifestyle doesn't work for everyone.

In the essay about the degenerative bone disease Legg-Calve-Perthes, the writer reminds the reader about the thesis, reflects on the explanation provided in the main part of the essay, and provides an important final thought.

> Legg-Calve-Perthes is like a cancer in how it affects an individual and her family. In Allie's case, the debilitating effects started with her painful efforts to walk and have continued with attempts to address the condition with operations, therapy, and braces. Through all of this, she and her family have missed out on so much. Her mother had to quit her job, and her sister felt ignored. As Allie recalled, "My sister has always felt jealous of all of the attention I get from my parents." But knowing that the condition should, in time, resolve itself certainly must help sufferers like Allie meet each new challenge. It must also help them to know that young people suffering from Legg-Calve-Perthes usually do quite well in the long term. Unfortunately, the chance of permanent hip damage exists as well.

Practice Write an ending paragraph (or two) based on one of the thesis statements that you have been working with in this chapter or in the previous one.

_____

_____

_____

_____

_____

_____

_____

_____

☑ Review and Enrichment

Reviewing the Chapter

Read and Write the Beginning Part

1. What information is usually found in the beginning part of a reading selection?

2. What are two strategies that you can use to introduce the topic in your writing?

Read and Write the Middle Part

3. What is the logical pattern of organization?

4. How can the thesis statement help you organize the main part of your essays?

5. What are three ways to organize the supporting information before you write?

Read and Write the Ending Part

6. How does an ending reinforce what is said in the main part of an essay?

7. What are two strategies to employ when ending an essay?

> "If an elephant has its foot on the tail of a mouse, and you say you are neutral, the mouse will not appreciate your neutrality."
>
> —Desmond Tutu

Reading for Enrichment

You will be reading an essay in which the writer takes a surprising, and perhaps unpopular, position on a crisis receiving national attention almost daily. Be sure to follow the steps in the reading process to help you gain a full understanding of the text.

About the Author

Nick Gillespie is editor of Reason.com and Reason.tv and the coauthor of *The Declaration of Independents: How Libertarian Politics Can Fix What's Wrong with America*. His writing has appeared in the *New York Times,* the *Los Angeles Times,* and *The Wall Street Journal.* And he has appeared on NPR, PBS, CNN, C-SPAN, and Fox News. The essay here first appeared in *The Wall Street Journal.*

Prereading

We hear of students bullied in schools, employees harassed in the workplace, and servicemen and -women bullied in the military. We even hear of bullying in professional football locker rooms, no less. As you probably know, technology has contributed to these problems because it allows perpetrators to harass and intimidate anonymously. In "Stop Panicking About Bullies," Gillespie responds specifically to bullying in our schools. Explore your own thoughts by freewriting about bullying. Try to write for at least five to eight minutes.

Consider the Elements

As you read this selection, pay careful attention to the basic **organization** of the essay—the beginning, middle, and ending. Do the three parts work together to form a meaningful whole? Also note the pattern of organization used in the middle or main part of the text. Does the pattern make it easy to follow the main idea and details?

El Greco, 2014 / Used under license from Shutterstock.com

What do you think?

How does Desmond Tutu's quotation relate to bullying? Why would the mouse not appreciate your "neutrality"?

Before you read, answer these three questions:

1. What do the title, the opening three paragraphs, and the first lines of other paragraphs tell you about the topic and thesis (the author's position)?

2. What are your first thoughts about the author's purpose and the intended audience?

3. What do you expect to learn?

Reading and Rereading

As you read, make it your goal to (1) identify the topic and thesis, (2) confirm the purpose and audience, (3) identify the three main parts of the essay, and (4) note the main pattern of organization used to develop the supporting information. Consider annotating the text and/or taking notes to help you keep track of important information during your reading. Be sure to reread as needed to confirm your understanding of the text and to analyze its ideas and organization.

The Reading Process

Prereading → Rereading

Reading → Reflecting

Stop Panicking About Bullies

"When I was younger," a remarkably self-assured, soft-spoken 15-year-old named Aaron tells the camera, "I suffered from bullying because of my lips—as you can see, they're kind of unusually large. So I would kind of get [called] 'Fish Lips'—things like that a lot—and my glasses too, I got those at an early age. That contributed. And the fact that my last name is Cheese didn't really help with the matter either. I would get [called] 'Cheeseburger,' 'Cheese Guy'—things like that, that weren't really very flattering. Just kind of making fun of my name—I'm a pretty sensitive kid, so I would have to fight back the tears when I was being called names."   1

As the parent now of two school-age boys, I also worry that my own kids will have to deal with such ugly and destructive behavior. And I welcome the common-sense antibullying strategies relayed in *Stop Bullying* (a Cartoon Network special): Talk to your friends, your   2 parents, and your teachers. Recognize that you're not the problem. Don't be a silent witness to bullying.

But is America really in the midst of a "bullying crisis," as so many now claim? I don't see it. I also suspect that our fears about the **ubiquity** of bullying are just the latest in a long line of well-intentioned yet **hyperbolic** alarms about how awful it is to be a kid today.

3

I have no interest in defending the bullies who dominate sandboxes, **extort** lunch money, and use Twitter to taunt their classmates. But there is no growing crisis. Childhood and adolescence in America have never been less brutal. Even as the country's overprotective parents whip themselves up into a moral panic about kid-on-kid cruelty, the numbers don't point to any explosion of abuse. As for the rising wave of laws and regulations designed to combat meanness among students, they are likely to lump together minor slights with major offenses. The antibullying movement is already conflating serious cases of gay-bashing and vicious harassment with things like . . . a kid named Cheese having a tough time in grade school.

4

How did we get here? We live in an age of helicopter parents so pushy and overbearing that Colorado Springs banned its annual Easter-egg hunt on account of adults jumping the starter's gun and scooping up treat-filled plastic eggs on behalf of their **winsome** kids. The Department of Education in New York City—once known as the town too tough for Al Capone—is seeking to ban such words as "dinosaurs," "Halloween," and "dancing" from citywide tests on the grounds that they could "evoke unpleasant emotions in the students," it was reported this week.

5

And it's not only shrinking-violet city boys and girls who are being treated as delicate flowers. Early versions of new labor restrictions still being hashed out in Congress would have barred children under 16 from operating power-driven farm equipment and kept anyone under 18 from working at agricultural co-ops and stockyards (the latest version would let kids keep running machines on their parents' spreads). What was once taken for granted—working the family farm, October tests with jack-o-lantern-themed

6

questions, hunting your own Easter eggs—is being threatened by paternalism run amok.

Now that schools are peanut-free, latex-free, and soda-free, *7* parents, administrators, and teachers have got to worry about something. Since most kids now have access to cable TV, the Internet, unlimited talk and texting, college, and a world of opportunities that was unimaginable even 20 years ago, it seems that adults have responded by becoming ever more overprotective and thin-skinned.

Kids might be fatter than they used to be, but by most standards *8* they are safer and better behaved than they were when I was growing up in the 1970s and '80s. Infant and adolescent mortality, accidents, sex, and drug use—all are down from their levels of a few decades ago. Acceptance of homosexuality is up, especially among younger Americans. But given today's rhetoric about bullying, you could be forgiven for thinking that kids today are not simply reading and watching grim, postapocalyptic fantasies like *The Hunger Games* but actually inhabiting such terrifying terrain, a world where *Lord of the Flies* meets *Mad Max 2: The Road Warrior*, presided over by **Voldemort**.

Even President Barack Obama has placed his stamp of approval *9* on this view of modern childhood. Introducing the Cartoon Network documentary, he solemnly intones: "I care about this issue deeply, not just as a president, but as a dad. . . . We've all got more to do. Everyone has to take action against bullying."

The state of New Jersey was well ahead of the president. Last *10* year, in response to the suicide of the 18-year-old gay Rutgers student Tyler Clementi, the state legislature passed the Anti-Bullying Bill of Rights. The law is widely regarded as the nation's toughest on these matters. It has been called both a "resounding success" by Steve Goldstein, head of the gay-rights group Garden State Equality, and a "bureaucratic nightmare" by James O'Neill, the interim school superintendent of the township of Roxbury. In Congress, New Jersey Sen. Frank Lautenberg and Rep. Rush Holt have introduced the federal Tyler Clementi Higher Education Anti-Harassment Act.

The Foundation for Individual Rights in Education has called *11* the Lautenberg-Holt proposal a threat to free speech because its "definition of harassment is vague, subjective, and at odds with Supreme Court precedent." Should it become law, it might well empower colleges to stop some instances of bullying, but it would also cause many of them to be sued for repressing speech. In New Jersey, a school anti-bullying coordinator told the *Star-Ledger* that the Anti-Bullying Bill of Rights has "added a layer of paperwork that actually inhibits us" in dealing with problems. In surveying the effects of the law, the *Star-Ledger* reports that while it is "widely used and has helped some kids," it has imposed costs of up to $80,000 per school district for training alone and uses about 200 hours per month of staff time in each district, with some educators saying that the additional effort is taking staff "away from things such as substance-abuse prevention and college and career counseling."

One thing seems certain: The focus on bullying will lead to   12
more lawsuits against schools and bullies, many of which will stretch the limits of empathy and patience. Consider, for instance, the current case of 19-year-old Eric Giray, who is suing New York's Calhoun School and a former classmate for $1.5 million over abuse that allegedly took place in 2004. Such cases can only become more common.

Which isn't to say that there aren't kids who face terrible   13
cases of bullying. The immensely powerful and highly acclaimed documentary *Bully*, whose makers hope to create a nationwide movement against the "bullying crisis," opens in selected theaters this weekend. The film follows the harrowing experiences of a handful of victims of harassment, including two who killed themselves in desperation. It is, above all, a damning indictment of ineffectual and indifferent school officials. No viewer can watch the abuse endured by kids such as Alex, a 13-year-old social misfit in Sioux City, Iowa, or Kelby, a 14-year-old lesbian in small-town Oklahoma, without feeling angry and motivated to change youth culture and the school officials who turn a blind eye.

But is bullying—which the stopbullying.gov Web site of the   14
Department of Health and Human Services defines as "teasing," "name-calling," "taunting," "leaving someone out on purpose,"

"telling other children not to be friends with someone," "spreading rumors about someone," "hitting/kicking/pinching," "spitting," and "making mean or rude hand gestures"—really a growing problem in America?

Despite the rare and tragic cases that rightly command our attention and outrage, the data show that things are, in fact, getting better for kids. When it comes to school violence, the numbers are particularly encouraging. According to the National Center for Education Statistics (NCES), between 1995 and 2009 the percentage of students who reported "being afraid of attack or harm at school" declined to 4% from 12%. Over the same period, the victimization rate per 1,000 students declined fivefold.   15

When it comes to bullying numbers, long-term trends are less clear. The makers of *Bully* say that "over 13 million American kids will be bullied this year," and estimates of the percentage of students who are bullied in a given year range from 20% to 70%. NCES changed the way it tabulated bullying incidents in 2005 and cautions against using earlier data. Its biennial reports find that 28% of students ages 12-18 reported being bullied in 2005; that percentage rose to 32% in 2007, before dropping back to 28% in 2009 (the most recent year for which data are available). Such numbers strongly suggest that there is no epidemic afoot (though one wonders if the new anti-bullying laws and media campaigns might lead to more reports going forward).   16

The most common bullying behaviors reported include being "made fun of, called names, or insulted" (reported by about 19% of victims in 2009) and being made the "subject of rumors" (16%). Nine percent of victims reported being "pushed, shoved, tripped, or spit on," and 6% reported being "threatened with harm." Though it may not be surprising that bullying mostly happens during the school day, it is stunning to learn that the most common locations for bullying are inside classrooms, in hallways and stairwells, and on playgrounds—areas **ostensibly** patrolled by teachers and administrators.   17

None of this is to be celebrated, of course, but it hardly paints a picture of contemporary American childhood as an unrestrained   18

Hobbesian nightmare. Before more of our schools' money, time, and personnel are diverted away from education in the name of this supposed crisis, we should make an effort to distinguish between the serious abuse suffered by kids in *Bully* and the sort of lower-level harassment with which the Aaron Cheeses of the world would have to deal.

In fact, Mr. Cheese, now a sophomore in high school with hopes 19 of becoming a lawyer, provides a model in dealing with the sort of jerks who will always, unfortunately, be a presence in our schools. At the end of *Stop Bullying*, he tells younger kids, "Just talk to somebody and I promise to you, it's going to get better." For Aaron, it plainly has: "It has been turned around actually. I am a generally liked guy. My last name has become something that's a little more liked. I have a friend named Mac and so together we are Mac and Cheese. That's cool."

Indeed, it is cool. And if we take a deep breath, we will realize 20 that there are many more Aaron Cheeses walking the halls of today's schools than there are bullies. Our problem isn't a world where bullies are allowed to run rampant; it's a world where kids like Aaron are convinced that they are powerless victims.

ubiquity
being everywhere, especially at the same time

hyperbolic
excessive, exaggerated

extort
to get something through force or threat

winsome
cheerful, lighthearted

Voldemort
leader of the Death Eaters, a group of evil wizards and witches in the *Harry Potter* series written by J.K. Rowling

Hobbesian
Related to the theory of Thomas Hobbes, English political philosopher (1588-1679), who argued that to maintain a civil society the citizenry must submit to the absolute power of a supreme ruler (king or queen)

ostensibly
outwardly appearing as such

Reflecting

1. What is the topic of the selection?

   _____

2. What is the author's thesis?

   _____

3. How does the author introduce his topic and thesis?

   _____

4. How are the supporting details in the middle part organized—*logically, spatially,* or *chronologically*? (Circle one.)

5. Do you feel the supporting information is reliable? Why or why not?

   _____

6. How does the ending part connect with the beginning part?

   _____

Vocabulary

For each word, define the identified word parts. Then try to explain the meaning of the complete word. (See Appendix D for a glossary of word parts.)

1. **conflating** (paragraph 4)   con + flat(e) + ing

   _____

2. **paternalism** (paragraph 6)   pater(n) + al + ism

   _____

3. **postapocalyptic** (paragraph 8)   post + apocalyp(se) + ic

   _____

Critical Thinking

- The author is a libertarian, a person who essentially believes that individuals should be allowed to say or do what they want, but within reason. How might this fact influence or affect his argument?
- Ultimately, whose responsibility is it to address the problem of bullying? Why?
- The media makes sure that we always have something to worry about. How would you respond to this claim?

Writing for Enrichment

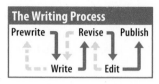

What follows are possible writing activities to complete in response to the reading.

Prewriting

Choose one of the following writing ideas, or decide upon an idea of your own related to the reading.

1. Describe an act of bullying you have experienced or witnessed.
2. Explain the most reasonable solutions to the problem of bullying.
3. Develop your own position on bullying in school, the workplace, or the military.
4. Analyze the causes of bullying.
5. Interview someone involved in this problem, and report on what you have learned.

When planning . . .

- Research the topic as needed, taking thorough notes as you go along.
- Establish a thesis for your essay.
- Review your notes for key ideas to support your thesis.

When writing . . .

- Develop effective beginning, middle, and ending parts in your essay.
- Present your thesis in the beginning part.
- Support the thesis in the middle part.
- Close your essay with final thoughts about your thesis.

When revising and editing . . .

- Carefully review your first draft.
- Ask at least one peer to review your writing as well.
- Improve the content as needed.
- Then edit your revised writing for style and correctness. (See Appendix B for an editing checklist.)

Chapter 6

"The chief virtue that language can have is clearness."
—Greek philosopher Hippocrates

Coherence

Many years ago, poet and essayist Matthew Arnold gave this wise advice to authors: "Have something to say and say it clearly as you can." Arnold's dictum is the ultimate test of any informational text you read: Does it clearly present important and/or useful information? And does it form a complete and unified whole? If the answer to these questions is "Yes," then the author has created a coherent text.

Likewise, your goal as a writer must be to create coherent essays and reports. That is, you must "have something to say" about important topics and express your ideas clearly and completely. This chapter will help you recognize coherency in a variety of informational texts and help you achieve it in your writing. Special attention is given to the use of transitions in the first part of the chapter.

Learning Outcomes

LO1 Recognize transitions in reading.
LO2 Use transitions in writing.
LO3 Read for coherence.
LO4 Write for coherence.

What do you think?

Why does Hippocrates call clearness "the chief virtue" of language and communication? Do you agree or disagree? Explain.

L01 Recognizing Transitions in Reading

The supporting details in informational texts are arranged according to patterns of organization, including chronological, spatial, cause-effect, comparison-contrast, and logical. Certain transitional words and phrases are commonly associated with the different patterns. For example, in an essay explaining a process, chronological transitions such as *first, second,* and *next* are often used to signal each new step. Transitions help unify a text by connecting ideas from sentence to sentence and paragraph to paragraph.

Recognizing the transitions will alert you to the type of text you are reading (for instance, a narrative or comparison essay) and help you follow the development of the ideas. This section identifies common transitions used with the different patterns.

Chronological Transitions

Table 6.1 includes common chronological transitions. These transitions are often used in narrative and process essays in which time order is followed.

Table 6.1 Common Chronological Transitions

after	next	in the future	now
second	today	during	for several years
yesterday	after that	then	in the past
meanwhile	before	soon after	first
over the past decade	later	in the beginning	third
	tomorrow	several years ago	fourth
as soon as	currently	finally	last

This paragraph uses transitional phrases (underlined) to establish the time frame of a discussion about a Salvadoran gang.

> Over the past decade, Salvadoran politicians passed a series of *mano dura,* or "firm hand," laws designed to crack down on criminal gang activity. These laws made it easier for police to detain suspects who exhibited certain characteristics such as having gang tattoos or loitering in known gang areas. Still, several years ago, MS-13 (the Mara Salvatrucha gang) members fired on two crowded buses in San Salvador, the country's capital, killing seventeen people and intensifying public outrage over gang violence. Three months later, in response, Salvadoran president Mauricio Funes signed the country's harshest antigang legislation to date. Under the new law, merely belonging to a gang is punishable by four to six years in prison, even if no other criminal activity is proved.

From GAINES/MILLER, *Criminal Justice in Action,* 6E. © 2011 Cengage Learning.

Spatial Transitions

Table 6.2 includes common spatial transitions. (Spatial means "of or relating to space.") These transitions are used to arrange the details in descriptions. Descriptions usually appear as part of another text, such as a narrative or informational essay.

Table 6.2 Common Spatial Transitions

top, on top of	beside	on the right	in the distance
below	on the left	across	behind
up close	in one place	down	over
in the middle	above	in front of	under
next, next to	between	high above	diagonally
beneath	in back of	along	far and near

This passage from Mark Twain's *Life on the Mississippi*, an autobiographical selection in which Twain recalls his training experiences as a riverboat pilot, describes one particular stunning sunset on the Mississippi River. The transitions Twain uses (underlined) help organize the description spatially, or by location.

> I still keep in mind a certain wonderful sunset, which I witnessed when steamboating was new to me. A broad expanse of the river was turned to blood; in the middle distance the red hue brightened into gold, through which a solitary log came floating black and **conspicuous**; in one place a long, slanting mark lay sparkling upon the water; in another [place] the surface was broken by boiling, tumbling rings that were as many tinted as an opal; where the ruddy flush was faintest was a smooth spot that was covered with graceful circles and radiating lines, ever so delicately traced; the shore on our left was densely wooded, and the somber shadow that fell from this forest was broken in one place by a long, ruffled trail that shone like silver; and high above the forest wall a clean-stemmed dead tree waved a single leafy bough that glowed like a flame in the unobstructed splendor that was flowing from the sun. There were graceful curves, reflected images, woody heights, soft distances; and over the whole scene, far and near, the dissolving lights drifted steadily, enriching it every passing moment with new marvels of coloring.   From *Life on the Mississippi* by Mark Twain. Used under the public domain.

---

conspicuous
easily seen or noticed

Example Transitions

Table 6.3 includes common transitions used to announce or introduce new examples in essays that explain, classify, and illustrate. Identifying these transitions will help you find the key point in a reading selection.

Table 6.3 Common Example Transitions

also	first	one approach	in addition
for instance	one example	another	further, moreover
for example	a second strategy	specifically	namely

This passage from an environmental textbook uses transitions (underlined) to identify each new approach or strategy to reduce forest fires.

Ecologists and forest fire experts have proposed several strategies for reducing fire-related harm to forests and to people who use the forests. One approach is to set small, contained surface fires to remove flammable small trees and underbrush in the highest-risk forest areas. Such prescribed burns require careful planning and monitoring to keep them from getting out of control. As an alternative to prescribed burns, local officials in populated parts of fire-prone California use herds of goats (kept in moveable pens) to eat away underbrush.

A second strategy is to allow some fires on public lands to burn, thereby removing flammable underbrush and smaller trees, as long as the fires do not threaten human structures and life.

A third strategy is to protect houses and other buildings in fire-prone areas by thinning a zone of about 60 meters (200 feet) around them and eliminating the use of highly flammable construction materials such as wood shingles.

A fourth approach is to thin forest areas that are vulnerable to fire by clearing away small fire-prone trees and underbrush under careful environmental controls. Many forest fire scientists warn that such thinning operations should not remove economically valuable medium-size and large trees. . . .

From Miller, *Living in the Environment*, 17E. © 2012 Cengage Learning

Cause-Effect Transitions

Table 6.4 includes common transitions used in cause-effect essays, one of the most important patterns of organization in informational writing. Some essays will focus more attention on the causes or effects of a problem. Other essays will give equal treatment to each.

Table 6.4 Common Cause-Effect Transitions			
Causes:	since	the reason is	the main cause is
	because	the main reason is	in fact
	results from		
Effects:	therefore	along with	hence
	consequently	as a result	thus
	as a consequence	the main effect is	then

This passage from a media textbook uses transitions (underlined) to identify a main cause and the resulting effects of the failure of magazines in the technology age.

Today, only one in three new magazines will survive more than five years. **1** The reason most magazines fail is that many new companies do not have the money to keep publishing long enough to be able to refine their editorial content, sell advertisers on the idea, and gather subscribers—in other words, until the magazine can make a profit.

All magazines are vulnerable to changing economic and even technology **2** trends. In 2005, *TV Guide* announced that it was discontinuing the magazine's role as a publisher of local TV schedules and, instead, re-launching the magazine in a new format exclusively devoted to celebrity news. Changing technology and the expansion of TV channels made it too hard for the magazine to keep up with TV programming, so the magazine chose to focus on the most popular part of the magazine—celebrity features. . . .

As a result, today's changing economic outlook means that people are less **3** willing to buy magazines when they believe they can find most of the information they want for free on the Internet. In 2009, when he announced that Condé Nast Publications was shutting down several popular magazines, including *Gourmet* and *Modern Bride*, CEO Chuck Townsend said, "In this economic climate it is important to narrow our focus to titles with the greatest prospects for long-term growth." From Biagi, *Media/Impact: An Introduction to Mass Media*, 11E. © 2014 Cengage Learning

Comparison-Contrast Transitions

Table 6.5 includes common transitions used in essays that compare and/or contrast. Some comparison-contrast essays focus more attention on the comparisons of the two topics; others focus more attention on the contrast of the topics. Still others are balanced in their treatment. Identifying the transitions will help you to follow any approach.

Table 6.5 Common Comparison-Contrast Transitions

Comparing:	also	similarly	just as
	both	likewise	so is
	in the same way	in comparison	in addition
	similar	as well	
Contrasting:	although	however	in contrast
	even though	yet	on the other hand
	but	while	
	or	despite	

This passage from a psychology textbook uses transitions (underlined) to help establish a comparison-contrast discussion of the two sides of the brain. More attention is given to differences than to similarities.

Right Brain/Left Brain . . . The brain divides its work in interesting ways. Roughly 95 percent of us use our left brain for language (speaking, writing, and understanding). In addition, the left hemisphere is superior in math, judging time and rhythm, and coordinating the order of complex movements, such as those needed for speech.   *1*

In contrast, the right hemisphere can produce only the simplest language and numbers. Working with the right brain is like talking to a child who can say only a dozen words or so. To answer questions, the right hemisphere must use nonverbal responses, such as pointing at objects.   *2*

Although it is poor at producing language, the right brain is especially good at perceptual skills, such as recognizing patterns, faces, and melodies, putting together a puzzle, or drawing a picture. It also helps us express emotions and detect the emotions that other people are feeling (Borod et al., 2002; Stuss & Alexander, 2000).   *3*

Even though the right hemisphere is nearly "speechless," it is superior at some aspects of understanding language. If the right side of the brain is damaged, people lose their ability to understand jokes, irony, sarcasm, implications, and other nuances of language.   *4*   From Coon/Mitterer. *Psychology*, 12E. © 2012 Cengage Learning

Logical Order Transitions

Some reading selections simply present information in a sensible order, moving logically from one point to the next. Table 6.6 includes transitions are commonly used in essays that follow logical order.

Table 6.6 Common Logical Order Transitions			
however	moreover	for this reason	nevertheless
other	besides	but	whenever
after all	in other words	insofar as	once in a while

In this paragraph from a sociology textbook, the transitions (underlined) indicate that the details progress logically or sensibly from one point to the next.

> Nobody can disagree with supporting fatherhood and stable family life. However, one problem with pro-fatherhood policies is that they are often intended to replace welfare programs, which are simultaneously being cut by both the federal and state governments. Moreover, critics of pro-fatherhood policies argue that what is essential for the healthy development of children is not just the father or, for that matter, even the mother. As psychologists have shown, what is essential is a lasting and loving relationship with at least one adult (Silverstein and Auerbach, 1999). In other words, it is not necessarily the presence of a nuclear family that ensures healthy family life. Insofar as the Fatherhood Initiative supports only one kind of family, it devalues other forms of family life, including single-parent households, homosexual couples, and so on.

From BRYM/LIE, *Sociology*, 2E. © 2007 Cengage Learning

Oksana Kuzmina, 2014 / Used under license from Shutterstock.com

Practice Underline the transitions used in each of the following texts based on the pattern of organization identified in bold print.

1. **Cause-Effect:** Even anthropologists whose fieldwork experience is less traumatic encounter some level of stress from culture shock, the psychological **disorientation** caused by trying to adjust to major differences in lifestyles and living conditions. Culture shock, a term introduced by anthropologist Kalervo Oberg (1960), ranges from mild irritation to out-and-out panic. This general psychological stress occurs when the anthropologist tries to play the game of life with little or no understanding of the basic rules. Due to this lack of understanding, the fieldworker, struggling to learn what is meaningful in the new culture, never really knows when she or he may be committing a serious social **indiscretion** that might severely jeopardize the entire fieldwork project, such as using the wrong hand when giving a gift or sharing food, or speaking out of turn.   *1*

    Consequently, when culture shock sets in, everything seems to go wrong. You may become irritated over minor inconveniences. You may begin to view things critically and negatively. For example, you might think the food is strange, the people don't keep their appointments, no one likes you, everything seems **unhygienic**, people don't look you in the eye, and on and on.   *2*

    From Ferraro/Andreatta, *Cultural Anthropology*, 9E. © 2012 Cengage Learning

    ---

    disorientation   **indiscretion**   **unhygienic**
    confusion   lack of good judgment   not healthful, unsanitary

2. **Examples:** Marriageable men were in short supply for years afterward, and the imbalance between men and women aged 20 to 35 influenced what was considered acceptable sexual conduct. After the war, for instance, it proved impossible to put young men and women back into the tight customary constraints of prewar society.   *1*

    In addition, the many millions of conscripts in the armies had been torn out of their accustomed and expected slots in life. For better or worse, many—especially rural youth—never returned to their prewar lifestyles. "How're you gonna keep them down on the farm after they've seen Paree [Paris]?" went a popular song in the United States. That was a relevant question and not just for Americans.   *2*

    From Adler/Pouwels, *World Civilizations*, 6E. © 2012 Cengage Learning

3. **Logical:** When my husband fasts, our relationship becomes a bland, lukewarm concoction that I find difficult to swallow. I'm not proud of this fact. After all, he isn't the only one in our house with a spiritual practice: I stumble out of bed in the dark most mornings and meditate in the corner of our room with my back to him, trying to find that bottomless truth beyond words. Once in a great while, I'll drag him to church on Sunday. Whenever I suggest we say grace at the table, he reaches willingly for my hand, and words of gratitude flow easily from him. He has never criticized my practices, even when they are wildly inconsistent or contradictory. But Ramadan is not ten minutes of meditation or an hour-long sermon; it's an entire month of deprivation. Ismail's God is the old-fashioned kind, omnipresent and stern, uncompromising with his demands. During Ramadan this God expects him to pray on time, five times a day—and to squeeze in additional prayers of forgiveness as often as he can.   Excerpted from *My Accidental Jihad: A Love Story.* Copyright 2014.

4. **Chronological:** One night while hitchhiking in Africa, [Denis Hayes] rested on a   *1*
hillside and started to put together what he had learned and what he had seen. He thought about how the principles of ecology apply to everything from **amoebas** to orangutans. Sometime shortly after that, Hayes decided to spend his life figuring out how human societies could benefit from organizing themselves around ecological principles. He has said: "Pretty much from birth, I had an awareness of the awesome natural beauty being torn apart by industrial processes."

Denis Hayes is currently president and CEO of The Bullitt Foundation of Seattle, Washington.
The foundation seeks to deal with key environmental problems in the U.S. Pacific Northwest. . . .   From Miller, *Living in the Environment,* 17E. © 2012 Cengage Learning

2

---

amoebas
one-celled organisms

L02   Using Transitions in Writing

When you develop your writing, use the appropriate transitions as needed to help you create a clear and unified piece of writing. Most assignments identify the pattern of organization for your writing, so you will know which type of transitions to use.

Identify the Pattern of Organization

Suppose your instructor made this assignment: *Describe a favorite location in the city, using plenty of sensory details. Arrange the details in an orderly way to help the reader visualize this setting.* In this assignment, it is clear that you are creating a description, so you would use spatial transitions to organize your details.

Or suppose you were given this assignment: *Explain the causes and effects of the Haymarket Riot of 1886. In your explanation, cite at least two sources provided in the reading list about this event.* It is clear in this assignment that you will be developing a cause-effect essay, so you would use transitions that identify causes and effects.

However, not all of your assignments will clearly identify a pattern of organization, such as this assignment: *Landscaping in cold climates poses specific challenges. Report on the best use of one type of plant as a cold-climate design feature.* For assignments like this, an organizing pattern usually emerges after you research your topic and establish a main idea for your writing. For example, if you decided to focus on the types of trees that work in cold climates, you could use example transitions (*one example, another example, also*) to organize the details (the trees) in the report.

Be Selective with Transitions

A piece of writing will sound forced or awkward if it contains too many transitions, so use them selectively. Transitions should be used as needed to help establish the organization of the text. This passage illustrates what can happen if a writer uses too many transitions. The transitions (underlined) actually bring undue attention on themselves and sound forced.

> Americans made many sacrifices during the 1973 energy crisis. First, homeowners voluntarily turned down their thermostats by an average of two degrees. Second, businesses voluntarily shortened the work week and cut back on energy use. Third, unneeded lights were turned off in homes and businesses. Fourth, slower driving was encouraged, and fifth, Sunday driving was discouraged.

Practice Identify appropriate transitions to complete each of these student texts.

1. Narrative following chronological order

Jammed in our aging royal blue Chevy Astro with limited legroom, my family journeyed along historic Route 66 near the New Mexico-Arizona border on our way to the Grand Canyon. This was not exactly my idea of a fun time. *First* the air conditioner was on the blink, so beads of sweat trickled down my brow and my back. That I was jammed between my two brothers, who generated their own heat, made the situation almost unbearable. *Next* I noticed the low-battery sign blinking on my mp3 player. Considering we were six hours from our destination, I would be soon without music to distract me while we motored along this godforsaken stretch of scrubland. How would I survive? *Then* what happened seemed like a scene from a bad comedy movie. Grayish smoke billowed from under the hood of the van, blocking my dad's view of the road. Dad pulled off the road, and a bad vacation *soon after* became the worst vacation ever.

2. Information essay providing examples

Different people pursue different levels of physical activity. _____ *1* a person with a sedentary lifestyle exercises fewer than three times per week. This type of lifestyle is linked to weight gain and an increased risk of developing diseases such as type 2 diabetes.

_____ level of physical activity is simply known as "lifestyle active." *2* This level describes a person who performs everyday lifestyle activities, such as walking to and from the store, doing yard work, or playing pick-up basketball. Engaging in regular lifestyle activities can help control cholesterol levels and reduce body fat.

Still _____ level called the "moderate physical lifestyle" describes *3* someone who follows a cardio-respiratory exercise program of 20 to 60 minutes of activity, three to five days per week. Such a person might be a regular runner, weight lifter, or power walker. A moderate physical lifestyle helps a person become fit while reducing the risk of chronic disease.

The highest level of physical activity is a "vigorous lifestyle." People on *4* this level exercise 20 to 60 minutes most days of the week and follow a routine of aerobic exercises, strength training, and stretching exercises. A vigorous physical lifestyle achieves the same benefits as moderate physical activities while promoting a greater level of fitness.

3. **Cause-effect essay**

Many people think that food gets better the closer you get to the equator. At   *1*
the poles, people eat seal blubber and **lutefisk**, but at the equator, people eat tacos
and teriyaki, curry, and jalapenos. People who don't like spicy foods wonder what
all the fuss is about. There are many reasons why people like spicy food and many
benefits from doing so.

~~The reason for~~ using spices makes food taste better and helps preserve it.   *2*
Without salt, pepper, and other spices, foods taste bland. In the Middle Ages,
explorers like Marco Polo set up trade routes to get desperately needed spices for
European foods. ~~Therefore~~ some spices were worth their weight in gold. These
spices didn't grow in northern climates, and they weren't needed as much for food
preservation as in the equatorial regions, but people still wanted them for taste.

New studies show that spicy foods have surprising health benefits. For   *3*
example, he British Journal of Medicine showed that women who added hot
peppers to their food ate fewer calories than women who didn't. ~~In fact~~
at the University of California, Los Angeles, scientists found that curcumin,
which makes **turmeric** yellow, clears plaque out of brains, helping to stop
Alzheimer's disease. And at the State University of New York, researchers found
that capsaicin—what makes hot peppers hot—causes endorphins to be released,
making the eater feel happy. . . .

---

lutefisk
dried codfish soaked in a water and lye solution
before cooking

turmeric
a powder used for flavoring and coloring
in Asian cooking

Practice ▶ Check the first draft you wrote in this chapter for transitions. Decide if your writing
would be improved with the use of appropriate transitions.

L03 Reading for Coherence

You can expect that your assigned readings will be coherent. That is, they will display the following characteristics:

- The details will explain or support a clearly identifiable topic and main idea.
- The supporting information will be organized and build sensibly from sentence to sentence, paragraph to paragraph, and section to section.
- Key points will be clarified and expanded upon to ensure understanding.
- Important words and phrases will be repeated to connect ideas.
- Pronoun references help connect ideas (for example, *it* for *automobile*).
- Transitions such as *in addition* or *in contrast* help readers follow the text.

In short, your readings will be clear, complete, and unified, which means they will be **coherent**. This selection from a cultural anthropology textbook illustrates important features of a coherent paragraph.

Language, which is found in all cultures of the world, is a symbolic system of sounds that, when put together according to a certain set of rules, conveys meanings to its speakers. The meanings attached to any given word in all languages are totally **arbitrary**; that is, the word *cow* has no particular connection to the large bovine animal that the English language refers to as a cow. The word *cow* is no more or less reasonable as a word for that animal than would be *kaflumpha, sporge,* or *four-pronged squirter.* The word *cow* does not look like a cow, sound like a cow, or have any particular physical connection to a cow. The only explanation for the use of the word is that somewhere during the evolution of the English language the word *cow* came to be used to refer to a large, milk-giving, domesticated animal. Other languages use different, and equally arbitrary, words to describe the very same animal. From Ferraro/Andreatta, *Cultural Anthropology,* 9E. © 2012 Cengage Learning.

---

arbitrary
not planned or chosen for a particular reason

Here are the key features that contribute to the coherence of the paragraph.

- **The paragraph is built around an identifiable topic** (*language*) **and main idea** (*is a symbolic system of sounds . . .*).
- **The information is organized.** The paragraph follows logical order.
- **Ideas are clarified or expanded upon to aid in understanding.** For example, the sentence "The only explanation for the use of . . ." expands upon the sentence before it.
- **Repeated words and phrases connect ideas and help the text progress sensibly.** Some of the repeated elements are underlined in the text.

This two-paragraph selection, which compares the Chinese and American attitudes about the home, illustrates coherence within each paragraph and between the paragraphs.

Chinese Place, American Space

Americans have a sense of space, not of place. Go to an American home in *1*
exurbia, and almost the first thing you do is drift toward the picture window. How curious that the first compliment you pay your host inside his house is to say how lovely it is outside the house! He is pleased that you should admire his vistas. This distant horizon is not merely a line separating earth from the sky; it is a symbol of the future. The American is not rooted in his place, however lovely; his eyes are drawn by the expanding space to a point on the horizon, which is his future.

By contrast, consider the traditional Chinese home. Blank walls enclose it. *2*
Step behind the spirit wall and you are in a courtyard with perhaps a miniature garden around a corner. Once inside his private compound, you are wrapped in an ambiance of calm beauty, an ordered world of buildings, pavement, rock, and decorative vegetation. But you have no distant view; nowhere does the space open out before you. Raw nature in such a home is experienced only as weather, and the only open space is the sky above. The Chinese [man] is rooted in his place. When he has to leave, it is not for the promised land on the terrestrial horizon, but for another world altogether along the vertical, religious axis of his imagination.

Yi-Fu Tuan, "Chinese Place, American Space."

exurbia	spirit wall	ambiance
a region beyond suburbs	a wall around a courtyard, to keep out evil spirits	a feeling or mood associated with a place

These features contribute to the coherency of "Chinese Place, American Space."

- **The excerpt is built around an identifiable topic** (*the American and Chinese sense of home*) **and main idea** (*is significantly different*).
- **The information is organized.** The comparison pattern is used—the first paragraph analyzes one topic; the next paragraph analyzes the second topic.
- **Ideas are clarified or expanded upon to aid in understanding.** For example, the sentence "The American is not rooted in place . . ." clarifies the idea that comes before it.
- **Repeated words and phrases link ideas and help the text progress sensibly.** A few of the repeated words and phases are underlined in the text.
- **Pronoun references also help link ideas.** For example, the pronoun "his" in the third sentence in paragraph 1 connects with "your host" in the same sentence.
- **Transitions alert readers to a condition or a change in the direction of the text.** For example, *by contrast* at the start of paragraph 2 announces a change in direction of the text.

This selection illustrates how coherency is established within an extended excerpt from a criminal justice textbook.

What Causes Crime?

Jessica Wolpaw Reyes, an economist at Amherst College in Massachusetts, has put forth an intriguing reason for the nation's crime decline. Numerous studies, Reyes points out, show that children with elevated levels of lead in their blood are more likely to act aggressively as adults. In the 1970s, the federal government banned lead in gasoline and many types of paint. A generation of lead-free children has reached adulthood since then, and Reyes believes its nonviolent tendencies are responsible for half of the recent drop in violent crime rates.   *1*

The scientific study of crime, known as criminology, is rich in different explanations as to why people commit crimes, from lead in the bloodstream to violent video games to low self-control. In this section, we discuss the most influential of these explanations put forth by criminologists, or researchers who study the causes of crime.   *2*

CORRELATION AND CAUSE

At the start, it is important to understand the difference between correlation and causation. Correlation between two variables means that they tend to vary together. Causation, in contrast, means that one variable is responsible for the change in the other. In her research described above, Reyes relied on the correlation between lead in the bloodstream and aggressive behavior to reach her conclusions about violent crime rates. No criminologist, however, has proved that high levels of lead cause criminal behavior. Rather, it is one variable that may contribute to violent behavior when combined with other variables.   *3*

So, correlation does not equal cause. Sales of ice cream and crime rates both rise in the summer, but nobody would say that increased ice cream sales cause higher crime rates. . . .   *4*

THE ROLE OF THEORY

Criminologists have uncovered a wealth of information concerning a different, and more practically applicable, inquiry: Given a certain set of circumstances, why do individuals commit criminal acts? This information has allowed criminologists to develop a number of theories concerning the causes of crime.   *5*

Most of us tend to think of a theory as some sort of guess or statement that is lacking in credibility. In the academic world, and therefore for our purposes, a theory is an explanation of a happening or circumstance that is based on observation, experimentation, and reasoning. . . . In the remainder of this section, we examine the most widely recognized of these theories, starting with one that relies on freedom of choice.   *6*

THE BRAIN AND THE BODY

Perhaps the most basic answer to the question of why a person commits a crime is that he or she makes a willful decision to do so. This is the underpinning of the **rational choice theory** of crime. . . .   *7*

"THRILL DEFENDERS" In expanding on rational choice theory, sociologist Jack Katz has stated the "rewards" of crime may be sensual as well as financial. The inherent danger of criminal activity, according to Katz, increases the "rush" a criminal experiences on successfully committing a crime. . . .   *8*

RATIONAL CHOICE THEORY AND PUNISHMENT The theory that wrongdoers choose to commit crimes is a cornerstone of the American criminal justice system. Because crime is seen as the end result of a series of rational choices, policymakers have reasoned that severe punishment can deter criminal activity by adding another variable to the decision-making process. Supporters of the death penalty—carried out in 33 states and by the federal government—emphasize its deterrent effects. . . .   *9*

From GAINES/MILLER, *Criminal Justice in Action*, 6E. © 2011 Cengage Learning

---

rational choice theory
wrongdoers act as if they weigh the possible benefits of criminal or delinquent activity against the expected costs of being apprehended

- **Design elements aid in a reader's understanding of a text.** The title, headings, subheadings, and defined term provide cues about the content to follow.
- **The selection is built around an identifiable topic** (*the cause of crime*) **and the main idea** (*the key explanations*).
- **The information is organized.** The beginning clearly establishes the thesis. The middle part generally follows logical order—first, explaining the difference between a cause and a correlation; next, discussing the nature of theories; and then identifying the first one, the rational choice theory.
- **Ideas are clarified or expanded upon to aid understanding.** For example, the sentence "A generation of lead-free children has reached adulthood . . ." in paragraph 1 expands upon the sentence that comes before it.
- **Repeated words and phrases link ideas and help the text progress sensibly.** Examples are underlined in the selection. Also the phrase "choose to commit crimes" in the first sentence of paragraph 9 repeats synonymously the phrase "rational choice theory" used in the same paragraph.
- **Pronoun references also help link ideas.** In paragraph 3, for example, the pronoun "it" in one sentence refers to "high levels of lead" in the previous sentence.
- **Transitions alert readers to a change in the text.** For example, *at the start* in paragraph 3 alerts readers that what follows is important to know right away.

Practice ▶ Answer the questions after each reading to analyze it for coherency.

1.   Mammals do have the largest brains of all animals. But we humans are not   *1*
the mammalian record holders. That honor goes to whales, whose brains tip the
scales at around 19 pounds. At three pounds, the human brain seems puny—until
we compare brain weight with body weight. We then find that a sperm whale's
brain is 1/10,000 of its weight. The ratio for humans is 1/60. And yet, the ratio for
tree shrews (very small squirrel-like insect-eating mammals) is about 1/30. So our
human brains are not noteworthy in terms of either **absolute weight** or **relative
weight** (Coolidge & Wynn, 2009).

        While a small positive correlation exists between intelligence and brain size,   *2*
overall size alone does not determine human intelligence (Johnson et al., 2008;
Witelson, Beresh, & Kigar, 2006). In fact, many parts of the brain are surprisingly
similar to corresponding brain areas in lower animals, such as lizards. It is your
larger **cerebral cortex** that sets you apart.

        The cerebral cortex covers most of the brain with a mantle of gray matter   *3*
(spongy tissue made up mostly of cell bodies). The cortex in lower animals is
small and smooth. In humans it is twisted and folded, and it is the largest brain
structure. The fact than humans are more intelligent than other animals is related
to this corticalization, or increase in the size and wrinkling of the cortex.

From Coon/Mitterer. *Psychology,* 12E. © 2012 Cengage Learning

---

| **absolute weight** | **relative weight** | **cerebral cortex** |
| weight of a body in a vacuum, or on its own | weight of a body in relation to a particular range | outer layer of the brain |

1. How is the paragraph organized—*chronologically, logically,* or *spatially* (by location)? Circle one.

2. What is an example of a sentence (or sentences) that clarifies or expands upon the sentence before it?

_____

3. What are two examples of key words repeated in the selection?

_____

4. What transitional words or phrases are included to help the reader understand the text? Name two.

_____

2.   Mate Selection: Whom Should You Marry?

Every society defines a set of kin with whom a person is to avoid marriage   *1*
and sexual intimacy. In no society is it permissible to mate with one's parents or
siblings (that is, within the nuclear family), and in most cases the restricted group
of kin is considerably wider. Beyond this notion of incest, people in all societies
are faced with rules either restricting their choice of marriage partners or strongly
encouraging the selection of certain people as highly desirable mates. These
are known as the rules of **exogamy** (marrying outside of a certain group) and
endogamy (marrying within a certain group).

Rules of Exogamy

Because of the universality of the incest taboo, all societies have rules about   *2*
marrying outside a certain group of kin. These are known as rules of exogamy.
In societies such as the United States and Canada, the exogamous group
extends only slightly beyond the nuclear family. It is considered either illegal or
inadvisable to marry one's first cousin, and in some cases, one's second cousin ,
but beyond that one can marry other more distant relatives and encounter only
mild disapproval. . . .

Rules of Endogamy

In contrast to exogamy, the rules of endogamy require a person to select a   *3*
mate from within one's own group. Hindu castes in traditional India are strongly
endogamous, believing that to marry below one's caste would result in serious
ritual pollution. Caste endogamy is also found in a somewhat less rigid form
among the Rwanda and Banyankole of eastern central Africa. . . .

Even though there are no strongly sanctioned legal rules of endogamy in the   *4*
United States, there is a certain amount of marrying with one's own group based
on class, ethnicity, religion, and race. This general **de facto** endogamy found in
the United States results from the fact that people do not have frequent social
contacts with people from different backgrounds. . . .

Arranged Marriages

Individuals in most contemporary Western societies are free to marry anyone   *5*
they please. In many societies, however, the interests of the family are so strong
that marriages are arranged. Negotiations are handled by family members of the

prospective bride and groom, and for all practical purposes, the decision of whom one will marry is made primarily by one's parents or other influential relatives. In certain cultures, such as parts of traditional Japan, India, and China, future marriage partners are betrothed while they are still children. . . .

From Ferraro/Andreatta, *Cultural Anthropology*, 9E. © 2012 Cengage Learning

| **exogamy** | **endogamy** | **de facto** |
| a rule requiring marriage outside of one's own social or kinship group | a rule requiring marriage within a specified social or kinship group | in effect, in practice |

1. What design elements aid in a reader's understanding of a text?

2. What is the topic and main idea of this selection?

3. How is the text organized—*chronologically, logically,* or by the *comparison-contrast pattern*? Circle one.

4. What is an example of a sentence (or sentences) that clarifies or expands upon the sentence before it?

5. What are two examples of key words repeated in the selection?

6. What is an example of a pronoun referring to a noun?

7. What transitional words or phrases are included to help the reader understand the text? Name two.

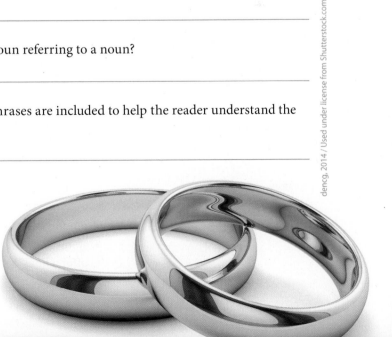

L04 Writing for Coherence

Producing a coherent piece of writing takes time, effort, and resolve. But if you're like many students, you may have a difficult time staying with a piece of writing long enough to do your best work. Here are some tips that can help you address this problem.

- **Write about topics that interest you.** If you're truly interested in a topic, you will naturally take more care when you write about it.
- **Approach your writing as a process, developing it step by step.** Then you will not try to get everything right in your first draft, which will only lead to frustration and poor results.
- **Share your writing as it develops.** You need at least two or three sets of eyes reviewing your writing as it progresses. Reviewers will help you see ways to improve the clarity and quality of your writing that you might miss.
- **Be willing to experiment or take risks.** One of your experiments may lead to a clearer or more complete explanation.
- **Remember the end game.** A coherent piece of writing should form a meaningful whole—with fully developed beginning, middle, and ending parts.

Checking for Overall Coherence

Your essays will be coherent in terms of overall structure if they form a unified whole. Each successive draft that you develop and each revision that you make should improve upon the clarity, completeness, and unity of each part. This is how experienced writers develop coherent writing. Even the most accomplished authors fail to get everything right the first, second, or even the third time. Use **Figure 6.1** as a basic guide when you check the structure of your writing for coherency.

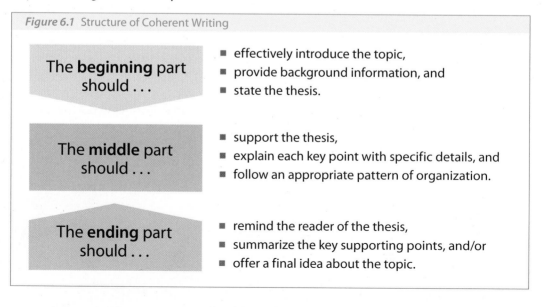

Figure 6.1 Structure of Coherent Writing

The **beginning** part should . . .
- effectively introduce the topic,
- provide background information, and
- state the thesis.

The **middle** part should . . .
- support the thesis,
- explain each key point with specific details, and
- follow an appropriate pattern of organization.

The **ending** part should . . .
- remind the reader of the thesis,
- summarize the key supporting points, and/or
- offer a final idea about the topic.

This student essay is labeled and assessed for general coherence to help you see how to use **Figure 6.1** as a guide.

Paddling Bliss

Beginning

Thesis (underlined)

Early in the morning, a light grey fog blanketed the lake. I could just make out the boats docked in the marina and a faint outline of trees to the side. Not a sound could be heard. But now, a few hours later, the fog has lifted, which means it's time to get on the water. Most mornings, I kayak for exercise and enjoyment.

1

Middle

Supporting details organized chronologically (transitions underlined)

To get started, I push off just 30 yards from my grandfather's cottage in O'Dell's Bay. By habit, I check the water quality soon after I start, looking for any patches of nasty algae that sometimes blooms on the surface. At its best, the lake water is a very light brown color, almost looking like root beer in the wake of a motorboat. At its worst, in the dog days of August, the water can shimmer with smelly, blue-green algae.

2

Once I'm out of the bay, I usually turn left, staying fairly close to the shoreline. On a good day, I'll see a lot of fish jumping, or at least I'll hear their splash and see the circular ripples that they've caused. Last year, for the first time, I saw a bald eagle flying away from its nest, which looked pretty much like a junk pile in the tree. I once came upon a crane with a fish in its mouth. As I paddled closer, it would move on, a few yards at a time. We played tag like this for a few moments before the crane had enough and took to the air to find a quiet spot for dinner.

3

After awhile, I'll mark out a spot, say a boat docked 50 yards away, and paddle like crazy until I reach that spot. This really gets my heart pumping and gives my upper body a good workout. Then, for a time, I'll just lazily drift along, taking in the quiet and calm that can be felt only on the water.

4

The lake is big enough that it makes me feel pretty small sometimes. When the wind picks up, the waves can build up a lot of power, making kayaking feel more like riding a roller coaster. And I swear that the sky is bigger here than it is back in the city. I like it best when it is partly cloudy, because the clouds look huge against the blue sky.

5

Ending

Offering final idea

Once I reach Half Moon Bay, I usually turn around and head back. The trip home might be easier or harder, depending on the wind's direction. I almost always focus less on nature and more on exercise on the return trip. I guess that's because I'm seeing the same things for a second time. When I finally make my last paddle and glide to a stop on the beach, I'm tired but happy for the trip.

6

Practice ▸ In a first draft, describe a common or uncommon experience in the outdoors. Afterward, check it for overall coherence using **Figure 6.1** as a guide.

Line-by-Line Writing Moves

Writing coherently may start at the general level, making sure that you have fully developed beginning, middle, and ending parts. But as you develop your essays, there are a number of line-by-line writing moves you can make to establish and maintain coherence. These moves are listed in **Figure 6.2**.

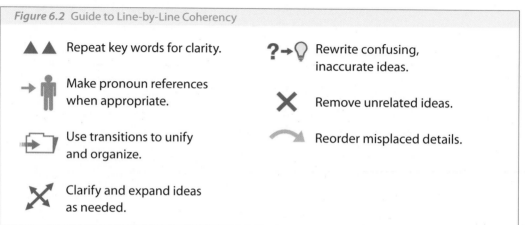

Figure 6.2 Guide to Line-by-Line Coherency

▲▲ Repeat key words for clarity.

→👤 Make pronoun references when appropriate.

Use transitions to unify and organize.

Clarify and expand ideas as needed.

?→💡 Rewrite confusing, inaccurate ideas.

✕ Remove unrelated ideas.

Reorder misplaced details.

Each of the writing moves identified in **Figure 6.2** is illustrated here. As you will see, each example helps establish or maintain coherence.

Repeat Key Words for Clarity

The repetition of key words is an essential feature of coherent writing. If, for example, the topic of your essay is clean drinking water, you would naturally repeat the word "water" as needed to ensure clarity as is done in this opening paragraph:

> One of the most overlooked luxuries of living in the United States is access to clean drinking water. Statistics show roughly one-eighth of the world's population lack access to safe water supplies, while as many as 2.5 billion people live without sanitized water. Untreated water is full of unhealthy chemicals and contaminants that, if consumed, lead to uncomfortable and sometimes fatal diseases, including dysentery and diarrhea. Purification plants remove these harmful impurities to make the water drinkable.

As you revise your writing, make sure the key words are repeated enough, but not too often. A word repeated too often can disrupt the flow of writing.

Make Pronoun References

If you repeat a key word too often, your writing may sound forced and awkward. When that happens, replace the key word with a pronoun. Suppose in an essay identifying famous detectives in crime fiction, you wrote this paragraph about Philip Marlowe.

> In the late 1930s, mystery writer Raymond Chandler created one of the first great American private investigators, Philip Marlowe. Marlowe is a hard-drinking tough guy who works in Los Angeles. Marlowe carries a gun and is not afraid of a fight, but he is also very intelligent. Marlowe learned to be an investigator by working for the district attorney and an insurance company. He often puts his life at risk against some real lowlifes during his investigations.

After reviewing the paragraph, you realize that you have at least one too many Marlowe references, so you substitute a pronoun for one of them to improve the readability.

> In the late 1930s, mystery writer Raymond Chandler created one of the first great American private investigators, Philip Marlowe. Marlowe is a hard-drinking tough guy who works in Los Angeles. He carries a gun and is not afraid of a fight, but he is also very intelligent. Marlowe learned to be an investigator by working for the district attorney and an insurance company. He often puts his life at risk against some real lowlifes during his investigations.

Use Transitions to Unify and Organize

Transitions are words or phrases that link ideas and alert the reader to a change or addition in a text. Suppose you are describing a typical laundry day, and while planning, you list the steps in your "process":

- haul laundry bags into basement laundry room
- sort the laundry for different washers
- study or read while waiting
- wrestle the heavy clothes into the dryers
- continue waiting
- fluff and fold dry clothes

To identify the steps, you would use chronological transitions (underlined).

> When you're a college student, doing laundry is a chore. I happen to clean my dirty clothes in the basement of my apartment building. First, I haul my two laundry baskets down four flights of stairs to the laundry room. Next, I go through the process of sorting the dirty clothes into two or three washers, depositing my quarters, and starting the machines. Then I either wait in an uncomfortable plastic chair in the room, studying or playing a game on my iPhone, or I head back to my apartment for 20 minutes or so. Upon return, I pry the wet clothes out of the washers and wrestle them into dryers. . . .

Explain and Clarify as Needed

A coherent piece of writing is clear and complete. To be complete, every detail in the writing must be fully explained. Suppose you are writing an essay about Ulysses S. Grant's unexpected rise to power, and you started it this way:

> A surprising story in the Civil War is the rise to power of U. S. Grant. At the   *1*
> start of the war, Grant was a clerk in his father-in-law's leather shop before signing
> on as lowly brigadier general in the Illinois Volunteers. But in a few years, he was
> appointed by President Lincoln to lead all of the troops in the Union Army. Grant
> earned this position by succeeding in three important battles in the West.
>
> Grant's first important victory came in February of 1862 at the Battle of Fort   *2*
> Donelson in Tennessee. The Confederate troops had entered the fort to regroup
> after a battle at Fort Henry. But before long, the Confederate troops agreed to
> Grant's terms of an unconditional surrender. After that, the "U.S." in U.S. Grant
> was said to stand for "unconditional surrender."

After reviewing this part, you realize that a key detail in the second paragraph is not complete enough, so you expand upon it (in *italics*):

> Grant's first important victory came in February of 1862 at the Battle of Fort
> Donelson in Tennessee. The Confederate troops had entered the fort to regroup
> after a battle at Fort Henry. *Grant ordered his men to make minor attacks on the fort,*
> *and they also stopped an attempt by the Confederacy to break out.* But before long,
> the Confederate troops agreed to Grant's terms of an unconditional surrender. After
> that, the "U.S." in U.S. Grant was said to stand for "unconditional surrender."

Rewrite Confusing, Inaccurate Ideas

Any ideas that are confusing or awkward must be revised until they are clear and smooth reading. Let's say you are explaining the cheese-making process, and one part reads as follows.

> After the cheese maker separates the curds from the whey, the process
> continues by reheating the curds, letting them settle, and stirring away as much
> liquid as possible. Repeat this step until the cheese becomes solid. When the
> cheese solidifies, it is poured into molds of different shapes and sizes. Then the
> cheese is placed in cooler temperatures so that it can ripen.

Upon review, you see that the second sentence is written in the second person (*you*) while the other sentences are in the third person (*he* or *she*). You rewrite the sentence to correct this error:

> This step is repeated until the cheese maker believes the cheese is sufficiently solid.

Remove Unrelated Ideas

Delete any details in your writing that do not directly relate to the main idea of your writing. Suppose you started an essay about head injuries in the NFL in this way.

> New studies conclude that concussions can lead to long-term, crippling brain damage. As a result, the National Football League (NFL) has improved its baseline testing for players who suffer head injuries during a game. The National Hockey League is also concerned about the long-term effects of head injuries on hockey athletes. Before gaining permission to re-enter an NFL game, the player in question must pass a lengthy test (six to eight minutes) that measures memory, balance, and concentration. The NFL is also cutting back on practice time and off-season programs, as well as limiting full-contact practices during the season.

Upon reviewing your work, you remove a detail (*crossed out*) because it is unrelated to the NFL and thus disrupts the unity of this part.

> New studies conclude that concussions can learn to long-term, crippling brain damage. As a result, the National Football League (NFL) has improved its baseline testing for players who suffer head injuries during a game. ~~The National Hockey League is also concerned about the long-term effects on head injuries on hockey athletes.~~ Before gaining permission to re-enter an NFL game, the player in question must pass a lengthy test (six to eight minutes) that measures memory, balance, and concentration. The NFL is also cutting back on practice time and off-season programs, as well as limiting full-contact practices during the season.

Reorder Misplaced Ideas

Always check the details in your writing to make sure that they are arranged in the best order. Let's say you're writing about a motorcycle trip, and in one passage you describe the soil along the open road:

> Even the color of the dirt changes as you travel. Missouri's soil, for example, is red clay, with lots of crumbly white rock in it. Illinois has rich, black dirt that fades to a dark gray when it's dry. Get to Arizona, and the "dirt" is yellow-gray dust or sand.

During revision, you realize the description would make better sense if it moved spatially from north to southwest.

> Even the color of the dirt changes as you travel. Illinois, for example, has rich, black dirt that fades to a dark gray when it's dry. Missouri's soil is red clay, with crumbly white rock in it. Get to Arizona, and the "dirt" is yellow-gray dust or sand.

Practice Answer the coherence-based questions after each of the following texts.

1.   The earth's biodiversity is a vital part of the natural capital that helps keep us alive and supports our economies. With the help of technology, we use biodiversity to provide us with food, wood, fibers, energy from wood and biofuels, and medicines. Biodiversity also plays critical roles in preserving the quality of the air and water, maintaining the fertility of topsoil, decomposing and recycling waste, and controlling populations that humans consider to be pests. Biodiversity should not be confused with biomes. In carrying out so many services, biodiversity helps us to sustain life on earth.   From Miller, *Living in the Environment*, 17E. © 2012 Cengage Learning

- What key word is repeated throughout the paragraph? _____
- What sentence disrupts the unity of the paragraph? _____

_____

2.   "Oh beautiful, for spacious skies, for amber waves of grain, for purple mountain majesties above the fruited plain." Sound familiar? These words begin the classic song "America the Beautiful." Unfortunately, a portion of the American landscape spoken of so eloquently in this song is quickly vanishing. The loss of farmland is putting our economy and food supply at risk for future generations. The American public must take greater measures to preserve the country's farmland.

- What transitional word is used to identify a condition? _____
- What key point would benefit from a clarifying detail? _____

_____

3.   A federal shield law should not provide journalists with unlimited protection from revealing their sources. If an unnamed source is an imminent threat to national security, the journalist should be compelled to reveal the source. However, in cases where an unnamed source is absolutely necessary, reporters should not have to fear imprisonment for honoring a confidentiality agreement with the source. Trust is essential between a reporter and his source. Lance Williams and Mark Fainru-Wada, who reported on steroid use in professional baseball, understood this and refused to reveal their source; they would have served jail time if the source had not confessed. The next journalist and his source might not be so lucky.

■ What key word (a noun) is repeated throughout the paragraph? _____

■ In what sentence or sentences would you substitute a pronoun for this key word to improve the coherence of the text? Rewrite those sentences. _____

_____

4.   *The Economist,* a London-based news magazine, reports that vertical farms make good sense. First of all, vertical farms need no soil. Crops are grown hydroponically, in a solution of essential minerals dissolved in water. The plants' roots absorb nutrients directly from this liquid. Second, since crops are grown in a controlled environment, few pesticides or herbicides are needed. Everything is recycled, so vertical farming uses far less water and nutrients than traditional farms use. Vertical farms will provide food to local areas, which saves on transportation costs ("Does It Really Stack Up?").

■ What two sentences would benefit from a transitional word to show that there are four reasons why vertical farms make good sense? _____

_____

■ What transition would you use for each of these sentences? _____

_____

5.   Scientists first survey the globe to predict which strains of the influenza virus will dominate the next flu season. These steps help decide which strains to put in the vaccine because a vaccine can protect against three different strains. Next, the World Health Organization confirms the dominant strains and submits its recommendation to the Food and Drug Administration (FDA). The FDA then distributes seeds of the three strains to manufacturers for production.

■ Which sentence seems confusing or inaccurate? _____

_____

■ How would you rewrite this sentence to make it clearer? _____

_____

Practice Check the first draft you wrote in this chapter for line-by-line coherence using **Figure 6.2** as a guide.

☑ Review **and** Enrichment

Reviewing the Chapter

Recognize Transitions in Reading

1. When are spatial transitions used?

   To show where things are in relation

2. What transitions alert a reader to the causes in cause-effect writing? Name two.

   _____

Use Transitions in Writing

3. Why should you use transitions selectively?

   _____

   _____

Read for Coherence

4. How do you know if a text that you read is coherent?

   _____

   _____

5. What are three characteristics of a coherent text?

   Main point , transitions, examples

   _____

Write for Coherence

6. What are the three parts of the overall structure of coherent writing?

   Intro., Body, conclusion

7. What specific writing moves ensure that your writing is coherent? List three.

   Specific details, transition, Key terms

"In the evolution of mankind there has always been a
certain degree of social coherence."

—Jim Rohn

Reading for Enrichment

In this section, you will read a selection entitled "Squeezing New Evidence into Old Beliefs." As you read, use the steps in the reading process to help you gain a full understanding of the text.

About the Authors

Cecie Starr, **Christine Evers**, and **Lisa Starr** are best-selling authors of several biology textbooks, including *Biology: Today and Tomorrow*, the source of this enrichment selection.

Prereading

Change is a common theme in nonfiction. For example, historians write about changes caused by significant events. Sociologists write about societal and familial changes. Meteorologists discuss changing weather patterns. "Squeezing New Evidence into Old Beliefs" examines early scientific theories regarding geological and biological change, including Charles Darwin's theory of evolution. What do you already know about Darwin's theory? Identify three things.

Consider the Elements

As you read this selection, check its **overall structure** for coherence; then pay careful attention to the **line-by-line techniques** used, such as repeating key words and using transitions to achieve coherence. Finally, ask yourself if these elements help to produce a clear, complete, and unified text.

1. _____

2. _____

3. _____

What do you think?

In the quotation, "social coherence" refers to the bonds that link people to one another and to the group. Knowing that, what point do you think Jim Rohn is trying to make?

Before you read, answer these three questions:

1. What do the title, the opening paragraph, the first few lines of other paragraphs, and the graphic tell you about the text?

_____

2. Who do you think are the "naturalists" referred to in the first line?

_____

3. What questions would you liked answered in your reading?

_____

Reading and Rereading

This selection introduces four important and interesting theories addressing evolution. As you read, make it your goal to (1) identify the main idea, (2) pay careful attention to details that support this idea, and (3) consider how the authors maintain coherence throughout the text. Consider annotating the text and/or taking notes as you read. Also reread parts of the selection as needed to help you fully understand its contents.

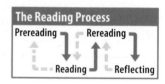

Squeezing New Evidence into Old Beliefs

In the nineteenth century, **naturalists** were faced with increasing   *1*
evidence that life on Earth, and even Earth itself, had changed over
time.

Around 1800, Georges Cuvier, an expert in zoology and   *2*
paleontology, was trying to make sense of the new information.
He had observed abrupt changes in the fossil record and knew that
many fossil species seemed to have no living counterparts. Given this
evidence, he proposed an idea startling for the time. Many species
that had once existed were now extinct. Cuvier also knew about
evidence that Earth's surface had changed. For example, he had seen
fossilized seashells on mountaintops far from modern seas. Like most

---

others of his time, he assumed Earth's age to be in the thousands, not billions, of years. He reasoned that **geological** forces unlike those operating in the present would have been necessary to raise seafloors to mountains in this short time span. Catastrophic geological events would have caused extinctions, after which surviving species repopulated in the planet. Cuvier's idea came to be known as catastrophism. We now know it is incorrect; geological processes have not changed over time.

Around this time another scholar, Jean-Baptiste Lamarck, was thinking about processes that drive evolution, or change in a line of descent. A line of descent is also called a lineage. Lamarck thought that a species gradually improved over generations because of an inherent drive toward perfection, up the chain of being. The drive directed an unknown "fluida" into body parts needing change. By Lamarck's hypothesis, environmental pressures cause an internal need for change in an individual's body, and the resulting change is inherited by offspring.   3

Try using Lamarck's hypothesis to explain why a giraffe's neck is very long. You might predict that some short-necked ancestor of the modern giraffe stretched its neck to browse on leaves beyond the reach of other animals. The stretches may have even made its neck a bit longer. By Lamarck's hypothesis, that animal's offspring would inherit a longer neck. The modern giraffe would have been the result of many generations that strained to reach ever loftier leaves. Larmarck was correct in thinking that environmental factors affect traits, but his understanding of how traits are passed to offspring was incomplete.   4

After an attempt to study medicine in college, Charles Darwin earned a degree in **theology** from Cambridge. All through school,   5 however, he had spent most of his time with faculty members and other students who embraced natural history. In 1831, botanist John Henslow arranged for the 22-year-old Darwin to become a naturalist aboard the *Beagle*, a ship about to embark on a survey expedition to South America. The young man who had no formal training in science quickly became an enthusiastic naturalist. During the *Beagle's* five-year voyage, Darwin found many unusual fossils and saw diverse species living in environments that ranged from the sandy shores of remote islands to plains high in the Andes. Along the way, he read the first volume of a new and popular book, Charles Lyell's *Principles of Geology*. Lyell was a proponent of what became known as the theory of uniformity, the idea that gradual, repetitive change had shaped Earth. For many years, geologists had been chipping away at the sandstones, limestones, and other types of rocks that form from accumulated sediments in lakebeds, river bottoms, and ocean floors. These rocks held evidence that gradual processes of geological change operating in the present were the same ones that operated in the distant past.

The theory of uniformity held that strange catastrophes 6 were not necessary to explain Earth's surface. Gradual, everyday geological processes such as erosion could have sculpted Earth's current landscape over great spans of time. The theory challenged the prevailing belief that Earth was 6,000 years old. According to traditional scholars, people had recorded everything that happened in those 6,000 years—and in all that time, no one had mentioned seeing a species evolve. However, by Lyell's calculations, it must have taken millions of years to sculpt Earth's surface. Darwin's exposure to Lyell's ideas gave him insights into the history of the regions he would encounter on his journey. Was millions of years enough time for species to evolve? Darwin thought it was.

Darwin sent to England thousands of specimens he collected   *7*
on his voyage. Among them were fossil glyptodons. These armored
mammals are extinct, but they have many traits in common with
modern armadillos. For example, both glyptodons and armadillos
have helmets and protective shells that consist of unusual bony
plates. Armadillos also live only in places were glyptodons once lived.
Could the odd shared traits and restricted distribution mean that
glyptodons were ancient relatives of armadillos? If so, perhaps traits
of their common ancestors had changed in the line of descent that led
to armadillos. But why would such changes occur?

Back in England, Darwin pondered his notes and fossils. He read   *8*
an essay by one of his contemporaries, economist Thomas Malthus.
Malthus had **correlated** increases in the size of human populations
with episodes of famine, disease, and war. He proposed the idea that
humans run out of food, living space, and other resources because
they tend to reproduce beyond the capacity of their environment to
sustain them. When that happens, the individuals of a population
must either compete with one another for the limited resources or
develop technology to increase their productivity. Darwin realized
that Malthus's ideas had wider application: All populations, not just
human ones, must have the capacity to produce more individuals
than their environment can support.

Reflecting on his journey, Darwin started thinking about how   *9*
individuals of a species are not always identical; they often vary a
bit in the details of shared traits such as size, coloration, and so on.
He saw such variation among many of the finch species that live on
isolated islands of the Galapagos **archipelago**. This island chain is
separated from South America by 900 kilometers of open ocean, so

most species living on the islands did not have the opportunity for interbreeding with mainland populations. The Galapagos island finches resembled finch species in South America, but many of them had unique traits that suited them to their particular island habitat.

Darwin was familiar with dramatic variations in traits that breeders of dogs and horses had produced through hundreds of years of selective breeding, or artificial selection. He recognized that an environment could similarly select traits that make individuals of a population suited to it. It dawned on Darwin that having a particular form of a shared trait might give an individual a survival or reproductive advantage over competing members of its species. Darwin realized that in any population, some individuals have forms of shared traits that make them better suited to their environment than others. In other words, individuals of a natural population vary in fitness. We define fitness as the degree of adaptation to a specific environment and measure it as relative genetic contribution to future generations. A trait that enhances an individual's fitness is called an evolutionary adaptation, or adaptive trait.   *10*

Over many generations, individuals with the most adaptive traits tend to survive longer and reproduce more than their less fit rivals. Darwin understood that this process, which he called natural selection, could be a mechanism by which evolution occurs. If an individual is better able to survive, then it has a better chance of living long enough to produce offspring. If individuals that bear an adaptive, heritable trait produce more offspring than those that do not, then the frequency of that trait will tend to increase in the population over successive generations.   *11*

Darwin wrote out his ideas about natural selection but let 10 years pass without publishing them. In the meantime, Alfred   *12*

Wallace, a naturalist who had been studying wildlife in the Amazon basin and the Malay Archipelago, wrote an essay and sent it to Darwin for advice. Wallace's essay outlined evolution by natural selection—the very same hypothesis as Darwin's. Wallace had written earlier letters to Darwin and Lyell about patterns in the geographic distribution of species; he, too, had connected the dots. Wallace is now called the father of **biogeography**.

Table 6.7 Principles of Natural Selection in Modern Terms

Observations about populations	■ Natural populations have an inherent reproductive capacity to increase in size over time. ■ As a population expands, resources that are used by its individuals (such as food and living space) eventually become limited. ■ When resources are limited, the individuals of a population compete for them.
Observations about genetics	■ Individuals of a species share certain traits. ■ Individuals of a natural population vary in the details of those shared traits. ■ Shared traits have a heritable basis in genes. Slightly different forms of those genes (**alleles**) give rise to variation in shared traits.

Inferences

■ A certain form of a shared trait may make its bearer better able to survive.
■ Individuals of a population that are better able to survive tend to leave more offspring.
■ Thus, an allele associated with an adaptive trait tends to become more common in a population over time.

In 1858, just weeks after Darwin received Wallace's essay, the hypothesis of evolution by natural selection was presented to a scientific meeting. Both Darwin and Wallace were credited as

13

authors. Wallace was still in the field and knew nothing about the meeting, which Darwin did not attend. The next year, Darwin published *On the Origin of Species*, which laid out detailed evidence in support of natural selection. Many people had already accepted the idea of descent with modification, or evolution. However, there was a fierce debate over the idea that evolution occurs by natural selection. Decades would pass before experimental evidence from the field of genetics led to its widespread acceptance as a theory by the scientific community.

From Starr/Evers/Starr, *Biology Today and Tomorrow with Physiology*, 4E. © 2013 Cengage Learning.

naturalist
a person who studies natural history

paleontology
science dealing with fossils of plants and animals that lived long ago

geological
physical history of the earth

theology
the study of religious faith

correlated
mutual relation or similarity of two or more things, parts, etc.

archipelago
a large group or chain of islands

biogeography
the branch of biology dealing with the geographical distribution of plants and animals

alleles
pairs or series of genes on a chromosome that determine hereditary characteristics

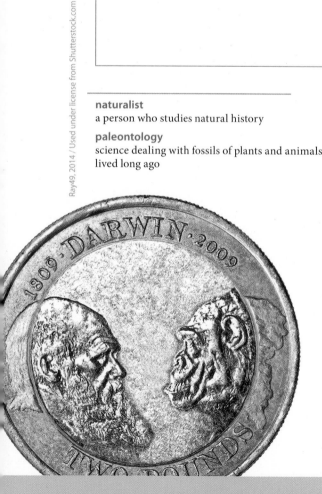

Summarizing

Write a summary of "Squeezing New Evidence into Old Beliefs." Rem[...]
summary presents the mains points in a clear, concise form using your own w[...]

Reflecting

1. What is the main idea of the selection? *Hint:* Refer to the beginning of the text.

   As time change everything changes.

2. The main part of the selection is essentially organized chronologically. What transitions are used at the beginning of certain paragraphs to indicate this pattern of organization?

   In the nineteenth century, Around 1800, when

3. How do the writers ensure coherence in paragraph two? Give examples of three techniques that they use.

   He observed changes in fossils, proposed an idea, assumed Earth's age, gave a reason.

4. In paragraph 6, the writers carefully and logically explain Charles Lyell's theory of uniformity. What does this theory suggest?

   ``Strange catastrophus were not necessary to explain Earth's surface

Vocabulary

Identify the context clues that help you define each term. Then define the term.

1. **lineage**
   (paragraph 3)

2. **sustain**
   (paragraph 8)

3. **evolution**
   (paragraph 13)

Critical Thinking

- How is the selection itself evolutionary?
- What does this selection tell you about scientific advancement—the process of forming, testing, and questioning hypotheses (theories)?
- How did Darwin's theory evolve from this process?

Technical Terms Academic texts will also contain content-related technical terms. Many texts provide definitions of these words either on the page where they occur or in a glossary. Otherwise, always keep a dictionary handy for reference, and record definitions of important terms in your notes. Here is a passage from an academic text discussing the genetic makeup of a certain group of people. The technical terms used in this passage are underlined.

> Despite centuries of <u>admixing</u>, a modern Catawba Indian was found to be, on average, 50 percent white and 50 percent Native American in <u>genetic composition</u> (Pollitzer et al., 1967). The results of the study surprised many who expected the percentage of <u>white genetic attributes</u> to be much higher. . . .

Insight **Jargon** is very specialized language that is commonly found in professional texts intended for readers trained in a particular field. In some cases, jargon can seem almost unintelligible to the average reader:

"To guarantee privacy, audio streams are obfuscated at the originating sensor device before they are transmitted."

Carefully Constructed Language In academic texts, writers choose their words carefully to maintain a certain level of formality. In addition, academic writers will use very few personal pronouns and few, if any, contractions. Notice below how the same idea is stated with carefully constructed language and then personally.

- **Academic, Formal Language:** "One of the best ways to maintain well-being, researchers found, is self-compassion, a healthy form of self-acceptance . . . of individual impediments."
- **Personal, Informal Language:** Researchers have found that we could be happier if we'd only learn how to accept and deal with life's setbacks.

Word Choice in Personal Texts

The language in narratives, personal essays, and feature articles is often relaxed and informal, reflecting the writer's purpose—to share personal thoughts, feelings, and/or experiences.

Relaxed Language Most personal texts will sound somewhat friendly in tone and make the reader feel comfortable and at ease. They may include personal pronouns, in particular first-person pronouns (I, we, us), contractions (it's, can't, weren't), and perhaps some familiar expressions ("Of course" and "It's too bad that . . ."). And overall, the words will be recognizable to most readers. Notice how easy it is to follow this passage from a personal essay.

jargon
very specialized language intended for readers trained in a particular field

- **Personal, Informal Language:** Of course, those were old memories. By the time I reached college, Grandpa wasn't as active anymore. Tired and overworked from his years of hard labor at the steel yard, his back eventually gave out and his joints swelled up with arthritis. And so I sat there, staring at the ceiling and reminiscing about him. Sure, I had a lump in my throat, and tears filled my eyes; but I also felt thankful for the times we had together and hopeful that one day I could be as good a grandfather as he had been to me. I owed him that much.

Practice Carefully read each of the following passages. Then identify the word choice as *academic* or *personal*. Underline words that support your answer.

1. This was not exactly my idea of a fun family vacation. Sweat beads trickled down my brow, and a feeling of dread washed over me as I noticed the low-battery sign blinking on my MP3 player.

   Word Choice: _____

2. While vertical farming may seem futuristic, it has roots in the past. A classic example is the Hanging Gardens of Babylon built in 600 BC. These gardens consisted of a series of stackable terraces.

   Word Choice: _____

3. When a paragraph is coherent, the parts stay together. A coherent paragraph flows smoothly because each sentence is connected to others by patterns in the language such as repetition and transitions.

   Word Choice: _____

4. And then there was Martha. She was a talker, talking openly and frequently, usually about her family—where they were all living and what they were doing. She'd get very excited anytime a relative came to visit.

   Word Choice: _____

5. I try to be supportive of Ismail's fast, but it's hard. The rules seem unnecessarily harsh to me, an American raised in the seventies by parents who challenged the status quo.

   Word Choice: _____

Diction Glossary

Diction is an author's choice of words based on their correctness, clearness, or effectiveness. The following are terms related to diction.

- **Colloquialisms** are expressions usually accepted in informal or casual texts or speaking situations, but not in a formal situations.

    "Anyway, the baby calf was standing underneath its mother, *just kind of* walking around, and the mother cow *took a 'dump'* on the baby calf's head." (Stephen Chbosky, *The Perks of Being a Wallflower*)

- **Jargon** (technical diction) is a specialized language used by a specific group.

    Computer jargon: *hypertext* (meaning "a system of web-like links among pages on the Internet or within a program")
    Police jargon: *code eight* (meaning "an officer needs immediate help")
    Medical jargon: *agonal* (meaning "a major, negative change in a patient's condition")
    Political jargon: *left wing* (meaning a "liberal, progressive approach")

- **Idioms** are words used in special ways that may be different from their literal meanings.

    as the crow flies (meaning "in a straight line")
    brain drain (meaning "the best graduates moving elsewhere")
    save face (meaning "fix an embarrassing situation")

- **Slang** is the nonstandard language used by a particular group of people among themselves; it is also language used in fiction and special writing situations to lend color and feeling. Slang may have a brief lifespan.

    emo (meaning "to be depressed, moody, and emotional over extended periods of time")
    iceman (meaning "someone with nerves of steel")

- **Trite** language lacks depth or original, fresh thinking.

    After the close call, the manager *leaped* from the dugout and *roared like a lion.*
    The sprinter *ran like a deer.*
    Larisa is a *deep thinker.*

- **Vulgarity** is abusive, vulgar, or disrespectful language.

    bastard (used as a crude insult)
    bitch (a rude reference to a woman)
    prick (an insulting reference for a person considered unpleasant)

Figures of Speech Glossary

Figures of speech are words or comparisons used in a non-literal sense to create meaning. These literary devices may contribute to a personal or satiric voice.

- **Metaphor** is a comparison of two unlike things in which no word of comparison (*as* or *like*) is used.

  > "When you write, you lay out a line of words. The line of words is a miner's pick, a woodcarver's gouge, a surgeon's probe."   —Annie Dillard, *The Writing Life*

- **Simile** is a comparison of two unlike things in which a word of comparison (*as* or *like*) is used.

  > "She stood in front of the altar, shaking like a freshly caught trout."
  > —Maya Angelou, *I Know Why the Caged Bird Sings*

- **Personification** is when an animal, object, or idea takes on a human characteristic.

  > "And what I remember next is how the moon, the pale moon with its one yellow eye . . . stared through the pink plastic curtains."   —Sandra Cisneros

- **Hyperbole** is an extreme exaggeration or overstatement.

  > "I have seen this river so wide it had only one bank."   —Mark Twain

- **Understatement** is stating an idea with restraint, often for humorous effect.

  > "He [our new dog] turned out to be a good traveler, and except for an interruption caused by my wife's falling out of the car, the journey went very well."   —E. B. White, *A Report in Spring*

Types of Irony

Irony is a twist or surprise in the story line, explanation, or set of circumstances that is designed to make a point. Irony may contribute to the creation of a satiric voice.

- **Verbal irony** occurs when a writer says one thing but really means another.

  > A chef critical of a greengrocer's produce might say, "The carrots were so fresh they bent easily to my touch."

- **Dramatic irony** occurs when the reader or viewer observes or knows a critical piece of information that the subject of a text (a character, or person) can't see him- or herself.

  > In *Lincoln*, viewers know that the president will be shot soon after he settles in at Ford's Theatre. He, obviously, has no idea that this is about to happen.

- **Irony of situation** occurs when there is a great difference between the purpose of an action and the result.

  > In *Romeo and Juliet*, Juliet takes a drug to fake her death, while Romeo poisons himself because he thinks Juliet is dead. Juliet awakes and discovers her lover is dead, so she kills herself.

"Whatever sentence will bear to be read twice, we may be sure was thought twice."
—Henry David Thoreau

Sentences

All sentences are built with the same parts—nouns, verbs, and modifiers. How an author works with these parts depends on his purpose for writing and his intended audience. Academic authors take special care that their sentences communicate content with a proper level of formality and depth. Authors of personal pieces are more interested in crafting sentences that essentially engage and/or entertain the reader.

Sentences in Academic Texts

Academic texts are characterized by longer sentences with multiple layers of meaning. Longer sentences often reveal careful thought and reflection on the part of the writer, who needs to impart information thoroughly and accurately. Consider these examples from academic texts. In each one, the core sentence is underlined. Notice all of the additional information added to each one.

> Once a country's forests are gone, <u>the companies move on to another country,</u> leaving ecological devastation behind.

> In Indonesia, Malaysia, and other areas of Southeast Asia, <u>tropical forests are being replaced with vast plantations of oil palm,</u> which produces an oil used in cooking, cosmetics, and biodiesel fuel for motor vehicles (especially in Europe).

> <u>Anorexia nervosa is an eating disorder</u> in which a person who has access to food does not eat enough to keep her weight within 15 percent of normal.

Sentences in Personal Texts

For the most part, the sentences in personal texts are relaxed and conversational in tone. As such, they are usually simple in structure, easy to follow, and move along at a quicker pace than sentences in academic texts. Notice how easy it is to read the following passages from personal narratives.

> My fate was in my hands—actually my feet. Funny. I had to reach back, do what was needed. I had to realize the future and pass the last runner. . . .

> Dad discovered the engine had overheated, and we were stuck. "Is this thing going to blow up?" asked my younger sister Michelle. "I have a bunch of clothes in there. . . ."

> On a good day, I'll see a lot of fish jumping, or at least I'll hear their splash. Last year, for the first time, I saw a bald eagle flying away from its nest.

Practice Carefully read the following sentences. Then identify each one as either *academic* or *personal* in structure.

1. I love watching the cranes fishing in the river. They look so prehistoric. It's too bad that they stay for such a short time.

   Sentence style: _____

2. While executions historically demand a certain degree of morbid curiosity, the last meals of the condemned seem to stimulate heightened interest.

   Sentence style: _____

3. Her face was dirty; her hair greasy and matted. A part of me felt sorry for her.

   Sentence style: _____

4. The basic unit of the Braille system is called a "cell," which is two dots wide and three dots high.

   Sentence style: _____

5. Consider, for example, the big bang, the **primordial** flash that brought our universe into existence.

   Sentence style: _____

6. Admitting I had a disorder was the hardest thing I've ever done. Now I manage my moods very carefully.

   Sentence style: _____

---

primordial
original, existing from the beginning

Before you read, answer these questions:

1. What do the title and first three paragraphs tell you about this essay?

_____

2. What are your first thoughts about the author's purpose and intended audience?

_____

3. What do you expect to learn?

_____

Reading and Rereading

As you read, make it your goal to (1) identify the topic and thesis, (2) confirm the purpose and audience, (3) note the author's developing thoughts and ideas, and (4) identify characteristics of her writing voice. Consider annotating the text as you read to help you interact with the text. Be sure to reread parts as needed to confirm your understanding of the content and voice in the text.

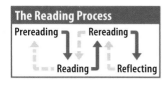

Campus Racism 101

There is a bumper sticker that reads: *TOO BAD IGNORANCE*   1
ISN'T PAINFUL. I like that. But ignorance is. We just seldom
attribute the pain to it or even recognize it when we see it. Like the
postcard on my corkboard. It shows a young man in a very hip jacket
smoking a cigarette. In the background is a high school with the
American flag waving. The caption says: "Too cool for school. Yet too
stupid for the real world." Out of the mouth of the young man is a
bubble enclosing the words "Maybe I'll start a band." There could be a
postcard showing a jock in a uniform saying, "I don't need school. I'm
going to the NFL or NBA." Or one showing a young man or woman
studying and a group of young people saying, "So you want to be
white." Or something equally demeaning. We need to quit it.

I am a professor of English at Virginia Tech. I've been here for   2 four years, though for only two years with academic rank. I am tenured, which means I have a teaching position for life, a rarity on a predominantly white campus. Whether from **malice** or ignorance, people who think I should be at a predominantly Black institution will ask, "Why are you at Tech?" Because it's here. And so are Black students. But even if Black students weren't here, it's painfully obvious that this nation and this world cannot allow white students to go through higher education without interacting with Blacks in authoritative positions. It is equally clear that predominantly Black colleges cannot accommodate the numbers of Black students who want and need an education.

Is it difficult to attend a predominantly white college? Compared 3 with what? Being passed over for promotion because you lack credentials? Being turned down for jobs because you are not college-educated? Joining the armed forces or going to jail because you cannot find an alternative to the streets? Let's have a little perspective here. Where can you go and what can you do that frees you from interacting with the white American mentality? You're going to interact; the only question is, will you be in some control of yourself and your actions, or will you be controlled by others? I'm going to recommend self-control.

What's the difference between prison and college? They both 4 prescribe your behavior for a given period of time. They both allow you to read books and develop your writing. They both give you time alone to think and time with your peers to talk about issues. But four years of prison doesn't give you a passport to greater opportunities. Most likely that time only gives you greater knowledge of how to get back in. Four years of college gives you an opportunity not only to lift yourself but to serve your people effectively. What's the difference when you are called nigger in college from when you are called nigger in prison? In college you can, though I admit with effort, follow procedures to have those students who called you nigger kicked out or suspended. You can bring issues to public attention without risking your life. But mostly, college is and always has been the future. We, neither less nor more than other people, need knowledge. There are discomforts attached to attending predominantly white colleges, though no more so than living in a racist world. Here are some rules to follow that may help:

Go to class. No matter how you feel. No matter how you think the professor feels about you. It's important to have a consistent presence in the classroom. If nothing else, the professor will know you care enough and are serious enough to be there. 5

Meet your professors. Extend your hand (give a firm handshake) and tell them your name. Ask them what you need to do to make an A. You may never make an A, but you have put them on notice that you are serious about getting good grades. 6

Do assignments on time. Typed or computer-generated. You have the syllabus. Follow it, and turn those papers in. If for some reason you can't complete an assignment on time, let your professor know before it is due and work out a new due date—then meet it. 7

Go back to see your professor. Tell him or her your name again. If an assignment received less than an A, ask why, and find out what you need to do to improve the next assignment. 8

Yes, your professor is busy. So are you. So are your parents who are working to pay or help with your tuition. Ask early what you need to do if you feel you are starting to get into academic trouble. Do not wait until you are failing. 9

Understand that there will be professors who do not like you; there may even be professors who are racist or sexist or both. You must discriminate among your professors to see who will give you the help you need. You may not simply say, "They are all against me." They aren't. They mostly don't care. Since you are the one who wants 10 to be educated, find the people who want to help.

Don't defeat yourself. Cultivate your friends. Know your 11
enemies. You cannot undo hundreds of years of prejudicial thinking.
Think for yourself and speak up. Raise your hand in class. Say what
you believe no matter how awkward you may think it sounds. You
will improve in your articulation and confidence.

Participate in some campus activity. Join the newspaper staff. 12
Run for office. Join a dorm council. Do something that involves
you on campus. You are going to be there for four years, so let your
presence be known, if not felt.

You will inevitably run into some white classmates who 13
are troubling because they often say stupid things, ask stupid
questions—and expect an answer. Here are some comebacks to some
of the most common inquiries and comments:

Q: What's it like to grow up in a ghetto? 14

A: I don't know. 15

Q: (from the teacher): Can you give us the Black perspective 16
on Toni Morrison, Huck Finn, slavery, Martin Luther King, Jr., and
others?

A: I can give you my perspective. (Do not take the burden of 17
22 million people on your shoulders. Remind everyone that you are
an individual, and don't speak for the race or any other individual
within it.)

Q: Why do all the Black people sit together in the dining hall? 18

A: Why do all the white students sit together? 19

Q: Why should there be an African-American studies course? 20

A: Because white Americans have not adequately studied the 21
contributions of Africans and African-Americans. Both Black and
white students need to know our total common history.

Q: Why are there so many scholarships for "minority" students? 22

A: Because they wouldn't give my great-grandparents their forty 23 acres and the mule.

Q: How can whites understand Black history, culture, literature, *24* and so forth?

A: The same way we understand white history, culture, *25* literature, and so forth. That is why we're in school: to learn.

Q: Should whites take African-American studies courses? *26*

A: Of course. We take white-studies courses, though the *27* universities don't call them that.

Comment: When I see groups of Black people on campus, it's *28* really intimidating.

Comeback: I understand what you mean. I'm frightened when I *29* see white students congregating.

Comment: It's not fair. It's easier for you guys to get into college *30* than for other people.

Comeback: If it's so easy, why aren't there more of us? *31*

Comment: It's not our fault that America is the way it is. *32*

Comeback: It's not our fault, either, but both of us have a *33* responsibility to make changes.

It's really very simple. Educational progress is a national *34* concern; education is a private one. Your job is not to educate white people; it is to obtain an education. If you take the racial world on your shoulders, you will not get the job done. Deal with yourself as an individual worthy of respect, and make everyone else deal with you the same way. College is a little like playing grown-up. Practice what you want to be. You have been telling your parents you are grown. Now is your chance to act like it.

demeaning
degrading or insulting

malice
desire to inflict injury, harm, or suffering

Summarizing

Write a summary of "Campus Racism 101." Remember that a su~~mmary~~ main idea and key supporting details in a clear, concise form using you~~~~

Reflecting

1. What main idea is developed?

   Rasim is involved in the Campus

2. Who is the intended audience for this essay?

   Students

3. Would you identify the author's voice as *academic* or *personal?* (Circle one.)

   [*personal?* circled]

4. What are two specific characteristics of Giovanni's voice?

   _____

   _____

5. What significance is there in the title?

   Racism is on a school campus

   _____

6. What, if anything, can you infer from this essay about Giovanni's attitude about education?

   Yes because not only is it on school campuses, it's also everywhere you go.

Vocabulary

For each word, define the identified word parts. Then try to explain the meaning of the complete word. (See Appendix D for a glossary of word parts.)

1. **predominantly** (paragraph 2)
   pre + domin + ant + ly

2. **discomforts** (paragraph 4)
   dis + comforts

Critical Thinking

- How would you characterize Giovanni's feelings about her audience?
- Giovanni states "Educational progress is a national concern; education is a private one" in the closing paragraph. What is she saying?

L02 Reading and Responding to Narrative Texts

When reading narratives, use a time line to keep track of the important events and a plot line to analyze the key parts in the story.

Using a Time Line

Part of the challenge when reading a narrative is keeping track of the key actions in the order that they occur. Placing the details in a time line (**Figure 8.1**) works well for this purpose because narratives are almost always organized chronologically. When completing a time line, focus on the essential actions in a story. You don't need to include all the specific details.

> **Figure 8.1** Time Line
>
> Order: Main Actions:
>
> 1 ── Two brothers go to a playground.
>
> 2 ── John's jacket is stolen.
>
> 3 ── Their mother scolds Daniel.
>
> 4 ── They go back and get the jacket.
>
> 5 ── They learn to protect each other.

Following a Plot Line

A narrative is essentially a story. And like the plot in a fictional story, a personal narrative should create suspense as it moves along. **Figure 8.2** shows the parts of the plot and how the level of reader interest should build as the story progresses. Tracing a narrative's plot will direct you to the most important parts of the story.

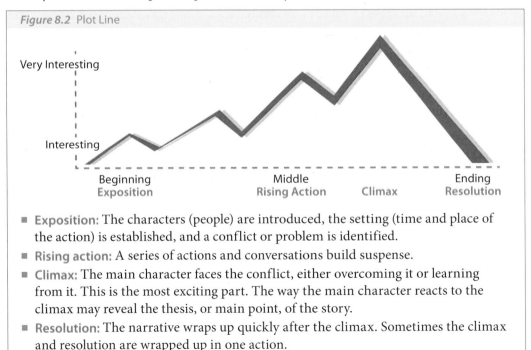

Figure 8.2 Plot Line

- **Exposition:** The characters (people) are introduced, the setting (time and place of the action) is established, and a conflict or problem is identified.
- **Rising action:** A series of actions and conversations build suspense.
- **Climax:** The main character faces the conflict, either overcoming it or learning from it. This is the most exciting part. The way the main character reacts to the climax may reveal the thesis, or main point, of the story.
- **Resolution:** The narrative wraps up quickly after the climax. Sometimes the climax and resolution are wrapped up in one action.

Reading and Reacting to a Professional Narrative

"My Accidental Jihad" first appeared in the magazine *The Sun* and was later adapted into a full memoir. The author's husband is a practicing Muslim; the author is not.

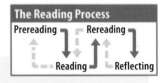

About the Author

Krista Bremer is an award-winning essayist whose writing has appeared in many publications, including the *New York Times Magazine; O, The Oprah Magazine;* and *CNN.com*. Her memoir, *My Accidental Jihad: A Love Story,* is published by Algonquin Books.

Before you read, answer these questions:

1. What do the title, first paragraph, and first lines of other paragraphs tell you about the text?

   _____

2. What type of experience will be shared?

   _____

3. What might be the author's purpose in sharing this story?

   _____

As you read, (1) follow the plot line, and (2) identify what the author comes to learn from the experience. Annotate the text during your reading, and create a time line to track key details.

My Accidental Jihad

Early one morning in September, when our house is pitch-dark and the entire family is still asleep, my husband, Ismail, sits upright at the first sound of his alarm, dresses quickly, and leaves our bedroom. Later, after I've woken up and made my way downstairs for a cup of coffee, I find him standing at the counter, stuffing the last of his breakfast into his mouth, his eye on the clock as if he were competing in a pie-eating contest at the fair. The minute hand clicks forward, and, on cue, Ismail drops the food he's holding. I'm momentarily confused. My husband and I usually sit down together over our first cup of coffee, and he rarely eats breakfast. Then I realize: Ramadan has begun.

For the next month, nothing will touch my husband's mouth between sunup and sundown: Not food. Not water. Not my lips. A chart posted on our refrigerator tells him the precise minute when his fast must begin and end each day. I will find him in front of this chart again this evening, staring at his watch, waiting for it to tell him he may eat.

Ramadan is the ninth month of the lunar calendar, the month during which the **Koran** was revealed to the Prophet Mohammed through the angel Gabriel. Each year, more than one billion Muslims observe Ramadan by fasting from dawn to dusk. In addition to avoiding food and drink during daylight hours, Muslims are expected to refrain from all other indulgences: sexual relations, gossip, evil thoughts—even looking at "corrupt" images on television, in magazines, or on the Internet. Ramadan is a month of purification, during which Muslims are called upon to make peace with enemies, strengthen ties with family and friends, cleanse themselves of impurities, and refocus their lives on God. It's like a month-long spiritual tune-up.

My husband found fasting easier when he lived in Libya, surrounded by fellow Muslims. Everyone's life changes there during the fast: People work less (at least those who work outside the home), take long naps during the day, and feast with family and friends late into the night. Now, with a corporate job and an American wife who works full time, my husband has a totally different experience of Ramadan. He spends most of his waking hours at work, just as he does every other month of the year. He still picks up our son from day care and shares cooking and cleaning responsibilities at home. Having no Muslim friends in our Southern college town, he breaks his fast alone, standing at our kitchen counter. Here in the United States, Ramadan feels more like an extreme sport than a spiritual practice. Secretly I've come to think of it as "Ramathon."

I try to be supportive of Ismail's fast, but it's hard. The rules seem unnecessarily harsh to me, an American raised in the seventies by parents who challenged the status quo. The humility required to submit to such a **grueling**, seemingly illogical exercise is not in my blood. In my family, we don't submit. We question the rules. We debate. And we do things our own way. I resent the fact that Ismail's life is being micromanaged by the chart in the kitchen. Would Allah really hold it against him if he finished his last bit of toast, even if the clock says it's a minute past sunrise? The no-water rule seems especially cruel to me, and I find the prohibition against kissing a little **melodramatic**. I'm tempted to argue with Ismail that the rules are outdated, but he has a billion Muslims in his corner, whereas I have yet to find another disgruntled American wife who feels qualified to rewrite one of the five pillars of **Islam**. . . .

When my husband fasts, our relationship becomes a bland, lukewarm concoction that I find difficult to swallow. I'm not proud of this fact. After all, he isn't the only one in our house with a spiritual practice: I stumble out of bed in the dark most mornings and meditate in the corner of our room with my back to him, trying to find that bottomless truth beyond words. Once in a great while, I'll drag him to church on Sunday. Whenever I suggest we say grace at the table, he reaches willingly for my hand, and words of gratitude flow easily from him. He has never criticized my practices, even when they are wildly inconsistent or **contradictory**. But Ramadan is not ten minutes of meditation or an hour-long sermon: It's an entire month of deprivation. Ismail's God is the old-fashioned kind, omnipresent and stern, uncompromising with his demands. During Ramadan this God expects him to pray on time, five times a day— and to squeeze in additional prayers of forgiveness as often as he can. My God would never be so demanding. My God is a **flamboyant** and **fickle** friend with a biting wit who likes a good party. My God is transgendered and tolerant to a fault; he/she shows up unexpectedly during peak moments, when life feel glorious and **synchronous**, then disappears for long stretches of time.   6

But Ramadan leaves little room for dramatic flair. There is no chorus of voices or public celebration—just a quiet and steady submission to Allah in the privacy of one's home. For some Muslims who live in the West, the holiday becomes even more private, since their friends and colleagues are not even aware of their fast.   7

During the early days of Ramadan, Ismail deals with his hunger by planning his next meal and puttering around the kitchen. In the last half-hour before the sun sets, he rearranges the food in our refrigerator or wipes down our already-clean counters. At night in bed, as I drift off to sleep, he reviews each ingredient in the **baklava** he intends to make the following evening. "Do you think I should replace the walnuts with pistachios?" he whispers. In the middle of the workday, when I call his cell phone, I hear the beeping of a cash   8 register in the background. He is wandering the aisles of our local grocery store. "I needed to get out of the office," he says matter-of-factly, as if all men escaped to the grocery store during lunch.

The last hours before he breaks his fast are the most difficult and volatile time of day for him. Coincidentally, they are the same hours at which I return home from work. I open the door and find him collapsed on the couch, pale and exhausted, our children running in circles around the room. Ismail is irritable, and his thoughts trail off in midsentence. I dread seeing him in this state. I count on my husband to speak coherently, to smile on a regular basis, and to enjoy our children. This humorless person on my couch is no fun. Every few days I ask (with what I hope sounds like innocent curiosity) what he's learned from his fast so far. I know this is an unfair question. How would I feel if he poked his head into our bedroom while I was meditating and asked, *How's it going? Emptied your mind yet?* 9

One **balmy** Saturday in the middle of Ramadan, we go to hear an outdoor lecture by a Sufi Muslim teacher who is visiting from California. The teacher sits cross-legged under a tree on a colorful pillow while the sun streams down on him through a canopy of leaves. After a long silence, he sweeps his arms in front of him, a **beatific** expression on his face, and reminds us to notice the beauty that surrounds us. "If you don't," he says, "you're not fasting—you're just going hungry." 10

I take a sidelong glance at Ismail. He is looking very hungry to me these days. I guess I imagined that during his fast a new radiance would emanate from him. I imagined him moving more slowly, but also more lovingly. I imagined a Middle Eastern Gandhi, sitting with our children in the garden when I got home from work. In short, I imagined that his spiritual practice would look more . . . well, spiritual. I didn't imagine the long silences between us or how much his exhaustion would irritate me. I didn't imagine him leaping out of bed in a panic, having slept through his alarm, and running downstairs to swallow chunks of bread and gulp coffee before the sun came up. I didn't imagine his **terse** replies to my attempts to start a conversation, or his impatience with our children. 11

I thought I understood the rules of Ramadan: the timetable on the refrigerator, the five daily prayers. But I didn't understand that the real practice is addressing a toddler's temper tantrum or a wife's hostile silence when you haven't eaten or drunk anything 12 in ten hours. I was like the children of Israel in the Bible, who once complained that, despite their dutiful fasting, God *still* wasn't answering their prayers. The children of Israel had it all wrong: God doesn't count calories. The fast itself only sets the stage. God is interested in our behavior and intentions *while* we are hungry. Through his prophet Isaiah, God gave the children of Israel peace of mind:

"Behold, in the day of your fast you seek your own pleasure, and oppress all your workers. Behold, you fast only to quarrel and to fight and to hit with a wicked fist. Fasting like yours this day will not make your voice to be heard on high" (Isaiah 58:3–4).   13

Ismail tells me that in the Middle East, Ramadan is a time of extremes: There are loving gatherings among family and friends at night, and a tremendous public outpouring of charity and generosity to those in need. At the same time, the daytime streets become more dangerous, filled with nicotine and caffeine addicts in withdrawal. People stumble through the morning without their green or black tea, drunk so dark and thick with sugar that it leaves permanent stains even on young people's teeth. Desperate smokers who light up in public risk being ridiculed or even attacked by strangers. The streets reverberate with angry shouts and car horns, and traffic conflicts occasionally escalate into physical violence.   14

Our home, too, becomes more volatile during Ramadan. Ismail's temper is short; my patience with him runs thin. I accuse him of being grumpy. He accuses me of being unsupportive. I tell him he is failing at Ramadan, as if it were some sort of exam. I didn't ask for this spiritual test, I tell him. As if I could pick and choose which parts of him to take into my life. As if he were served up to me on a plate, and I could primly push aside what I didn't care for—his temper, his doubt, his self-pity—and keep demanding more of his delicious tenderness.   15

And then there is my husband's unmistakable Ramadan scent. Normally I love the way he smells: the faint scent of soap and laundry detergent mixed with the warm muskiness of his skin. But after a few days of fasting, Ismail begins to smell *different*. Mostly it's his breath. The odor is subtle but distinct and persists no matter how many times he brushes or uses mouthwash. When I get close to him, it's the first thing I notice. I do a Google search for "Ramadan and halitosis" and learn that this is a common side effect of fasting—so   16 common that the Prophet Mohammed himself even had something to say about it: "The smell of the fasting person's breath is sweeter to Allah than that of musk." Allah may delight in this smell, but I don't. I no longer rest my head on Ismail's chest when we lie in bed at night. I begin to avoid eye contact and increase the distance between us when we speak. I no longer kiss him on impulse in the evening. I sleep with my back to him, resentful of this odor, which hangs like an invisible barrier between us.

The purpose of fasting during Ramadan is not simply to suffer   *17* hunger, thirst, or desire, but to bring oneself closer to *taqwa*: a state of sincerity, discipline, generosity, and surrender to Allah; the sum total of all Muslim teachings. When, in a moment of frustration, I grumble to my husband about his bad breath, he responds in the spirit of *taqwa*: He listens sympathetically and then apologizes and promises to keep his distance. He offers to sleep on the couch if that would make me more comfortable. He says he wishes I had told him earlier so he could have spared me any discomfort. His humility catches me off guard and makes my resentment absurd.

This month of Ramadan has revealed to me the limits of   *18* my compassion. I recall a conversation I had with Ismail in the aftermath of September 11, 2001, when the word *jihad* often appeared in news stories about Muslim extremists who were hell-bent on destroying the United States. According to Ismail, the Prophet Mohammed taught that the greatest jihad, or struggle, of our lives is not the one that takes place on a battlefield, but the one that takes place within our hearts—the struggle to increase self-discipline and become a better person. This month of Ramadan has thrown me into my own accidental jihad, forcing me to wrestle with my intolerances and self-absorption. And I have been losing ground in this battle, forgetting my husband's intentions and focusing instead on the petty ways I am inconvenienced by his practice.

Ramadan is meant to break our rigid habits of overindulgence,   *19* the ones that slip into our lives as charming guests and then refuse to leave, taking up more and more space and stealing our attention away from God. And it's not just the big habits, the ones that grab us by the throat—alcohol, coffee, cigarettes—but the little ones that take us gently by the hand and lead us stealthily away from the truth. I begin to notice my own compulsions, the small and socially acceptable ones that colonize my day: The way I depend on regular exercise to bolster my mood. The number of times I check my email. The impulse to watch a movie with my husband after our children are in bed, rather than let the silence envelop us both. And the words: all the words in books, in magazines, on the computer; words to distract me from the mundane truth of the moment. I begin to notice how much of my thinking revolves around what I will consume next.

I am plump with my husband's love, overfed by his kindness, yet [20] I still treat our marriage like an all-you-can-eat buffet, returning to him over and over again to fill my plate, as if our vows guaranteed me unlimited nourishment. During Ramadan, when he turns inward and has less to offer me, I feel **indignant**. I want to make a scene. I want to speak to whoever is in charge, to demand what I think was promised me when I entered this marriage. But now I wonder: Is love an endless feast, or is it what people manage to serve each other when their cupboards are bare?

In the evening, just before sundown, Ismail arranges three dates [21] on a small plate and pours a tall glass of water, just as the Koran instructs him to do, just as the Prophet Mohammed himself did long ago. Then he sits down next to me at the kitchen counter while I thumb through cookbooks, wondering what to make for dinner. He waits dutifully while the phone rings, while our daughter practices scales on the piano, while our son sends a box of LEGOs crashing onto our wood floor. Then, at the moment the sun sets, he lifts a date to his mouth and closes his eyes.

Bremer, Krista. Excerpted from *My Accidental Jihad: A Love Story*. Algonquin. Copyright 2014. Reprinted by permission of the author.

Jihad
an individual's attempt at spiritual self-perfection; a Muslim holy war or struggle

Koran
the sacred text of Muslims

grueling
long and very difficult

melodramatic
exaggerated behavior, showing lots of emotion

Islam
Muslim religion

contradictory
illogical; a statement that disagrees with another statement or action

flamboyant
showy, bright, colorful

fickle
likely to change

synchronous
happening at the same time

baklava
a Middle-Eastern pastry filled with ground nuts

balmy
hot and humid

beatific
a happy, satisfied state

terse
abrupt or blunt in manner

volatile
unpredictable anger or hostility

taqwa
Islamic concept of enlightenment

indignant
feeling displeasure at something that you declare is unjust or unfair

Summarizing

Write a summary of "My Accidental Jihad." Remember that a summary presents the main points in a clear, concise form using your own words.

Reflecting

1. Create a time line that lists the main actions and conversations from this story in chronological order.

2. What stands out in the development of the essay—the explanations, the dialogue, and/or the sensory details? Explain.

3. How much time is covered in the narrative?

4. What is the climax in this story?

5. What does the author learn from this experience?

Vocabulary

Create vocabulary entries for these words. For each word, identify the pronunciation and helpful word parts, give a primary definition, and use the word in a sentence.

1. **fast** (paragraph 2)
2. **indulgences** (paragraph 3)
3. **self-absorption** (paragraph 18)

Critical Thinking

- What two words come to mind when you think of the husband? Explain your choices.
- What two words come to mind when you think of the author? Explain your choices.
- What does the author mean when she says, "This month of Ramadan has thrown me into my own accidental jihad?"
- What were your perceptions of the word *jihad* before reading this narrative? Did the narrative confirm or contradict your feelings about the word? How so?
- Why is it important that the author is a part of the story? Would the story be as effective if it was written from the perspective of an outsider looking in on the relationship between the husband and wife during Ramadan?

L03 Planning a Personal Narrative

Now that you've read a professional narrative, start thinking about what you would like to focus on in your own narrative. Prewriting begins by selecting a topic and identifying the key moments in the narrative. A narrative topic should be an event, an experience, or a moment from your life that had an impact on you. It could be a surprise, a setback, a turning point, or something else meaningful.

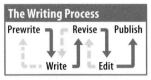

Once you pick a topic, think carefully about and record the actions and conversations related to your topic. List as many of the important details as you can. If you have trouble recalling details about the experience, complete one or more of these activities.

- Talk about the experience with a classmate or with someone else associated with it.
- Review any photographs or videos of the experience.
- Write nonstop about the experience for 5–7 minutes to see what actions and details come to mind.

Practice List four experiences from your own life to consider for a personal narrative. Consider experiences that covered a brief span of time, from a few minutes to a few hours. Then choose one of the experiences to write about and list key actions and conversations related to the topic.

Creating a Time Line

Once you have gathered the main actions of your story, organize the details chronologically using a time line. The time line will serve mainly as a reference point for writing the narrative, so don't worry about adding all the specific details. Figure 8.3 shows a prewriting time line of key events in the narrative "Remembering Gramps."

Practice Complete a time line to organize the key details of your narrative in chronological order.

Figure 8.3 Prewriting Time Line

1 — Saturday morning phone call

2 — Mom says, "Grandpa died."

3 — Drop on the couch

4 — Remember all our times together

5 — Thank him for his good character

Viorel Sima, 2014 / Used under license from Shutterstock.com

Gathering Details

The most vivid narratives use plenty of sensory details that allow the reader to picture, hear, and touch what you describe. You can use a sensory chart like the one in Figure 8.4 to gather the sensory details for your writing. Your narrative may not address all of the senses, but adding a variety of sensory details can help you recreate the experience in a way that makes your readers feel like they are experiencing the event with you.

Figure 8.4 Sensory Chart

Sights	Sounds	Smells	Tastes	Textures
ceiling fan	buzz of the phone	eggs frying	burn of the bourbon drink	lump in the throat
egg in the frying pan	conversation with Mom			watery eyes
sparkle of brown eyes	Grandpa's deep laugh			
arthritic hands				

Practice Create a sensory chart by listing the sights, sounds, smells, tastes, or textures related to your experience. (Your experience may not have details in every category.)

Showing Details

Sensory details help you "show" an experience rather than simply tell about it. Other "showing" details that can help your narrative come alive include dialogue, personal reflections, and references to the setting.

- **Dialogue** shares conversations between people.

  > "Are you awake?" she asked, her voice cracking.
  > Sensing her distress, I asked, "What's wrong?"

- **Personal reflections** reveal your thoughts and feelings at the time.

  > I felt thankful for the times we had together. . . .

- **References to the setting** (time and place of the action) help the reader visualize the experience.

  > It was sometime after eight o'clock on a Saturday morning. . . .

Practice Consider dialogue for your narrative. Though it may be almost impossible to recall every last detail or conversation from a past experience, you can still capture the spirit of the time and place by creating realistic conversations.

LO4 Writing the First Draft

Follow your prewriting plan to help you write the first draft of your narrative. "Remembering Gramps" is about a vivid moment in the writer's life.

Practice ▶ Read the personal narrative, noting how the writer created effective opening and closing parts. Also note how the writer developed ideas in the middle part: Are all of the details arranged chronologically? Does the writer include any personal thoughts and feelings about the experience?

Remembering Gramps

Opening Paragraph

It was sometime after eight o'clock on a Saturday morning when I received the call about my grandfather's death. I was already awake, cracking eggs into a skillet, when my cell phone buzzed on the countertop. A little early for a phone call, I thought. It was my mom. "Are you awake?" she asked, her voice cracking. Sensing her distress, I asked, "What's wrong?" She told me my grandfather had suffered a stroke during the night and didn't make it.

1

Middle Paragraph 1

After talking through the funeral plans, I wobbled over to my cushy, leather couch and stared blankly at the circulating blades on the ceiling fan. Memories of my grandfather spun around in my head, like the time he taught me how to throw a curveball, and the fishing trip we took together on the Gulf Coast, and the day he poured me a Coke but instead mistakenly handed me his glass of bourbon and ice.

2

Middle Paragraph 2

Of course, those were old memories. By the time I reached college, Grandpa wasn't as active anymore. Tired and overworked from his years of hard labor at the steel yard, his back eventually gave out and his joints swelled up with arthritis. He lived alone in the modest two-bedroom home he built for my grandmother after they married. But even after she was gone, he never lost the sparkle in his brown eyes. Nor did he lose his sense of humor, punctuated by a deep baritone laugh.

3

Closing Paragraph

And so I sat there, staring at the ceiling and reminiscing about Grandpa. Sure, I had a lump in my throat, and tears filled my eyes; but I felt thankful for the times we had together and hopeful that one day I could be as good a grandfather as he had been to me. I owed him that much—and so much more.

4

Developing an Opening Paragraph

The opening part should capture the readers' attention and lead the audience into the story. Here are three strategies for beginning a narrative:

- **Jump right into things.**

  Jammed in our aging royal blue Chevy Astro van with no air conditioning, no radio, and limited legroom sat my parents, my two sisters, and our dog, Max.

- **Set the stage.**

  It was sometime after eight o'clock on a Saturday morning when I received the call about my grandfather's death.

- **Offer an interesting thought.**

  I should have listened to my brother and never walked into that room.

Creating the Middle Paragraphs

In the middle part of your narrative, share the main details about the experience. In other words, this is where you tell your story. Here are some reminders:

- **Organize details chronologically,** referring back to your time line as necessary.
- **Include explanations, sensory details, dialogue, and other "showing" details** to recreate the experience and build your audience's interest.
- **When necessary, use transition words that show time:** *after, before, during, later, now, soon, suddenly, then, when, while, first, second, finally, lastly.*

Creating a Closing Paragraph

The closing part can wrap up the experience after the most exciting action has happened, or it can provide an analysis of the experience by explaining its value and importance. Here are three strategies to consider:

- **Include a final piece of dialogue.**

  We did eventually make it to the Grand Canyon, but not before Mom admitted, "A pool would feel really nice right now."

- **Conclude with the last important action.**

  John and Dan triumphantly strolled home. Dan had John's jacket in his hand.

- **Offer a final analysis of the experience.**

  I felt thankful for the times we had together and hopeful that one day I could be as good a grandfather as he had been to me.

Practice ▸ Create your first draft, using your planning and these opening, middle, and closing tips as a guide.

L05 Revising the Writing

Revising a first draft involves adding, deleting, rearranging, and reworking parts of the writing. Revision often begins with a peer review. Sharing your work with peers helps you gain a fresh perspective on your first draft, and the feedback will help you make changes to improve your narrative.

Peer Review Sheet

Narrative title: Remembering Gramps

Writer: Jody Parker

Reviewer: Toby Wallis

1. Which part of the narrative works best—opening, middle, or closing? Why?
   Opening, because it makes you want to read the rest and find out what is going to happen.

2. Which part of the narrative needs work—opening, middle, or closing? Why?
   Middle, because I want more details about the relationship between the writer and the grandfather.

3. Which details in the story caught your attention? Name three.
   a. buzzing phone
   b. cracking voice
   c. modest two-bedroom home

4. Does the writer include appropriate dialogue? Explain.
   Yes, a short exchange between mother and son gets the reader's attention.

5. Identify a phrase or two that show the writer's level of interest in his or her story.
   Lines 9 and 10 in the essay

Practice ▸ Ask a classmate to read your first draft and answer peer review questions about it. Consider the reviewer's suggestions as you revise your first draft. If a classmate asks you to complete a peer review sheet, keep your comments helpful and positive. Then share the sheet with the writer.

Adding Specific Verbs and Modifiers

Strengthen your narrative by replacing general verbs and modifiers with more specific ones as in **Figure 8.5**. Doing so will energize the writing and help readers visualize the story.

Figure 8.5 Specific Verbs and Modifiers

Verbs		Modifiers	
General	**Specific**	**General**	**Specific**
grew	swelled	**baseball** cap	**flat-billed Yankees** cap
came	advanced	**curly** hair	**wavy auburn** hair
run	sprint	**deep** laugh	**baritone** laugh
lives	roams	**sweet** sauce	**tangy barbecue** sauce
wear	don	**dangerous** pier	**wobbly** pier

Read aloud the first draft and then the revised version of the excerpt. Study how the specific verbs and adjectives add life to the writing.

> wobbled   cushy, leather   stared   circulating   ceiling
> I ~~walked~~ over to my couch and ~~looked~~ blankly at the blades on the fan.

Practice ▸ Improve your writing by replacing general verbs and modifiers with more specific ones. Finally, use a revising checklist like the one in **Figure 8.6** to check your ideas, organization, and voice. Continue working until you can check off each item in the list.

Figure 8.6 Revising Checklist

Ideas

_____ 1. Do I focus on one specific experience or memory?
_____ 2. Do I include sensory details and dialogue?
_____ 3. Do I use specific verbs and modifiers?

Organization

_____ 4. Does the narrative have an opening, a middle, and a closing?
_____ 5. Is the story organized chronologically?
_____ 6. Have I used transitions to connect my sentences?

Voice

_____ 7. Is my interest in the story obvious to the reader?
_____ 8. Does my writing voice sound natural?

L06 Editing the Writing

The main work of editing is correcting the revised first draft for spelling, grammar, and usage.

Quotation Marks and Dialogue

Most narratives include dialogue, which enlivens the story and reveals the personalities of its characters. When you write conversations between people using their exact words, place quotation marks before and after the **direct quotation**. However, when you write *about* what someone has said, not using the speaker's exact words, omit the quotation marks before and after the **indirect quotation**.

Direct Quotation

Before we left class, Mr. Lopez said, "Next week's final will be comprehensive."

Indirect Quotation

Mr. Lopez told the class that the final will be comprehensive.

NOTE: The word *that* often indicates dialogue that is being reported rather than quoted.

Practice Read the sentences. Indicate where quotation marks ("") should be placed before and after the speaker's exact words in direct quotations. If the sentence contains no direct quotations, write "C" for correct on the blank line following the sentence. The first example has been done for you.

1. "I'm having the worst day," Jessie said, "I left my cell phone at home." _____

2. Who is your favorite actress? asked Veronica. _____

3. The salesperson suggested that I should take the truck for a test-drive. _____

4. Frank said that if we want to make it in time, we should leave by noon. _____

5. Pull over to the side of the road, said the police officer. _____

6. After glancing at her test score, Jillian said, Spring break can't come soon enough. _____

7. And with this new car model, said the salesperson, you will save money on gas. _____

Practice Read your narrative. If you included any dialogue (with direct quotations), make sure that it is properly marked with quotation marks. If you did not include any dialogue, consider adding some.

Punctuation of Dialogue

As you edit your narrative, check the dialogue for punctuation errors. Familiarize yourself with these three rules:

- **When a period or comma follows the quotation**, place the period or comma *before* the quotation mark.

  > "You should check your voice messages," advised Mr. Lee.

  > "As you will soon discover," Reggie said, "the wrap station in the cafeteria is the best choice for lunch."

- **When a question mark or an exclamation point follows the quotation**, place it before the quotation mark if it belongs with the quotation. Otherwise, place it after.

  > Sheryl asked, "Where can I get some good soul food?"

  > Did you hear Veronica say, "I quit"?

- **When a semicolon or colon follows the quotation**, place it after the quotation mark.

  > Trey simply said, "I have other plans"; he didn't mention his fear of heights.

Practice Correct the punctuation of the dialogue in each sentence.

1. "Let's focus on solutions, not problems", offered Haley.

2. Jack promised he would "try my best to make it;" however, I know he's not coming.

3. "It's not the size of the dog in the fight", suggested Mark Twain ", it's the size of the fight in the dog."

4. "It's about time you showed up"! exclaimed Karen.

5. "Should I apply for the job"? asked my roommate.

6. What did you mean when you said, "There is more to the story than you think?"

7. "We are doing everything in our power to regain your trust", said the company spokesperson.

Practice Review your narrative closely for the punctuation of any dialogue.

Marking a Narrative

Before you finish editing your revised draft, practice on a model narrative.

Practice Read the narrative, looking for problems listed in the editing checklist in **Figure 8.7**. Then correct the model using correction marks. One correction has been done for you.

Whale Watchers

On a sunny afternoon off the coast of San Diego, my friend Natalie and I set off on our great whale watching adventure. In the winter months some 20,000 gray whales migrate through the Pacific waters along the coast of california, and we wanted to see the majestic creatures in there natural habitat.   1

As we stepped aboard the 100-foot tour boat nicknamed *Night and Day*, Natalie reminded me to take some medication to prevent seasickness. Good thing she did, because the captain announced we would hit six-foot swells on our journey. Their were about 40 other passengers onboard with us.   2

About 15 minutes off the shoreline, a passenger shouted, "There she blows"! Indeed, about 20 yards ahead of us, I seen a spray of white water rocket vertically from the ocean surface we had spotted our first whale! As the boat crept closer, we could see the bumpy, gray backs of two more whales rising above the undulating waves. I was so excited that I high-fived Natalie so hard it made my hand sting.   3

We ended up seeing five diffrant gray whales two packs of dolphins, and too many pelicans to count. seeing this beautiful sea life in the wild was an experience I'll never forget. Learning that the whales are endangered goes to show that we must boost our efforts to protect them from extinction.   4

Correction Marks

℣ delete	⋀ add comma	word ⋀ add word
≡ᵈ capitalize	? ⋀ add question mark	⊙ add period
ø lowercase	⋁ insert an apostrophe	◯ spelling
⋀ insert		⊓⊔ switch

Using an Editing Checklist

Use an editing checklist to edit the remainder of your narrative for style and correctness.

Practice Prepare a clean copy of your revised narrative, and then use the checklist in Figure 8.7 to look for errors. Continue working until you can check off each item in the list.

Figure 8.7 Editing Checklist

Words

_____ 1. Have I used specific nouns and verbs?

_____ 2. Have I used more action verbs than "be" verbs?

Sentences

_____ 3. Have I used sentences with varying beginnings and lengths?

_____ 4. Have I avoided improper shifts in sentences?

_____ 5. Have I avoided fragments and run-ons?

Conventions

_____ 6. Do I use correct verb forms (*he saw*, not *he seen*)?

_____ 7. Do my subjects and verbs agree (*she speaks*, not *she speak*)?

_____ 8. Have I used the right words (*their, there, they're*)?

_____ 9. Have I capitalized first words and proper nouns and adjectives?

_____ 10. Have I used commas after long introductory word groups and to separate items in a series?

_____ 11. Have I correctly punctuated any dialogue?

_____ 12. Have I carefully checked my spelling?

Adding a Title

Finish the narrative by adding an attention-getting title. Here are three simple strategies.

- **Use a phrase from the piece:**

  Remembering Gramps

- **Use alliteration**, the repetition of a consonant sound:

  Whale Watchers

- **Use a play on words:**

  Tripped-Up Road Trip

"All writers who have produced anything have done it out of their specific experience and making that experience reverberate in other people."

—Gloria Naylor

☑ Reading for Enrichment

You will be reading an excerpt from *Lipstick Jihad*, a memoir about an Iranian-American's search for identity within two contrasting cultures. Follow the reading process and refer back to what you've learned about narratives to gain a full understanding of the text. Afterward, you'll find a number of writing ideas for creating your own narrative related to the reading.

About the Author

Azadeh Moaveni is an accomplished journalist who has reported throughout the Middle East for publications such as *Time, The Washington Post,* and the *New York Times Book Review*. Much of Moaveni's reporting focuses on happenings in Iran, where she is one of the few American journalists since 1999 to be given the freedom to write and report from within the country. Along with *Lipstick Jihad,* Moaveni has authored *Honeymoon in Tehran* and co-authored *Iran Awakening*. She currently works as a Middle East correspondent for *The Guardian*.

Prereading

Azadeh Moaveni narrates a childhood trip that altered her perspective of her heritage. Have you ever experienced a trip or vacation that changed your preconceived notions of a place, people, or culture? Think about it to get a sense of what Moaveni might have experienced while writing her memoir.

ArtisticPhoto, 2014 / Used under license from Shutterstock.com

What do you think?

What does Gloria Naylor's quotation say about the importance of personal experiences in a writer's life?

Before you read, answer these questions:

1. What do the title, the opening two paragraphs, and the first lines of the other paragraphs tell you about the topic?

_____

2. What might be the author's intended purpose and audience?

_____

3. What questions do you want answered by this reading?

_____

Reading and Rereading

As you read, make it your goal to note the key moments in the narrative, confirm the purpose and audience, and answer the questions you posed during prereading. Annotate the text, and create a time line to help you keep track of important information.

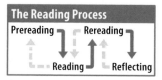

Reread as needed to confirm your understanding of the text. Consider the types of details used to make the story come to life and to hold the reader's interest.

Lipstick Jihad

It was so cool and quiet up in the *toot* (mulberry) tree that I never wanted to come down. I didn't have to; the orchard was so dense that I could scramble from the limb of one tree to another, plucking the plump, red berries as I went along. The sweet juice made my fingers stick together, but I couldn't stop climbing. The trees stretched out as far as I could see, a glorious forest of mulberries, ripe for my picking. I loved mulberries, but until that summer in Tehran, I had only tasted them dried, from little plastic packets sold in the Iranian grocery store in San Jose. Riveted by the abundance, and the squishy texture of the berry in its fresh form—a whole new delight—I had spent the better part of the afternoon perched in the shady canopy of the orchard. "Azadeh jan, I am going to count to three, and you had better come down," came Maman's glaring voice from somewhere far below. I gave in, but only because of the preliminary pangs of the hideous stomachache to come. Sedigheh Khanoum, one of the farmers who took care of the orchards at Farahzad and who had tended Maman's stomach when she was little, made me tea with sugar crystals, to soothe the cramps. And I lay content on my back on the Persian rug outside, as Maman chatted with Sedigheh about our life in America, debating whether tomorrow I should go after the delicate white toot, or the dark red.

Only a very small child in the safety of a walled family compound would have felt liberated in Iran one year after the **Islamic Revolution**, but I was blissfully unaware of such matters. Finally, I was unleashed, and wanted to stay forever in this country where I could romp about freely. In Iran I could play wherever and with whomever I wanted—in the street, in the backyard, with the caretaker's daughter, with my brand-new duck. When my cousins and I played at our grandparents' apartment complex in California, we had to be visible and within hearing distance at all times. We were tethered to our parents' fears: that we might consort with "street children"—which I later realized only meant normal kids who were allowed to play outside—or that some terrible fate might **befall** us in this as yet foreign country. If we were to blip off the radar for more than a few minutes, a search and rescue squad would fan out in our pursuit. Neither I nor my cousins tolerated this **cloying** protectiveness well, and occasionally we would dial 911 in revenge, for the pleasure of watching our poor grandmother or aunt explain to a stern policeman who knocked on the door that "Surely, sir, there is mistake; here we are having no emergency."

In Tehran that summer, I wasn't the only one unleashed. My mother could barely stay put, flitting from house to house, from Tehran to the Caspian and back again; even when she was at home, sitting down, she was gulping in space-high ceilings, drawing rooms vast enough that I could race a tricycle down from one end to the other—as though her lungs had only been partially breathing the whole time she'd been away. I finally saw Maman, my beautiful, proud, mad mother, laughing gustily, instead of the tight-lipped smile she wore as she chauffeured me around San Jose, to piano lessons, to ice skating lessons, to gymnastics, back and forth to

became one of the leaders in the uprising. They had been friendly in those college days, and when at the dawn of the revolution my uncle was taken to prison, he contacted his old roommate Chamran. No reply. "Your type must go," came a message, through a friend.

Leaving Tehran broke my heart. My pet duck died the week we were to go, and Maman tried to console me with promises of a kitten back home. I was too young to understand that what I didn't want to part with was a newfound sense of wholeness—a sense of belonging in a world that embraced us. The memories of those few months colored the rest of our life in America. They flooded back vividly, when my grandmother cooked jam, when Maman took me with her to the bank, to visit the safety-deposit box where she kept all the jewelry she no longer wore, the gold bangles and dainty earrings our relatives had bestowed on me in Tehran. In times of acute alienation, they were a reminder that things could be different; proof that the often awkward fusion of East and West in our American lives didn't necessarily point to our failure, but the inherent tension of the attempt. At those times when I was most furious with Maman, I would recall the lightness of our days in Tehran, her easy smile and fluid movements, and remind myself of the strength it took for her to build a life in a strange country, alone.

9

Moaveni, Azadeh. Excerpted from *Lipstick Jihad: A Memoir of Growing Up Iranian in America and American in Iran*. The Perseus Books Group. Copyright 2006. Permission conveyed by the Copyright Clearance Center.

Islamic Revolution
a 1979 Iranian revolution that overthrew the Pahlavi dynasty and instituted Islamic rule in Iran

befall
to happen or occur

cloying
overbearing; too much of something

Shah
the highest title given to kings and emperors of Iran

vigilantes
people who purposely reject all law, often violently

sycamores
a type of tree characterized by spotted trunks

aromatic
having a strong and distinct smell

dissimulation
disguising or concealing the truth

alienation
to feel withdrawn or isolated

Summarizing

Write a summary of "Lipstick Jihad." Remember that a summary presents the main points in a clear, concise form using your own words.

Reflecting

1. What do the details in paragraph 3 reveal about the author's mother?

   _____

2. Provide examples of each sensory detail from the selection.

Sights	Sounds	Smells	Tastes	Textures

3. What paragraph reveals the climax of the story, the author's realization about the significance of this trip to Iran?

   _____

4. What is the purpose of this narrative—to entertain, to persuade, to inform, to humor, or a combination of these? Explain.

   _____

Vocabulary

Use context clues to explain or define the following words from the text.

1. **tethered**
   (paragraph 2)

2. **flitting**
   (paragraph 3)

Critical Thinking

- Do you think the experience helped the author gain a better understanding of her mother? Explain.
- How would you explain what the title "Lipstick Jihad" means?
- What do the details about Pahlavi Boulevard in paragraph 4 reveal about Iran?
- What does the narrative reveal about childhood?
- Both this reading and Krista Bremer's "My Accidental Jihad" include the word *jihad* in their titles. Why do you think the authors made this choice? Does "jihad" mean the same thing in each reading? Explain.

Writing for Enrichment

Choose one of the following writing ideas, or decide upon an idea of your own related to the reading.

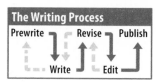

1. Have you ever experienced a trip or vacation that impacted the way you view the world? Describe the experience in narrative essay.

2. Write about a time when you learned about a custom or culture different than yours. Narrate the experience and show what you learned.

3. Share a story or moment when you gained a greater appreciation for a parent, sibling, or other close relative.

4. Write a personal narrative that is set in a place that made your senses come to life. Make the experience come to life for readers with many sensory details.

5. Develop a narrative about a significant childhood experience.

When planning . . .

- Make sure that your topic is specific enough for a personal narrative.
- Use a time line and a sensory chart to gather details (sensory details, reflections, dialogue, and/or actions) to make the story come alive for readers.

When writing . . .

- Include an opening, a middle, and a closing in your narrative.
- Understand that you don't have to describe or show everything. You can leave some things to the reader's imagination.

When revising . . .

- Search for any dead spots that need more detail or should be cut.
- Determine if readers will be able to visualize (see in their minds) the experience as it unfolds.
- Decide if the dialogue seems realistic.
- Edit your revised writing for style and correctness.

Reflecting on Narrative Writing

Answer the following questions about your narrative reading and writing experiences.

1. Why do writers find it valuable to write about their personal experiences?
2. Which is the most helpful reading strategy in the chapter? Explain.
3. What do you like the most about the narrative you wrote in this chapter? What one thing would you like to change in it?
4. What is the most important thing you have learned about narrative writing?

Jan S., 2014 / Used under license from Shutterstock.com

Chapter

9

"The mediocre teacher tells. The good teacher explains. The superior teacher demonstrates. The great teacher inspires."

—William Arthur Ward

Reading and Writing Expository Texts

Expository writing explains or informs. Expository articles provide information to readers, helping them learn about new topics and grapple with ideas. But great expository writing goes beyond just explaining. It demonstrates and inspires, making the reader say, "Wow, I didn't know that!"

The expository models in this chapter inspire amazement and reflection in equal measure. The first reading reveals a history of women warriors among the ancient Maya, and the second describes a conflict in marriage customs in the modern United States.

In each of these readings, you'll see how professional writers explain, demonstrate, and inspire. Afterward, you'll get the chance to write your own expository texts.

Learning Outcomes

LO1 Understand expository texts.

LO2 Read and respond to expository texts (using a gathering grid and recognizing signal words).

LO3 Plan an expository essay.

LO4 Write the first draft.

LO5 Revise the writing.

LO6 Edit the writing.

What do you think?

What is the difference between explaining and inspiring? What topics most inspire you?

"Either write something worth reading or do
something worth writing."

—Benjamin Franklin

L01 Understanding Expository Texts

Expository writing provides information, so whenever you learn something new, expository writing is probably involved. In that sense, expository writing is the workhorse of learning.

Expository writing is common in trade magazines, which present information on many different topics. The first professional reading in this chapter comes from *Discover* magazine and focuses on archaeological discoveries about warrior women in ancient Mayan societies. The author uses facts, descriptions, definitions, anecdotes, examples, and quotations to explain these discoveries. Textbooks also specialize in expository writing because experts have a lot of information to impart about their areas of expertise.

When you write expository texts, you should choose a form that fits your purpose. Select from one of the forms of expository texts listed here.

Illustration An illustration explains or clarifies a main idea with specific reasons, facts, and details. As the name suggests, an illustration "paints a picture" for the reader, helping him or her see the topic clearly.

For over 2000 years, audiences have enjoyed shadow-puppet shows in China. The stage is simple: a white cloth screen with a light shining behind it. The puppets, too, are simple: profile cutouts of princes, sages, soldiers, and queens with joints held together by thread, allowing movement. Five performers use these simple materials to bring a story to life. A puppeteer operates all of the puppets while a singer sings their story and adds voices to each character. The other three performers play instruments: a fiddle, a flute, and a drum. Traditionally, this entertainment began when Emperor Wu of the Han dynasty lost a favorite concubine. A minister arranged the first shadow puppetry using children's dolls behind a screen to remind the emperor of his lost love. From that time, the art of shadow puppetry has remained strong, though it now is in danger of dying out, like other traditional art forms.

Definition A definition explores the meaning of an important word or concept. The writing may include synonyms, antonyms, etymology (history), examples, and comparisons.

English includes three articles: *a, an,* and *the.* The words *a* and *an* are called indefinite articles because they show that the noun they describe is not a specific one. The command "bring me a book" means that the speaker wants any book. The articles *a* and *an* derive from the German word *ein,* which means "one." The word *the* is called a definite article because it shows that the noun that follows it is a specific one known to the speaker and the listener. The command "bring me the book" means that the speaker wants a specific book (not just any old book). The article *the* derives from the same word as *that,* pointing to a particular person, place, or thing.

Process A process text gives step-by-step instructions for completing a task, usually employing command verbs that tell the reader just what to do. Some process texts focus instead on how something works, such as the process of amending the constitution or of transforming from pupa to butterfly.

Before this old-school role-playing session can begin, each player must generate a character using a player-character sheet. First, players choose a gender (male or female), a race (human, elf, dwarf), and a class (fighter, mage, rogue, or priest). Afterward, players roll three 6-sided dice and add up the total. They do so seven times in total, discarding the lowest score and assigning each remaining score to one of their character attributes (strength, dexterity, constitution, intelligence, wisdom, or charisma). Finally, players choose skills from the list of options located in the *Player's Handbook.*

Classification A classification breaks a subject into categories, explaining each category and relating them to the larger whole. This type of text focuses on groups, types, varieties, and kinds, sorting them and organizing them in a structure sometimes called a "taxonomy."

The modern orchestra uses three basic types of instruments: strings, winds, and percussion. String instruments produce sound through bowing, plucking, or strumming tightened strings, which vibrate in response. Violins, violas, cellos, and basses are the most common string instruments in orchestras, though guitars also may be used. Wind instruments produce sound by vibrating a volume of air in a cylinder. Some winds, like flutes and piccolos, create sound by blowing across an opening; others, like clarinets and saxophones, do so by blowing over or through a reed; and still more do so by vibrating lips on a mouthpiece. Percussion instruments make sound by striking an object. This category includes drums, cymbals, triangles, and even the piano.

Cause-Effect A cause-effect text identifies the reasons that a certain event, condition, or set of circumstances occurred and explores what resulted from it. The text links causes to effects, exploring chains of events.

> Lead is a naturally occurring element in the earth's crust, but it is also a deadly neurotoxin. The amount of exposure people have to natural sources of lead tends to be low, but human-made products and activities can make lead much more prevalent. Prior to 1978 in the United States, paint, toys, and gasoline often contained lead. To this day, some houses contain lead pipes or copper pipes soldered with lead. When lead is ingested—whether from water that runs through old pipes, chips of old paint, or flecks of soil contaminated by years of lead-laden exhaust—lead poisoning can occur. In children, lead poisoning often causes vomiting, diarrhea, loss of appetite, and weight loss and may result in developmental delays. In adults, lead poisoning can result in high blood pressure, memory loss, and mood disorders.

Comparison-Contrast A comparison-contrast text explains how two or more subjects are alike and different. Some comparisons focus on similarities and others on differences. Some focus first on one subject and then the other, while others consider each subject point by point.

> When selecting an alternative to traditional gas guzzlers, consumers can choose between hybrid and electric vehicles. Hybrid cars have both electric and gasoline motors. They use electricity at slow speeds, with light payloads, and when traveling downhill, but hybrids shift to gasoline at high speeds, when hauling loads, or when climbing hills. The gasoline engine also helps to recharge the electric battery. Electric cars use electricity exclusively, getting their energy from wall sockets or swapping out their used batteries for fully-charged ones at charging stations. Hybrids have excellent fuel economy, averaging about 45 miles to the gallon. They also produce fewer emissions than regular gas-powered vehicles. Electric cars use no gasoline at all and produce no emissions. However, their batteries take four to eight hours to fully recharge, drawing on electricity that is often generated by burning fossil fuels such as coal. Hybrid vehicles can travel more than 500 miles without stopping to refuel, while electric vehicles have a range of 100 to 200 miles.

Nerthuz, 2014 / Used under license from Shutterstock.com

The Power and Glory of the Maya Queens

The great pyramids of Naachtun lie shrouded in the emerald forest of northern Guatemala. They are part of one of the most remote, inaccessible sites in the entire ancient Maya world. At the height of Maya civilization, this prosperous city lay in a perilous heartland, caught between two clashing superpowers: Tikal and Calakmul. [1]

To study Naachtun and its alliances in treacherous times, University of Calgary **archaeologist** Kathryn Reese-Taylor made her way to the site in 2004. For three months, she and an international research team mapped Naachtun's architecture and recorded ancient texts inscribed on altars and limestone blocks (known as **stelae**). One of these, Naachtun Stela 18, a massive stone that once towered 14 feet in the air, depicts a fierce-looking Naachtun queen. . . . With a battle shield strapped to her arm, this queen stands majestically on the back of an enemy captive, a lord of Calakmul. [2]

Surprised by this find, Reese-Taylor returned from her trip wondering, "Was it possible that there were warrior queens in ancient Maya societies? Did some royal Maya women actually take part in the violence sparked by ruling houses hungry for power and resources?" [3]

A decade ago, most archaeologists would have flatly dismissed the idea, seeing Maya royal women mainly as marriage pawns, **consorts** and mothers of kings, says Reese-Taylor, a warm, energetic woman in her early 50s. But now she and other researchers are amassing striking new evidence of warrior queens who may have risen to the heights of battle glory during the latter half of Maya civilization, between A.D. 600 and 800. [4]

Dressed to Kill

Maya artists frequently portrayed the military **prowess** of their kings by showing them trampling over cowering prisoners. The [5] sculptures that Reese-Taylor found in Naachtun, however, depict both king and queen as conquering heroes, literally crushing into the ground a member of one of the most powerful dynasties in the Maya world. Reese-Taylor combed through hundreds of published inscriptions and royal portraits housed at university libraries in Canada and the U.S., looking for imagery of other warrior queens from the Maya lowlands around Naachtun.

Finding and identifying these women wasn't easy. Most illustrations and sculptures from the time depicted kings and queens alike in an **ambiguous** ceremonial garment—a beaded net skirt. Reese-Taylor turned to the work of Peter Mathews, a former University of Calgary archaeologist who specialized in the Maya of Naachtun. Mathews had already started to decode the subtleties of these ancient Maya costumes, noticing that the images associated with the names of women feature warriors dressed in full, loose, calf-length skirts. Men's garb was tighter and more revealing. Reese-Taylor confirmed this trend, finding the same costume differences in images of queens from several Maya cities beyond Naachtun.

6

She determined, by identifying characters in loose beaded skirts, that the lowland Maya had many warrior queens. In four Maya city-states—Coba, Naranjo, Calakmul and Naachtun—ancient artists illustrated at least 10 different royal women standing on bound captives or towering over prisoners. Some queens sported symbols of war in their headdresses; others armed themselves with battle shields or waved war banners aloft. And on a famous altar stone from the site of Sak Nikte', also in modern-day Guatemala, a queen known as Ix Naah Ek' wore the helmet of the Maya god of war and stood atop a large battle palanquin, or platform, the size of a Macy's parade float.

7

Politics and Hieroglyphics

Hieroglyphic inscriptions offered clues about the role of Maya queens, too. During the early part of the 20th century, archaeologists

8

from the Carnegie Institution for Science in Washington, D.C., deciphered the dates on a Calakmul stela featuring a warrior queen. This and subsequent similar findings led Reese-Taylor to believe that most of the warrior queens in Maya society rose to power after 623, during a **seismic geopolitical** shift in the Maya world. Around this time, a northern royal family known as the Kaan or Snake Dynasty moved into the rainforests of the central lowlands, in the middle of the Yucatan Peninsula, explains Reese-Taylor. The Kaan claimed the throne of Calakmul and rose to great power and influence.

As Reese-Taylor began sifting through more hieroglyphs looking **9** for inscriptions and dates associated with queens, she determined that the northern Maya dynasties prized their female ancestors, and the Kaan seem to have placed great value on royal women. After 623, Kaan princesses married into many local ruling houses in the lowlands, carrying these new ideas with them. There was "a real expansion of the role that women played in politics," says Reese-Taylor. "A woman's role was not in the background. It was up front and center."

Then Reese-Taylor found the epigraphic, or inscription, work of **10** Maya scholar Linda Schele, which revealed that at the height of the rainy season in 682, a Maya princess from Dos Pilas, in what is now west-central Guatemala, arrived in the shattered city of Naranjo, just west of the Belize-Guatemala border. Enemy kings had long fought over the region's **lucrative** river trade. The king of Dos Pilas dispatched his daughter, Ix Wak Chan Ajaw, to marry the king of the region. While this leader died shortly after marriage, he left Ix Wak Chan Ajaw in charge. She did not disappoint. Deftly stepping into the throne, she launched eight major military campaigns over five years, torching the cities of her enemies. Her early battlefield record helped Reese-Taylor understand the **trajectory** of women warriors through Maya history.

Buried Evidence

Ix Wak Chan Ajaw was not the only Maya princess who   11
scooped up the reins of power. Reese-Taylor's attempt to piece
together the history of Maya queens brought her to archeologist Traci
Ardren at the University of Miami. Ardren, too, has sifted through
evidence from royal tombs and inscriptions, searching for traces of
female rulers. In all, she says, excavators have recorded nearly two
dozen tombs of royal women.

While some, such as a burial chamber found at Nakum, west   12
of Naachtun, are relatively modest, containing only a few painted
pots, others clearly advertise the great wealth and influence of
the occupant. At Copan, to the south, for example, fifth-century
mourners dressed their dead queen in burial garments shimmering
with precious greenstone beads, shell ornaments and feathered bird
heads, and they laid her to rest on a massive carved **funerary** slab in
what is known today as the Margarita Tomb. Then they sprinkled
her remains with costly imported red pigments from the minerals
cinnabar and hematite.

Ardren has "brought together studies from throughout the   13
ancient Maya world to show that women were not sidebars in Maya
society, but significant actors in their own right," says Reese-Taylor,
who is now building on Ardren's work as she looks for clues about
powerful queens who were also fierce warriors.

In 2012, more evidence emerged from Guatemala. While   14
excavating the ancient royal Maya city El Peru-Waka', archaeologists
from Washington University in St. Louis uncovered the tomb of a
royal woman. Her bones lay resting beneath a shrine, surrounded
by jewels and two figurines. Hieroglyphs nearby indicated her name
was Lady K'abel, also know as Lady Waterlily-Hand and Lady Snake
Lord. Lady Ka'bel's name had been etched on a seventh-century stela
next to a picture of a woman dressed in royal garb, and holding a
warrior shield.

Before the Fall

For Reese-Taylor, Ardren, and many others, these new   15
findings reveal much that previous researchers have missed when
it came to Maya queens. "I think it shows that power was a lot
more complicated than our models have suggested," concludes
Ardren. "And clearly we have a long way to go in understanding the
biographies of the most extraordinary women."

By analyzing hieroglyphic inscriptions and illustrations of   16
costumed queens, poring over evidence from royal tombs and
reconstructing royal dynasties, Reese-Taylor and her colleagues
have revealed for the first time how some Maya queens ruled alone
in turbulent times, securing their dynasties and their kingdoms
from **usurpers**, while others led their subjects to war, presiding over
battles of **attrition** against enemy kings. "These queens are really
important," says Reese-Taylor, "and we had just given them lip
service before."

archaeologist
person who studies ancient settlements

stelae
limestone blocks carved by Maya

consort
royal spouse, lover

prowess
valor, skill, ability

ambiguous
uncertain, indistinct, unclear

hieroglyphic
picture writing

seismic
earthshaking, world changing

geopolitical
related to control of territory

lucrative
profitable, producing wealth

trajectory
path, course, career

funerary
related to rites of the dead

usurpers
those attempting to take a throne

attrition
loss of forces or resources

Summarizing

Write a summary of the "The Power and Glory of Maya Queens." Remember that a summary presents the main points in a clear, concise form using your own words.

Reflecting

1. What is the purpose of this selection?

   to entertain   *to explain*   *to persuade*   *to evaluate*

   _____

   _____

2. What is the main idea of this text? (If you can't find a statement, infer one.)

   _____

   _____

3. Choose two of the subheadings in the text and use them to create a gathering grid. See **Figure 9.1** for an example.

4. This article originally appeared in a science magazine. How does the author's voice reflect the context of the publication?

   _____

   _____

5. What detail do you find most interesting or valuable? Why?

   _____

   _____

Vocabulary

Create vocabulary entries for these words. For each word, identify the pronunciation and helpful word parts, give a definition, and use the word in a sentence.

1. **shrouded** (paragraph 1)   2. **ceremonial** (paragraph 6)

Critical Thinking

- Why has it taken so long for archaeologists to discover the importance of warrior women among the Maya?
- How do these discoveries impact previous beliefs about the role of women in some traditional societies?
- What can the study of ancient civilizations teach us about modern society?

L03 Planning Expository Writing

Your topic should be focused enough to explore in an essay. Start by identifying a general subject that interests you. Then select a specific topic that you can address. Be sure that you select a topic that truly interests you.

The Writing Process

Prewrite → Revise → Publish

Write → Edit

General Subject	Specific Topic
marriage	marriage customs in traditional societies

Practice In the first box, write a general subject that interests you. In the second box, write a specific topic. Repeat this exercise until you have a topic to write about.

General Subject	Specific Topic

Selecting Sources and Gathering Details

Once you have selected a topic, you need to gather details about it. Occasionally, you may know enough about a topic to draw solely from your prior knowledge. Usually, though, you will need to conduct research. Consider both primary and secondary sources.

Primary Sources
- events or experiences
- interviews
- museum exhibits
- surveys/questionnaires
- letters/diaries/journals

Secondary Sources
- textbooks
- magazine/journal articles
- news reports
- Web sites
- books

Practice List sources you will explore to conduct research about your topic. Then gather details.

_____

_____

_____

Forming a Thesis

Your thesis statement should identify your topic and provide a focus for your essay—a thought or feeling that you would like to emphasize about the topic. The following formula will help you write this statement.

Specific Topic		Thought or Feeling About It		Thesis Statement
marriage customs in traditional cultures	**+**	conflict with American practices	**=**	Marriage customs from some societies might bring criminal charges in the United States.

Practice Create your thesis statement using the formula as a guide. If necessary, write two or three versions until your thesis says what you want it to say.

Specific Topic		Thought or Feeling About It		Thesis Statement
	+		**=**	

Arranging Your Details

Consider how you will arrange the details in your essay. You might center your essay around a specific event, as is done in "Is Marriage a Crime?" Or you might explain different categories of a topic, as the model "Exploitation Caused by Gender Ideology" does. Consider the following organizational patterns.

Organizational Patterns

- **Classification:** Explain each category of a larger group.
- **Cause-Effect:** Trace the causes and effects of a phenomenon.
- **Comparison:** Show how two subjects are alike and different.
- **Logic:** Build a case based upon claims and support.

Practice Consider how you want to arrange the details in your essay. Write down an organizational pattern and indicate why you chose it.

_____

_____

_____

LO4 Writing the First Draft

After you have completed your planning, you are ready to write your first draft.

Practice ▶ Read this text, paying attention to the opening, middle, and closing parts.

Is Marriage a Crime?

Opening Paragraph

In 1996 a recent Iraqi refugee was the proud father of two brides in a traditional double wedding ceremony for his two eldest daughters at their home in Lincoln, Nebraska (Terry 1996). An Islamic cleric was flown in from Ohio to perform the ceremony in front of more than a hundred friends and relatives. For all attending it was a festive social event celebrating the sacredness of matrimony. But for local authorities, it was the scene of a crime.

1

Middle Paragraph 1

The problem stemmed from the fact that the two Iraqi brides, who were thirteen and fourteen years old, were marrying men who were twenty-eight and thirty-four. According to marital law in Nebraska, seventeen is the minimum legal age for marriage. Authorities charged the father with two counts of child abuse, while the mother was charged with contributing to the delinquency of a minor. Moreover it is illegal for anyone older than eighteen to have sexual relations with anyone younger than eighteen. Because the two grooms consummated their marriages on the night of the wedding, both men were charged with statutory rape, which carries a maximum sentence of fifty years in prison. Both the parents and their two sons-in-law were shocked when police came to arrest them.

2

Middle Paragraph 2

The issue in this tragic case revolves around two very different definitions of marriage. According to both law and custom in the United States, marriage represents a voluntary union between two consenting individuals. . . . . Traditional Iraqi marriage is viewed more as a union between two large families than as a way of providing happiness and individual fulfillment for the husband and wife. In addition, traditional Iraqi parents fear that their daughters will engage in premarital sexual relations and thereby dishonor the entire family. To their way of thinking, the best way to protect their daughters and their families from such disgrace is to marry them off at an early age.

3

Closing Paragraph

Clearly this case presented a real dilemma for Nebraska law enforcement officials. The Iraqis . . . had no intention of violating the law. Nevertheless their traditional marriage practices did violate some strongly held American values and some strongly sanctioned laws. Many Americans want to be sensitive to the cultural pluralism. . . . At the same time, Americans need to be true to their core values of protecting the rights of women and children. Should culture be taken into consideration when dealing with civil and criminal cases, and if so, to what extent? How would you resolve this case if you were serving on the jury?

4

From Ferraro/Andreatta, *Cultural Anthropology: An Applied Perspective*, 2012 Edition. © 2014 Cengage Learning.

Developing an Opening Paragraph

Your opening paragraph should identify your topic, gain the reader's interest, and state your thesis. Here are three strategies for gaining the reader's interest.

- **Set the scene.**

  The great pyramids of Naachtun lie shrouded in the emerald forest of northern Guatemala. They are part of one of the most remote, inaccessible sites in the entire ancient Maya world. . . .

- **Make a shocking statement.**

  For thousands of years, the amazing reality of Maya queens has been literally set in stone and staring us in the face. . . .

- **Start with an interesting story.**

  In 1996 a recent Iraqi refugee was the proud father of two brides in a traditional double wedding ceremony for his two eldest daughters at their home in Nebraska. . . . But for local authorities, it was the scene of a crime.

Creating the Middle Paragraphs

In the middle paragraphs, develop your explanation with the different types of details you gathered and the planning you did.

- Try to include at least two types of details per middle paragraph.
- Provide enough information to make each point clear to the reader.
- Follow the organizational pattern you selected in prewriting, or decide on a different pattern.
- Use transitions to help you move smoothly from one point or detail to the next.

Creating the Closing Paragraph

The closing paragraph should restate the thesis, summarize the main supporting points, or provide a final thought or two about the topic. Here are two strategies to consider.

- **Provide a strong final quotation.**

  "I think it shows that power was a lot more complicated than our models have suggested," concludes Ardren. "And clearly we have a long way to go in understanding the biographies of the most extraordinary women."

- **Pose a thought-provoking question.**

  How would you resolve this case if you were serving on the jury?

Practice ▶ Create your first draft, using your planning and these opening, middle, and closing tips as a guide.

L05 Revising the Writing

Revising your first draft involves adding, deleting, rearranging, and reworking parts of your writing. Revision can begin with a peer review. Sharing your writing at various stages is important, especially when you review and revise a first draft. The feedback that you receive will help you improve and strengthen your essay.

Peer Review Sheet

Essay title: _____

Writer: _____

Reviewer: _____

1. Which part of the essay seems to work best—opening, middle, or closing? Why?

   _____

   _____

2. Which part of the essay needs work—opening, middle, or closing? Why?

   _____

   _____

3. Do the middle paragraphs clearly explain the thesis? How so?

   _____

   _____

4. Do you understand the topic after reading the essay?

   _____

   _____

5. Identify a phrase or two that show the writer's level of interest.

   _____

   _____

Practice Ask a classmate to read your first draft and answer peer review questions about it. Consider the reviewer's suggestions as you revise your first draft. If a classmate asks you to complete a peer review sheet, keep your comments helpful and positive. Then share the sheet with the writer.

Adding Clarifying Details

In some cases, it may not be enough to simply state an idea and expect the reader to understand what you mean. You may need to add details before an idea becomes clear.

Key point: Courage means different things to different people.

Major detail: For my brother it means using the "river swing" on the Black River. *(Not clear enough)*

Minor detail: The platform to swing from is about 30 feet up in a huge oak tree, and the rope to grab onto is attached to an even higher tree. *(Clearer)*

Minor detail: Once you climb up to the platform, you must grab above a knot on the rope. Then, at the call of " Go," you swing way out and let go right at the top of your swing. *(Much clearer)*

Read aloud the unrevised and then the revised version of the following passage. Note how the added minor details make the information clearer.

"Human trafficking" is a difficult term to define. To begin with, human trafficking, migration, and smuggling are distinct but related situations, and incorrect understanding of them could wrongly label people. $\wedge$

For example, Public Law 106-386 forbids the U.S. government from jailing victims of human trafficking. On the other hand, illegal immigration subjects may . . .

Practice Improve your writing using the revising checklist in Figure 9.2 and your partner's comments on the Peer Review Sheet as a guide.

Figure 9.2 Revising Checklist

Ideas

_____ 1. Do I focus on one specific, interesting topic to explain?
_____ 2. Do I state the focus of my essay in a thesis statement?
_____ 3. Do I include different types of details to provide support?
_____ 4. Do I explain each new main idea with enough details?

Organization

_____ 5. Does my essay have effective opening, middle, and closing paragraphs?
_____ 6. Have I arranged the supporting details in an effective pattern?

Voice

_____ 7. Do I sound knowledgeable and interested?

L06 Editing the Writing

The main work of editing is correcting your revised first draft. Errors can distract the reader and take away from the effectiveness of your writing.

Avoiding Fragments

Formal expository writing should use sentences instead of fragments. A sentence has a subject and verb and expresses a complete thought. If a group of words lacks a subject or verb or does not express a complete thought, it is a fragment. To fix a fragment, supply the part that it is missing.

Fragments	Sentences
One Maya queen (lacks verb)	One Maya queen **fought eight battles**.
Excavated nearby (lacks subject)	**Reese-Taylor** excavated nearby.
In the past (lacks subject and verb)	In the past, **female rulers were forgotten**.
When she arrived (incomplete thought)	When she arrived, **Kathryn saw the stelae**.
Who became rulers (incomplete thought)	**She sought women** who became rulers.

Practice For each fragment below, use your imagination to supply what is missing (subject, verb, or complete thought).

1. The ruling dynasties of the Maya world

2. Interpreted the clothing style on different stelae

3. On the west side of the pyramid

4. Who dressed more modestly than their male counterparts

5. When archaeologists examined other, similar stelae

6. In the early hours, with mist suffusing the forest

7. Due to the work of Reese-Taylor

8. A new view of the role of women in ancient Maya society

9. Because archaeologists expected Maya rulers to be male

10. Provided solid evidence of Maya warrior queens

Practice Read your writing, watching for fragments. Add a subject, verb, or something else to complete the thought to any fragments you discover to make them into complete sentences.

Avoiding Run-Ons and Comma Splices

When two sentences are short and express related ideas, you may want to combine them into a compound sentence. Place a comma after the first sentence, and use a coordinating conjunction (*and, but, or, nor, for, so, yet*) to connect it to the second sentence.

Two Sentences	Compound Sentence
Rob phoned Bill. Jean called Clare.	Rob phoned Bill, **and** Jean called Clare.
I swim. Lorna jogs.	I swim, **but** Lorna jogs.
I packed a lunch. We went out to eat.	I packed a lunch, **yet** we went out to eat.

Two sentences joined without a comma or coordinating conjunction form a run-on sentence, which is an error. Two sentences joined with just a comma and no coordinating conjunction form a comma splice, another kind of error. To fix them, use both a comma and a coordinating conjunction to join two sentences.

Run-On Sentence	Corrected Sentence
Jana played sax I played piano.	Jana played sax, **and** I played piano.

Comma Splice	Corrected Sentence
A storm is coming, let's load the van.	A storm is coming, **so** let's load the van.

Practice Correct each run-on, comma splice, or comma error by inserting what is missing.

1. Each culture has marriage customs, often they conflict with each other.
2. Western cultures prize romantic love eastern cultures prize family bonds.
3. Romance does not guarantee compatibility but neither do arranged marriages.
4. Any marriage requires trust and cooperation love grows and changes over time.
5. In many cultures, husbands are dominant, in many marriages, wives actually are.
6. Both members can't be in charge of everything spouses have to split up duties.
7. Money problems create many stresses, couples must agree about spending.
8. Abuse is never acceptable in relationships abuse can take many forms.
9. Marriage balances partnership and attraction the two people must be a team.
10. Customs seek to control relationships in the end it's up to the people in them.

Practice Reread your essay, making sure all compound sentences are correctly formed.

Marking an Essay

Edit the following model before you edit a revised version of your own essay.

Practice ▶ Carefully read the following essay, looking for the problems listed in Figure 9.3. Correct the model using the marks listed here. The first correction has been done for you.

Trafficking in Slaves

At some point, most nations histories include periods of either being enslaved   *1*
or enslaving others. Unfortunately, the condition continue today. In fact, different
types of slavery exist today in developing countries as well as in prosperous
countrys such as the United States. Current trends show that human trafficking or
slavery is a very complex problem. With few realistic options for ending it.

"Human trafficking" is a difficult term to define. To begin with, human   *2*
trafficking, migration, and smuggling are distinct but related situations, and
an incorrect understanding of them could wrongly labal people. For example,
Public Law 106-386 forbids the U.S. government from jailing victims of human
trafficking, illegal immigration subjects many people to criminal charges and
possible deportation. Smuggling, the illegal transport of people into a country, is
also considered a matter of immigration rather than human trafficking.

Human trafficking is different it abuses the victims and forces them to   *3*
travel or work against there will. With this idea in mind. The United Nations
Convention Against Transnational Organized Crime has developed this
definition of human trafficking: "The recruitment, transportation, transfer,
harbouring, or receipt of persons, by means of the threat or use of force or having
control over another person for the purpose of exploitation." under this definition,
smuggling can become trafficking if a smuggler's actions include any means of
force or threats.

Due to globalization, there's probably no illegal activity more serious than   *4*
human trafficking. Because of human trafficking in today's world. Millions of
people experience multiple forms of slavery, from sexual slavery to debt slavery.

Correction Marks

ᗐ delete	⋏ add comma	ᵂᵒʳᵈ⋀ add word
ḏ capitalize	? ⋀ add question mark	⊙ add period
⌀ lowercase	⌄ insert an apostrophe	◯ spelling
⋀ insert		⊓ switch

Using an Editing Checklist

Now it's time to correct your own expository essay.

Practice ▷ Prepare a clean copy of your revised essay, and then use the checklist in Figure 9.3 to look for errors. Continue working until you can check off each item in the list.

Figure 9.3 Editing Checklist

Words

_____ 1. Have I used specific nouns and verbs?
_____ 2. Have I used more action verbs than "be" verbs?
_____ 3. Have I used signal words to help my reader follow the ideas?

Sentences

_____ 4. Have I used sentences with varying beginnings and lengths?
_____ 5. Have I avoided improper shifts in sentences?
_____ 6. Have I avoided fragments, run-ons, and comma splices?

Conventions

_____ 7. Do I use correct verb forms (*he saw*, not *he seen*)?
_____ 8. Do my subjects and verbs agree (*she speaks*, not *she speak*)?
_____ 9. Have I used the right words (*their, there, they're*)?
_____10. Have I capitalized first words and proper nouns and adjectives?
_____11. Have I used commas after long introductory word groups and to separate items in a series?
_____12. Have I correctly punctuated any dialogue?
_____13. Have I used apostrophes correctly in contractions and to show possession?

Adding a Title

Make sure to add an attention-getting title. Here are three strategies to try.

- Highlight the thesis:
   - The Power and Glory of the Maya Queens

- Think creatively:
   - Hypnosis—Look into My Eyes

- Make a dramatic pronouncement:
   - Trafficking in Slaves

"He who looks outside, dreams; he who looks within, awakens."

—Carl Jung

☑ Reading for Enrichment

The following selection, "Hypnosis—Look into My Eyes" comes from a psychology textbook entitled *Psychology: A Journey*. Read the selection, following the steps in the reading process. Afterward, you'll find a number of writing ideas for creating an expository essay related to the reading.

About the Authors

Dennis Coon teaches, writes, edits, and consults in Tucson, where he earned a doctorate in psychology from the University of Arizona. Previously, he spent 22 years teaching introductory psychology at Santa Barbara City College. Dr. Coon enjoys hiking, photography, painting, woodworking, and music, including designing, building, and playing guitars. **John O. Mitterer** teaches at Brock University, St. Catherines, Ontario. He focuses on how psychology relates to learning. He teaches introductory psychology classes and consults with numerous companies. An avid birder, Dr. Mitterer has traveled to the Galapagos Islands, Papua New Guinea, Brazil, Australia, and South Africa in hopes of spotting every species of bird during his lifetime.

Prereading

The selection you are about to read discusses hypnotism. Activate your prior knowledge about this topic by thinking about each of these terms, which you will encounter as you read.

1. **Hypnosis**

2. **Consciousness**

3. **Sensation**

What do you think?

How does Carl Jung's quotation relate to hypnosis?

Before you read, answer these questions:

1. What do the title, opening, and headings tell you about the topic of the reading?

   _____

2. What uses of hypnosis are familiar to you?

   _____

3. What questions do you have about the topic?

   _____

Reading and Rereading

The authors of this selection focus on the history of hypnosis, theories about how it works, and the realities of the practice. As you read, (1) identify just what hypnosis is; (2) note the types of information in each part; and (3) reread to aid understanding. Focus first on ideas—the thesis (main idea), supporting points, and details that explain it. Then consider organization—the way that the opening, middle, and closing parts are constructed. Annotate the text and take notes.

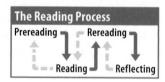

Hypnosis—Look into My Eyes

"Your body is becoming heavy. You can barely keep your eyes   1
open. You are so tired you can't move. Relax. Let go. Relax. Close
your eyes and relax." These are the last words a textbook should ever
say to you, and the first a hypnotist might say.

Interest in hypnosis began in the 1700s with Austrian doctor   2
Franz Mesmer, whose name gave us the term *mesmerize* (to
hypnotize). Mesmer believed he could cure disease with magnets.
Mesmer's strange "treatments" are related to hypnosis because
they actually relied on the power of suggestion, not magnetism
(Waterfield, 2002). For a time, Mesmer enjoyed quite a following. In
the end, however, his theories of "animal magnetism" were rejected,
and he was branded a fraud.

The term *hypnosis* was later coined by English surgeon James   3
Braid. The Greek word *hypno* means "sleep," and Braid used it to

describe the hypnotic state. Today we know that hypnosis is *not* sleep. Confusion about this point remains because some hypnotists give the suggestion, "Sleep, sleep." However, **EEG** patterns recorded during hypnosis are different from those observed when a person is asleep or pretending to be hypnotized (Barabasz, 2000).

Theories of Hypnosis

If hypnosis isn't sleep, then what is it? That's a good question. 4
Hypnosis is often defined as an altered state of **consciousness**, characterized by narrowed attention and an increased openness to suggestion (Kallio & Revonsuo, 2003; Kosslyn et al., 2000). Notice that this definition assumes that hypnosis is a distinct state of consciousness.

The best-known *state theory* of hypnosis was proposed by Ernest 5
Hilgard (1904–2001), who argued that hypnosis causes a *dissociative state*, or "split" in awareness. To illustrate, he asked hypnotized subjects to plunge one hand into a painful bath of ice water. Subjects told to feel no pain said they felt none. The same subjects were then asked if there was any part of their mind that did feel pain. With their free hand, many wrote, "It hurts," or "Stop it, you're hurting me," while they continued to act pain free (Hilgard, 1977, 1994). Thus, one part of the hypnotized person says there is no pain and acts as if there is none. Another part, which Hilgard calls the hidden observer, is aware of the pain but remains in the background. The *hidden observer* is a detached part of the hypnotized person's awareness that silently observes events.

In contrast, *nonstate theorists* argue that hypnosis is not a 6
distinct state at all. Instead it is merely a blend of **conformity**, relaxation, imagination, obedience, and role-playing (Kirsch, 2005). For example, many theorists believe that all hypnosis is really self-hypnosis (autosuggestion). From this perspective, a hypnotist merely helps another person to follow a series of suggestions. These suggestions, in turn, alter sensations, perceptions, thoughts, feelings,

and behaviors (Lynn & Kirsch, 2006).

Regardless of which theoretical approach finally prevails, both   7
views suggest that hypnosis can be explained by normal principles. It
is not mysterious or "magical," despite what stage hypnotists might
have you think.

The Reality of Hypnosis

How is hypnosis done? Could I be hypnotized against my   8
will? Hypnotists use many different methods. Still, all techniques
encourage a person (1) to focus attention on what is being said, (2) to
relax and feel tired, (3) to "let go" and accept suggestions easily, and
(4) to use vivid imagination (Druckman & Njork, 1994). Basically,
you must cooperate to become hypnotized.

What does it feel like to be hypnotized? You might be surprised   9
at some of your actions during hypnosis. You also might have mild
feelings of floating, sinking, **anesthesia**, or separation from your
body. Personal experiences vary widely. A key element in hypnosis
is the basic suggestion effect (a tendency of hypnotized persons to
carry out suggested actions as if they were involuntary). Hypnotized
persons feel like their actions and experiences are automatic—they
seem to happen without effort. Here is how one person described his
hypnotic session:

I felt **lethargic**, my eyes going out of focus and wanting to close.   10
My hands felt real light. . . . I felt I was sinking deeper into the chair.
. . . I felt like I wanted to relax more and more. . . . My responses were
more automatic. I didn't have to wish to do things so much or want
to do them. . . . I just did them. . . . I felt floating. . . . very close to
sleep (Hilgard, 1968).

Contrary to the way hypnosis is portrayed in movies,   11
hypnotized people generally remain in control of their behavior and
aware of what is going on. For instance, most people will not act out
hypnotic suggestions that they consider immoral or repulsive (such
as disrobing in public or harming someone) (Kirsch & Lynn, 1995).

Hypnotic Susceptibility

Can everyone be hypnotized? About 8 people out of 10 can be   *12*
hypnotized, but only 4 out of 10 will be good hypnotic subjects.
People who are imaginative and prone to fantasy are often highly
responsive to hypnosis (Kallio & Revonsuo, 2003). But people who
lack these traits may also be hypnotized. If you are willing to be
hypnotized, chances are good that you could be. Hypnosis depends
more on the efforts and abilities of the hypnotized person than
the skills of the hypnotist. But make no mistake, people who are
hypnotized are not merely faking their responses.

Hypnotic susceptibility refers to how easily a person can   *13*
become hypnotized. It is measured by giving a series of suggestions
and counting the number of times a person responds. A typical
hypnotic test is the Stanford Hypnotic Susceptibility Scale. In the
test, various suggestions are made, and the person's response is
noted. For instance, you might be told that your left arm is becoming
more and more rigid and that it will not bend. If you can't bend your
arm during the next 10 seconds, you have shown susceptibility to
hypnotic suggestions.

Effects of Hypnosis

What can (and cannot) be achieved with hypnosis? Many   *14*
abilities have been tested during hypnosis, leading to the following
conclusions (Burgess & Kirsch, 1999; Chaves, 2000):

1. **Superhuman acts of strength.** Hypnosis has no more effect   *15*
   on physical strength than instructions that encourage a
   person to make his or her best effort.

2. **Memory.** There is some evidence that hypnosis can enhance   *16*
   memory (Wagstaff et al., 2004). However, it frequently
   increases the number of false memories as well. For this
   reason, many states now bar persons from testifying in court
   if they were hypnotized to improve their memory of a crime
   they witnessed.

3. **Amnesia.** A person told not to remember something heard   17
during hypnosis may claim not to remember. In some
instances, this may be nothing more than a deliberate
attempt to avoid thinking about specific ideas. However,
brief memory loss of this type actually does seem to occur
(Barnier, McConkey, & Wright, 2004).

4. **Pain relief.** Hypnosis can relieve pain (Keefe, Abernethy, &   18
Campbell, 2005). It can be especially useful when chemical
painkillers are ineffective. For instance, hypnosis can reduce
phantom limb pain (Oakley, Whitman, & Halligan, 2002).

5. **Age regression.** Given the proper suggestions, some   19
hypnotized people appear to "regress" to childhood.
However, most theorists now believe that "age-regressed"
subjects are only acting out a suggested role.

6. **Sensory changes.** Hypnotic suggestions concerning   20
sensations are among the most effective. Given the proper
instructions, a person can be made to smell a bottle of
ammonia and respond as if it were a wonderful perfume.
It is also possible to alter color vision, hearing sensitivity,
time sense, perception of illusions, and many other sensory
responses.

Hypnosis is a valuable tool. It can help people relax, feel less   21
pain, and make better progress in therapy (Chapman, 2006).
Generally, hypnosis is more successful at changing **subjective**
experience than it is at modifying behaviors such as smoking or
overeating.   From Coon/Mitterer, *Psychology: A Journey*, 4e. © 2011 Cengage Learning.

EEG
electroencephalogram, a device
that measures brain waves

consciousness
awareness; sensation, emotion, and
thought

conformity
tendency to obey authority

anesthesia
inability to sense, especially pain,
pressure, and temperature

lethargic
sluggish, lacking energy

superhuman
beyond normal human ability

subjective
personal; perceived rather than
objective reality

Summarizing

Write a summary of "Hypnosis—Look into My Eyes." Remember th
presents the main points in a clear, concise form using your own words.

Reflecting

1. How does the essay begin?

   With a quote~~on~~

2. What is the main idea of the selection? Is it directly stated or implied?

   Hypnosis → Directly stated.

3. How is the selection organized? (Circle one.)
   (chronologically)   spatially   comparison-contrast   logically

4. What is the state theory of hypnosis discussed in paragraph 5?

   Hypnosis causes a dissociative
   state, or "split" in awareness.

5. What is the nonstate theory of hypnosis discussed in paragraph 6?

   Hypnosis is not a distinct
   state at all.

6 What is the purpose of the numbered list near the end of the selection?

   Effects of Hypnosis

Vocabulary

Create vocabulary entries for these terms. For each term, identify the pronunciation and
helpful word parts (see Appendix D), give a primary definition, and use the word in a sentence.

1. **animal magnetism**   (paragraph 2)   3. **involuntary**   (paragraph 9)
2. **dissociative**   (paragraph 5)   4. **phantom limb pain**   (paragraph 18)

Critical Thinking

- How has reading this text changed your perspective of hypnosis?
- In what other application could hypnosis be helpful? How so? In what other
  applications could it be harmful? Explain.

Writing for Enrichment

Choose one of the following writing ideas, or decide upon an idea of your own related to the reading.

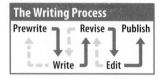

1. Explore the causes and effects of a hypnotic state.
2. Explain the use of hypnosis in health and medicine.
3. Compare hypnosis to meditation.
4. Provide step-by-step instructions for putting someone in a hypnotic state.
5. Report on the latest research on techniques for improving memory.

When planning . . .

- Start with a general subject that interests you.
- Establish a thesis for your essay.
- Gather a variety of details from a variety of sources.
- Decide how you would like to organize the details in your writing.

When writing . . .

- Pay attention to each part of your essay—opening, middle, and closing.
- Use major and minor details to make your ideas clear.

When revising and editing . . .

- Determine if your essay answers key questions readers have about your topic.
- Be prepared to do some additional research if necessary.
- Edit your revised writing for style and correctness.

Reflecting on Expository Writing

Answer the following questions about your expository reading and writing experiences.

1. What is the purpose of expository writing?
2. What value does expository writing have for the reader?
3. Which reading strategy in this chapter seems the most helpful? Explain.
4. Why is it important to use a variety of details in expository texts?
5. What do you like best about your expository essay?
6. What is one thing you would like to change in your essay?

Chapter

10

> "Nothing is as frustrating as arguing with someone who knows what he's talking about."
>
> —Sam Ewing

Reading and Writing Arguments

One definition of *argument* is "a quarrel or dispute," as when a brother and a sister engage in a shouting match with heated words. Another definition of *argument* is "a discussion aimed at demonstrating truth or falsehood." Levelheadedness is important in this type of argument.

This chapter focuses on reasonable arguments that let the facts speak for themselves. A well-crafted argumentative essay informs and explains. It prompts logical thinking rather than emotion, guiding the reader toward informed conclusions about important, sometimes controversial issues.

In this chapter, you will learn about the working parts of argumentation and the importance of analyzing arguments for their logic and completeness. Then you will write an argumentative essay of your own.

Learning Outcomes

LO1 Understand argumentation.

LO2 Read and respond to arguments.

LO3 Plan an argument essay.

LO4 Write the first draft.

LO5 Revise the writing.

LO6 Edit the writing.

What do you think?

According to the quotation, what can lead to frustration? Do you agree with Sam Ewing? Why or why not?

L01   Understanding Argumentation

In ancient Greece and Rome, anyone lucky enough to receive an education was trained in argumentation. The belief was (and still is) that those who develop argumentative skills become clear thinkers and leaders. Believe it or not, the basic structure used to build arguments in those ancient civilizations is still used today.

An argument is only as good as the thoughts and ideas that go into it. A strong argument develops a logical or reasonable claim (the thesis) with solid evidence (the details). It acknowledges important opposing points of view and either counters (disputes) them or concedes (admits) their value. And overall, an argument provides a meaningful and logical examination of an issue. Arguments, of course, are made about issues on which people have differing points of view. There's nothing to argue about if everyone agrees on something.

Arguments are weakened by logical fallacies or false statements. These appear unintentionally in quickly fashioned persuasive texts or intentionally in manipulative arguments, such as advertisements: "Temptrol is the best cold medicine in the world!" or "One call to my law office will take care of all of your bankruptcy problems!"

You'll encounter argumentation in each of the following forms of writing.

Editorial   An editorial is an opinion piece seeking to sway readers to its point of view on a currently debated topic. Historically, editorials have often been written by editors of newspapers or magazines. You may even find them listed under the heading "Opinions" in those periodicals.

> You've seen the anti-vaccine slogans: "If you mixed mercury, aluminum phosphate, ammonium sulfate, and formaldehyde with viruses, then got a syringe and injected it into your child, you would be arrested and sent to jail for child endangerment and abuse. Then why is it legal for a doctor to do it?"   1
>
> Have you seen these parody slogans? "If you burst into the bedroom of children you didn't know while wielding an axe, then forcibly carried them away, you would be arrested. So why are firefighters allowed to do it?" "If you packed scores of people into a pressurized metal tube, then used refined kerosene to launch them 35,000 feet into the air, you would be arrested. So why are airlines allowed to do it?" Endless variations are possible.   2
>
> The point is clear. The anti-vaccine movement is alarmist, ill-informed, and downright silly. It has been with us ever since Jonas Salk invented the first polio vaccine—you know, the one that virtually wiped polio off the face of the planet. Yet today it makes less sense than ever before. . . .   3

Personal Commentary Like editorials, personal commentaries are opinion pieces. But while editorials are officially sanctioned by the editorial staff of a periodical and are usually actually written by those editors, a personal commentary may appear nearly anywhere, from blogs to book prefaces to professional essays. Similarly, while editorials tend to discuss current events, personal commentaries may deal with nearly any topic.

> We live in a time of chaos and uncertainty. Every day we are bombarded with news of strife and tragedy somewhere in the world. Stories of terrorist strikes and military counterstrikes are commonplace. At times it appears the world is coming apart at the seams. This is when the lessons of history become essential. By comparing conflict and crime in the world today with that of earlier times, we see a pattern emerging. It is a pattern of progress and of hope. . . .

Problem-Solution Essay A problem-solution essay is a particular type of argument that seeks to explain a problem and provide a convincing solution or set of solutions for it. This sort of essay involves argumentation in that the writer seeks to convince the reader to take a particular course of action. In explaining the problem, it may also need to persuade the reader concerning specific causes.

> Texting while driving is undeniably dangerous. Studies have shown that this distraction is every bit as much an impairment as driving while intoxicated. Yet people are tempted to respond whenever their cell phone gives an alert. *1*
>
> Given how "smart" phones are now, one solution is to make them incapable of texting while moving at driving speeds. A phone's GPS could simply freeze its texting apps, perhaps except when use is voice activated and hands free. . . . *2*

Position Paper Many college courses, especially those in the humanities—from literary criticism to history to philosophy—ask students to write position papers on a regular basis. The purpose of these essays (often about two pages in length) is to demonstrate a student's thoughts about the material being covered in class or readings related to it.

> Some critics complain that *Crime and Punishment*'s epilogue doesn't fit the rest of the novel. They claim that it just continues to dwell on Raskolnikov's moral confusion, which has already been thoroughly treated in the story. Others complain about the sudden change of direction in the final paragraph, as if Dostoevsky planned to write a sequel but never lived to do so. *1*
>
> My own feeling is that this ending is perfectly suited to the novel. It gives meaning to the mental suffering throughout by offering a hint of better things to come. It shows that Sofia's faithfulness is infectious. And it does so without stooping to a "fairy-tale" ending. . . . *2*

Analyzing Parts of an Argument

Essays of argumentation are meant to convince readers to accept a point of view or rethink their opinion about something. Critical reading of these texts is necessary for making informed decisions about whether to accept or dismiss the writer's position.

To critically examine an argument, you need to recognize its basic parts. Analyzing the parts and their functions will help you trace the author's logic.

- **Main claim:** The main claim (or thesis) generally appears early in the essay, usually in one of the first paragraphs, after background information about the topic. A claim presents a viewpoint about the topic that cannot be directly proven true like a fact can be. However, a claim can be strengthened by evidence:

  > Laws should be enacted to reduce our dependence on nitrogen-based fertilizers and detergents.

- **Supporting claims (reasons):** A supporting claim is a statement that provides a reason for accepting the main claim. Body paragraphs in essays of argumentation often begin with a new supporting claim. Each claim is then supported with evidence.

  > Nitrogen runoff in our waterways leads to algal blooms and red tides, blocking sunlight to other water plants and staining our shorelines.

- **Evidence:** A claim succeeds or fails based on its supporting evidence. The evidence in a strong argument can be checked, backed up, and relied upon. Common types of evidence include the following:

  - **Facts and statistics:** According to a 2011 study by the DNR, a murky bottom predicts an algae cover greater than 80 percent.
  - **Examples:** Lake Erie experienced an unusually high buildup of algae in 2014.
  - **Expert testimony:** Sarah Follet, a water resource official, stated, "There are . . ."

- **Counterarguments:** A strong argument addresses opposing points of view, either conceding or countering them. A concession admits the value of an opposing point. A counter shows why the opposing point lacks value. Opposing points of view may be introduced with words or phrases such as *admittedly, granted, it is true that, I accept that,* and *no doubt.*

  - **Opposing point of view:** It is true that the appearance of the algae is limited to late summer, and according to some people, it occurs only if the weather is very still and hot.
  - **Counter:** In saying this, people are simply ignoring the problem. The algae will still be there regardless of the weather, just waiting to bloom.
  - **Concession:** Fixing the algae problem is admittedly a pricey endeavor.

- **Call to action:** Many arguments end by requesting that the reader respond to the argument by thinking or acting in a certain way.

  > We must demand that our elected officials address this troublesome side effect of nitrogen-based fertilizers and detergents.

Analyzing Logic

The relative strength of an argument depends on its logic. Logic is the science of reasonable and accurate thinking. An argument is logical if it contains relevant and provable evidence to support a reasonable claim.

Reliable and Logical Evidence

Different types of evidence provide different types of support for an argument. The best evidence is fact based, meaning it is provable. Conversely, opinions, which are personally held tastes or attitudes, are not provable and are not reliable forms of evidence.

- **Fact:** Nuclear power is a nonrenewable energy source. *(You can check this statement for accuracy.)*
- **Opinion:** I think nuclear power is unsafe. (*This simply offers a personal feeling.*)

For an essay that argues "Nuclear power is not an appropriate source of energy," the following types of evidence would be provable:

- **Observation:** Ugly nuclear reactors litter the countryside in Europe.
- **Quotation:** Former Japan Prime Minister Naoto Kan says, "Nuclear arms and atomic power represent a technology in which coexistence with man is extremely difficult."
- **Statistic:** The explosion of the nuclear reactor at the Chernobyl Nuclear Power Plant in Ukraine exposed more than 600,000 people to the effects of radiation poisoning.
- **Comparison:** Using fossil fuels for energy is much less expensive than uranium.
- **Explanation:** The World Nuclear Association points out that although the Fukushima Daiichi nuclear accident caused no deaths or sickness from radiation, more than 100,000 people had to be evacuated from their homes, and 1,000 people died as a result of the evacuation.
- **Inference:** Scientific discovery, such as nuclear fission, can have unintended consequences for mankind.

The quantity of evidence used is not the only factor that makes an argument logical. The quality and variety of the evidence are similarly important factors. When analyzing the supporting evidence for an argument, make sure the evidence is:

- **Accurate:** Do most experts agree on the information? Is it up to date?
- **Complete:** Does the evidence tell the "whole story"? Or do some legitimate counterarguments seem to be ignored?
- **Relevant:** Is all evidence related to the main argument?

Faulty Logic

A logical fallacy is a faulty or false statement that weakens an argument by distorting an issue, drawing a false conclusion, misusing evidence, or misusing language. Avoid logical fallacies in your own writing, and be aware of them while reading argumentative texts.

Common Logical Fallacies

- **Exaggerating the Facts:** This fallacy distorts facts in order to make an extreme claim in favor of an argument.

  > Eating chocolate can cause all kinds of diseases, even if you eat only one or two pieces a day.

- **Offering Extremes:** This fallacy offers extreme or outlandish consequences for not acting a certain way.

  > Either people should give up chocolate, or we are going to face incredible increases in heath-care costs.

- **Half Truths:** A half truth contains part but not the whole truth. It fails to tell "the whole story," making it both true and false simultaneously.

  > The increase in tuition is a good idea because it will lower taxes for county residents. (But the increase might hurt low-income residents.)

- **Appealing to Popular Position:** Also known as "bandwagoning," this fallacy argues for something on the basis that many other people like it.

  > The new tuition increase is a good idea because it passed unanimously at the last board meeting.

- **Straw Man:** This logical fallacy distorts an issue by exaggerating or misinterpreting an opponent's position.

  > Those who consider themselves caring people cannot approve of the death penalty.

- **Broad Generalization:** This logical fallacy makes an all-or-nothing claim based on little evidence. The claim will often include an intensifier, such as *all, every,* or *never.*

  > All professional athletes will cheat if that is the only way they can maintain their competitive edge.

- **Impressing with Numbers:** In this case, a writer attempts to overwhelm the reader with a deluge of statistics, some of which may be unrelated to the issue at hand.

  > At 35 ppm, CO levels factory-wide are an insignificant 10 ppm above the OSHA guideline of 25 ppm. This "pollution" pales in comparison to such things as "noise pollution" in other industries, where a dBA as high as 115 is allowed.

- **Red Herring:** This fallacy presents an observation or detail to distract the reader from the actual claim.

  > Although the student parking problem is real, and the proposed solutions seem valid, we already have a full agenda of other topics to discuss.

- **Ad Populum:** This fallacy appeals to the reader's emotions instead of to logic.

  > The fashion industry is essentially corrupt. Hugo Boss designed Nazi uniforms.

L02   Reading and Responding to Arguments

Reading arguments requires a close examination of the main claim, supporting claims, and evidence.

Using a Line Diagram

You can use a line diagram to trace the key parts of an author's argument. Fill in the top of the diagram with the main claim. Fill in the second level of branches with the supporting claims. Fill in the bottom levels of branches with evidence used to strengthen each supporting claim. **Figure 10.1** shows the key parts of Ronald Reagan's "Remarks at the Brandenburg Gate."

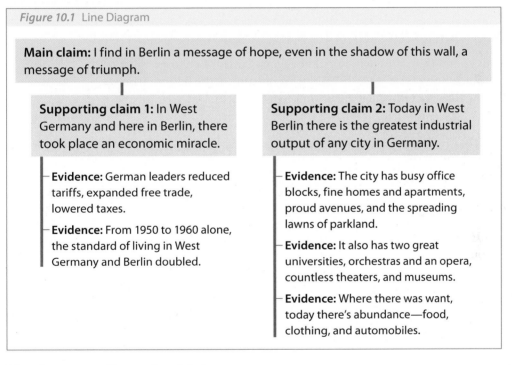

Figure 10.1 Line Diagram

Main claim: I find in Berlin a message of hope, even in the shadow of this wall, a message of triumph.

Supporting claim 1: In West Germany and here in Berlin, there took place an economic miracle.

Evidence: German leaders reduced tariffs, expanded free trade, lowered taxes.

Evidence: From 1950 to 1960 alone, the standard of living in West Germany and Berlin doubled.

Supporting claim 2: Today in West Berlin there is the greatest industrial output of any city in Germany.

Evidence: The city has busy office blocks, fine homes and apartments, proud avenues, and the spreading lawns of parkland.

Evidence: It also has two great universities, orchestras and an opera, countless theaters, and museums.

Evidence: Where there was want, today there's abundance—food, clothing, and automobiles.

Understanding the Voice

Voice refers to the author's writing personality and attitude toward the topic and the reader. Use these questions as a guide for judging voice in an argument.

- Does the author seem honest and sincere?
- Does he or she make a realistic claim?
- Does he or she seem respectful and understanding?
- Does he or she focus on issues rather than personalities?
- Does the author engage the reader, rather that lecture him or her?

Understanding Bias

Sometimes a writer's strong feelings about a topic can result in argumentation that is not balanced. Beware "catch phrases" that appeal to emotion instead of logic, and watch for ignored counterarguments. Both indicate an argument that is not well thought out, as demonstrated in the following example.

> Clearly, marijuana needs to be legalized. Marijuana relieves stress and anxiety and has been known to prevent Alzheimer's disease and glaucoma. It's obvious that marijuana is not any more addictive than alcohol and is less dangerous than other drugs.

Words and phrases like "clearly" and "it's obvious that" appeal to emotion, and the argument fails to fully address any legitimate counterarguments about the risks of marijuana.

Reading and Reacting to a Professional Argument

This comes from President Ronald Reagan's famed "Remarks at the Brandenburg Gate" speech, calling for opening of the Berlin Wall. Note how the individual parts work together.

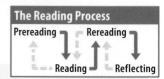

About the Author

Ronald Reagan was the 40th president of the United States, serving two terms from 1981–1989. Originally a Hollywood actor, he served as president of the Screen Actors Guild, where he was drawn into disputes about Communism in the industry. His political views shifted from liberal to conservative, and he was elected governor of California for two terms before running for the U.S. presidency. In that office, he focused upon reducing the role of government in public affairs and improving public confidence in citizen efforts.

Before you read, answer these questions:

1. What do the title, the first few paragraphs, and the final few paragraphs tell you about the text?

   _____

2. What is your position related to the topic?

   _____

3. What do you expect to learn?

   _____

As you read, (1) identify the author's main claim, (2) follow his reasoning and argument, and (3) reread any parts as needed. Annotate the text and take notes using a line diagram.

Remarks at the Brandenburg Gate

I find in Berlin a message of hope, even in the shadow of this wall, a message of triumph.

In this season of spring in 1945, the people of Berlin emerged from their air-raid shelters to find devastation. Thousands of miles away, the people of the United States reached out to help. And in 1947 Secretary of State—as you've been told—George Marshall announced the creation of what would become known as the Marshall Plan. Speaking precisely 40 years ago this month, he said: "Our policy is directed not against any country or doctrine, but against hunger, poverty, desperation, and chaos."

In the Reichstag a few moments ago, I saw a display commemorating this 40th anniversary of the Marshall Plan. I was struck by a sign—the sign on a burnt-out, gutted structure that was being rebuilt. I understand that Berliners of my own generation can remember seeing signs like it dotted throughout the western sectors of the city. The sign read simply: "The Marshall Plan is helping here to strengthen the free world." A strong, free world in the West—that dream became real. Japan rose from ruin to become an economic giant. Italy, France, Belgium—virtually every nation in Western Europe saw political and economic rebirth; the European Community was founded.

In West Germany and here in Berlin, there took place an economic miracle, the Wirtschaftswunder. Adenauer, Erhard, Reuter, and other leaders understood the practical importance of liberty—that just as truth can flourish only when the journalist is given freedom of speech, so prosperity can come about only when the farmer and businessman enjoy economic freedom. The German leaders—the German leaders reduced tariffs, expanded free trade, lowered taxes. From 1950 to 1960 alone, the standard of living in West Germany and Berlin doubled.

Where four decades ago there was rubble, today in West Berlin   5 there is the greatest industrial output of any city in Germany: busy office blocks, fine homes and apartments, proud avenues, and the spreading lawns of parkland. Where a city's culture seemed to have been destroyed, today there are two great universities, orchestras and an opera, countless theaters, and museums. Where there was want, today there's abundance—food, clothing, automobiles—the wonderful goods of the **Kudamm**. From devastation, from utter ruin, you Berliners have, in freedom, rebuilt a city that once again ranks as one of the greatest on earth. Now, the Soviets may have had other plans. But, my friends, there were a few things the Soviets didn't count on: *Berliner Herz, Berliner Humor, ja, und Berliner Schnauze* [Berliner heart, Berliner humor, yes, and a Berliner snout].

In the 1950s—In the 1950s Khrushchev predicted: "We will bury   6 you."

But in the West today, we see a free world that has achieved   7 a level of prosperity and well-being unprecedented in all human history. In the Communist world, we see failure, technological backwardness, declining standards of health, even want of the most basic kind—too little food. Even today, the Soviet Union still cannot feed itself. After these four decades, then, there stands before the entire world one great and inescapable conclusion: Freedom leads to prosperity. Freedom replaces the ancient hatreds among the nations with **comity** and peace. Freedom is the victor.

And now—now the Soviets themselves may, in a limited way,   8 be coming to understand the importance of freedom. We hear much from Moscow about a new policy of reform and openness. Some political prisoners have been released. Certain foreign news broadcasts are no longer being jammed. Some economic enterprises have been permitted to operate with greater freedom from state control.

Are these the beginnings of profound changes in the Soviet   *9*
state? Or are they token gestures intended to raise false hopes in the West or to strengthen the Soviet system without changing it? We welcome change and openness, for we believe that freedom and security go together, that the advance of human liberty—the advance of human liberty can only strengthen the cause of world peace.

There is one sign the Soviets can make that would be   *10*
unmistakable, that would advance dramatically the cause of freedom and peace.

General Secretary **Gorbachev**, if you seek peace, if you seek   *11*
prosperity for the Soviet Union and Eastern Europe, if you seek liberalization: Come here to this gate.

Mr. Gorbachev, open this gate.   *12*

Marshall Plan
American aid program to help European economies recovery from World War II

Kudamm
shopping district in Berlin

comity
courtesy and cooperation for mutual benefit

Mikhail Gorbachev
then the general secretary of the Soviet Union

Summarizing

Write a summary of "Remarks at the Brandenburg Gate." Remember that a summary presents the main points in a clear, concise form using your own words.

Reflecting

1. Review the line diagram in **Figure 10.1**. In the essay, locate the main claim, supporting claims, and evidence from that line diagram.

2. What, if any, opposing points of view does the author address? Does he counter or concede them?

   _____

   _____

3. Consider the "inescapable conclusion" of paragraph 7. In what way does this qualify as a logical fallacy?

   _____

   _____

4. What other logical fallacies can you find in the argument?

   _____

   _____

5. Overall, how would you evaluate the validity of this argument? Why?

   _____

   _____

Vocabulary

Create vocabulary entries for these words. For each word, identify the pronunciation and helpful word parts, give a primary definition, and use the word in a sentence.

   1. **commemorating** (paragraph 3)   2. **abundance** (paragraph 5)

Critical Thinking

- Why is it important to analyze the parts of an argument in political speeches and rhetoric?
- How would listening to this speech differ from reading it? Would the argument be more or less convincing?
- What do you know about Germany today? How does it compare to the Germany described in Reagan's famous speech?

L03 Planning an Argument Essay

Consider a debatable topic that you feel strongly about. It could be about an issue that impacts your school or community. If you can't think of a topic, browse newspapers, magazines, and the Internet for current issues. Choose the one that is important to you.

The Writing Process

Prewrite Revise Publish

Write Edit

Practice List three or four debatable issues you could write about in an essay.

Making a Claim

Once you choose a topic, consider your initial position or opinion about the issue. Create a main claim that you wish to defend. The claim should introduce the topic and express your opinion about it. Use the formula in **Figure 10.2** to create a claim.

Figure 10.2 Main Claim Formula

Specific Topic		**Opinion or Position About It**		**Main Claim**
Federal shield law	**+**	needs to be passed to protect the public's right to information	**=**	Passing a federal shield law is a necessary step to ensure the general public's right to know.

Practice Create your own main claim using the formula as a guide. If necessary, write two or three versions until your claim says what you want it to say.

Specific Topic		**Opinion or Position About It**		**Main Claim**
	+		**=**	

Now develop and refine your main claim so that you are certain you have strong feelings about it. You can do so by:

- Researching different positions on your topic.
- Determine if the most compelling evidence supports or opposes your initial claim.

If necessary, rewrite your statement to reflect your research.

L06 Editing the Writing

The main work of editing is correcting your revised first draft. Because clarity is so important in an essay of argumentation, take special care to avoid ambiguous wording.

Correcting Ambiguous Wording

Ambiguous wording creates uncertainty for the reader. Such wording results in sentences that have multiple possible meanings. Avoid indefinite pronoun references, incomplete comparisons, and unclear wording.

Vague or Indefinite Pronoun Reference

When it is unclear which word or phrase a pronoun refers to, the wording is ambiguous.

Ambiguous: When Mike moved the lamp onto the wobbly chair, it fell on the floor.

Clear: When Mike moved the lamp onto the wobbly chair, the lamp fell on the floor.

Ambiguous: Monica reminded Misha that she needed to buy a new black dress for the party. *(Who needed to buy a black dress—Monica or Misha?)*

Clear: Monica reminded Misha to buy a new black dress for the party.

Practice Rewrite each sentence so that it does not contain any ambiguous pronoun references.

1. When Andy placed the box of macaroni back on the shelf, it tipped over.

   When Andy placed the box of macaroni back on the shelf, the box tipped over.

2. The professor told Tim that he needed to pursue the research opportunity.

   _____

   _____

3. As Brad drove his motorcycle into the garage, it shook.

   _____

   _____

Practice Read your argument essay and watch for indefinite pronoun references. Correct any errors you find.

Incomplete Comparisons

Don't confuse the reader by leaving out a word or words that are necessary to complete a comparison.

> **Ambiguous:** The head chef said the Kobe steak is tastier. *(The Kobe is tastier than what?)*
>
> **Clear:** The head chef said the Kobe steak is tastier **than the porterhouse.**

Unclear Wording

Avoid writing a statement that can have two or more meanings.

> **Ambiguous:** Jill decided to take her sister to a movie, which turned out to be a real bummer. *(It is unclear what was a real bummer—taking her sister to the movie or the movie itself.)*
>
> **Clear:** Jill decided to take her sister to a movie, **but the film turned out to be a real bummer.**

Practice Rewrite each of the following sentences so that it does not contain incomplete comparisons or unclear wording.

1. Going bowling is more fun.

   Going bowling is more fun than video games.

2. I can handle Mel's personality better.

   I can handle Mel's personality better than Tay's.

3. Vera wanted to complete her economics report after reading the latest research, but she didn't.

   _____

   _____

Practice Read your argument essay and watch for incomplete comparisons or unclear wording. If you find any examples, correct them.

Marking an Essay

Before you finish editing your revised essay, practice by editing the following model.

Practice ▸ Read the following argument essay and correct it using the marks shown.

Ban Burmese Pythons

An invasive species are taking the southern tip of Florida by storm. Thousands of Burmese pythons—giant snakes native to southern asia—are thriving in the tropic-like environment of Everglades National Park. Their presence in the park is a product of irresponsible pet owners, who intentionally release the snakes into the wild when they become too difficult to care for. as a result, Florida lawmakers have passed a law making it illigal for individuals to own burmese pythons. In order to protect native wildlife and treasured ecosystems of the southern United States, this law should expand nationally.   1

Reports show some 144,000 pythons have been imported into the United States, many of which end up in homes of irresponsible pet owners. "All of the Burmese pythons that we see in the park are a product of the international pet trade" said Skip Snow, a wildlife biologist at Everglades National Park. The problem is many pet owners doesn't fully understand the responsibility of taking care of a python often the python, which grow to between 10 and 20 feet becomes too big and to expensive to be kept in a home. In the end, the owner releases the pet into the wild.   2

It is in the wild where Burmese pythons is causing havoc. The tropical environment of the Everglades provides perfect conditions for the pythons to breed and feed. With no natural competitor the strong and stealthy python is feeding at will on native Everglades species, Scientists worry that the ecological effects could be devastating. Second to habitat loss, invasive species are the leading cause of species endangerment.   3

To be fair, there are no doubt thousands of responsible pet owners across the United States. But the drawbacks of owning Burmese pythons outweigh the benefits. These snakes are not meant to be pets. If the United States wants to maintain its fragile southern ecosystem, it should take a hard look at making the importation of burmese pythons illegal.   4

Correction Marks

⌿ delete	⋀ add comma	word ⋀ add word
d̳ capitalize	? add question mark ⋀	⊙ add period
⌿ lowercase		◯ spelling
⋀ insert	⋁ insert an apostrophe	⊓ switch

Using an Editing Checklist

Now it's time to edit your own essay.

Practice ▷ Prepare a clean copy of your revised essay, and then use the checklist in Figure 10.4 to look for errors. Continue working until you can check off each item in the list.

Figure 10.4 Editing Checklist

Words

_____ 1. Have I used specific nouns and verbs?

_____ 2. Have I used more action verbs than "be" verbs?

Sentences

_____ 3. Have I varied the beginnings and lengths of sentences?

_____ 4. Have I combined short, choppy sentences?

_____ 5. Have I avoided improper shifts in sentences?

_____ 6. Have I avoided fragments and run-ons?

_____ 7. Have I avoided vague pronoun references, incomplete comparisons, and unclear wording?

Conventions

_____ 8. Do I use correct verb forms (*he saw,* not *he seen*)?

_____ 9. Do my subjects and verbs agree (*she speaks,* not *she speak*)?

_____ 10. Have I used the right words (*their, there, they're*)?

_____ 11. Have I capitalized first words and proper nouns and proper adjectives?

_____ 12. Have I used commas after long introductory word groups?

_____ 13. Have I punctuated dialogue correctly?

_____ 14. Have I carefully checked my spelling?

Adding a Title

Make sure to add an attention-getting title. Here are three simple strategies for writing titles.

- Use a phrase from the essay:

  | America the Developed

- Make a dramatic statement:

  | A Necessary Protection

- Use alliteration or another poetic technique.

  | Ban Burmese Pythons

"The best argument is that which seems merely an explanation."

—Dale Carnegie

☑ Reading for Enrichment

You will be reading an argumentative essay entitled "The George W. Bush Presidency" from the history text *The American Pageant* to read and react to. As you read this essay, be sure to follow the steps in the reading process. The reading activities are followed by writing ideas to choose from to write an argumentative essay of your own.

About the Authors

David M. Kennedy is an economic and cultural scholar who teaches at Stanford University. **Lizabeth Cohen** teaches American Studies at Harvard University.

Prereading

President George W. Bush first took office under the cloud of a contested election and presided over one of the most conflicted periods of American history. Before you read, make a list of things you already know about this period of history. Write your current opinion about his presidency, and briefly explain why you feel that way. Discuss your answers with a fellow student. Then read and consider the essay.

Consider the Elements

As you read the essay that follows, focus first on the **ideas**—the main claim, the evidence, and any counterarguments. Then consider the **organization**—the arrangement of the details in the main part of the essay. Also think about the writers' **voice**—their unique way of speaking to the reader. And finally, ask yourself if these traits combine to produce a satisfying reading experience.

_____

_____

_____

_____

_____

_____

What do you think?

According to Dale Carnegie's quotation, a strong argument "seems merely an explanation." What does this idea mean to you?

Before you read, answer these three questions:

1. Scan the title and the internal headings of the essay. What organizational structure do you notice?

2. Who is the intended audience for this essay? How does that influence the wording?

   Students

3. What do you expect to learn from this essay?

   George's Presidency

Reading and Rereading

This essay presents president George W. Bush's actions in the face of unprecedented events. It concludes with a summation of his effectiveness in office. Read the essay carefully, considering the facts that are presented. Create a line diagram as you read to trace the main claim, supporting claims, and evidence.

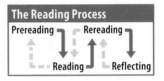

The Reading Process
Prereading — Rereading
Reading — Reflecting

The George W. Bush Presidency

As the son of the forty-first president, George W. Bush became 1 the first presidential offspring since John Quincy Adams to reach the White House. Raised largely in Texas, the younger Bush publicly distanced himself from his family's privileged New England heritage and affected the chummy manner of a self-made good ol' boy, though he held degrees from Yale and Harvard. (His adversaries sniped that he had been born on third base and claimed to have hit a triple.) He promised to bring to Washington the **conciliatory** skills he had honed as the Republican governor of Texas, where he had worked well with the Democratic majority in the state's legislature.

But as president, Bush soon proved to be more of a divider 2 than a uniter, less a "compassionate conservative" than a crusading **ideologue**. Religious traditionalists cheered but liberals jeered when he withdrew American support from international health programs that sanctioned abortion, advocated federally financed faith-based social-welfare initiatives, and sharply limited government-sponsored research on embryonic stem cells, which many scientists believed held the key to conquering diseases such as Parkinson's and Alzheimer's. He pleased corporate chieftains but angered environmentalists by challenging scientific findings on groundwater contamination and global warming, **repudiating** the Kyoto Treaty limiting greenhouse gas emissions (negotiated by the Clinton administration but never **ratified** by the Senate), advocating new oil exploration in the Arctic National Wildlife Refuge on Alaska's ecologically fragile north coast, and allowing Vice President Cheney to hammer out his administration's energy policy in behind-closed-doors meetings with representatives of several giant oil companies. Even many fiscal conservatives thought him reckless when he pressed ahead with a whopping $1.3 trillion tax cut. Together with a softening economy and the increasing costs of war in Iraq, the tax cut turned the federal budget surpluses of the late 1990s into yawning deficits, reaching more than $400 billion in 2004.

Terrorism Comes to America

On September 11, 2001, the long era of America's **impregnable** 3 national security violently ended. On a balmy late-summer morning, suicidal terrorists slammed two hijacked airliners, loaded with passengers and jet fuel, into the twin towers of New York City's World Trade Center. They flew a third plane into the military nerve center of the Pentagon, near Washington, D.C., killing 189 people. Heroic passengers forced a fourth hijacked aircraft to crash in rural Pennsylvania, killing all 44 aboard but depriving the terrorists of an additional weapon of mass destruction. As the two giant New York skyscrapers thunderously collapsed, some three thousand innocent victims perished, including people of many races and faiths from more than sixty countries, as well as hundreds of New York's police-

and fire-department rescue workers. A stunned nation blossomed with flags, as grieving and outraged Americans struggled to express their sorrow and **solidarity** in the face of the catastrophic terrorism of 9/11.

President Bush responded with a sober and stirring address to Congress nine days later. His solemn demeanor and the gravity of the situation helped to dissipate the cloud of illegitimacy that had shadowed his presidency since the disputed election of 2000. While emphasizing his respect for the Islamic religion and Muslim people, he identified the principal enemy as Osama bin Laden, head of a shadowy terrorist network known as Al Qaeda ("the base" in Arabic). A wealthy extremist exiled from his native Saudi Arabia, bin Laden was associated with earlier attacks on American embassies in East Africa and on the USS *Cole* in Yemen. He had taken refuge in landlocked Afghanistan, ruled by Islamic **fundamentalists** called the Taliban. (Ironically, the United States had indirectly helped bring the Taliban to power by supporting religious rebels resisting the Soviet invasion of Afghanistan in the 1980s.) Bin Laden was known to harbor venomous resentment toward the United States for its growing military presence in the Middle East (especially on the sacred soil of the Arabian Peninsula) and its unyielding support for Israel in the face of intensifying Palestinian nationalism. Bin Laden also fed on worldwide resentment of America's enormous economic, military, and cultural power. Ironically, America's most **conspicuous** strengths had made it a conspicuous target.

When the Taliban refused to hand over bin Laden, Bush ordered a massive military campaign against Afghanistan. Within three months American and Afghan rebel forces had overthrown the Taliban but failed to find bin Laden, and Americans continued to live in fear of future attacks. Confronted with this unconventional, **diffuse** menace, antiterrorism experts called for a new kind of "asymmetrical warfare," employing not just traditional military muscle but also counter-insurgency tactics like innovative intelligence gathering, training of local police forces, economic reprisals, infiltration of suspected organizations, and even assassinations.

The terrorists' blows diabolically coincided with the onset of a recession. The already gathering economic downturn worsened as edgy Americans shunned air travel and the tourist industry withered. In this anxious atmosphere, Congress in October 2001 rammed through the USA Patriot Act. The act permitted extensive telephone and email surveillance and authorized the detention and deportation of immigrants suspected of terrorism. Just over a year later, Congress created the new cabinet-level Department of Homeland Security to protect the nation's borders and ferret out potential attackers. The Justice Department meanwhile rounded up hundreds of immigrants and held them without *habeas corpus* (formal charges in an open court). The Bush administration further called for trying suspected terrorists before military tribunals, where the usual rules of evidence and procedure did not apply. As hundreds of Taliban fighters captured in Afghanistan languished in legal limbo and demoralizing isolation in the Guantánamo Detention Camp on the American military base at Guantánamo, Cuba, public-opinion polls showed Americans sharply divided on whether the terrorist threat fully warranted such drastic encroachments on America's **venerable** tradition of protecting civil liberties.

Catastrophic terrorism posed an unprecedented challenge to the United States. The events of that murderous September morning reanimated American patriotism, but they also brought a long chapter in American history to a dramatic climax. All but unique among modern peoples, Americans for nearly two centuries had been spared from foreign attack on their homeland. That unusual degree of virtually cost-free national security had **undergirded** the values of openness and individual freedom that defined the distinctive character of American society. Now American security and American liberty alike were dangerously imperiled. . . .

Re-Electing George W. Bush

Americans had rarely been as divided as they were in the first years of the twenty-first century. Civil libertarians worried that the government was trampling on personal freedoms in the name of fighting terrorism. Revelations in 2002 about flagrant corporate fraud fed rampant popular disillusion with the business community. Cultural tensions brewed over the rights of gay and lesbian Americans when leaders in San Francisco and Massachusetts permitted same-sex couples to marry in 2004. Affirmative action continued to spark sharp debate, as the Supreme Court permitted some preferential treatment in admitting minority undergraduate and law students to the University of Michigan in 2003.

8

Amid this division George W. Bush positioned himself to run for re-election. He proclaimed that his tax cuts had spurred economic growth. Targeting what he called "the soft bigotry of low expectations," he championed the No Child Left Behind Act of 2002, which mandated sanctions against schools that failed to meet federal performance standards. He played to cultural conservatives in opposing stem cell research and called for a constitutional amendment to ban gay marriage. But most of all, he promoted himself as a stalwart leader in wartime, warning the country not to "change horses midstream."

9

After a bruising round of primary elections, the **embattled** Democrats chose lanky and long-jawed Massachusetts senator John Kerry to represent their ticket. Kerry pushed progressive visions of government and counted on his Vietnam War record to counter charges that he would be weak in the face of terrorism. But that plan

10

backfired as Kerry fell under attack for his very public opposition to Vietnam once he had returned from battle in the early 1975. In spite of increased public misgivings about the war in Iraq, Bush nailed down a decisive victory in November 2004. He received the first popular vote majority by a presidential candidate in more than a decade—60,639,281 to 57,355,978—and won the Electoral College, 286 to 252, if by only one state (this time Ohio). This time his victory was clear, constitutional, and uncontested.

Bush's Second Term

Re-election, George W. Bush announced, gave him "political capital," which he intended to spend on an aggressive domestic agenda. The appointment of two new conservative Supreme Court justices (John G. Roberts and Samuel A. Alito, Jr.) upon the retirement of Sandra Day O'Connor and the death of Chief Justice William Rehnquist seemed to bode well for his ambitions. But Bush soon overplayed his hand. Attacking the core of New Deal liberalism, he proposed a radical program to privatize much of Social Security. A massive outcry led by the American Association of Retired Persons (AARP) and other liberal groups reminded Americans how much they loved Social Security, warts and all. Bush's proposal faded away within six months of his re-election. The same fate befell a proposed constitutional amendment to ban same-sex marriage, which had been a major "values" issue in the 2004 campaign.   *11*

The president also took (faulty) aim at the **contentious** issue of immigration reform. Here he parted company with the conservative wing of his party, many of whom wanted to deport the nearly 12 million undocumented people in the United States. His compromise plan to establish a guest-worker program and a "path to citizenship" for the undocumented ended up pleasing no one. Congress rejected it in the summer of 2007, and the issue was dead for the rest of Bush's term.   *12*

Every second-term president since the 1960s had seen scandal [13] mar his later years in office. Nixon had Watergate, Reagan had Iran-contra, and Clinton had Lewinsky. The Bush White House was no exception, but this time the accusations were political, not personal. In the fall of 2005, Vice President Dick Cheney's chief of staff was convicted of perjury in an investigation into the source of a leak that had exposed the identity of an undercover CIA agent as political retaliation against her antiwar husband. Then in December of that year, journalists discovered that the government was conducting illegal wiretap surveillance on American citizens inside the United States in violation of federal law. Perhaps the most tragic and avoidable of Bush's missteps came in the botched response to the deadly Hurricane Katrina, which devastated New Orleans and much of the Gulf Coast in late August 2005, flooding 80 percent of the historic city and causing over 1,300 deaths and $150 billion in damages. The Federal Emergency Management Agency (FEMA) proved pathetically inept in New Orleans, and Bush came in for still more criticism. A consensus began to build that Bush was a **genial** personality but an **impetuous**, unreflective, and frequently feckless leader, a president in over his head in a sea of complex problems that he seemed incapable of mastering.

From Kennedy/Cohen, Cengage Advantage Books: *The American Pageant*, 15E. © 2014 Cengage Learning

conciliatory
unifying, goodwill

ideologue
a person who intensely argues for a certain belief or agenda with disregard to opposition

repudiating
rejecting

ratified
made official

impregnable
offering great resistance; unbreakable

solidarity
unity and togetherness arising from a common interest

Islamic fundamentalists
people who strictly follow Islamic law and believe that the Koran (holy book) is the literal word of God

conspicuous
easily seen

diffuse
widely spread, not concentrated

venerable
respected for age and character

rampant
spreading without opposition

undergirded
secured and supported

embattled
under attack, surrounded

contentious
of great debate

genial
warm and cheerful

impetuous
characterized by sudden, or rash, actions and decisions

Summarizing

Write a summary of "The George W. Bush Presidency." Remember that a summary presents the main points clearly and concisely in your own words.

Reflecting

1. What is the authors' main claim?

   George Bush's presidency brought the nation down.

2. What evidence do they provide in support of their claim? Give at least two examples.

   Terrorism to America & the down-side of the economy

3. What opposing arguments, if any, are addressed? Does the writer concede or counter them?

4. How would you describe the writers' voice or tone? Do they engage readers or lecture them? Do you find any logical fallacies? Explain.

   The writer is very aggressive and informative

Vocabulary

Create vocabulary entries for these words. For each word, identify the pronunciation and helpful word parts, give a primary definition, and use the word in a sentence.

1. **adversaries**   (paragraph 1)
2. **asymmetrical**   (paragraph 5)
3. **feckless**   (paragraph 13)

Critical Thinking

- In paragraph 12 the author says the president took "faulty" aim. Explain what you think the author means by "faulty." Was this a good word choice, in your opinion?
- Does the writing seem biased, either for or against this president? Point out examples.

Writing for Enrichment

Choose one of the following writing ideas, or decide upon an idea of your own related to the reading. Use the writing process to help you develop your work.

The Writing Process

Prewrite → Revise → Publish → Write → Edit

1. Write a personal blog or journal entry in which you explore the value (or lack of it) of a high school or college class you have attended. Support your opinion with effective details.

2. Develop an argument based on an issue from world affairs. Write an essay that develops a main claim and supports it with supporting details and evidence.

3. Develop an argument for another debatable issue that you listed earlier.

4. Rewrite your essay that you wrote in this chapter by reordering your supporting evidence or by adding a different opposing argument.

5. Write an argumentative essay that counters an argument made in one of the example essays in this chapter.

When planning . . .
- Choose a topic that is debatable and that truly interests you.
- Gather information and evidence that effectively supports your claim.
- Also consider questions the reader may have about the topic.
- Review the essays in the chapter to see how the writers shaped their ideas.

When writing . . .
- Use specific details to support your claims.
- Address opposing points of view with concessions or counterpoints.
- Make a strong connection between the opening and closing parts of your essay.

When revising and editing . . .
- Restate weak ideas, making them logical and clear.
- Check the organization to make sure your supporting arguments are in an order that best suits the topic.
- Double-check for any logical fallacies in your argument.
- Add any missing key details about the topic.
- Ask yourself if you have engaged your reader.
- Edit your revised writing for style and correctness. See Appendix B for an editing checklist.

Reflecting on Argument Writing

Answer the following questions about your reading and writing experiences in this chapter.

1. What is the purpose of an argument essay—to inform, to persuade, to entertain, combination of purposes? Explain.

2. What reading strategy seems the most helpful for reading this type of essay? Explain.

3. How does the writer's voice affect the impact of an argument essay?

4. What are the key parts of an argument essay?

5. What do you like best about your argument essay?

6. What is one thing you would like to change in it?

7. What is the most important thing you have learned about argument writing?

Key Terms to Remember

When you read and write argument essays, keep in mind the following terms.

- **Argumentation**—the process of proving the strength of a certain line of thinking
- **Persuasion**—the process of trying to convince an audience
- **Claim**—the position or thesis developed in an argument essay
- **Evidence**—the facts and details that support the claim
- **Counterarguments**—opposing positions or arguments
- **Concession**—a writer's admission that an opposing viewpoint deserves merit
- **Counter**—a type of counterargument that states an opposing view and explains why the opposing point is flawed
- **Logical fallacy**—a faulty or false statement that weakens an argument by distorting an issue, drawing a false conclusion, misusing evidence, or misusing language

PART 4:

Research

Part 4: Research

Chapter

11

"Research is formalized curiosity. It is poking and prying with a purpose."

—Zora Neale Hurston

Understanding Research

Who actually conducts research? The simple answer is that everyone does. You may have reviewed reports about the latest cell phones before buying one. Or you might study different careers before choosing a college major. Or you may talk to experienced travelers before planning a trip. An academic research project is a similar process, though it follows guidelines and time lines established by your instructor and your field of study.

In this chapter, you will learn about a key aspect of the research process—using outside sources of information. The knowledge that you gain in this chapter will help you conduct effective research and write effective research reports.

Learning Outcomes

LO1 Understand sources of information.

LO2 Evaluate sources of information.

LO3 Cite sources of information.

LO4 Avoid plagiarism.

LO5 Understand summarizing, paraphrasing, and quoting.

What do you think?

Zora Neale Hurston describes research as "poking and prying with a purpose." How do you interpret her description?

L01   Understanding Sources of Information

Sources of information fall into two general categories: primary sources and secondary sources.

Primary Sources

Primary sources are sources of facts that you collect through firsthand experiences. They involve you directly in the topic of your research.

- Conducting interviews and surveys
- Doing experiments or other hands-on activities
- Observing events
- Attending presentations (art exhibits, museum displays, political speeches)
- Studying original documents (court records, letters, journals, diaries)

Secondary Sources

Secondary sources provide information that you collect indirectly, through the efforts and perspectives of other people.

- Reference books
- Nonfiction books
- Periodicals (magazines and journals)
- Newspapers
- Web sites
- Documentaries

Practice List examples of primary and secondary sources of information that you have used recently for academic or personal purposes. Share these researching experiences with your classmates.

Primary sources

Interviews

Observations

Experiments

Presentations

Secondary sources

Web sites

Magazines

Professors

Using Primary Sources

Primary sources are useful for gaining direct, firsthand information on a topic from sources close to the issue or question.

Conducting Interviews

During an interview you either (1) talk in person with an expert who knows about your topic, (2) communicate with that person in real time by phone or Internet connection, or (3) email questions you would like answered by the person.

> **Advantage:** Interviewing allows you to learn about your topic from an expert.
>
> **Disadvantage:** Interviewing requires more time than many other sorts of research, from contacting possible interviewees, to scheduling and conducting the interview, to recording and transcribing responses.

When conducting an interview, follow these guidelines.

1. **Schedule the interview**—in person, by phone, or online.
2. **Prepare a list of important questions.** Arrange them in a sensible order.
3. **Be polite** during the interview.
4. **Give background information** about yourself and your research.
5. **Listen carefully** to the person's answers and write them down or record them (with permission from the interviewee).
6. **Be prepared to reword a question** or to ask follow-up questions to get the information you need.
7. **Thank the person** for her or his help.
8. **Review your notes,** and contact the person to clarify anything you are unsure about.

Making Observations

Some topics can be studied by watching people, places, events, and things in action. Observations can help you formulate and test concepts, ideas, or theories related to the topic.

> **Advantage:** Making observations allows you to experience your topic for yourself.
>
> **Disadvantage:** Depending on the topic, it may be difficult to schedule or carry out an observation. Also, if you miss a detail, that moment cannot be recaptured.

When making an observation, follow these guidelines.

1. **Know what you want to accomplish**—your goal.
2. **Learn about your topic** before you observe it.
3. **Get permission to observe** if a location or an event isn't open to the public.
4. **Come prepared with the proper equipment**—pens, notebook, camera.
5. **Record sights and sounds** as you experience them.
6. **Review your notes** carefully to determine what you have learned.

Using Secondary Sources

Most of your research will deal with secondary sources. This information is one step removed from the origin. As such, it may offer quality information on your research topic based on expert perspectives and analysis by other people.

Books

Reference books and other nonfiction books are common sources of secondary information. Because of the time spent producing them, these sources tend to be well edited and trustworthy.

Reference Books

Reference books are general sources of information, and they are available to you in print and online. Common reference books include encyclopedias, atlases, and almanacs.

> **Advantage:** Reference books serve as a trustworthy starting point for research.
>
> **Disadvantage:** Reference books often contain only general information, and they may not include the most recent knowledge on a subject.

When using reference books, follow these guidelines.

1. **Learn about the structure of the reference.** Check the table of contents and index, and read the introductory material. These will reveal how best to explore and document the work.
2. **Understand what the reference covers.** Also think about what types of details it does not include.
3. **Use precise words in searches.** For example, the word "vegetarian" will lead to different information than the word "vegan" will.
4. **Take careful notes on your reading,** being sure to accurately record the information and details of how to document it.
5. **Refer to these notes during your further research** to remind yourself what you have learned and what you still need to find out.

Nonfiction Books

Nonfiction books traditionally have been a main source of information in college-level research projects. Books are storehouses of information about every sort of topic imaginable.

> **Advantage:** Nonfiction books usually provide far more information about a topic than you will find in reference books.
>
> **Disadvantage:** Books may not be as up-to-date as other sources. Also not every author is a recognized authority in your field of study. Choose your books wisely.

When using nonfiction books, follow these guidelines.

1. **Learn how the book is put together** and which parts are important to your research.
2. **Use the reading process** to fully understand the text.
3. **Take careful notes,** using a proven strategy.
4. **Identify the source** of your notes (title and author) and the page numbers of the information.
5. **Use quotation marks** to enclose words and ideas taken directly from the text.
6. **Refer to the notes as a reminder** during your further research.

Periodicals

Periodicals are magazines and journals that are published on a regular basis (often weekly, monthly, or quarterly). Magazines usually focus on general areas of interest. Journals usually address professional areas of study.

> **Advantage:** Periodicals provide recent information on a topic.
>
> **Disadvantage:** Information in periodicals may be as yet unproven or under debate. Magazine articles may be written by people who are not true experts in the field, while journal articles may be written in a scholarly style that is challenging to understand.

1. **Learn about the periodical**—its purpose, structure, and features.
2. **Use the reading process** to fully understand the text.
3. **Take careful notes,** using a proven strategy.
4. **Identify the source of your notes**—the title and author of the article, page number, title of the periodical, volume number, and date.
5. **Use quotation marks to enclose** the exact words that you record.
6. **Refer to the notes as a reminder** of what you have learned and what research questions remain unanswered.

With so many periodicals available, it can be a challenge to find the most helpful articles. To get started, learn about the search tools your library offers.

Your library may subscribe to EBSCOhost, Lexis-Nexis, or another database service. Review the keyword search instructions for your service to find the best articles on your topic. When you locate promising articles, you may be able to print them, save them, or email them to yourself. If not, look for a print version. Check with your instructor or a librarian for help.

Practice Learn about the procedure for finding periodicals in your school's library. Test the procedure for a topic of your choice.

Web Sites

The Internet will probably be one of the first places you turn to for beginning your research. Just make sure that it isn't the only place you turn to. Your instructors may, in fact, limit the number of Internet sources you can cite in your research.

> **Advantage:** The Internet provides a vast amount of information that is easy to access.
>
> **Disadvantage:** The information load can be overwhelming, some sites are unreliable sources, and it's easy to get distracted as you browse the Web.

When using the Internet for research, follow these guidelines.

1. **Check with a librarian** for special online searching options, such as the Library of Congress, EBSCOhost (a database of newspapers, magazines, and journals), and national and state government sites.
2. **Know the basics of Internet searching.** Check each site for its keyword guidelines.
3. **Review a number of choices** before deciding which ones to use. Finding good information takes time.
4. **Check the reliability** of sites that interest you.
5. **Take careful notes** or annotate copies of the information.
6. **Identify the key source of your information** (title of the article or Web page, author, name of the Web site, date of posting, and Web address).
7. **Refer to your notes often** as a reminder of what you have learned and what questions remain unanswered.

A Guide to Keyword Searching

The success of your Internet search depends on your understanding of search tools and the quality of the keywords you use. Although search sites are becoming more predictive of your intent, simple changes to a keyword can often provide very different results.

1. Start by typing in your topic: *salmon, robotics.*
2. Add a word to call up pages containing any of the words: *wild salmon, home robotics.*
3. Enclose the phrase in quotation marks to call up just the pages containing that phrase: *"wild salmon."*
4. Use words such as *and* (+) or *not* (-) to narrow or focus your search: *salmon and harvesting* or *salmon not farmed.*
5. Experiment with word order to receive different results: *home robotics* versus *robotics home.*

L02 Evaluating Sources of Information

When you conduct research, be sure that your sources are reliable or trustworthy. The following information will help you check sources for reliability.

Experts and Other Primary Sources

- Before deciding to interview an "expert," learn about the person. Does she or he have the education and experience to be an expert? Research the person's biography and other experts' opinions of him or her. And during an interview, consider the quality and depth of the person's responses.

Books and Other Print Materials

- When selecting print material, also learn about the author. Does she or he have the proper background for the subject? Check the material's publisher and the date of publication to make sure that the information comes from a reputable source and is current. As you read, decide if the information seems fair and balanced and raises no questions about its reliability. Checking with other sources will help you do this.

Telecasts and Broadcasts

- When considering a TV or radio program, be aware that it may address a topic unfairly. Documentaries and straight news reports are generally more reliable than talk-radio conversations. Always consider the show's intended audience, its sponsors, and the particular broadcaster's approach to news and current events.

Web Sites

- Be sure that the author of a site (if identified) is respected in the field by learning what you can about his or her credentials (education, connection to the topic). Also check the type of site; government (.gov), education (.edu), and nonprofit (.org) sites often are more reliable than commercial (.com) sites. In addition, determine if the site presents current information that seems balanced and accurate. If you have questions about a site, check the information against other sources.

Insight While wikis like Wikipedia can be a quick way to learn the basics of a topic and discover links to other sources, wiki entries are often incomplete or even subject to the original author's biases. For these reasons, they are not respected sources for a scholarly research paper.

The quality of a Web site's design is another clue for determining its reliability. A professional, error-free text with effective graphics is a good sign. Sites with poor design features, many grammatical errors, and broken links signal problems.

Practice ▶ Team up with a partner to evaluate the effectiveness of two specific sources of information (Web site, magazine article, book). Refer to tips you just learned as needed.

L03 Citing Sources of Information

You must give credit to the sources of ideas or words that you use in your academic essays and reports. Doing so avoids *plagiarism*, which is using the words and thoughts of others without crediting them in your writing.

Academic research uses a number of different styles for citing sources. For example, the Modern Language Association (MLA) style is generally used for research in the humanities (literature, philosophy, art history), and the American Psychological Association (APA) style is generally used for research in the social sciences (sociology, psychology, political science). Check with your instructor before choosing a citation style.

Insight *Plagiarism* is a serious offense that can damage your reputation. Penalties for plagiarism vary but can range from having a research paper rejected to losing financial aid to being dismissed from a university.

Table 11.1 shows the basic guidelines for using the MLA and APA styles for crediting sources in the text of a research report.

Table 11.1 MLA and APA Guidelines

Sources	MLA	APA
Work with one author	*Author name and page number* (Waye 27)	*Author name, year of publication, and page number* (Waye, 2008, p. 27)
Work with two (or three) authors	(Waye and Joniz 27) (Sams, Banks, and Ory 31)	(Waye & Joniz, 2008, p. 27) (Sams, Banks, & Ory, 2010, p. 31)
Work with four (or five) authors	(Waye et al. 27)	(Waye, Joniz, Damik, & Martin, 2008, p. 27)
Work with six or more authors	(Waye et al. 27)	(Waye et al., 2008, p. 27)
Author identified within the sentence	According to Mariah Waye, fishery expert, wild salmon need human help (27).	According to Mariah Waye, fishery expert, wild salmon need human help (2008, p. 27).
Work with no author specified	*First main word(s) of the title and page number* ("Salmon in Crisis" 27)	*First main word(s) of the title, date, and page number.* ("Salmon in Crisis," 2008, p. 27)
Work with no page number specified (as in a Web page)	*Author name only (or first main word[s] of title if no author is specified)* (Waye)	*Author name (or first main word[s] of title if no author is specified) and date* (Waye, 2008)

Using In-Text Citations

You can learn more about basic documentation by studying the following passages from a research report, demonstrating first the MLA style and then the APA style.

MLA Style

Source is cited in the sentence. — According to the Consumer Product Safety Commission, almost 25,000 children are treated in hospital emergency rooms each year as a result of shopping-cart injuries. The National Safe Kids Campaign says "the number of children ages 5 and under injured in shopping-cart incidents

Title only; this Web site names no author. — has increased more than 30 percent since 1985" ("Secure Children").

B. Potential Injuries

Shopping-cart injuries include cuts, bruises, fractures, internal injuries, and head injuries—even skull fractures. In fact, children have

Four authors, with page — died as a result of shopping-cart falls (Smith et al. 161). For the sake of our number customers, Jonesville Home Mart needs to take steps to ensure shopping-cart safety.

C. Solutions

A solution to this problem comes from a sister store in Anchorage,

Single author, with page — which has made safety its motto (Clepper 47). Like this store, Jonesville . . . number

APA Style

According to the Consumer Product Safety Commission, almost 25,000 children are treated in hospital emergency rooms each year as a result of

Online material — shopping-cart injuries (2009). The National Safe Kids Campaign says "the with no page number number of children ages 5 and under injured in shopping-cart incidents numbers specified — has increased more than 30 percent since 1985" ("Secure Children," 2009).

B. Potential Injuries

Shopping-cart injuries include cuts, bruises, fractures, internal injuries, and head injuries—even skull fractures. In fact, children have

Four authors, with year and — died as a result of shopping-cart falls (Smith, Dietrich, Garcia, & Shields, page number 2010, p. 161). For the sake of our customers, Jonesville Home Mart needs to take steps to ensure shopping-cart safety.

C. Solutions

A solution to this problem comes from a sister store in Anchorage,

Single author, with year and — which has made safety its motto (Clepper, 2010, p. 47). Like this store, page number Jonesville . . .

Creating a Source List

At the end of your report, you must list your sources—either a **works-cited list** (MLA) or a **references list** (APA)—so that your reader can locate them. Table 11.2 shows the differences between the styles. In both the MLA and APA formats, any source listed must also be cited in your paper, and any source cited in your paper must appear in the source list. The exception, in APA format, is personal communication such as interviews and email, which should be cited in text but not included in the references list.

Whether your sources are books, magazine articles, pamphlets, or Web sites, the citations should include all of the following elements that are available:

1. **Author name(s)**
2. **Title** (When including two parts of a publication, list the smaller part first.)
   - "Book chapter" / *Book title*
   - "Magazine article" / *Magazine title*
   - "Web site article" / *Web site title*
3. **Publication facts** (the date, the place of publication, the publisher; or appropriate Web information)

Table 11.2 MLA and APA Source List Differences

	Author	Title	Publication Facts
MLA	Give the name as it appears on the title page.	Capitalize all important words.	Place the date after the publication information, followed by the medium—Print, Web, CD-ROM, etc.
	Waye, Mariah S. *Environmental Watch: Salmon in Danger.* **New York: Pudding Press, 2010. Print.**		
APA	Use initials for the first and middle names.	Capitalize only the first word in a title, the first word in a subtitle, and any proper nouns. Capitalize titles of periodicals normally.	Place the date after the author's name.
	Waye, M. S. (2010). *Environmental watch: Salmon in danger.* **New York, NY: Pudding Press.**		

---

works-cited list
list of sources prepared according to MLA style

references list
list of sources prepared according to APA style

MLA Style

Works Cited

Magazine
article
— Clepper, Irene. "Safety First: Alaska Retailer Attracts Customers with Safe-and-Sound Seminars." *Playthings* 97 (2010): 46-47. Print.

Web article
— Consumer Product Safety Commission. "Shopping Cart Injuries: Victims 5 years old and younger." CPSC. 25 July 2012. Web. 22 Sept. 2014.

Web article
— "Secure Children Properly in Shopping Carts." Texas Medical Center. 2009. Web. 22 Sept. 2014.

Book
— Shelov, Steven P., ed. *Caring for Your Baby and Young Child: Birth to Age 5.* 5th ed. New York: Bantam, 2009. Print.

Article, four
authors
— Smith, Gary A., et al. "Injuries to Children Related to Shopping Carts." *Pediatrics* 97 (2010): 161-65. Print.

APA Style (for the same sources)

References

Magazine
article
— Clepper, I. (2010). Safety first: Alaska retailer attracts customers with safe-and-sound seminars. *Playthings*, 97, 46-47.

Web article
— Consumer Product Safety Commission. (2012). "Shopping Cart Injuries: Victims 5 years old and younger." Retrieved September 22, 2014 from https://www.cpsc.gov/en/Media/Documents/Research--Statistics/ Injury-Statistics/Public-Facilities-and-Products/Shopping-Cart-Injuries-Victims-5-years-old-and-younger

Web article
— Secure children properly in shopping carts. (2009). Retrieved September 22, 2014, from http://www.tmc.edu/tmcnews/ 06_15_00/page_16.html

Book
— Shelov, S. P. (Ed.). (2009). *Caring for your baby and young child: Birth to age 5.* New York, NY: Bantam.

Article, four
authors
— Smith, G. A., Dietrich, A., Garcia, T., & Shields, B. (2010). Injuries to children related to shopping carts. *Pediatrics*, 97, 161-165.

L04 Avoiding Plagiarism

The following article and explanations demonstrate different types of plagiarism. Use this information as a guide to check your own work and to avoid plagiarizing the sources you've used.

People in Need

On a chilly February afternoon, an old man stands on a city sidewalk and leans against a fence. In his hands a sign reads: "Will work for food. Please help!" Imagine, for a moment, the life this man leads. He probably spends his days alone on the street begging for handouts and his nights searching for shelter from the cold. He has no job, no friends, and nowhere to turn.

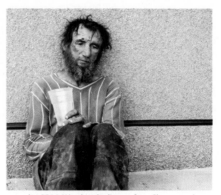

wrangler, 2014 / Used under license from Shutterstock.com

Most Americans would like to believe that cases like this are rare. However, the National Coalition for the Homeless estimates that as many as 3 million people in this country share this man's condition. Who are these people we call "the homeless," and what factors have contributed to their plight?

According to Pastor Joel Warren, the director of the Greater Mission Shelter in San Angela, most of the homeless are unemployed males, and from 40 to 60 percent have alcohol- or drug-related problems. Warren notes that the image of the typical homeless person is changing. He says that the average age of the homeless has dropped from 55 to 30 in the last ten years. National studies have also shown that this population is changing.

A recent study by the United States Conference of Mayors found that one-third of the homeless population consists of families with small children, and 22 percent of the homeless have full- or part-time jobs. Statistics seem to show that more and more of the homeless are entire families who have simply become the victims of a bad economy.

Common Types of Plagiarism

The highlighted examples of plagiarism below are linked to the "People in Need" article from which the information was taken.

Copying Text Without Credit

Here the writer copies word-for-word from the original source without giving any credit.

It's not hard to imagine what life is like for a homeless person. He probably spends his days alone on the street begging for handouts and his nights searching for shelter from the cold. He has no job, no friends, and nowhere to turn. Such a life is becoming all too familiar to many because of the poor economy.

Neglecting Quotation Marks

Here the writer credits the source but forgets to place quotation marks around exact words borrowed from it.

Many people have no real connection with a homeless man like the one just described, and so they do not think much about this serious problem. In "People in Need," Anna Morales states that most Americans would like to believe that cases like this are rare. However, the National Coalition for the Homeless estimates that as many as 3 million people share this man's condition. Still, many of us seem to live in places far removed from the homeless.

Paraphrasing Ideas Without Citing Them

Here the writer paraphrases information from a specific passage from an original article or book without identifying the source.

The economy has changed the profile of the homeless population. Studies indicate that families with young children now make up more than 30 percent of this population. In addition, more and more homeless have part-time or full-time jobs.

Insight Other types of source abuse include *self-plagiarism* and *copyright violation*. Self-plagiarism means using material you have written elsewhere, without giving credit. In school, this generally involves using a paper in more than one class without permission. In professional life, it can mean neglecting to cite your previously published work. Copyright violation means using text, images, or audio files without permission and credit. It can result in criminal charges and lawsuits.

L05 Summarizing, Paraphrasing, and Quoting

Summarizing, paraphrasing, and quoting are three main ways of incorporating sources.

Summarizing

A summary condenses a source to its most basic ideas while retaining their original order. It is usually no more than one-third the length of the original material. In a research paper, you might spend a few paragraphs summarizing a major resource.

Example Summary of this Chapter:

Kemper et al. say that everyone does research, whether comparing cell phones, evaluating college careers, planning a trip, or writing an academic research paper. Guidelines are provided to help you use sources in your research paper. *1*

Research resources can be either primary or secondary. Primary sources include interviews with experts and personal observation of events. Using these requires careful planning but gives you direct access to information. Secondary sources include books, periodicals, and Web sites. Using these can save time, but they may be limited by someone else's purpose and understanding. You are responsible for evaluating the validity and completeness of all sources you use. *2*

You must also cite your sources to avoid plagiarizing, which can damage your reputation and college career. Most college papers use either MLA or APA style. Working sources into your paper involves accurately summarizing, paraphrasing, and quoting (345–358). *3*

Paraphrasing

A paraphrase restates an idea in your own words. This both demonstrates your understanding and best fits the voice of your paper and the flow of your ideas.

Example Paraphrase of the Previous Sentences:

Paraphrasing puts an idea into your own words, to show your understanding and to suit your paper's voice and structure (Kemper et al. 358).

Quoting

Quotations add authority to your work by integrating the best words of experts. But too many quotations can make a paper seem to be a patchwork of other people's ideas. Working a quotation into your writing smoothly may require replacing or leaving out some words. Take care that the results represent the original source accurately.

Example Quotation from the Previous Sentences:

Avoid having your paper seem a "patchwork of other people's ideas" from too many quotations (Kemper et al. 358).

Practice ▷ Read the following excerpt and complete the bulleted activities. In each case use MLA documentation style to give credit for the material you have borrowed.

- Write a summary of the entire selection.
- Choose one of the three paragraphs and write a paraphrase of it.
- Write a personal response in which you incorporate a quotation from the selection.

This excerpt comes from a college textbook on health. It is part of a larger section dealing with proper use of prescription drugs.

The Reading Process

Prereading → Rereading

↓ ↑

→ Reading → Reflecting

About the Author

Dianne Hales is an award-winning freelance journalist with writing credits in numerous national periodicals and more than a dozen published nonfiction books.

Drug Interactions

OTC [over the counter] and prescription drugs can interact in a variety of ways. For example, mixing some cold medications with tranquilizers can cause drowsiness and coordination problems, thus making driving dangerous. Moreover, what you eat or drink can impair or completely wipe out the effectiveness of drugs or lead to unexpected effects on the body. For instance, aspirin takes five to ten times as long to be absorbed when taken with food or shortly after a meal than when taken on an empty stomach. If tetracyclines encounter calcium in the stomach, they bind together and cancel each other out.

1

To avoid potentially dangerous interactions, check the label(s) for any instructions on how or when to take a medication, such as "with a meal." If the directions say that you should take a drug on an empty stomach, take it at least one hour before eating or two or three hours after eating. Don't drink a hot beverage with a medication; the temperature may interfere with the effectiveness of the drug.

2

Whenever you take a drug, be especially careful of your intake of alcohol, which can change the rate of metabolism and the effects of many different drugs. Because it dilates the blood vessels, alcohol can add to the dizziness sometimes caused by drugs for high blood pressure, angina, or depression. Also, its irritating effects on the stomach can worsen stomach upset from aspirin, ibuprofen, and other anti inflammatory drugs.

3

From Hales, *An Invitation to Health*, 7E. © 2012 Cengage Learning

☑ Reviewing the Chapter

Understand Sources of Information

1. Define or explain the two types of sources and the particular advantage of each.

   ■ Primary Sources

   Information gathered through first hand experience

   ■ Secondary Sources

   Information collected by others & used by you or others.

2. Explain two possible problems with using the Internet for research.

   Not accurate & copied from other sources

Evaluate Sources of Information

3. Explain how you can determine the reliability of two of the following sources: an expert, a book, a TV program, a Web site.

Cite Sources of Information

4. Explain what it means to cite sources of information within your writing.

5. Identify the two common documentation styles.

   MLA & APA

Avoid Plagiarism

6. Explain how you can avoid plagiarism in your writing.

   Citation

Summarize, Paraphrase, and Quote

7. Explain the difference between paraphrasing and quoting.

"Somewhere, something special is
waiting to be known."

—Carl Sagan

Research Report

Everyone has at least one favorite pastime or interest. You may, for example, enjoy hair design and like learning and talking about the latest styles. Or you may follow the NASCAR circuit and enjoy keeping up with the latest standings and discussing them with friends. Then again, you may be attracted to music, movies, gaming, or working out. Your choices are endless.

Writing a research report is a similar experience: A topic interests you, and after learning enough about it, you share what you have learned. While the research described in the first paragraph may seem pure enjoyment, you put effort into that learning. A research report rewards that same effort with a deeper understanding of the world around you.

In this chapter, you will read and react to a research report and then write one of your own. In the process, you will learn about a number of important strategies that will help you with research writing in all of your classes.

Learning Outcomes

LO1 Understand research.
LO2 Learn reading strategies.
LO3 Read and react to a research report.
LO4 Plan a research report.
LO5 Write a research report.
LO6 Revise and edit a report.

What do you think?

How does Carl Sagan's quotation relate to research? What is something special that you would like to know?

"All my knowledge comes from research."

—Stan Sakai

L01 Understanding a Research Assignment

When an instructor asks you to write a research report, he or she is asking you to do two things: (1) become knowledgeable about a topic and (2) share this information in a clear, organized paper.

A research report is a carefully planned form of informational writing, usually at least three pages long. It cites information from books, periodicals, Web sites, interviews, or observations following MLA, APA, or another recognized documentation style. It may also include graphics—charts, diagrams, maps, or photographs. Each instructor will have specific guidelines for researching your topic and compiling your report.

The Internet serves as an easy first source of information, accessing an unlimited number of resources almost immediately. Unfortunately, all of this information can overwhelm you. Effective research requires the ability to narrow your choices by recognizing the difference between quality and questionable sources of information and then choosing those that best apply to your specific purpose.

Since a research report is an extended writing assignment, it requires careful planning and patience. During the first part of the process, you need to learn about your topic. During the second part, you need to plan and write your report. Your instructor may provide a timetable for accomplishing your work; if not, you'll need to establish your own timetable.

Research Report Versus Research Paper

In a research *report*, you collect, organize, and compile information about a topic. You share important facts and details from reliable sources in order to enhance or expand upon your own ideas. In a research *paper*, you select a topic that is open for debate, research it, and develop a position based on your own thinking and findings. In short, a research report shares information, and a research paper defends or develops a point of view. You will write both during your college career.

Insight Report writing is common not only in school, but also in the workplace. Depending on your job, you may be asked to write a marketing report, a budget report, or a safety report. These all require careful research and clear writing.

Practice List three personal interests that you could discuss authoritatively with friends and classmates. Share your list with your classmates. Be prepared to identify a few interesting ideas related to one of these interests.

1. _____

2. _____

3. _____

LO2 Learning Reading Strategies

Using an Organized List

The purpose of reading a report is to learn about a particular topic. Using an organized list is one strategy that will help you keep track of all the supporting information. **Figure 12.1** shows how this simple strategy works.

Understanding the Writer's Approach

Research reports, always full of information, require careful reading. When reading a report, it may be helpful to understand the writer's basic approach. Often a writer presents information objectively, letting the facts and details speak for themselves. Sometimes a writer takes a subjective approach, including personal thoughts and feelings throughout. Objective reports are written in the third person (*he*, *she*, *it*, and *they*), subjective reports in the first person (*I*, *me*, and *we*). These two passages show the difference:

> *Figure 12.1* Organized List
>
> ### Organized List
>
> **Report topic/thesis:**
>
> 1. Main idea or topic sentence of the first middle paragraph
>   + (Key supporting points)
>   +
>   +
>
> 2. Main idea or topic sentence of the second middle paragraph
>   +
>   +
>   +
>
> 3. Main idea or topic sentence of the third middle paragraph
>
> **TIP:** If needed, add another level of detail under the (+) key supporting points introduced by another symbol (-).

Objective: Squatters often live by simple, straightforward rules. They know that rule number one is keep the lights off to avoid being noticed. Rule number two is don't bother people when they are sleeping. Rule number three involves . . .

Subjective: I chose to investigate a funeral home to cure myself of the grim-reaper syndrome. When I walked inside Vander Furniture Store/Funeral Home, I half expected to see a well-dressed, evil individual standing by a counter, sharpening his sickle. . . .

Insight Writers who are especially involved in their research sometimes include subjective personal thoughts and feelings in their reports. Some such reports may seem more like personal stories. However, both the subjective and the objective report have their place and value.

L03 Reading and Reacting to a Research Report

Read the following report that explores a new form of agriculture called vertical farming. The report follows MLA documentation style. Use the reading process to help you fully appreciate and understand the text and how it incorporates sources of information.

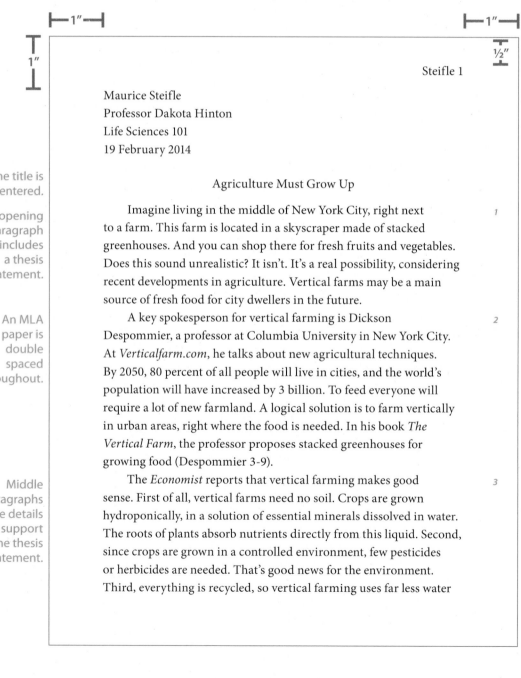

Steifle 1

Maurice Steifle
Professor Dakota Hinton
Life Sciences 101
19 February 2014

The title is centered.

Agriculture Must Grow Up

The opening paragraph includes a thesis statement.

Imagine living in the middle of New York City, right next to a farm. This farm is located in a skyscraper made of stacked greenhouses. And you can shop there for fresh fruits and vegetables. Does this sound unrealistic? It isn't. It's a real possibility, considering recent developments in agriculture. Vertical farms may be a main source of fresh food for city dwellers in the future.

An MLA paper is double spaced throughout.

A key spokesperson for vertical farming is Dickson Despommier, a professor at Columbia University in New York City. At *Verticalfarm.com*, he talks about new agricultural techniques. By 2050, 80 percent of all people will live in cities, and the world's population will have increased by 3 billion. To feed everyone will require a lot of new farmland. A logical solution is to farm vertically in urban areas, right where the food is needed. In his book *The Vertical Farm*, the professor proposes stacked greenhouses for growing food (Despommier 3-9).

Middle paragraphs give details to support the thesis statement.

The *Economist* reports that vertical farming makes good sense. First of all, vertical farms need no soil. Crops are grown hydroponically, in a solution of essential minerals dissolved in water. The roots of plants absorb nutrients directly from this liquid. Second, since crops are grown in a controlled environment, few pesticides or herbicides are needed. That's good news for the environment. Third, everything is recycled, so vertical farming uses far less water

Steifle 2

and nutrients than traditional farms use. Finally, vertical farms will provide food to local areas, which saves on transportation costs ("Does It Really Stack Up?").

Two key technologies already exist for vertical farming— greenhouses and hydroponics. *The Economist* mentions a number of experiments already in place. For example, the South Pole Growth Chamber is a semi-automated hydroponic facility that produces food for scientists and technicians working in Antarctica. The Science Barge in New York has also been growing food hydroponically ("Does It Really Stack Up?"). Another example is Plantlab, a 12-year-old company in the Netherlands that has grown strawberries, corn, and beans on three floors, all underground (Kretschmer and Kollenberg).

Closer to home, Joe Heineman and Johanna Hearron-Heineman have been growing butter lettuce on two floors of an old building in Racine, Wisconsin. As the *Milwaukee Journal Sentinel* reports, the couple uses treated wastewater from tilapia fish tanks to grow the lettuce. In this building, they hope to produce the same amount of lettuce that would take 40 acres of traditional farmland to grow. The couple also wants to grow a half-million pounds of tomatoes in a rooftop greenhouse (Herzog).

The idea of vertical farming on a grand scale, however, still needs work. There are no stacked greenhouses yet, as Despommier has envisioned them. As a matter of fact, environmental scientists and engineers have serious questions about the efficiency of vertical farming.

The Economist explains one main concern: "Light has to be very tightly controlled to get uniform production of very high-quality food," says British engineer Peter Head. Often this means

4

5

6

7

Text cues indicate where borrowed ideas begin.

Parenthetical citations show the sources of borrowed ideas.

The exact words of a source are placed in quotation marks.

Steifle 3

using expensive artificial light. Dr. Ted Caplow, a pioneer in rooftop greenhouses, believes vertical farming will work only if it uses natural light ("Does It Really Stack Up?"). Vertical farms also need power for heating and cooling. In Racine, the Heinemans say that lighting and temperature control are expensive. It costs 40 cents worth of electricity for every head of lettuce, which sells for $1.50. Joe Heineman hopes to cut this cost in half (Herzog). As it is, the electric bill for vertical farming could wipe out the savings in transportation costs.

The Economist mentions ideas for addressing these concerns. In single-story structures, for example, movable trays can give plants the best exposure to natural and artificial light. The magazine also shares Dr. Caplow's idea for farming in existing multistory buildings: "plants growing around edges of the building, sandwiched between two glass layers and rotating on a conveyor." Another idea is rooftop gardens, which get the best natural light, as Peter Head explains. Members of the Science Barge project have started a business to create a huge commercial rooftop farm in Queens. Powered by solar panels, it will produce 30 tons of vegetables per year ("Does It Really Stack Up?").   8

The conclusion revisits the thesis statement.

Whether urban farming ultimately follows the Despommier model or takes some other form, it looks like it will become an important part of the urban landscape. What the pioneers in the field learn today may lead to multilevel, integrated systems that can feed large cities in a cost-effective way. Greenhouses may one day reach into the sky.   9

Steifle 4

A separate page lists works cited in the report.

Sources are formatted with hanging indentation.

Works Cited

Despommier, Dickson. *The Vertical Farm.* New York: St. Martins, 2010. Print.

---. *Verticalfarm.com.* Np., n.d. Web. 31 Jan. 2012.

"Does It Really Stack Up?" *The Economist* 11 Dec. 2010: 15-16. Print.

Herzog, Karen. "Urban Farm in Racine Is No Fish Tale." *Milwaukee Journal Sentinel* 15 July 2010: B3. Print.

Kretschmer, Fabian, and Malte E. Kollenberg, "Can Urban Agriculture Feed a Hungry World?" *Spiegel.de. Spiegel* Online, 22 July 2011. Web. 31 Jan. 2012.

Practice Answer the questions below about the report you just read about vertical farming. Then discuss your responses with your classmates.

1. What is the main idea or thesis in this report?

   _____

2. How is the thesis supported or developed? Consider using an organized list to identify the key details and their source in each middle paragraph. The number of key supporting points (+) may vary from paragraph to paragraph.

Organized List

Report topic/thesis: _____

1. _____

   +

   +

   +

   +

2. _____

   +

   +

3. _____

   +

   +

3. What is the main purpose of this report—to entertain, to inform, or to persuade?

   _____

4. Does the writer approach the topic objectively or subjectively? Explain.

   _____

5. How would you evaluate the sources cited in this report? Are they reliable?

   _____

6. Circle a paragraph that paraphrases a source. Why did the author paraphrase there?

   _____

7. Now circle two quotations. Why are they used instead of paraphrases?

   _____

8. What did you learn from this report? What questions do you still have?

   _____

L04 Planning a Research Report

A research report requires a lot of planning, which takes time. You won't write an effective report if you wait until the last minute to start your work. Be sure to use the writing process to do your best work.

The Writing Process

Prewrite → Write → Revise → Edit → Publish

Scheduling Your Work

Follow the schedule or timetable that your instructor provides. If you must make your own schedule, use the timetable in **Figure 12.2** as a guide. It gives you approximately three weeks to complete the assignment, but you may adjust the schedule as necessary.

Figure 12.2 Research Timetable

1. Prewriting, researching, and planning (4 or 5 days)

2. Writing the first draft (2 or 3 days)

3. Revising (3 days)

4. Editing (2 days)

5. Preparing a final copy (1 day)

Planning a research paper, like any other project, involves predicting how long each step will take. You should also allow extra time for unforeseen problems.

To begin, mark your due date on the calendar. Then work backward, estimating the time needed for each step. If possible, also include a few days away from the paper between writing and revising to let yourself see it with fresh eyes.

As you work, keep checking your schedule. If a step is running long, you will have to adjust later dates to compensate. If a step runs shorter than expected, you can do added research or more extended revising and editing.

Practice Prepare a timetable for your report.

Selecting a Topic

Write your report about a new trend or development in energy, agriculture, technology, health, careers, or another topic that fits your instructor's guidelines.

Practice For two or more of these categories, list three possible subjects for your report. One idea has been provided under each heading.

energy	agriculture	technology	health	careers

Practice Carefully review your lists of topics before choosing one. It may help to talk about your ideas with a classmate. Also consider the following points. Finally, circle the topic you want to write about.

Be sure that . . .

- the topic is well suited to your interests.
- the topic is neither too general nor too specific. (*Alternative energy sources* is too general; *biking to school* may be too specific.)
- you can find enough information about the topic.
- you have enough time to research and write about this topic.

Practice In a few sentences, explain the reason for your topic choice. Doing this will help you establish a focus for your research.

_____

_____

_____

_____

_____

Researching Your Topic

Effective research begins with questions that will direct you as you gather information about your topic.

Establishing a Starting Point

You can establish a starting point for your research by identifying what you already know about the topic and what you need to learn about it.

Practice In a chart like **Figure 12.3**, list things that you already know about the topic and things you would like to find out:

Figure 12.3 Research Chart

Topic: Vertical Farming

Things I Know	Things I Need to Find Out
examples of vertical farming	where vertical farming is used
	what benefits vertical farming offers
	what problems vertical farming faces

Forming Research Questions

As a guide for your research, turn your "Things I Need to Find Out" list into a series of questions.

Practice Write four to six important questions about your topic. As you conduct your actual research, you may add more questions to your list, depending on what you discover.

Research Questions

_____

_____

_____

_____

_____

_____

Identifying Your Sources

Once you have formed a series of questions, you can begin your research. Always follow your instructor's guidelines for the number and types of resources to consult. Whether you refer to books, periodicals, or Web sites, determine first that your sources are current and reliable.

Practice ▸ Fill in a chart with sources of information that seem promising for your research. (You may or may not use all of the different types listed.) Include enough information— title, author, key page numbers, location, publisher—so that you can easily find or refer to each source. This list is often called a **preliminary bibliography**.

Sources for My Research Report

Web sites	
Articles (from journals, magazines, and newspapers)	
Books	
People to interview	
Places to visit	

---

preliminary bibliography
an early list of resources for your research

Insight Plan any interviews and visits right away so that you can benefit from these valuable primary sources.

Olga Danylenko, 2014 / Used under license from Shutterstock.com

Reflecting on Research Writing

Answer the following questions about your reading and writing experiences in this chapter.

1. What is the purpose of a research report—to inform, to persuade, or to entertain? Explain.

2. What is the difference between a research report and a research paper?

3. Which reading strategy seems most helpful when reading a report? Explain.

4. What do you find most convincing in the model report?

5. What is the strongest part of your own report?

6. How could your report be stronger, more convincing, or more informative?

7. What are two important things that you learned about writing a research report?

Key Terms to Remember

When you read and write reports, it is important to understand the following terms.

- **Research report**—a carefully planned form of informational writing, ranging in length from two or three pages on up
- **Documentation guidelines**—rules to follow for giving credit for the ideas of others used in a report; commonly MLA *(Modern Language Association)* or APA *(American Psychological Association)*
- **Citations**—sources cited or referred to in research; occur within the text and in a listing at the end of the report
- **Organized list**—an outline-like graphic used to keep track of the information in a report
- **Writer's stance**—the writer's approach to her or his reporting; either objective *(sticking to the facts)* or subjective *(including personal reflections)*

PART 5:

Sentence Workshops

Part 5: Sentence Workshops

Chapter

13

"An idea can only become a reality once it is broken down into organized, actionable elements."

—Scott Belsky

Sentence Basics

Sentences are built from some very simple parts—nouns, verbs, and modifiers. Every sentence has, at its base, the pairing of a noun and a verb, or a few of them. The other words in the sentence merely modify the noun and verb.

These are sentence basics—the building blocks of thought. With these blocks, you can build tiny towers or magnificent mansions. It all comes down to understanding how to put the pieces together and deciding what you want to create.

Learning Outcomes

LO1 Subjects and Predicates (Verbs)
LO2 Special Types of Subjects
LO3 Special Types of Predicates
LO4 Adjectives
LO5 Adverbs
LO6 Prepositional Phrases
LO7 Clauses

What do you think?

How do ideas become real for you? In what way can writing make things happen?

L01 Subjects and Predicates (Verbs)

The subject of a sentence tells what the sentence is about. The predicate of a sentence tells what the subject does or is.

Dogs bark.

Subject: what the
sentence is about

Predicate: what
the subject does

► Simple Subject and Simple Predicate

The **simple subject** is the subject without any modifiers, and the **simple predicate** is the verb and any helping verbs without modifiers or objects.

The black and white schnauzer was barking all day long.

simple subject   simple predicate

► Complete Subject and Complete Predicate

The **complete subject** is the subject with modifiers, and the **complete predicate** is the verb with modifiers and objects. Modifiers add information to the subject and predicate.

The black and white schnauzer was barking all day long.

complete subject   complete predicate

In this example, the words "black and white" modify, or give more information about, the schnauzer. The words "all day long" give more information about the simple predicate.

► Implied Subject

In commands, the subject *you* is implied. Commands are the only type of sentence in English that can have an **implied subject**.

(You)

implied subject

Stop barking!

complete predicate

► Inverted Order

Most often in English, the subject comes before the predicate. However, in questions and sentences that begin with *here* or *there*, the subject comes after the predicate.

subject

Why are you so loud?

predicate

subject

Here is a biscuit.

predicate

Practice For the following sentences, identify and label the simple subject (SS) and simple predicate (SP). Then write a similar sentence of your own and identify the simple subject and simple predicate in the same way.

1. For thousands of years, humans bred dogs.

_____

2. All dog breeds descended from wolf ancestors.

_____

3. At the end of the Ice Age, humans lived nomadically with their dogs.

_____

4. Ever since that time, dogs have enjoyed going for walks.

_____

Practice For the following sentences, identify and label the complete subject (CS) and complete predicate (CP). Then write a similar sentence of your own and identify the complete subject and complete predicate in the same way.

1. An Irish wolfhound stands as tall as a small pony.

_____

2. Wolfhounds were bred to hunt their ancestors.

_____

3. Wolfhounds also were used for hunting boar.

_____

4. Why are boars extinct in Ireland?

_____

5. There were too many wolfhounds.

_____

---

simple subject
the subject without any modifiers

simple predicate
the verb and any helping verbs
without modifiers or objects

complete subject
the subject with modifiers

complete predicate
the verb with modifiers and objects

implied subject
the word *you* implied in command
sentences

L02 Special Types of Subjects

As you work with subjects, watch for these special types.

► Compound Subjects

A **compound subject** is two or more subjects connected by *and* or *or*.

My <u>sister</u> and <u>I</u> swim well.   <u>Terri, Josh,</u> or <u>I</u> will dive.
compound subject   compound subject

► Infinitives as Subjects

An **infinitive** can function as a subject. An infinitive is a verb form that begins with *to* and may be followed by objects or modifiers.

<u>To become a park ranger</u> is my dream.
infinitive subject with modifiers

► Gerunds as Subjects

A **gerund** can function as a subject. A gerund is a verb form that ends in *ing* and may be followed by objects or modifiers.

<u>Hiking</u> builds strong calves.   <u>Hiking the Appalachian trail</u> is amazing.
gerund subject   gerund subject with modifiers

► Noun Clauses as Subjects

A **noun clause** can function as a subject. The clause itself has a subject and a verb but cannot stand alone as a sentence. Noun clauses are introduced by words like *what, that, when, why, how, whatever,* or *whichever.*

<u>Whoever hikes the trail</u> should bring replacement boots.
noun clause subject

<u>Whatever you need</u> must be carried on your back.
noun clause subject

> Insight   Note that each of these special subjects functions as a noun. A sentence is still, at root, the connection between a noun and a verb.

Say It   Pair up with a partner and read each sentence aloud. Take turns identifying the type of subject—compound subject, infinitive subject, gerund subject, or noun-clause subject. Discuss your answers.

1. You and I should go hiking sometime.
2. To reach the peak of Mount Rainier would be amazing.
3. Whoever wants to go should train with a mountaineer.
4. Hiking the Rockies at high altitudes is challenging.

Practice For the following sentences, identify the complete subject as a compound subject (CPS), infinitive (I), gerund (G), or noun clause (NC). Then write a similar sentence of your own and identify the complete subject in the same way.

1. Planning for success is the key to success.

   _____

2. To complete the course in two years is my main goal.

   _____

3. A donut, a cup of coffee, and good conversation make my morning.

   Compound subject

4. Whoever finds the money can keep it.

   Noun clauses

5. Are Hannah, Michelle, and Sharissa going?

   Compound subject

6. Whenever he arrives is the starting time.

   _____

---

compound subject
two or more subjects connected by *and* or *or*

infinitive
a verb form that begins with *to* and can be used as a noun (or as an adjective or adverb)

gerund
a verb form that ends in *ing* and is used as a noun

noun clause
a group of words that begins with words like *that, what, whoever, whatever, why,* and *when* and contains a subject and a verb but is unable to function as a sentence

L03 Special Types of Predicates

As you work with predicates, watch for these special types.

► Compound Predicates

A **compound predicate** consists of two or more verbs joined by *and* or *or*.

I <u>watched</u> and <u>laughed</u>. My cat <u>stalks, pounces, or tumbles</u>.
compound predicatecompound predicate

► Predicates with Direct Objects

A **direct object** follows a transitive verb and tells what or who receives the action of the verb. A **transitive verb** is an action verb that transfers action to a direct object.

I pointed the <u>laser</u>. My cat saw the <u>spot</u>. He batted <u>it</u> and nipped the <u>ground</u>.
direct object direct object direct object direct object

► Predicates with Indirect Objects

An **indirect object** comes between a transitive verb and a direct object and tells to whom or for whom an action was done.

I gave <u>him</u> a rest. My cat shot <u>me</u> a puzzled look.
indirect object indirect object

► Passive Predicates (Verbs)

When a verb is **passive**, the subject of the sentence is being acted upon rather than acting. Often, the actor is the object of the **preposition** in a phrase that starts with *by*. To make the sentence **active**, rewrite it, turning the object of the preposition into the subject.

Passive	**Active**
My <u>cat</u> <u>was exhausted</u> by the <u>game</u>.	The <u>game</u> <u>exhausted</u> <u>my cat</u>.
subject passive verb object of the preposition	subject active verb direct object

Say It

Pair up with a partner and read each sentence. Take turns identifying the sentence as active or passive. If the sentence is passive, speak the active version out loud.

1. My cat was mesmerized by the laser.
2. The light danced in his paws.
3. The light was chased up and down the hallway by my cat.

Practice For the following sentences, identify and label any compound predicate (CPP), direct object (DO), and indirect object (IO) that you find. Then write a similar sentence of your own and identify the same items.

1. Our pet rabbits hopped and thumped.

   _____

2. The lop-ear leaped the gate.

   _____

3. I gave her a carrot.

   _____

4. She crouched or nibbled.

   _____

Practice For the following sentences, identify and label the simple subject (S), the passive predicate (PP), and the object of the preposition *by* (O). Then rewrite each sentence, making it active.

1. The rabbits are fed by my sister.

   _____

2. She is seen by them as their food goddess.

   _____

---

compound predicate
two or more predicates joined by *and* or *or*

direct object
a word that follows a transitive verb and tells what or who receives the action of the verb

indirect object
a word that comes between a

transitive verb and a direct object and tells to whom or for whom an action was done

passive
the voice created when a subject is being acted upon

active
the voice created when a subject is acting

transitive verb
an action verb that transfers action to a direct object

preposition
a word or group of words that is used with a noun, pronoun, or noun phrase to show direction, location, time, or to introduce an object

L04 Adjectives

To modify a subject (noun), use an adjective. You may also use a phrase or clause that acts as an adjective.

Adjectives answer these basic questions: *which? what kind of? how many? how much?*

To modify the noun athletes, ask . . .

Which athletes? ——▶ **college** athletes

What kind of athletes? ——▶ **female** athletes

How many athletes? ——▶ **few** athletes

few female college athletes

▶ ### Adjective Phrases and Clauses

Phrases and clauses can also act as adjectives to modify nouns. A phrase is a group of words that lacks a subject or predicate or both. A clause is a group of words that has a subject and a predicate but does not form a complete sentence.

To modify the noun athletes, ask . . .

Which athletes? ——▶ athletes **who are taking at least 12 credit hours**

What kind of athletes? ——▶ athletes **with a 3.0 average**

The administration will approve loans for athletes **with a 3.0 average who are taking at least 12 credit hours.**

Insight   If a group of words answers one of the basic adjective questions, the words are probably functioning as an adjective.

Say It   Pair up with a classmate to find adjectives—words, phrases, or clauses—that modify the following nouns. Take turns asking the questions while the other person answers.

1. **Sports**
   Which sports?
   What kind of sports?
   How many sports?

2. **Classes**
   Which classes?
   What kind of classes?
   How many classes?

Practice For each noun, answer the questions using adjectives—words, phrases, or clauses. Then write a sentence using two or more of your answers.

1. **Tournaments**

   Which tournaments? _____

   What kind of tournaments? _basketball_____

   How many tournaments? _two_____

   Sentence: _Our basketball team has have two tournaments this year._

2. **Opponents**

   Which opponents? _____

   What kind of opponents? _____

   How many opponents? _____

   Sentence: _____

   _____

3. **Victories**

   Which victories? _____

   What kind of victories? _____

   How many victories? _____

   Sentence: _____

   _____

L05 Adverbs

To modify a verb, use an adverb. You may also use phrase or clause that acts as an adverb.

Adverbs answer these basic questions: *how? when? where? why? how long? how often?*

To modify the verb dance, ask . . .

How did they dance? ⟶ danced **happily**

When did they dance? ⟶ danced **yesterday**

Where did they dance? ⟶ danced **there**

How often did they dance? ⟶ danced **often**

Yesterday, the bride and groom danced **happily**
and **often there** in the ballroom.

▶ ## Adverb Phrases and Clauses

Phrases and clauses can also act as adverbs to modify verbs.

To modify the verb dance, ask . . .

How did they dance? ⟶ danced **with great joy**

When did they dance? ⟶ danced **from the first song**

Where did they dance? ⟶ danced **all around the room**

Why did they dance? ⟶ danced **to celebrate their wedding**

How often did they dance? ⟶ danced **until the last song**

From the first song until the last song, the couple danced **all around the room**
with great joy to celebrate their wedding.

Insight   Read the last sentence aloud. Though it may look imposing on the page, it sounds natural, probably because adverbs are a common part of our speech. Experiment with these modifiers in your writing as well.

Practice For each verb, answer the questions using adverbs—words, phrases, or clauses. Then write a sentence using three or more of your answers.

1. **Ran**

   How did they run? _Slowly_

   When did they run? _Yesterday_

   Where did they run? _up & down the mtn._

   Why did they run? _Exercise_

   How long did they run? _3hrs_

   How often did they run? _Everyday_

   Sentence: _____

   _____

2. **Jumped**

   How did they jump? _____

   When did they jump? _____

   Where did they jump? _____

   Why did they jump? _____

   How long did they jump? _____

   How often did they jump? _____

   Sentence: _____

   _____

L06   Prepositional Phrases

One of the simplest and most versatile types of phrases in English is the **prepositional phrase**. A prepositional phrase can function as an adjective or an adverb.

► Building Prepositional Phrases

A prepositional phrase is a preposition followed by an object (a noun or pronoun) and any modifiers.

Preposition	+	Object	=	Prepositional Phrase
at		noon		at noon
in		an hour		in an hour
beside		the green clock		beside the green clock
in front of		my aunt's vinyl purse		in front of my aunt's vinyl purse

As you can see, a propositional phrase can be just two words long or many words long. As you can also see, some prepositions are themselves made up of more than one word. Table 13.1 shows a list of common prepositions.

Table 13.1 Prepositions

aboard	back of	except for	near to	round
about	because of	excepting	notwithstanding	save
above	before	for	of	since
according to	behind	from	off	subsequent to
across	below	from among	on	through
across from	beneath	from between	on account of	throughout
after	beside	from under	on behalf of	'til
against	besides	in	onto	to
along	between	in addition to	on top of	together with
alongside	beyond	in behalf of	opposite	toward
alongside of	but	in front of	out	under
along with	by	in place of	out of	underneath
amid	by means of	in regard to	outside	until
among	concerning	inside	outside of	unto
apart from	considering	inside of	over	up
around	despite	in spite of	over to	upon
as far as	down	instead of	owing to	up to
aside from	down from	into	past	with
at	during	like	prior to	within
away from	except	near	regarding	without

Insight   A preposition is pre-positioned before the other words it introduces to form a phrase. Other languages have post-positional words that follow their objects.

Practice For the following items, create a prepositional phrase by writing a preposition and an object (and any modifiers). Then write a sentence using the prepositional phrase.

1.

Preposition	**+**	**Object** (and any modifiers)

Sentence: _____

2.

Preposition	**+**	**Object** (and any modifiers)

Sentence: _____

3.

Preposition	**+**	**Object** (and any modifiers)

Sentence: _____

4.

Preposition	**+**	**Object** (and any modifiers)

Sentence: _____

5.

Preposition	**+**	**Object** (and any modifiers)

Sentence: _____

prepositional phrase
a group of words beginning with a preposition and including an object
(noun or pronoun) and any modifiers

L07 Clauses

A clause is a group of words with a subject and a predicate. If a clause can stand on its own as a sentence, it is an **independent clause**; but if it cannot, it is a **dependent clause**.

▶ Independent Clause

An independent clause has a subject and a predicate and expresses a complete thought. It is the same as a simple sentence.

Clouds piled up in the stormy sky.

▶ Dependent Clause

A dependent clause has a subject and a predicate but does not express a complete thought. Instead, it is used as an **adverb clause**, an **adjective clause**, or a **noun clause**.

Say It Read the dependent clauses (in red) out loud. Can you hear how they sound incomplete? A dependent clause must connect with an independent clause to form a complete thought and make sense.

■ An **adverb clause** begins with a subordinating conjunction (see Table 13.2) and functions as an adverb. To form a complete sentence, it must be connected to an independent clause.

Table 13.2 Subordinating Conjunctions

after	because	in order that	though	where
although	before	provided that	unless	whereas
as	even though	since	until	while
as if	given that	so that	when	
as long as	if	that	whenever	

<u>Even though the forecast said clear skies</u>, the storms rolled in.
adverb clause (dependent)

■ **An adjective clause** begins with a relative pronoun (*which, that, who*) and functions as an adjective, so it must be connected to an independent clause to be complete.

I don't like a meteorologist <u>who often gets the forecast wrong.</u>
adjective clause (dependent)

■ **A noun clause** begins with words like those in Table 13.3 and functions as a noun. It is used as a subject or an object in a sentence.

Table 13.3 Subordinating Conjunctions

how	what	whoever	whomever
that	whatever	whom	why

I wish he had known <u>that the afternoon would bring rain and hail.</u>
noun clause (dependent)

Practice For the following sentences, identify and label any adverb clauses (ADVC), adjective clauses (ADJC), or noun clauses (NC). Then write a similar sentence of your own and identify the clauses.

1. I wonder why weather is so unpredictable.

   _____

2. Storms still surprise meteorologists who have years of experience.

   _____

3. Many different factors determine what will happen in the sky.

   _____

4. Until we can track all factors, we can't predict perfectly.

   _____

5. Whoever gives a forecast is making a guess.

   _____

6. Since weather is so uncertain, predictions include percentages.

   _____

7. A 50 percent chance of rain means that a 50 percent chance of fair weather also exists.

   _____

8. When air crosses a large lake, it picks up moisture that often turns into rain or snow.

   _____

9. Buffalo gets whatever moisture Lake Erie dishes up.

   _____

---

independent clause
a group of words with a subject and predicate that expresses a complete thought

dependent clause
a group of words with a subject and predicate that does not express a complete thought

adverb clause
a dependent clause beginning with a subordinating conjunction and functioning as an adverb

adjective clause
a dependent clause beginning with a relative pronoun and functioning as an adjective

noun clause
a dependent clause beginning with a word like *what, how, that,* or *why* and functioning as a noun

🌐 Real-World Application

Practice In the following email, identify the <u>simple subjects</u>, <u>simple predicates</u>, and (dependent clauses). (Use underlining and circling as shown.)

✉ 📎 📇 🖊   •••

To: Terri Bell

Subject: Revision Suggestions

Hi, Teri:

I enjoyed your article, "Taking On the New *BattleTown 2*," which you submitted for publication on MMORPNews2.com. We like your article but request a few revisions before we send contracts.

This is a quick rundown of our revision suggestions:

1. The opening could be more gripping. The title works well to grab the reader's interest, but the opening feels flat. Perhaps you could provide a glimpse of new features of game play or even give a scenario that was not possible in *BattleTown 1*.

2. A direct quotation from Todd Allen would strengthen the center section. Though you allude to your interview on many occasions, Todd never speaks for himself, and he is a definite name in the industry.

3. Can you get permission to use the visuals? AssemblyArts would love the free publicity, but you need written permission to include the screenshots.

If you could make these changes, we would be very interested in publishing your article. Once I see the revised piece, I can send a contract for you to sign.

Thanks,

Richard Prince

Chapter

14

Robsonphoto, 2014 / Used under license from Shutterstock.com

"A complex system that works is invariably found to
have evolved from a simple system that works."

—John Gaule

Simple, Compound, and Complex Sentences

Most leaves have a central stem with veins extending from it. Sometimes this structure forms a simple oval, but at other times, two or more ovals connect to form a compound leaf. And the shape of some leaves is complex, as if a number of leaves were fused together.

Sentences are similar. All have a subject and a predicate, and some stop at this simple structure. In other cases, two or more sentences combine to make a compound sentence. And when a sentence has one or more dependent clauses fused to it, it becomes complex.

This chapter shows how to create simple, compound, and complex sentences. As with leaves, variety makes sentences beautiful.

Learning Outcomes

LO1 Simple Sentences

LO2 Simple Sentences with Compound Subjects

LO3 Simple Sentences with Compound Predicates

LO4 Compound Sentences

LO5 Complex Sentences

LO6 Complex Sentences with Relative Clauses

What do you think?

Which type of leaf is most beautiful—a simple, compound, or complex leaf? Why?

L01 Simple Sentences

A **simple sentence** consists of a subject and a predicate. The subject is a noun or pronoun that names what the sentence is about. The predicate is verb that tells what the subject does or is.

My roommate plays.

Subject   Predicate

► Modifiers

Other words can be used to modify the subject. Words that modify the subject answer the adjective questions: *which? what kind of? how many? how much?*

My college roommate plays. *(Which roommate?)*

Other words can also modify the verb. These words and phrases answer the adverb questions: *how? when? where? why? to what degree? how often?*

My college roommate plays in the pep band. *(Where does my roommate play?)*

► Direct and Indirect Objects

The verb might also be followed by a noun or pronoun that receives the action of the verb. Such a word is called the **direct object**, and it answers the question *what?* or *whom?*

My college roommate plays the tuba. *(What does my roommate play?)*

Another noun or pronoun could come between the verb and the direct object, telling *to whom* or *for whom* an action is done. Such a word is the **indirect object**.

The college gives him one credit per semester for playing.
(The college gives one credit to whom?)

---

simple sentence
a subject and a predicate that together form a complete thought

direct object
a noun or pronoun that follows a verb and receives its action

indirect object
a noun or pronoun that comes between a verb and a direct object, telling *to whom* or *for whom* an action is done

Say It   Team up with a partner and follow these steps: One of you speaks the sentence aloud, and the other asks the question in italics. Then the first person says the sentence again, inserting an answer.

1. The band marched. *(When did the band march?)*
2. The routine was our favorite. *(Which routine was your favorite?)*
3. The brass section played. *(What did they play?)*
4. The crowd gave loud cheers. *(To whom did the crowd give cheers?)*

Practice   For the following items, write a noun for the subject, a verb, and words to answer the question. Put all the words together to form a sentence.

1.

| **Subject** | + | **Verb** |

Which? _____

Simple Sentence: _____

2.

| **Subject** | + | **Verb** |

What kind of? _____

Simple Sentence: _____

3.

| **Subject** | + | **Verb** |

How many? _____

Simple Sentence: _____

4.

| **Subject** | + | **Verb** |

Whom? _____

Simple Sentence: _____

L02 Simple Sentences with Compound Subjects

A simple sentence can have a **compound subject** (two or more subjects).

► Two Subjects

To write a simple sentence with two subjects, join them using *and* or *or*.

One Subject: Lee worked on the Rube Goldberg machine.

Two Subjects: Lee and Jerome will add the lever arm to tip the bucket.
Lee or Jerome will add the lever arm to tip the bucket.

One Subject: Ms. Claymore will attach the flywheel.

Two Subjects: Ms. Claymore and her aide will attach the flywheel.
Either Ms. Claymore or her aide will attach the flywheel.

► Three or More Subjects

To write a simple sentence with three or more subjects, create a series. Use commas between all subjects, and place *and* or *or* before the last subject.

Three Subjects: Jerome, Lee, and Sandra are finishing the machine soon.

Five Subjects: Jerome, Lee, Sandra, Ms. Claymore, and her aide will enter the machine in a contest.

When a compound subject is joined by *and*, the subject is plural and requires a plural verb. When a compound subject is joined by *or*, the verb should agree with the last subject.

Ms. Claymore and her aide need to submit the entry form.

Ms. Claymore or her aide needs to submit the entry form.

---

compound subject
two or more subjects joined by *and* or *or*

Insight   A compound subject does not make the sentence compound. As long as all of the subjects connect to the same predicate, the thought is still a simple sentence.

Say It Speak each of the following sentences out loud.
1. Jerome *loves* the Rube Goldberg project.
2. Jerome *and* Sandra *love* the Rube Goldberg project.
3. Jerome *or* Sandra *works* on it every day after school.
4. Jerome, Sandra, *and* Lee *are* good team members.
5. Jerome, Sandra, *or* Lee often *makes* a helpful comment.

Practice Write a subject in each box. Then write a sentence using a compound subject joined by *and* or *or*.

1.
Subject	Subject

Simple Sentence: _____

2.
Subject	Subject

Simple Sentence: _____

3.
Subject	Subject	Subject

Simple Sentence: _____

4.
Subject	Subject	Subject

Simple Sentence: _____

5.
Subject	Subject	Subject	Subject

Simple Sentence: _____

6.
Subject	Subject	Subject	Subject

Simple Sentence: _____

L03 Simple Sentences with Compound Predicates

A simple sentence can have a **compound predicate** (two or more verbs).

► Two Verbs

To create a compound predicate, join two verbs using *and* or *or*.

One Verb: The band rocked.

Two Verbs: The band rocked and danced.

Remember that the predicate includes not just a verb but also words that modify or complete the verb.

One Verb plus Other Words: The band played their hit single.
                                            predicate

Two Verbs plus Other Words: The band played their hit single and covered other songs.
                                            compound predicate

► Three or More Verbs

To create a compound predicate with three or more verbs, use a series. Put commas between all the verbs, and place *and* or *or* before the last verb.

Three Verbs: The singer crooned, wailed, and roared.

Five Verbs: The fans clapped, screamed, danced, cheered, and swayed.

If each verb also includes modifiers or completing words (direct and indirect objects), place the commas after each complete predicate.

The crowd members got to their feet, waved their hands back and forth, and sang along with the band.

Insight   Remember that the predicate tells what the subject is doing or being. As long as both predicates connect to the same subject, the sentence is still a simple sentence.

Practice For the following subjects, write a verb in each box. Then write a simple sentence joining the verbs with *and* or *or* to create a compound predicate. You may also add modifiers and completing words.

1. The reporters

Verb

Verb

2. The police

Verb

Verb

3. The manager

Verb

Verb

4. The bouncer

Verb

Verb

Verb

---

compound predicate
two or more predicates joined by *and* or *or*

L05 Complex Sentences

A **complex sentence** joins an independent clause to one or more dependent clauses. The independent clause can stand alone as a sentence, but a dependent clause cannot. (Remember that a clause is a group of words with a subject and verb.)

► Using a Subordinating Conjunction

You can create a complex sentence by placing a **subordinating conjunction** before the clause that is less important. Table 14.1 shows common subordinating conjunctions:

Table 14.1 Common Subordinating Conjunctions

after	before	so that	when
although	even though	that	where
as	if	though	whereas
as if	in order that	till	while
as long as	provided that	'til	
because	since	until	

The subordinating conjunction shows that one clause depends on the other to make sense.

Two Simple Sentences: We played flawless offense. We won the football game.

Complex Sentence: Because we played flawless offense, we won the football game.
                                              dependent clause
                    We won the football game because we played flawless offense.
                                                           dependent clause

NOTE: The subordinating conjunction goes at the beginning of the less important clause, but the two clauses could go in either order. When the dependent clause comes second, it usually is not set off by a comma.

► Compound-Complex Sentences

You can create a **compound-complex sentence** by placing a subordinating conjunction before a simple sentence and connecting it to a compound sentence.

Say It
Read the example complex and compound-complex sentences aloud. Despite their daunting names, you use these kinds of sentences in speech. Experiment with them in your writing.

Simple Sentence: I threw two touchdowns.

Compound Sentence: Jake kicked the extra points, and we took the lead.

Compound-Complex: After I threw two touchdowns, Jake kicked the extra points, and we took the lead.

Practice Write a simple sentence to answer each prompt. Then select a subordinating conjunction from Table 14.1, place it at the beginning of one sentence, and combine the two sentences into a single complex sentence.

1. What and how did you play? _Volleyball, good_

   Did you win or lose? _Won_

   Complex sentence: _Because cassy played volleyball pretty good, she won the game_

2. What person or team did you play? _Duke, Jason_

   Why did you play the opponent? _tournament_

   Complex sentence: _____

   _____

3. Who won the game? _____

   Why did that side win? _____

   Complex sentence: _____

   _____

4. Where did you play? _____

   Where else could you have played? _____

   Complex sentence: _____

   _____

5. What surprised you? _____

   Why did it surprise you? _____

   Complex sentence: _____

   _____

complex sentence
a sentence with one independent clause and one or more dependent clauses

compound-complex sentence
a sentence with two or more independent clauses and one or more dependent clauses

subordinating conjunction
word or word groups that connect clauses of different importance

🌐 Real-World Application

Practice Read the following email message about a meeting. Note how every sentence is a simple sentence. Rewrite the message, combining some sentences into compound or complex sentences to improve the flow.

✉️ 📎 📇 📝   ● ● ●

To: Melvin Lindau

Subject: Production Meeting Summary

Dear Mr. Lindau:

You asked about the Monday production meeting. I will summarize it. The production staff met with the writers. The writers explained their new project. It focuses on twenty-first-century skills. The writers presented two chapters. They will become a prototype.

The new project needs to be visual. It should appeal to students and teachers. The design needs to make text accessible. The writing has an open quality. It still feels academic. The book should be available for sale in the fall. A teacher's edition will follow.

The designers are beginning work on a prototype. The writers continue to create chapters.

I hope this answers your questions.

Sincerely,

Amy Lentz

Dear Mr. Lindau:

_____

_____

_____

_____

_____

_____

_____

_____

_____

_____

Chapter

15

"My idea of an agreeable person is a person who agrees with me."

—Benjamin Disraeli

Agreement

When two people agree, they can work together. They have the same goals and outlook, and they can become a team.

Subjects and verbs are much the same. If the subject is plural, the verb needs to be plural as well, or they can't work together. Pronouns also need to agree in number with their antecedents, which are the nouns the pronouns replace. Without agreement, these words fight each other, and instead of conveying ideas, they disrupt communication.

This chapter focuses on the agreement between subjects and verbs and between pronouns and antecedents. It also tackles other pronoun problems. After you work through the exercises here, you'll find it easy to write sentences that agree.

Learning Outcomes

LO1 Subject-Verb Agreement
LO2 Agreement with Compound Subjects
LO3 Agreement with *I* and *You*
LO4 Agreement with Indefinite Pronouns
LO5 Pronoun-Antecedent Agreement
LO6 Other Pronoun Problems

What do you think?

What makes a person agreeable? What makes subjects and verbs agreeable?

L01 Subject-Verb Agreement

A verb must **agree in number** with the subject of the sentence. If the subject is singular, the verb must be singular. If the subject is plural, the verb must be plural.

Plural subjects often end in *s*, but plural verbs usually do not. Also note that only present-tense verbs and certain *be* verbs have separate singular and plural forms. Table 15.1 shows the singular and plural forms of common present- and past-tense verbs.

Table 15.1 Singular and Plural Forms of Common Verbs

Present:	Singular	Plural	Past:	Singular	Plural
	walks	walk		walked	walked
	sees	see		saw	saw
	eats	eat		ate	ate
	is/am	are		was	were

- To make most verbs singular, add just an *s*.

  run—runs   write—writes   stay—stays

- The verbs *do* and *go* are made singular by adding an *es*.

  do—does   go—goes

- When a verb ends in *ch*, *sh*, *x*, or *z*, make it singular by adding *es*.

  latch—latches   wish—wishes   fix—fixes   buzz—buzzes

- When a verb ends in a consonant followed by a *y*, change the y to *i* and add *es*.

  try—tries   fly—flies   cry—cries   quantify—quantifies

---

agree in number
match, as when a subject and verb are
both singular or both plural.

Say It   Read the following word groups aloud, emphasizing the words in *italics*.

1. The bird *sings* / The birds *sing* / The phone *rings* / The phones *ring*
2. He *works* / They *work* / She *learns* / They *learn*
3. The woman *does* / The women *do* / The man *goes* / The men *go*
4. She *wishes* / They *wish* / He *boxes* / They *box*

Practice For the following sentences, write the correct form of the verb in parentheses.

1. A philosophy major _____ about thinking. (know)

2. A philosopher _____ to find philosophical work. (try)

3. An employer rarely _____ to hire philosophers. (wish)

4. But a philosopher often _____ outside the box. (think)

5. My roommate _____ philosophy. (study)

6. He also _____ to study the want ads for jobs. (need)

7. He _____ employers need thinkers. (say)

8. That idea _____ sense. (make)

Practice Correct any agreement errors you find by crossing out the verb and writing the correct present-tense verb.

        The philosopher Plato say in his writing that the material world aren't the real world. He say we sees shadows on a cave wall. Plato believe in eternal forms of perfection. Every real table in the world are patterned after the perfect form of a table. In that way, people, too, is patterned after the perfect form of people. Though Plato lived more than three hundred years before Jesus, many Christian thinkers likes his concept of eternal forms. The idea fit well with the ideas of a soul and a creator. Many modern thinkers, though, has the opposite idea. They says that only physical things is real. Plato's teachings, of course, disagree.

Practice For each plural verb, write one sentence using the verb in its singular form.

1. fly   3. fish
2. do   4. wax

L02 Agreement with Compound Subjects

Sentences with **compound subjects** have special agreement rules.

- When a sentence has two or more subjects joined by *and*, the verb should be plural.

Mani and Sutu march.

- When a sentence has two or more subjects joined by *or* or *nor*, the verb should agree with the last subject.

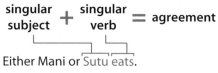

Either Mani or Sutu eats.

or

The sentence has two subjects joined by *or*. The second subject (*Sutu*) is singular, so a singular verb (*eats*) is needed for the sentence to agree.

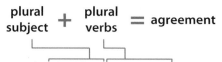

Neither the rhino nor the elephants eat or sleep by each other.

The sentence has two subjects joined by *nor*. The second subject (*elephants*) is plural, so plural verbs (*eat, sleep*) are needed for the sentence to agree.

> **Say It** Read the following sentences aloud, emphasizing the words in *italics*.
>
> 1. Mani *and* Sutu *swim*. Mani *or* Sutu *swims*.
> 2. The man *and* woman *dance*. The man *or* woman *dances*.
> 3. The Democrat *and* the Republican *agree*. The Democrat *or* the Republican *agrees*.
> 4. Neither the pets *nor* their owner *likes* thunder.
> 5. The dog, cat, *and* guinea pig *greet* me. The dog, cat, *or* guinea pig *greets* me.

---

compound subject
two or more subjects that share the same verb or verbs

Practice For the following sentences, write the correct form of the verb in parentheses.

1. The band and the director _____ the crowd. (entertain)

2. The music or the marching _____ plenty of applause. (get)

3. The director and trumpet soloist _____ an ovation. (receive)

4. Neither the band nor the audience ____wants____ the performance to end. (want)

5. The brass section or the director _____ an encore. (signal)

6. Teamwork and practice _____ brought success. (have)

7. Either Todd or Lewis _____ to join the band. (plan)

8. Sweat and hard work _____ Todd or Lewis. (await)

9. Both Todd and Lewis ____are____ freshmen. (are)

10. Either a recorded performance or an audition ____is____ required. (are)

Practice Correct any agreement errors you find by crossing out the verb and writing the correct present-tense verb.

Childhood dreams and fantasies rarely comes true. A firefighter or police

officer ~~are~~ is what many children dream of being. Imagine a world filled with

firefighters and police! Neither the accountant nor the landscaper figure~~s~~ big in

childhood plans. A princess or a wizard ~~are~~ is also a popular choice for kids. Job

openings and pay for either career ~~is~~ are pretty unlikely. Even being an astronaut or

exploring faraway places ~~have~~ has become a scary choice. The trials of joblessness

and the responsibilities of adulthood conspires to convince people to seek other

careers. Childhood stars sometimes get "real" jobs, too. Johnny Whitaker and Wil

Wheaton works with computers. They traded childhood dreams for adult ones.

Practice Write a sentence with a compound subject joined by *and*. Write a sentence with a compound subject joined by *or*. Check subject-verb agreement.

L03 Agreement with *I* and *You*

The pronouns *I* and *you* usually take plural verbs, even though they are singular.

plural verb

Correct: I go to Great America and ride roller coasters. You do, too.

singular verb

Incorrect: I goes to Great America and rides roller coasters. You does, too.

NOTE: The pronoun *I* takes the singular verbs *am* and *was*.
Do not use *I* with *be* or *is*. Table 15.2 shows when to use *am*, *is*, *are*, *was*, and *were*.

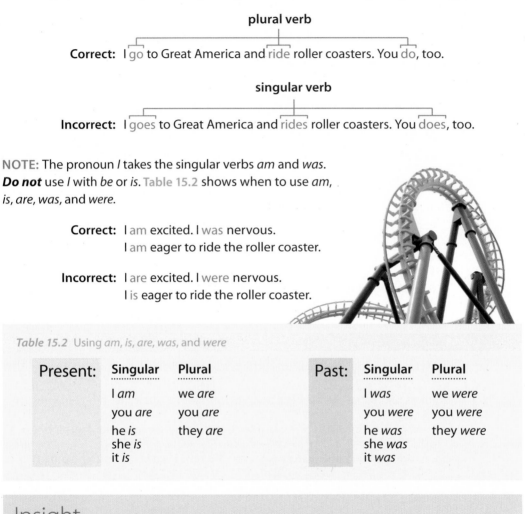

> **Correct:** I am excited. I was nervous.
> I am eager to ride the roller coaster.
>
> **Incorrect:** I are excited. I were nervous.
> I is eager to ride the roller coaster.

Table 15.2 Using *am, is, are, was,* and *were*

Present:	Singular	Plural	Past:	Singular	Plural
	I *am*	we *are*		I *was*	we *were*
	you *are*	you *are*		you *were*	you *were*
	he *is*	they *are*		he *was*	they *were*
	she *is*			she *was*	
	it *is*			it *was*	

Insight The word *am* exists for one reason only—to be used with the word *I*. There is no other subject for the verb *am*. In academic or formal writing, *I* should never be used with *be* or *is*. Think of René Descartes saying, "I think, therefore I am."

Say It Read the following sentences aloud, emphasizing the words in *italics*.

1. I *laugh* / You *laugh* / She *laughs* / They *laugh*
2. I *work* / You *work* / He *works* / They *work*
3. I *do* / You *do* / He *does* / They *do*
4. I *am* / You *are* / She *is* / They *are*

Practice For the following sentences, write the correct form of the verb in parentheses. (Do not change the tense.)

1. I _____ louder than he _____ . (laugh)

2. You _____ as well as she _____ . (climb)

3. We _____ together, or you _____ alone. (work)

4. Stan _____ silverware, while I _____ pans. (wash)

5. I _____ often, but he _____ rarely. (help)

6. The group _____ on Sunday, but I _____ later. (watch)

7. I _____ first, and she _____ next. (eat)

8. You _____ tired, and I _____ , too. (are)

9. Last year, I _____ short, but you _____ tall. (were)

10. You _____ helpful; I hope I _____ also. (are)

Practice Correct any agreement errors you find by crossing out the verb and writing the correct verb.

I is starting a class in astronomy, and I wonders if I can borrow your telescope. You rarely uses it anymore, and I needs it to be able to look at the moons of Jupiter. My professor says that even a moderate-size telescope will show the moons. She have instructions for finding Jupiter. I knows how to use the telescope, but if you is afraid I would break it, you could set it up for me.

I has a yard away from city lights, and I has lawn chairs and blankets we could use. If you agrees to come out and set up the telescope, I agrees to provide snacks for us.

What do you think? I hopes I'm not asking too much and that you are willing to help. I is just excited to see Jupiter's moons, and I thinks you might like to see them, too.

Practice Write two sentences using *I* as the subject. Then write two more using *you* as the subject. Check your subject-verb agreement.

L04   Agreement with Indefinite Pronouns

An **indefinite pronoun** is intentionally vague. Instead of referring to a specific person, place, or thing, an indefinite pronoun refers to something general or unknown.

▶ Singular Indefinite Pronouns

Singular indefinite pronouns (see Table 15.3) take singular verbs:

Someone cooks every night.

No one gets out of kitchen duty.

Everyone benefits from the chore schedule.

Table 15.3 Singular Indefinite Pronouns

someone	somebody	something
anyone	anybody	anything
no one	nobody	nothing
everyone	everybody	everything
one	each	either / neither

Note that indefinite pronouns that end in *one, body,* or *thing* are singular, just as these words themselves are singular. Just as you would write "That thing is missing," you would write "Something is missing."

Using *one, each, either,* and *neither* as subjects can be tricky because these words are often followed by a prepositional phrase that contains a plural object. The verb must still be singular.

One of my friends is a great cook.
    prepositional phrase

Each of us wants to cook as well as he does.
    prepositional phrase

Remember that a compound subject joined with *or* needs a verb that matches the last subject.

No one or nothing keeps him from making a wonderful meal.

Say It   Read the following word groups aloud, emphasizing the words in *italics*.
1. No one *is*   /   Nobody *has*   /   Nothing *does*
2. Everyone *is*   /   Everybody *has*   /   Everything *does*
3. One of my friends *is*   /   Each of my friends *has*   /   Either of my friends *does*

---

indefinite pronoun
a special type of pronoun that does not refer to a
specific person, place, or thing

Practice For the following sentences, write the correct form of the verb in parentheses. (Do not change the tense.)

1. Everyone _____complete_____ an application. (complete)

2. Somebody _____has_____ to get the job. (have)

3. Each of the jobs _____is_____ available. (are)

4. Neither of the applicants _____is_____ qualified. (are)

5. Either of the prospects _____hopes_____ to be trained. (hope)

6. Nobody _____wants_____ to go home empty-handed. (want)

7. Everybody _____has_____ bills to pay. (have)

8. Someone or something _____has_____ to give. (have)

9. Either of the positions _____pays_____ well. (pay)

10. One of my friends _____waits_____ for word on the job. (wait)

Practice For the following sentences, write a sentence using the indefinite pronoun as a subject. Choose present-tense verbs and check subject-verb agreement.

1. Someone _____

   _____

2. Nothing _____

   _____

3. Neither _____

   _____

4. Everyone _____

   _____

5. Each _____

   _____

6. Anybody _____

   _____

Other indefinite pronouns are plural, and some indefinite pronouns can be singular *or* plural depending on how they are used.

► Plural Indefinite Pronouns

Plural indefinite pronouns take plural verbs (see **Table 15.4**).

Table 15.4 Plural Indefinite Pronouns	
both	many
few	several

> Many of us follow classical music.
>
> Several are big fans.
>
> Few musicians are greater than Mozart.

► Singular or Plural Indefinite Pronouns

Some indefinite pronouns are singular or plural (see **Table 15.5**). If the object of the prepositional phrase following the pronoun is singular, the pronoun takes a singular verb; if the object is plural, the pronoun takes a plural verb.

Table 15.5 Singular or Plural Indefinite Pronouns	
all	most
any	none
half	some
part	

NOTE: The *object* of the prepositional phrase is the noun that follows the preposition. It is needed to complete the phrase's meaning.

Most of the song thrills us.

| indefinite | singular | singular |
| pronoun | object | verb |

Most of the songs thrill us.

| indefinite | plural | plural |
| pronoun | object | verb |

Notice the shift in meaning, depending on the prepositional phrase. "Most of the song" means that one song is mostly thrilling. "Most of the songs" means that all but a few of several songs are thrilling. Here's another example.

> Half of the concert features Mozart.
>
> Half of the concerts feature Mozart.

In the first sentence, half of one concert features Mozart's compositions. In the second sentence, half of several concerts feature Mozart's music. Here's a final example.

> Some of class was devoted to studying Mozart's music.
>
> Some of the classes were devoted to studying Mozart's music.

In the first sentence, some of one class was devoted to studying Mozart's music. In the second sentence, some of multiple classes were devoted to studying Mozart's music.

Say It Read the following word groups aloud, emphasizing the words in *italics*.

1. Both *are* / Few *have* / Many *do* / Several *were*
2. All of the piece *is*   /   Any of the pieces *are*   /   Half of the piece *does*
3. Part of the song *is*   /   Most of the songs *are*

Practice For the following sentences, write the correct form of the verb in parentheses. (Do not change the tense.) Check your work by saying each sentence aloud, emphasizing the underlined verbs.

1. Several _____ attending, and all of us _____ sitting in the balcony. (are)

2. All of the songs _____ dramatic; all of the drama _____ intentional. (are)

3. Everyone _____ Tchaikovsky, but few _____ only him. (like)

4. One of my friends _____ to classical radio; several _____ to Internet radio. (listen)

5. Half of the album _____ symphonies, and half of the symphonies _____ brass fanfares. (feature)

6. Most of us _____ about music, and some of us _____ music, too. (read)

7. Of the music lovers, several _____ hard-core fans, but none of them _____ composers. (are)

8. One of my friends _____ trombone, and some of my friends _____ piano. (play)

9. Few _____ played in an orchestra, but one of us _____ played in a band. (have)

Practice For the following items, write a sentence using the indefinite pronoun as the subject. Choose present-tense verbs and check subject-verb agreement.

1. Part _____

2. Most _____

3. Few _____

4. Several _____

5. Both _____

6. All _____

L05 Pronoun-Antecedent Agreement

A pronoun must agree in **person**, **number**, and **gender** with its **antecedent** (see Table 15.6). The antecedent is the noun that the pronoun refers to or replaces.

antecedent
(third-person, singular, feminine) **+** **pronoun**
(third-person, singular, feminine) **=** **agreement**

The woman brought her briefcase but forgot her computer.

Table 15.6 Pronoun-Antecedent Agreement

	Singular	Plural
First Person:	I, me, my, mine	we, us, our, ours
Second Person:	you, your, yours	you, your, yours
Third Person:		
masculine	he, him, his	they, them, their, theirs
feminine	she, her, hers	they, them, their, theirs
neuter	it, its	they, them, their, theirs

► Two or More Antecedents

When two or more antecedents are joined by *and*, the pronoun should be plural.

> Kali and Teri want to fill their baskets with eggs.

When two or more singular antecedents are joined by *or* or *nor*, the pronoun or pronouns should be singular.

> Either Alice or Dave planned the hunt, so she or he hid the eggs.

> Neither Kali nor Teri filled her basket with eggs.

> Either Alice or Dave will search for her or his favorite hiding spots next year.

NOTE: Avoid sexism when choosing a pronoun to replace a general noun. Don't assume the pronoun refers to only males or only females.

> **Sexist:** Each child should bring his basket.
> **Correct:** Each child should bring her or his basket.
> **Correct:** Children should bring their baskets.

Practice In the following sentences, write the pronoun that agrees with the underlined word or words.

1. <u>Ted</u> has written a patriotic poem, and _____ will read _____ poem at the Fourth of July festival.

2. <u>Shandra</u> and <u>Shelli</u> will bring _____ lawn chairs to the fireworks display.

3. Either <u>John</u> or <u>Grace</u> will play _____ or _____ favorite marches over the sound system.

4. <u>John</u> and <u>Dave</u> play trombone and will bring _____ instruments to play with the band.

5. Each <u>person</u> should bring _____ or _____ own flag.

6. <u>Mayor Jenny White</u> or <u>Congressperson Mark Russell</u> will give the invocation, and then _____ or _____ will introduce the main speaker.

7. <u>Rick</u> and <u>Linda</u> will sing _____ rendition of the national anthem.

8. <u>Acrobats</u> will stroll through the park on _____ ten-foot-tall stilts.

9. Each <u>acrobat</u> will have to keep _____ or _____ balance on uneven ground among running children.

10. <u>Ducks</u> and <u>ducklings</u> in the lake will have to make _____ way to quieter waters when the fireworks begin.

Practice Rewrite each of the following sentences to avoid sexism.

1. Every acrobat should check his equipment.

_____

2. Each acrobat must keep her balance.

_____

3. One of the acrobats left his stilts at the park.

_____

---

person
the person speaking (first person—*I, we*), the person being spoken to (second person—*you*), or the person being spoken about (third person—*he, she, it, they*)

number
indication of whether a word is singular or plural

gender
masculine, feminine, neuter, or indefinite

antecedent
the noun that a pronoun refers to or replaces

L06 Other Pronoun Problems

▶ Missing Antecedent

If no clear antecedent is provided, the reader doesn't know what or whom the pronoun refers to.

Confusing: In Illinois, they claim Lincoln as their own.
(To whom does the pronoun "they" refer?)

Clear: In Illinois, the citizens claim Lincoln as their own.

▶ Vague Pronoun

If the pronoun could refer to two or more words, the passage is **ambiguous**.

Indefinite: Sheila told her daughter to use her new tennis racket.
(To whom does the pronoun "her" refer, Sheila or her daughter?)

Clumsy: Sheila told her daughter to use Sheila's new tennis racket.

Clear: Sheila loaned her new tennis racket to her daughter.

▶ Incorrect Case

Pronouns have three cases. That means they can be used in three ways—as subjects, objects, or possessives. Table 15.7 outlines which pronouns to use in each case. One common error is using an object pronoun as a subject.

Table 15.7 Cases of Personal Pronouns

Subject	Object	Possessive
I	me	my, mine
we	us	our, ours
you	you	your, yours
he	him	his
she	her	her, hers
it	it	its
they	them	their, theirs

Incorrect: Them are funny videos.
Him and I laughed hard.

Correct: They are funny videos.
He and I laughed hard.

Also remember to use *my* before the thing possessed and *mine* afterward: *my cat*, but *that cat is mine*. Do the same with *our/ours*, *your/yours*, *her/hers*, and *their/theirs*.

▶ Double Subject

If a pronoun is used right after the subject, an error called a double subject occurs.

Incorrect: Your father, he is good at poker.

Correct: Your father is good at poker.

pukach, 2014 / Used under license from Shutterstock.com

Practice In the following sentences, write the correct pronoun from the choices in parentheses.

1. _____ need to help _____ with the taxes.
   (I, me, my, mine)   (you, your, yours)

2. _____ should help _____ and see what _____ needs.
   (you, your, yours)   (she, her, hers)   (she, her, hers)

3. _____ can show _____ that account of _____ .
   (he, him, his)   (I, me, my, mine)   (you, your, yours)

4. _____ gave _____ permission for _____ to see it.
   (you, your, yours)   (you, your, yours)   (I, me, my, mine)

5. _____ asked _____ accountant to help _____ .
   (we, us, our, ours)   (we, us, our, ours)   (we, us, our, ours)

Practice Rewrite each of the following sentences, correcting the pronoun problems.

1. Him and I worked on the project in class.

   _____

2. Lupita needed to visit with Kelly, but she had no time.

   _____

3. Before we climbed in, it collapsed.

   _____

4. They say that a cure for cancer is coming.

   _____

5. Trina and Lois, they bought frozen custard.

   _____

6. Carl asked Tim to make his lunch.

   _____

ambiguous
unclear, confusing

🌐 Real-World Application

Practice ▷ In the following email, correct the agreement errors and any other pronoun problems.

To: Jean Leuinski

Subject: Thank You for Your Recommendation

Hi, Ms. Leuinski:

Thank your for recommending me for the position of research analyst at Bismark Laboratories. During the interview last Monday, Dr. Jason Lemark said that she had received your letter and had talked with you by phone. On both occasions, him noted, you described mine work as "well researched, meticulous, and professional." I deeply appreciates your comments and you trust.

The outcome of the application process could not be more positive. Dr. Lemark are offering me not just one job, but two! The first position is the one that I applied for in Bismark's San Diego office. The second position have more responsibility and higher pay, but they is in the company's Houston office.

Thanks again for your strong recommendation, Ms. Leuinski! Your positive words clearly affected the decision made by Dr. Lemark and the Research and Development Department. You has my deepest gratitude.

Best wishes,

Rodell

Robsonphoto, 2014 / Used under license from Shutterstock.com

"I love my car . . . especially when it's taking
me places."

—Anonymous

16

Sentence Problems

Cars are great when they go, but when they break down, they're a huge headache. After a look under the hood, a bit of scrabbling beneath the thing, maybe a push, maybe a jack, and probably a tow truck, there's probably going to be a big bill.

Sentences also are great until they break down. But you don't need to be stuck with the confusing mess for long. This chapter outlines a few common sentence problems and explains how to fix them.

Learning Outcomes

LO1 Common Fragments

LO2 Tricky Fragments

LO3 Comma Splices

LO4 Run-On Sentences

LO5 Rambling Sentences

LO6 Dangling and Misplaced Modifiers

LO7 Shifts in Sentence Construction

What do you think?

How is reading unclear sentences similar to driving with a flat tire?

L01 Common Fragments

In everyday speech and informal writing, sentence fragments are occasionally used. In academic conversations and formal writing, fragments should be avoided because they are too easily misunderstood.

► Missing Parts

A sentence requires a subject and a verb. If one or the other or both are missing, the sentence is a **fragment**. Such fragments can be fixed by supplying the missing part.

Fragment:	Went to the concert.
Fragment + Subject:	We went to the concert.
Fragment:	Everyone from Westville Community College.
Fragment + Verb:	Everyone from Westville Community College may participate.
Fragment:	In the interest of student safety.
Fragment + Subject and Verb:	The president acted in the interest of student safety.

► Incomplete Thoughts

A sentence also must express a complete thought. Some fragments have a subject and a verb but do not express a complete thought. These fragments can be corrected by providing words that complete the thought.

Fragment:	The concert will include.
Completing Thought:	The concert will include an amazing light show.
Fragment:	If we arrive in time.
Completing Thought:	If we arrive in time, we'll get front-row seats.
Fragment:	That opened the concert.
Completing Thought:	I liked the bluegrass band that opened the concert.

(Say It)   Read these fragments aloud. Then read each one again, but this time supply the necessary words to form a complete thought.

1. The student union building.
2. Where you can buy used books.
3. Walked to class every morning.
4. When the instructor is sick.
5. The cop was.

Practice ▷ Add words to turn the following fragments into complete sentences.

1. Went to the office.

_____

2. The photographer standing at the door.

_____

3. Will debate the pros and cons of tanning.

_____

4. Native Americans.

_____

Practice ▷ The following paragraph contains numerous fragments. Either add what is missing or combine fragments with other sentences to make them complete. Use the correction marks shown.

> Some classes ask you to learn lots of facts. Art-history classes, for example. Require strong memorization skills. I panicked once. When a semester's worth of art-history notes went missing. The test was the next day. Had just been studying. Those miles and miles of notes. And then a phone call. My friend had found them. Soggy but intact.

Correction Marks

⌐ delete	⋏ add comma	˄ᵂᵒʳᵈ add word
ᵈ̲ capitalize	? ˄ add question mark	⊙ add period
⌀ lowercase	˅ insert an apostrophe	⬭ spelling
⋏ insert		⊓⊔ switch

Practice ▷ Correct the following fragments by supplying the missing parts. Use your imagination.

1. In the newspaper.   2. We bought.   3. The purpose of math.

_____

fragment
a group of words that is missing a subject, a verb, or other words
that keep it from expressing a complete thought

L02 Tricky Fragments

Some fragments are more difficult to find and correct. They creep into our writing because they are often part of the way we talk.

► Absolute Phrases

An **absolute phrase** may look like a sentence, but it isn't. An absolute phrase can be made into a sentence by adding a **helping verb** or by connecting the phrase to a complete sentence.

> **Absolute Phrase**
> **(Fragment):** Our legs trembling from the hike.
>
> **Absolute Phrase +**
> **Helping Verb:** Our legs were trembling from the hike.
>
> **Absolute Phrase +** We collapsed on the couch, our legs trembling
> **Complete Sentence:** from the hike.

► Informal Fragments

Fragments that are commonly used in speech should be eliminated from formal writing. Avoid the following types of fragments unless you are writing dialogue.

> **Interjections:** Hey! Yeah!
>
> **Exclamations:** What a nuisance! How fun!
>
> **Greetings:** Hi, everybody. Good afternoon.
>
> **Questions:** How come? Why not? What?
>
> **Answers:** About three or four. As soon as possible.

Sentences that begin with *here* or *there* have a **delayed subject**, which appears after the verb. Other sentences (commands) have an **implied subject** (*you*). Such sentences are not fragments.

> **Delayed Subject:** Here are some crazy fans wearing wild hats.
>
> **Implied Subject:** Tackle him! Bring him down!

Say It Read each fragment aloud. Then add words to form a complete thought.

1. Are three types of laptop computers.
2. Our instructor explaining the assignment.
3. About three in the morning.
4. Is my favorite Web site.
5. My friend working at a half-priced book store.

Practice ▶ Rewrite each of the following fragments, making it a sentence.

1. Our boisterous behavior announcing our approach.

_____

2. A tidy hedge surrounding the trimmed lawn.

_____

3. The owner's gaze tracking us from the front porch.

_____

4. His dogs barking loudly from the backyard.

_____

5. Our welcome feeling less likely with each step.

_____

Practice ▶ The following paragraph contains a number of informal fragments. Identify and cross out each one. Reread the paragraph and listen for the difference.

Wow! It's amazing what archaeologists can discover from bones. Did you know that Cro-Magnon (our ancestors) and Neanderthal tribes sometimes lived side by side? Sure did! In other places, when climate change drove our ancestors south, Neanderthals took their place. Neanderthals were tough and had stronger arms and hands than Cro-Magnons had. Neanderthal brains were bigger, too. What? So why aren't there any Neanderthals around now? Huh? Well, although Neanderthal tribes used spears and stone tools, our ancestors were much better toolmakers. Yeah! Also, Neanderthals ate mainly big animals, while Cro-Magnon ate anything from fish to pigs to roots and berries. So in the long run, Cro-Magnon hominids prospered, while Neanderthal tribes dwindled away.

absolute phrase
a group of words with a noun and a participle (a word ending in *ing*) and the words that modify them

helping verb
verb that works with a main verb to form a sentence

delayed subject
a subject that appears after the verb, as in a sentence that begins with *here* or *there* or a sentence that asks a question

implied subject
the word *you*, assumed to begin command sentences

L03 Comma Splices

Comma splices occur when two sentences are connected with only a comma. A comma splice can be fixed by adding a coordinating conjunction (*and, but, or, nor, for, so,* or *yet*) or a subordinating conjunction (*while, after, when, before, because, although*). The two sentences can also be joined by a semicolon (;) or separated by a period.

Comma Splice: The Eiffel Tower was a main attraction at the Paris Exposition, the Ferris wheel was its equivalent at the Chicago Exposition.

Corrected by adding a coordinating conjunction:	The Eiffel Tower was a main attraction at the Paris Exposition, and the Ferris wheel was its equivalent at the Chicago Exposition.
Corrected by adding a subordinating conjunction:	While the Eiffel Tower was a main attraction at the Paris Exposition, the Ferris wheel was its equivalent at the Chicago Exposition.
Corrected by replacing the comma with a semicolon:	The Eiffel Tower was a main attraction at the Paris Exposition; the Ferris wheel was its equivalent at the Chicago Exposition.

Insight A comma without a conjunction is not strong enough to join two sentences. A semicolon can join two related sentences, or a period can separate them.

Comma Splice: An engineer named George Washington Gale Ferris planned the first Ferris wheel, many people thought he was crazy.

Corrected by adding a coordinating conjunction:	An engineer named George Washington Gale Ferris planned the first Ferris wheel, but many people thought he was crazy.
Corrected by adding a subordinating conjunction:	When an engineer named George Washington Gale Ferris planned the first Ferris wheel, many people thought he was crazy.
Corrected by replacing the comma with a period:	An engineer named George Washington Gale Ferris planned the first Ferris wheel. Many people thought he was crazy.

---

comma splice
a sentence error that occurs when two sentences are connected with only a comma

Practice ▷ Correct the following comma splices by adding a coordinating conjunction (*and, but, yet, or, nor, for, so*), adding a subordinating conjunction (*when, while, because, before, after*), or replacing the comma with a semicolon or period. Use the approach that makes the sentence read most smoothly.

1. We set out for a morning hike, it was raining.

2. The weather cleared by the afternoon, we hit the trail.

3. Both Jill and I were expecting wonderful scenery, we were not disappointed.

4. The view of the valley was spectacular, it was like a portrait.

5. We snacked on granola bars and apples, we enjoyed the view.

6. Then we strapped on our backpacks the final leg of the hike awaited us.

7. The trail became rockier, we had to watch our step.

8. We reached the end of our hike, the sun was setting.

9. We're on the lookout for a new trail, it will be tough to beat this one.

10. We're done with our physical activities, it is time to watch a movie.

Practice ▷ Correct any comma splices in the following email message.

To: HR Staff

Subject: Agenda for Conference

HR Staff:

At 8:15 a.m. on Friday, we will meet in Conference Room B, breakfast will be provided.

We will discuss our strategy for the show, we will then set up our materials at show table 15. The busiest crowd flow is expected from 10 a.m. to 11 a.m., the second busiest should be from 1 p.m. to 3 p.m.

Please bring plenty of energy and enthusiasm to the show, be ready to discuss the strengths of our products.

Thanks,

Phil Dawson

L04 Run-On Sentences

A **run-on sentence** occurs when two sentences are joined without punctuation or a connecting word. A run-on can be corrected by adding a comma and a conjunction or by inserting a semicolon or period between the two sentences.

Run-On: Horace Wilson taught in Tokyo in 1872 he introduced the Japanese to baseball.

Corrected by adding a comma and coordinating conjunction: Horace Wilson taught in Tokyo in 1872, and he introduced the Japanese to baseball.

Corrected by adding a subordinating conjunction and a comma: While Horace Wilson taught in Tokyo in 1872, he introduced the Japanese to baseball.

Corrected by inserting a semicolon: Horace Wilson taught in Tokyo in 1872; he introduced the Japanese to baseball.

Run-On: The first team in Japan was formed in 1878 no one knew how popular the sport would become.

Corrected by adding a comma and coordinating conjunction: The first team in Japan was formed in 1878, yet no one knew how popular the sport would become.

Corrected by adding a subordinating conjunction: The first team in Japan was formed in 1878 although no one knew how popular the sport would become.

Corrected by inserting a period: The first team in Japan was formed in 1878. No one knew how popular the sport would become.

Here's an additional way to correct a run-on sentence: Turn one of the sentences into a phrase or series of phrases; then combine it with the other sentence.

The first team in Japan was formed in 1878 without a thought about how popular the sport would become.

Practice Correct the following run-on sentences. Use the approach that makes the sentence read most smoothly.

1. In 1767 English scientist Joseph Priestley discovered a way to infuse water with carbon dioxide this invention led to carbonated water.
   , so

2. Carbonated water is one of the main components of soft drinks it gives soft drinks the fizz and bubbles we enjoy.
   because

3. The first soft drinks in America were dispensed out of soda fountains they were most often found at drug stores and ice-cream parlors.
   and

4. Interestingly, soda was sold at drug stores it promised healing properties.
   ; and

5. Most of the formulas for American soft drinks were invented by pharmacists the idea was to create nonalcoholic alternatives to traditional medicines.
   ^

6. The first carbonated-drink bottles could not keep bubbles from escaping it was more popular to buy a soda from a soda fountain.
   ^

7. A successful method of keeping bubbles in a bottle was not invented until 1892 it was called a crowned bottle cap.
   and

8. The first diet soda to be sold was known as "No-Cal Beverage" in 1959 the first diet cola hit the stores.
   ^ therefore;

Practice Rewrite the following paragraph, correcting any run-on sentences that you find.

Arbor Day is an undervalued holiday in America. On this holiday, people are encouraged to plant trees it is celebrated on the fourth Friday of April. It was created by J. Sterling Morton he was President Grover Cleveland's secretary of agriculture. The holiday is now observed in a number of other countries.

_____

_____

_____

_____

run-on sentence
a sentence error that occurs when two sentences are
joined without punctuation *or* a connecting word

L05 Rambling Sentences

A **rambling sentence** occurs when many separate ideas are connected by one *and, but,* or *so* after another. The result is an unfocused sentence that goes on and on. To correct a rambling sentence, break it into smaller units, adding and cutting words as needed.

Rambling: When we signed up for the two-on-two tournament, I had no thoughts about winning, but then my brother started talking about spending his prize money and he asked me how I would spend the share so we were counting on winning when we really had little chance and as it turned out, we lost in the second round.

Corrected: When we signed up for the two-on-two tournament, I had no thoughts about winning. Then my brother started talking about spending the prize money. He even asked me how I would spend my share. Soon we were counting on winning when we really had little chance. As it turned out, we lost in the second round.

Say It Read the following rambling sentences aloud. Afterward, circle all of the connecting words (*and, but, so*). Then think of a way to break each rambling sentence into smaller units. Say the sentences out loud.

1. I enjoyed touring the hospital and I would enjoy joining the nursing staff and I believe that my prior work experience will be an asset but I also know that I have a lot more to learn.

2. The electronics store claims to offer "one-stop shopping" and they can take care of all of a customer's computer needs and they have a fully trained staff to answer questions and solve problems so there is really no need to go anywhere else.

---

rambling sentence
a sentence error that occurs when many separate ideas are connected by one *and, but,* or *so* after another

Practice Correct the following rambling sentences by dividing them into separate sentences. Afterward, share your corrections with a classmate.

1. The dancer entered gracefully onto the stage and she twirled around twice and then tiptoed to the front of the stage and the crowd applauded.

   _____

   _____

2. I went to the movies last night and when I got to the theater, I had to wait in a super-slow line and when I finally got to the front, the show I wanted to see was sold out.

   _____

   _____

3. I like to listen to music everywhere but I especially like to rock out in my car so I scream and dance and I don't care if anyone sees me through the windows.

   _____

   _____

Practice Answer the following questions about rambling sentences.

1. How can you recognize a rambling sentence?

   _____

   _____

2. Why is a rambling sentence a problem?

   _____

   _____

3. How can you correct a rambling sentence?

   _____

   _____

L06 Dangling and Misplaced Modifiers

► Dangling Modifiers

A modifier is a word, phrase, or clause that functions as an adjective or adverb. When the reader cannot find the word that is being described by the modifier, the modifier is called a **dangling modifier**. This error can be corrected by inserting the missing word or rewriting the sentence.

Dangling Modifier: After putting some raw chicken in the bowl, my cat began to purr. *(The cat could put chicken in the bowl?)*

Corrected: After I put some raw chicken in the bowl, my cat began to purr.

Dangling Modifier: Trying to gobble the food quickly, the bowl got tipped over. *(The bowl was trying to gobble the food?)*

Corrected: Trying to gobble the food quickly, the cat tipped over the bowl.

► Misplaced Modifiers

When a modifier is placed beside a word that it does not modify, the modifier is misplaced. This often results in an amusing or **illogical** statement. The reader must ask, "Who or what is actually being described?" The **misplaced modifier** can be corrected by moving it next to the word that it modifies.

Misplaced Modifier: My cat was diagnosed by the vet with fleas. *(The vet has fleas?)*

Corrected: The vet diagnosed my cat with fleas.

Misplaced Modifier: The vet gave a pill to my cat that tastes like fish. *(The cat tastes like fish?)*

Corrected: The vet gave my cat a pill that tastes like fish.

Avoid placing any adverb modifiers between a verb and its direct object.

Misplaced: I will throw quickly the ball.

Corrected: I will quickly throw the ball.

Also, do not separate two-word verbs with an adverb modifier.

Misplaced: Please take immediately out the trash.

Corrected: Please immediately take out the trash.

Say It   Read the following sentences aloud, noting the dangling or misplaced modifier in each one.

1. After tearing up the couch, I decided to get my cat a scratching post.
2. I have worked to teach my cat to beg for three weeks.

Practice   Rewrite the following sentences, correcting the misplaced and dangling modifiers.

1. I bought a hound dog for my brother named Rover.

   _____

2. The doctor diagnosed me and referred me to a specialist with scoliosis.

   _____

3. The man was reported murdered by the coroner.

   _____

4. Please present the recommendation that is attached to Mrs. Burble.

   _____

5. Jack drove me to our home in a Chevy.

   _____

6. I couldn't believe my brother would hire a disco DJ who hates disco.

   _____

Practice   For each sentence, correct the placement of the adverb.

1. Give quickly the report to your boss.

   _____

2. We will provide immediately an explanation.

   _____

3. Fill completely out the test sheet.

   _____

dangling modifier	**illogical**	**misplaced modifier**
a modifying word, phrase, or clause that appears to modify the wrong word or a word that isn't in the sentence	without logic; senseless, false, or untrue	a modifying word, phrase, or clause that has been placed incorrectly in a sentence, often creating an amusing or illogical idea

L07 Shifts in Sentence Construction

▶ Shift in Person

A **shift in person** is an error that occurs when first, second, and third person are improperly mixed in a sentence.

> **Shift in Person:** If you exercise and eat right, an individual can lose weight. (The sentence improperly shifts from second person—*you*—to third person—*individual*.)
>
> **Corrected:** If you exercise and eat right, you can lose weight.

▶ Shift in Tense

A **shift in tense** is an error that occurs when more than one verb tense is improperly used in a sentence.

> **Shift in Tense:** He tried every other option before he agrees to do it my way. (The sentence improperly shifts from past tense—*tried*—to present tense—*agrees*.)
>
> **Corrected:** He tried every other option before he agreed to do it my way.

▶ Shift in Voice

A **shift in voice** is an error that occurs when active voice and passive voice are mixed in a sentence.

> **Shift in Voice:** When she fixes the radiator, other repairs may be suggested. (The sentence improperly shifts from active voice—*fixes*—to passive voice—*may be suggested*.)
>
> **Corrected:** When she fixes the radiator, she may suggest other repairs.

(Say It)   Read the following sentences aloud, paying careful attention to the improper shift each contains.

1. David exercises daily and ate well.
2. Marianne goes running each morning and usually friends are met.
3. After you choose an exercise routine, a person should stick to it.
4. Lamar swam every morning and does ten laps.
5. The personal trainer made a schedule for me, and a diet was suggested by her.

Practice ▸ Rewrite the following sentences, correcting any improper shifts in construction.

1. You should be ready for each class in a person's schedule.

   _____

2. I work for my brother most days and classes are attended by me at night.

   _____

3. When you give me a review, can he also give me a raise?

   _____

4. As we walked to school, last night's football game was discussed by us.

   _____

Practice ▸ Correct the improper shifts in person, tense, or voice in the following paragraph. Use the correction marks shown when you make your changes.

Some people are early adopters, which means technology is adopted by them when it is new. Other people are technophobes because you are afraid of technology, period. I am not an early adopter or a technophobe, but a person has to see the value in technology before I use it. Technology has to be cheap, intuitive, reliable, and truly helpful before you start using it. I let others work out the bugs and pay the high prices before a piece of technology is adopted by me. But when I decide it is time to get a new gadget or program, you buy it and use it until it is worn out. Then I look for something else that is even cheaper and more intuitive, reliable, and helpful, which is then bought by me.

Correction Marks

ℳ delete	⋀ add comma	ᵂᵒʳᵈ⋀ add word
ᵈ̲ capitalize	? ⋀ add question mark	⊙ add period
⌀ lowercase	ᵛ, insert an apostrophe	⌒ spelling
⋀ insert		⊓ switch

shift in person
an error that occurs when first, second, and third person are improperly mixed in a sentence

shift in tense
an error that occurs when more than one verb tense is improperly used in a sentence

shift in voice
an error that occurs when active voice and passive voice are mixed in a sentence

🌐 Real-World Application

Practice⟩ Correct any sentence fragments in the following business memo. Use the correction marks shown.

Slovik Manufacturing

Date: August 8, 2014
To: Jerome James, Personnel Director
From: Ike Harris, Graphic Arts Director
Subject: Promotion of Mona Veal from Intern to Full-time Graphic Artist

For the past five months, Mona Veal as an intern in our Marketing Department. I recommend that she be offered a position as a full-time designer. Are the two main reasons behind this recommendation.

1. Mona has shown the traits that Slovik Manufacturing values in a graphic designer. Creative, dependable, and easy to work with.

2. Presently, we have two full-time graphic designers and one intern. While this group has worked well. The full-time designers have averaged 3.5 hours of overtime per week. Given this fact. Our new contract with Lee-Stamp Industries will require more help, including at least one additional designer.

If you approve this recommendation. Please initial below and return this memo.

Yes, I approve the recommendation to offer Mona Veal a full-time position.

———————

Attachment: Evaluation report of Mona Veal

cc: Elizabeth Zoe
    Mark Moon

Correction Marks

୬ delete	⋀ add comma	word ⋀ add word
ᵈ capitalize	? ⋀ add question mark	⊙ add period
⁄ lowercase	⸲ insert an apostrophe	◯ spelling
⋀ insert		⊓⎵ switch

Practice ▸ In the following email, correct any comma splices or run-on sentences using correction marks.

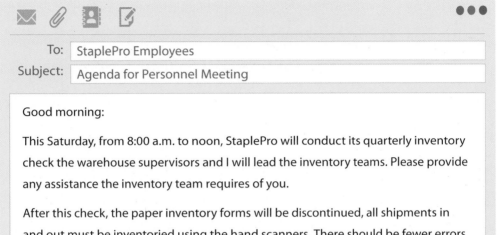

To: StaplePro Employees

Subject: Agenda for Personnel Meeting

Good morning:

This Saturday, from 8:00 a.m. to noon, StaplePro will conduct its quarterly inventory check the warehouse supervisors and I will lead the inventory teams. Please provide any assistance the inventory team requires of you.

After this check, the paper inventory forms will be discontinued, all shipments in and out must be inventoried using the hand scanners. There should be fewer errors when using StaplePro's electronic system, the supervisors will schedule training for the employees who are unfamiliar with the scanners.

Thanks for your cooperation StaplePro's new system will help us store and ship staples more effectively and provide better service for our customers.

Best regards,

Kevin Dooley

Warehouse Director

Practice ▸ Reflect on what you have learned about comma splices and run-on sentences by answering the following questions.

1. What is the difference between a comma splice and a run-on sentence?

    _____

    _____

2. How can you correct a comma splice? (Name at least three ways.)

    _____

    _____

Practice In the following email, correct any shifts in sentence construction and dangling or misplaced modifiers using correction marks.

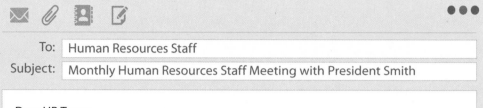

To: Human Resources Staff

Subject: Monthly Human Resources Staff Meeting with President Smith

Dear HR Team:

Monday, September 12, will be the Human Resources staff meeting with the first monthly president. A person should plan to attend these meetings on the second Monday of each month from 8:30 to 9:30 a.m., and you should go to the Human Resources conference room.

To help make these meetings productive, a staff member can prepare in two ways:

1. You should review and bring any periodic reports that are generated by you—hiring stats, exit interviews, medical or workers' comp claims, and so on. He or she should bring 11 copies and an electronic file of each document.

2. You should bring any questions or concerns. However, if an issue is significant, the person should review it with Richard before you bring it to a monthly meeting.

These monthly meetings are a big commitment for everyone of time, and attendance is required. If you can't make a meeting, send an email and attach for Richard a note.

Thanks for your cooperation. If you have questions or suggestions about September's meeting, Richard or I should be contacted by you.

Thanks,

Julia

Correction Marks

ᖀ delete	⋀ add comma	word ⋀ add word
ᵈ capitalize	? add question mark	⊙ add period
∅ lowercase	ᵛ insert an apostrophe	⬭ spelling
⋀ insert		⊓ switch

Practice Rewrite the following sentences, fixing misplaced modifiers, dangling modifiers, and improper shifts in construction.

1. After finishing the project, the teacher got our report.

   _____

2. I will shortly arrive.

   _____

3. The washing machine has nearly been running two hours straight.

   _____

4. Having rearranged the new furniture, the cat lost her favorite sleeping spot.

   _____

5. Students going on the volunteer trip should report to the Union after he or she signs their waivers.

   _____

6. I'm currently scanning the cereal aisle and searched for deals.

   _____

7. The man apprehended was suspected of burglary by the police officer.

   _____

8. Customers can pay when ordering or when you receive the items.

   _____

9. The casting director selected me and told me to go celebrate for the role in the play.

   _____

10. When people get great advice, he or she should share what they learned with their colleagues.

    _____

Practice ⟩ Rewrite the following passages, fixing any fragments by supplying the missing part or combining parts to form a complete sentence.

1. After finishing the trail, the bikers reached the bridge. On the bridge.

   _____

2. My friends ready to leave. I wanted to stay.

   _____

3. If we go now. Make it home in time for the show.

   _____

4. All of the workers in the office except for Harold. He missed the memo.

   _____

5. When we got our dog. The addition brought great responsibility.

   _____

Practice ⟩ Each of the following sentences contains a sentence problem. Circle the type of sentence problem. Then rewrite the sentence to fix the problem.

1. Craig prepared for the presentation, but he caught the flu and couldn't make it, so Candice replaced him, and she did great, so our project might be accepted in the research conference, and I am excited for it.

   run-on sentence   *comma splice*   *rambling sentence*

   _____

   _____

2. We arrived at the gate on time the plane had already departed.

   run-on sentence   *comma splice*   *rambling sentence*

   _____

3. A good job should be enjoyable, it also should pay well.

   run-on sentence   *comma splice*   *rambling sentence*

   _____

4. The Galaxy won the soccer match, they scored three goals.

   run-on sentence   *comma splice*   *rambling sentence*

   _____

PART 6:

Word Workshops

Part 6: Word Workshops

Kevin Key, 2014 / Used under license from Shutterstock.com

17

"If you want to make an apple pie from scratch,
you must first create the universe."

—Carl Sagan

Noun

Astrophysicists tell us that the universe is made up of two things—matter and energy. Matter is the stuff, and energy is the movement or heat of the stuff.

Grammarians tell us that thoughts are made up of two things—nouns and verbs. Nouns name the stuff, and verbs capture the energy. In that way, the sentence reflects the universe itself. You can't express a complete thought unless you are talking about matter and energy. Each sentence, then, is the basic particle of thought.

This chapter focuses on nouns, which describe not just things you can see—such as people, places, or objects—but also things you can't see—such as love, justice, and democracy.

Learning Outcomes

L01 Classes of Nouns
L02 Number of Nouns
L03 Count and Noncount Nouns
L04 Articles with Nouns
L05 Other Noun Markers

What do you think?

What is the most beautiful noun? What is the ugliest one? What makes a noun beautiful or ugly?

L01   Classes of Nouns

All nouns are either *common* or *proper*. They can also be *collective, concrete,* or *abstract*.

▶ Common or Proper

A **common noun** names a general person, place, thing, or idea and is not capitalized. A **proper noun** names a specific person, place, thing, or idea and is capitalized. Table 17.1 shows common and proper nouns.

Table 17.1 Common and Proper Nouns

	Common Nouns	Proper Nouns
Person:	politician	Barack Obama
Place:	park	Yellowstone
Thing:	marker	Sharpie
Idea:	religion	Hinduism

▶ Collective

A **collective noun** names a group or unit of people, animals, or things: *team, class, family, committee, herd.*

▶ Concrete or Abstract

A **concrete noun** can be seen, heard, smelled, tasted, or touched. An **abstract noun** (a condition, an idea, or a feeling) cannot be sensed. Table 17.2 demonstrates each type.

Table 17.2 Concrete and Abstract Nouns

Concrete Nouns	Abstract Nouns
judge	impartiality
brain	mind
heart	courage
train	transportation

L02   Number of Nouns

The **number** of a noun indicates whether it is singular (one) or plural (more than one). Table 17.3 shows singular and plural nouns.

Table 17.3 Singular and Plural Nouns

Singular Nouns	Plural Nouns
sister	sisters
church	churches
child	children
tooth	teeth

NOTE: Form the plural of most nouns by adding *s*. For nouns ending in *ch, s, sh, x* or *z*, add *es*. Also note that some nouns take a special spelling in the plural form.

Practice ▸ In the following sentences, identify the underlined nouns as common (C) or proper (P). Also indicate if the underlined noun is collective (CL).

1. William Faulkner wrote about the death of the Old South.

2. His novel *The Unvanquished* tells about the aftermath of the Civil War.

3. He chronicles the end of slavery but also of the genteel class in the South.

4. His novel *Absalom, Absalom!* describes the creation and end of a plantation.

5. The character Quentin Compson appears often in Faulkner's writings.

6. His family is the centerpiece of Yoknapatawpha County.

Practice ▸ Identify each word as concrete (CT) or abstract (A).

flag _____   wisdom _____   joy _____   laughter _____

joke _____   humor _____   symbol _____   love _____

wind _____   freedom _____   field _____

Practice ▸ Write the plural form of each noun. Use a dictionary if necessary.

automobile _____   sister _____

child _____   professor _____

ox _____   foot _____

woman _____   fish _____

mess _____   box _____

common noun
noun referring to a general person, place, thing, or idea; not capitalized as a name

proper noun
noun referring to a specific person, place, thing, or idea; capitalized as a name

collective noun
noun referring to a group or unit of people, animals, or things

concrete noun
noun referring to something that can be sensed

abstract noun
noun referring to an idea, a condition, or a feeling—something that cannot be sensed

number of noun
indicates whether a noun is singular (one) or plural (more than one)

L03 Count and Noncount Nouns

Some nouns name things that can be counted, and other nouns name things that cannot be counted. Different rules apply to each type.

► Count Nouns

A **count noun** names something that can be counted—*pens, people, votes, cats*. It can be singular or plural and be preceded by a number or an article (*a, an,* or *the*): *two* pens, *a* room, *an* apple, *the* iguanas. Table 17.4 shows singular and plural count nouns.

Table 17.4 Count Nouns

Singular	Plural
apple	apples
iguana	iguanas
thought	thoughts
room	rooms

Insight Many native English speakers, although unaware of count and noncount nouns, naturally use these nouns correctly. Listen to how these speakers use count and noncount nouns.

► Noncount Nouns

A **noncount noun** names something that cannot be counted. It is used in singular form and can be preceded by *the*, but rarely by *a* or *an*. Table 17.5 lists noncount nouns by category.

This semester, I'm taking mathematics and biology as well as Spanish.

Table 17.5 Noncount Nouns

Substance	Foods	Activities	Science	Languages	Abstractions
wood	water	reading	oxygen	Spanish	justice
cloth	milk	boating	weather	English	harm
ice	wine	smoking	heat	Mandarin	publicity
plastic	sugar	dancing	sunshine	Farsi	advice
wool	rice	swimming	electricity	Greek	happiness
steel	meat	soccer	lightning	Latin	health
aluminum	cheese	hockey	biology	French	joy
metal	flour	photography	history	Japanese	love
leather	pasta	writing	mathematics	Afrikaans	anger

► Two-Way Nouns

Two-way nouns can function as either count or noncount nouns.

Please set a glass in front of each place mat. (count noun)

The display case was made of tempered glass. (noncount noun)

Practice Read the following list of nouns and sort the words into columns of count and noncount nouns.

window	shoe	Japanese	rain
English	plum	health	ice
bowling	holiday	poetry	teaspoon
aluminum	tricycle	lawyer	

Count Nouns

_____

_____

_____

_____

_____

_____

_____

Noncount Nouns

_____

_____

_____

_____

_____

_____

_____

Practice Read the following paragraph and correct the noun errors. The first line has been corrected for you.

Our kitchen redesign involved tearing out the plastic*s* that covered the

counter and removing the flashings around the edges. We installed new

aluminums to replace the old metals. Also, the cupboard doors, which used to

be made of woods, were replaced by doors made of glasses. We have a new jar

for holding flours and a new refrigerator with a special place for milks and a

dispenser for waters. Everything is illuminated by new lightings, and a larger

window lets more sunlights in.

---

count noun
a noun that names things that can be counted (*pens, votes, people*)

noncount noun
a noun that names things that cannot be counted (*ice, plastic, sunshine*)

two-way nouns
a noun that can function as either count or noncount noun (*glass, light, paper*)

L04   Articles with Nouns

Articles show whether a noun refers to a specific thing or to a general thing. Articles are either definite or indefinite.

▶ Definite Article

The **definite article** is the word *the*. It signals that the noun refers to one specific person, place, thing, or idea.

> Look at the rainbow.
> (*Look at a specific rainbow.*)

NOTE: *The* can be used with most nouns, but usually not with proper nouns.

> **Incorrect:** The Joe looked at the rainbow.
> **Correct:** Joe looked at the rainbow.

Insight If your native language does not use articles, pay close attention to the way native English speakers use *the* when referring to a specific thing.

▶ Indefinite Articles

The **indefinite articles** are the words *a* and *an*. They signal that the noun refers to a general person, place, thing, or idea. The word *a* is used before nouns that begin with consonant sounds, and the word *an* is used before nouns that begin with vowel sounds.

> I enjoy seeing a rainbow.
> (*The speaker is talking about any rainbow, as indicated by "a rainbow."*)

> It was an honor to work with you.
> (*"Honor" is a general idea and begins with a vowel sound.*)

NOTE: Don't use *a* or *an* with noncount nouns or plural count nouns.

> **Incorrect:** I love a sunshine.
> **Correct:** I love the sunshine.

NOTE: If a word begins with an *h* that is pronounced, use *a*. If the *h* is silent, use *an*.

> **Incorrect:** I stared for a hour.
> **Correct:** I stared for an hour.

Practice Add the appropriate indefinite article (*a* or *an*) to the following words. The first one has been done for you.

1. __an__ orchard

2. _____ petunia

3. _____ hose

4. _____ honor

5. _____ avocado

6. _____ evening

7. _____ house

8. _____ hour

9. _____ shark

10. _____ eye

11. _____ error

12. _____ opportunity

13. _____ honest person

14. _____ emblem

15. _____ handkerchief

Practice Either cross out the incorrect article or replace it with the correct one. The first sentence has been done for you.

Climate scientists see a shift in ~~a~~ *the* weather. With rising levels of carbon dioxide in an environment, the atmosphere is trapping a heat of the sun. More heat in an air means more heat in the oceans. If a oceans get warmer, the storms they create are more intense. An hurricane could advance to an higher category, with stronger winds and more lightning. A Earth is already an stormy world, but with a rise in global temperatures, a weather could become even more extreme.

---

article
the most common type of noun marker (*a, an,* or *the*)

definite article
the word *the,* used to mark a noun that refers to a specific person, place, or thing

indefinite article
the words *a* or *an,* used to mark a noun that refers to a general person, place, or thing

Real-World Application

Practice Correct the article and noun marker errors in the following email.

✉ 📎 👤 📝   • • •

To: | Design and Printing Staff

Subject: | Internship Program for University Students

Hi, Team:

Could you use a assistant—a intern who is ready to work hard?

The head of the Graphic Arts Department at Northwestern College has asked us if we'd be interested in developing internships for third-year students in a university's four-year graphic-arts program.

Internships could be an solution to our current staff shortage. Interns would:

- work on tasks that you assign.
- get excellent professional experience by working with you.
- give us an opportunity to work with potential employees.

Please consider working with an student intern during the fall semester. If you are interested, let me know before January 28.

Thanks for considering these invitation to help future members of a graphic arts profession.

Melissa

FiledIMAGE, 2014 / Used under license from Shutterstock.com

Chapter

18

"Clothes make the man. Naked people have little
or no influence on society."

—Mark Twain

Pronoun

An old saying goes that clothes make the man. Well, not quite. Just because a suit is standing on a mannequin in the window doesn't mean that a living, breathing, and thinking person is in the room. The clothes are just temporary stand-ins.

Pronouns, similarly, are stand-ins for nouns. They aren't nouns, but they suggest nouns or refer back to them. That's why it's especially important for the pronoun to clearly connect to whatever it is replacing.

This chapter will help you make sure your pronoun stand-ins work well.

Learning Outcomes

LO1 Personal Pronouns
LO2 Pronoun-Antecedent Agreement
LO3 Indefinite Pronouns
LO4 Relative Pronouns
LO5 Other Pronoun Types

What do you think?

How could clothes make the man (or woman)? How do pronouns help nouns?

L01 Personal Pronouns

A **pronoun** takes the place of a noun or another pronoun. **Personal pronouns** indicate whether the person is speaking (first person), is being spoken to (second person), or is being spoken about (third person). Table 18.1 lists the personal pronouns.

Table 18.1 Personal Pronouns

Person	Singular			Plural		
	Nom.	Obj.	Poss.	Nom.	Obj.	Poss.
First *(speaking)*	I	me	my/mine	we	us	our/ours
Second *(spoken to)*	you	you	your/yours	you	you	your/yours
Third *(spoken about)*						
masculine	he	him	his	they	them	their/theirs
feminine	she	her	her/hers	they	them	their/theirs
neuter	it	it	its	they	them	their/theirs

Nom. = nominative case / **Obj.** = objective case / **Poss.** = possessive case

► ## Case of Pronouns

The **case** of a pronoun indicates how it can be used.

■ **Nominative** pronouns are used as subjects or as subject complements. Subject complements follow the linking verbs (*am, is, are, was, were, be, being,* or *been*) and refer to the subject. The subject complement in the following example follows the linking verb "was" and refers to the subject "it."

> He ate the pie. It was he.
> subject   subject   subject complement

■ **Objective** pronouns are used as direct objects, indirect objects, or objects of prepositions.

> The police officer warned us about them.
>   direct object   object of the preposition

■ **Possessive** pronouns show ownership.

> Her lawn looks much greener than mine.
> possessive   possesive

► ## Gender

Pronouns can be **masculine**, **feminine**, or **neuter**.

> He showed her how to fix it.
> masculine   feminine   neuter

Say It Read the following aloud.

1. *I* am / *You* are / *He* is / *She* is / *It* is / *We* are / *They* are

2. Show *me* / Show *you* / Show *him* / Show *her* / Show *them* / Show *us*

3. *My* car / *Your* car / *His* car / *Her* car / *Their* car

4. The car is *mine*. / The car is *yours*. / The car is *his*. / The car is *hers*. / The car is *theirs*.

Practice Select the correct personal pronoun in parentheses.

1. (*I, Me, My*) love to hang out at the corner coffee shop.

2. (*I, Me, My*) friends and I go there on Saturday morning.

3. One friend, Zach, is making a film, and (*he, him, his*) asked me to be in it.

4. We read over the lines, and other patrons listened to (*we, us, our*).

Practice Correct the pronoun errors in this paragraph.

Zach, Rachel, and me went to the coffee shop on Saturday afternoon when them is usually closed. The owners agreed to let we film there. Zach rearranged the tables a little to make room for the camera, and him and me set up the equipment. The camera rolled, and Rachel and me started reading our lines. A couple of times, we had to stop because the owners were laughing, and that made we laugh, too. Rachel and me had a hard time being straight with ours kissing scene. But it went well, and her and me got through it in one take.

---

pronoun
a word that takes the place of a noun or other pronoun

personal pronoun
indicates whether the person is speaking, is spoken to, or is spoken about

nominative pronoun
used as a subject or subject complement

objective pronoun
used as a direct object, an indirect object, or an object of a preposition

possessive pronoun
used to show ownership

gender
masculine (male), feminine (female), or neuter (neither male nor female)

L02 Pronoun-Antecedent Agreement

The **antecedent** is the word that a pronoun refers to or replaces. A pronoun and its antecedent agree when they have the same person, number, and gender.

Colleen thought she would need a lift, but her car started.

Third-person: singular feminine

► Agreement in Person

A pronoun needs to match its antecedent in **person** (first, second, or third).

	third person	second person
Incorrect:	If people keep going, you can usually reach the goal.	

Correct: If you keep going, you can usually reach the goal.

Correct: If people keep going, they can usually reach the goal.

► Agreement in Number

A pronoun needs to match its antecedent in **number** (singular or plural).

singular   plural

Incorrect: Each lifeguard must buy their own uniform.

Correct: Lifeguards must buy their own uniforms.

Correct: Each lifeguard must buy her or his own uniform.

► Agreement in Gender

A pronoun needs to match its antecedent in **gender** (masculine, feminine, or neuter).

feminine   masculine

Incorrect: Mrs. Miller will present his speech.

Correct: Mrs. Miller will present her speech.

---

antecedent
the word that a pronoun refers to or replaces

pronoun-antecedent agreement
matching a pronoun to its antecedent in person, number, and gender

person
first (speaking), second (spoken to), third (spoken about)

number
singular or plural

Practice Rewrite each sentence to correct the agreement in person error.

1. When you go to the multiplex, a person has a lot of movies to choose from.

   _____

2. We must buy your own ticket and snacks.

   _____

3. If the viewer arrives early enough, you can see a triple feature.

   _____

4. People may be overwhelmed by how many movies you can see.

   _____

Practice Rewrite each sentence to correct the agreement in number error.

1. The moviegoers choose which movies he or she may want to see.

   _____

2. A snack-counter attendant serves treats, and they also clean up messes.

   _____

3. Movie critics give his or her opinions about different films.

   _____

4. If a critic gives away the ending, they will ruin the movie for viewers.

   _____

Practice Rewrite each sentence to correct the agreement in gender error.

1. When a viewer loves a movie, he often tells others about it.

   _____

2. The multiplex is impressive; she looks like a palace on the hill.

   _____

L03 Indefinite Pronouns

An **indefinite pronoun** does not have an antecedent, and it does not refer to a specific person, place, thing, or idea. These pronouns pose unique issues with subject-verb and pronoun-antecedent agreement.

► Singular Indefinite Pronouns

The indefinite pronouns in Table 18.2 are singular. When they are used as subjects, they require a singular verb. As antecedents, they must be matched to singular pronouns.

Table 18.2 Personal Pronouns

each	anyone	somebody	everything
either	someone	everybody	nothing
neither	everyone	nobody	
another	no one	anything	
one	anybody	something	

Nobody on our camping trip is expecting to see Bigfoot.
singular subject   singular verb

Someone used his or her own money to buy a Bigfoot detector at a novelty shop.
singular antecedent   singular pronouns

► Plural Indefinite Pronouns

The indefinite pronouns in Table 18.3 are plural. As subjects, they require a plural verb, and as antecedents, they require a plural pronoun.

Table 18.3 Plural Indefinite Pronouns

both	several
few	many

A few of the campers hear thumps in the night.
plural subject   plural verb

Several of my friends swear they can see eyes glowing eight feet off the ground.
plural antecedent   plural pronoun

► Singular or Plural Indefinite Pronouns

The indefinite pronouns in Table 18.4 can be singular or plural, depending on the object of the preposition in the phrase that follows them.

Table 18.4 Singular or Plural Indefinite Pronouns

all	most	some
any	none	

plural object   singular object
Most of us are too frightened to sleep. Most of the night is over anyway.
plural subject   plural verb   singular subject   singular verb

Practice Rewrite each sentence to correct the agreement errors. (*Hint:* All the sentences are about a group of female campers.)

1. Everyone needs to set up their own tent.

   _____

2. No one are getting out of work.

   _____

3. Anyone who wants to be dry put up a rain fly.

   _____

4. Nothing are more miserable than lying in a wet sleeping bag.

   _____

5. Few wants to end up drenched.

   _____

6. Several has gone hiking to look for Bigfoot.

   _____

7. Many has doubts that Bigfoot exists.

   _____

8. A few says they might have dated him in high school.

   _____

9. One of the Bigfoot hunters remind the others to bring their cameras.

   _____

10. Most of the hunters is also going to carry a big stick.

    _____

11. Most of the afternoon are available for different activities.

    _____

12. None of the girls is planning to hike after dark.

    _____

13. None of the food are left out to attract animals or Bigfoot.

    _____

---

indefinite pronoun
a pronoun that does not refer to a specific person, place, thing, or idea

L04 Relative Pronouns

A **relative pronoun** (*who, whom, which, whose, whoever, whomever, that*) introduces a dependent clause. (The dependent clauses in the examples that follow are indicated by **bold** type.)

> I would like to meet the person who **discovered dark matter**.

- **Who/Whoever** and **Whom/Whomever**—These pronouns refer to people. *Who* and *whoever* are used as subjects, while *whom* and *whomever* are used as objects.

  > The astronomer who **imagined invisible matter** amazes me. The astronomer, whom **I was honored to meet**, is Vera Rubin.

- **That** and **Which**—These pronouns usually refer to things. Clauses beginning with *that* are not set off with commas, while those that begin with *which* are set off with commas.

  > I saw a show that **explained dark matter**. The show, which **is called** *Into the Wormhole*, is on the Science Channel.

- **Whose**—This pronoun indicates ownership or connection.

  > Morgan Freeman, whose **voice is soothing**, hosts the show.

L05 Other Pronoun Types

Other types of pronouns have specific uses in your writing.

- An **interrogative pronoun** asks a question (*who, whose, whom, which, what*).

  > What shall we call our band? Who will be in it?

- A **demonstrative pronoun** points to a specific thing (*this, that, these, those*).

  > That is a great name! This will get attention.

- A **reflexive pronoun** reflects back to the subject of a sentence (*myself, ourselves, yourself, yourselves, himself, herself, itself, themselves*).

  > We gave ourselves credit for thinking of an awesome name.

- An **intensive pronoun** emphasizes the noun or pronoun it refers to (*myself, ourselves, yourself, yourselves, himself, herself, itself, themselves*).

  > I myself suggested the name Psycho Drummer.

- A **reciprocal pronoun** refers to the individuals within a plural antecedent (*each other, one another*).

  > The band members always support one another.

Practice For each sentence, select the correct relative pronoun.

1. Vera Rubin, (*who, whom*) first discovered dark matter, wasn't seeking fame.

2. In the 1960s, she avoided black holes, (*that, which*) were a hot topic.

3. Instead, Rubin focused on the rotation of spiral galaxies, (*that, which*) few other people studied.

4. She expected stars (*that, which*) were on the outside of galaxies would move faster than stars (*that, which*) were near the center.

5. Instead, Rubin discovered that all of the galaxy's stars, (*that, which*) are in many different positions within the galaxy, move at the same speed.

6. The only way for the galaxy to move that way required it to have ten times the mass (*that, which*) was visible.

7. Rubin, (*who, whom, whose*) had never courted fame, became a very controversial figure when she presented her findings about dark matter.

8. Other astrophysicists (*who, whom*) did not believe Rubin did similar observations and calculations and confirmed her findings.

Practice Write the type of each underlined pronoun: *interrogative, demonstrative, reflexive, intensive,* or *reciprocal.*

1. That is why this band needs a road crew. _____

2. What are we supposed to do without power cords? _____

3. I myself would not mind playing unplugged. _____

4. You need to remind yourself that we don't have acoustic guitars. _____

5. That is the whole problem. _____

6. The guitars themselves prevent us from playing unplugged. _____

7. Who could hear an unplugged electric guitar? _____

8. As a band, we should help one another solve this problem. _____

---

relative pronoun
a pronoun that begins a relative clause, connecting it to a sentence

relative clause
a type of dependent clause that begins with a relative pronoun

🌐 **Real-World** Application

Practice ▷ Correct any pronoun errors in the letter that follows.

✗ **Psycho Drummer**
12185 W. 22nd Avenue, Elkhorn, WI 53100 Ph: 262.555.7188

July 30, 2014

Ms. Marcia Schwamps, Manager
Piedog Studios
350 South Jackson Street
Elkhorn, WI 53100

Dear Ms. Schwamps:

One of your recording technicians says that you are looking for session musicians whom could play instruments for other artists. My bandmate Jerome and me would like to offer ours services.

Jerome and me are the power duo whom is called Psycho Drummer, a name that refers to Jerome hisself. He is a master percussionist, and him has trained hisself in many styles, from heavy metal to rock, pop, jazz, blues, and even classical.

I am the guitarist in Psycho Drummer. I play electric and acoustic (6- and 12-string) guitars as well as electric bass, and I, too, have taught me to perform different styles of music.

Attached, you will find ours résumés, a list of recent gigs us have played, and a review of we from the *Walworth County Week*.

Please consider Jerome and I for work as session musicians at Piedog Studios. We look forward to hearing from yous and would very much appreciate an interview/audition.

Sincerely,

Terrance "Tear-It-Up" Clark

Terrance "Tear-It-Up" Clark
Guitarist
Enclosures 3

Chapter

19

> "Theater is a verb before it is a noun,
> an act before it is a place."
> —Martha Graham

Verb

You've probably heard that a shark has to keep swimming or it suffocates. That's not entirely true. Yes, sharks breathe by moving water across their gills, but they can also lie on the bottom and push water through their gills or let currents do the work. Still, most sharks stay on the move, and when a shark is still, it has to work harder to breathe.

Verbs are much the same way. They like to stay on the move. Most verbs are action words, describing what is happening. Some verbs describe states of being—much like sharks sitting on the bottom, breathing. Either way, though, the verb gives life to the sentence. This chapter takes you into the compelling world of verbs.

Learning Outcomes

LO1 Classes of Verbs
LO2 Number and Person
LO3 Voice
LO4 Basic Tenses
LO5 Progressive-Tense Verbs
LO6 Perfect-Tense Verbs
LO7 Verbals
LO8 Verbals as Objects

What do you think?

Do you prefer *doing* or *being*? Why?

L01 Classes of Verbs

Verbs show action or express a state of being.

► Action Verbs

Verbs that show action are called **action verbs**. Some action verbs are **transitive**, which means that they transfer action to a direct object.

> Trina hurled the softball.
> (The verb *hurled* transfers action to the direct object *softball*.)

Others are **intransitive** and do not transfer action to a direct object.

> Trina pitches.
> (The verb *pitches* does not transfer action to a direct object.)

► Linking Verbs

Verbs that link the subject to a noun, a pronoun, or an adjective are **linking verbs**. They express a state of being. Table 19.1 lists common linking verbs.

> Trina is a pitcher.
> (The linking verb *is* connects *Trina* to the noun *pitcher*.)

> She seems unbeatable.
> (The linking verb *seems* connects *She* to the adjective *unbeatable*.)

Table 19.1 Linking Verbs

is	was	being	seem	look	sound
am	were	been	grow	smell	appear
are	be	become	feel	taste	remain

The farmers grow corn.
(The verb *grow* transfers action to the direct object *corn*.)

Hungry deer smell and taste the young plants.
(The verbs *smell* and *taste* transfer action to the direct object *plants*.)

► Helping Verbs

A **helping** (or auxiliary) verb works with an action or a linking verb to form a certain tense, mood, or voice. Table 19.2 lists common helping verbs.

> Trina has pitched two shut-out games, and today she may be pitching her third. (The helping verbs *has* and *may be* work with the main verbs *pitched* and *pitching* to form special tenses.)

Table 19.2 Helping Verbs

am	have	are	is	be	may
been	might	being	must	can	shall
could	should	did	was	do	were
does	will	had	would	has	

Practice ▷ For the following sentences, identify the underlined verbs as transitive action verbs (T), intransitive action verbs (I), linking verbs (L), or helping verbs (H).

1. I love fast-pitch softball, but I rarely pitch.

2. I play first base; it is a pressure-filled position.

3. Runners charge first base, and I must tag them out.

4. Double plays require on-target throws, clean catches, and timing.

5. If a runner steals, the pitcher and second baseperson work with me.

6. We can catch the runner in a "pickle" and tag her out.

7. Softball is exciting, and I will play all summer.

8. I look worn out after a game, but I feel completely exhilarated.

---

action verb
word that expresses action

transitive verb
action verb that transfers action to a direct object

intransitive verb
action verb that does not transfer action to a direct object

linking verb
verb that connects the subject with a noun, a pronoun, or an adjective in the predicate

helping (auxiliary) verb
verb that works with a main verb to form a certain tense, mood, or voice

L02   Number and Person

Verbs reflect number (singular or plural) and person (first person, second person, or third person).

▶ Number

The **number** of the verb indicates whether the subject is singular or plural.

Singular: A civil war re-enactment involves infantry, cavalry, and artillery units.

Plural: Actors stage amazing battle scenes from the war.

NOTE: Third-person present-tense singular verbs end in *s*; third-person present-tense plural verbs do not.

▶ Person

The **person** of a verb indicates whether the subject is speaking, being spoken to, or being spoken about. Table 19.3 shows the number and person of *be* verbs.

Table 19.3   *Be* Verbs (Number and Person)

	Singular	Plural
First Person:	(I) am	(we) are
Second Person:	(you) are	(you) are
Third Person:	(he, she, it) is	(they) are

NOTE: The pronoun *I* takes a special form of the *be* verb—*am*—in present tense and is paired with *was* in past tense.

Incorrect: I is eager to see the cannons fire.

Correct: I am eager to see the cannons fire.

Incorrect: I were not at the re-enactment last year.

Correct: I was not at the re-enactment last year.

NOTE: No matter its use, *you* takes the plural form of the *be* verb.

Incorrect: You is in for a treat when the battle begins.

Correct: You are in for a treat when the battle begins.

Incorrect: You was here early this morning.

Correct: You were here early this morning.

---

number
singular or plural

person
first (subject is speaking), second (subject is spoken to), third (subject is spoken about)

Practice For the following sentences, provide the present-tense verb (*is, am, are*) that agrees with the subject in person and number.

1. We _____ at the Civil War encampment.

2. It _____ a gathering of Union and Confederate regiments.

3. You _____ in a uniform of Union blue.

4. I _____ in the gray of the Confederacy.

5. A light-artillery brigade _____ a group of mobile cannons.

6. A cavalry regiment _____ a group of mounted soldiers.

7. The camp doctors _____ equipped to do amputations.

8. The medicine they use _____ sometimes worse than the disease.

9. I _____ amazed by all of the tents.

10. Many people _____ interested in the Civil War.

Practice Rewrite the following sentences, correcting the verbs to agree with their subjects in number and person.

1. I jumps the first time a cannon goes off.

_____

2. The guns blows huge white smoke rings; they whirls into the air.

_____

3. The cavalry regiments charges, and they battles with sabers.

_____

4. In the fray, one cavalry officer fall from his horse.

_____

5. We is acting as infantry soldiers. We lines up in two rows to send out volleys of bullets.

_____

6. After the battle, President Lincoln deliver a solemn address.

_____

L03 Voice

The **voice** of the verb indicates whether the subject is acting or being acted upon.

▶ Active Voice and Passive Voice

In **active voice**, the subject is acting. In **passive voice**, the subject is being acted upon. Table 19.4 gives examples of active and passive voice.

Active: The cast sang the song "Our State Fair."

Passive: The song "Our State Fair" was sung by the cast.

Table 19.4 Active Voice and Passive Voice

	Active Voice		Passive Voice	
	Singular	**Plural**	**Singular**	**Plural**
Present Tense	I see you see he/she/it sees	we see you see they see	I am seen you are seen he/she/it is seen	we are seen you are seen they are seen
Past Tense	I saw you saw he saw	we saw you saw they saw	I was seen you were seen it was seen	we were seen you were seen they were seen
Future Tense	I will see you will see he will see	we will see you will see they will see	I will be seen you will be seen it will be seen	we will be seen you will be seen they will be seen
Present Perfect Tense	I have seen you have seen he has seen	we have seen you have seen they have seen	I have been seen you have been seen it has been seen	we have been seen you have been seen they have been seen
Past Perfect Tense	I had seen you had seen he had seen	we had seen you had seen they had seen	I had been seen you had been seen it had been seen	we had been seen you had been seen they had been seen
Future Perfect Tense	I will have seen you will have seen he will have seen	we will have seen you will have seen they will have seen	I will have been seen you will have been seen it will have been seen	we will have been seen you will have been seen they will have been seen

Active voice is preferred for most writing because it is direct and energetic.

Active: The crowd gave the cast a standing ovation.

Passive: The cast was given a standing ovation by the crowd.

Passive voice is preferred when the focus is on the receiver of the action or when the subject is unknown.

Passive: A donation was left at the ticket office.

Active: Someone left a donation at the ticket office.

Practice Read the following sentences. Rewrite them, changing passive verbs to active verbs. Think about who or what is performing the action and make that the subject. The first one is done for you.

1. *State Fair* was put on by the community theater group.

   The community theater group put on State Fair.
   _____

2. The Frake family is featured in the musical.

   _____

3. Many songs were sung by the cast.

   _____

4. Pickles and mincemeat are rated by judges at the fair.

   _____

5. Mrs. Frake's mincemeat is spiked with too much brandy.

   _____

6. The judges are overcome by the strength of the mincemeat.

   _____

7. Two couples are shown falling in love at the fair.

   _____

8. The singers were assisted by a stalwart piano player in the orchestra pit.

   _____

9. The first act is climaxed by the song "It's a Grand Night for Singing."

   _____

10. The cast was applauded gratefully by the crowd.

    _____

voice
active or passive

active voice
voice created when the subject is performing the
action of the verb

passive voice
voice created when the subject is receiving the action
of the verb

L05 Progressive-Tense Verbs

The basic tenses tell when action takes place—past, present, or future. The progressive tenses indicate that action is ongoing.

- **Progressive tenses** are formed by using a helping verb along with the *ing* form of the main verb. Each uses a helping verb in the appropriate basic tense—either past, present, or future.

For thousands of years, most humans were working in agriculture. (past progressive)

Currently in the West, most humans are working in nonagricultural jobs. (present progressive)

In the future, people will be working in unimaginable occupations. (future progressive)

vovan, 2014 / Used under license from Shutterstock.com

Forming Progressive Tense					
Past:	was/were	+	main verb	+	ing
Present:	am/is/are	+	main verb	+	ing
Future:	will be	+	main verb	+	ing

Insight **Avoid** using the progressive tense with . . .

- Verbs that express thoughts, attitudes, and desires: *know, understand, want, prefer*
- Verbs that describe appearances: *seem, resemble*
- Verbs that indicate possession: *belong, have, own, possess*

Incorrect: I am knowing your name.

Correct: I know your name.

Incorrect: Stan was owning a new car.

Correct: Stan owned a new car.

---

progressive tense
verb tense that expresses ongoing action

Practice Rewrite each sentence three times, changing the tenses as requested in parentheses.

- Agribusiness makes food production very efficient.

1. (present progressive) _____

_____

2. (past progressive) _____

_____

3. (future progressive) _____

_____

- Businesses provide various products or services.

4. (present progressive) _____

_____

5. (past progressive) _____

_____

6. (future progressive) _____

_____

- The products and services in greatest demand produce the greatest wealth.

7. (present progressive) _____

_____

8. (past progressive) _____

_____

9. (future progressive) _____

_____

L06   Perfect-Tense Verbs

The perfect tenses tell that action is finished, not ongoing, whether in the past, present, or future.

Perfect tenses are formed by using a helping verb along with the past-tense form of the main verb. Each uses a helping verb in the appropriate basic tense—either past, present, or future.

> By the end of my first year on the job, I had learned the basic sales procedures. (past perfect)
>
> This year, I have learned new technology skills. (present perfect)
>
> By this time next year, I will have learned how to be an effective salesperson. (future perfect)

Forming Perfect Tense			
Past:	had	+	past-tense main verb
Present:	has/have	+	past-tense main verb
Future:	will have	+	past-tense main verb

► Perfect Tense with Irregular Verbs

To form the perfect tenses with irregular verbs, use the past participle instead of the past-tense form. Table 19.6 shows the past participles of common irregular verbs.

Table 19.6 Present Tense and Past Participles of Irregular Verbs

Pres.	Past Part.	Pres.	Past Part.	Pres.	Past Part.	Pres.	Past Part.	Pres.	Past Part.	Pres.	Past Part.
am, are	been	dig	dug	fly	flown	hide	hidden	see	seen	stand	stood
become	become	do	done	forget	forgotten	keep	kept	shake	shaken	steal	stolen
begin	begun	draw	drawn	freeze	frozen	know	known	shine	shone	swim	swum
blow	blown	drink	drunk	get	gotten	lead	led	show	shown	swing	swung
break	broken	drive	driven	give	given	pay	paid	shrink	shrunk	take	taken
bring	brought	eat	eaten	go	gone	prove	proven	sing	sung	teach	taught
buy	bought	fall	fallen	grow	grown	ride	ridden	sink	sunk	tear	torn
catch	caught	feel	felt	hang	hung	ring	rung	sit	sat	throw	thrown
choose	chosen	fight	fought	have	had	rise	risen	sleep	slept	wear	worn
come	come	find	found	hear	heard	run	run	speak	spoken	write	written

---

perfect tense
verb tense that expresses completed action

Practice Rewrite each sentence three times, changing the tenses as requested in parentheses.

- I work hard and listen carefully.

1. (past perfect) _____

   _____

2. (present perfect) _____

   _____

3. (future perfect) _____

   _____

- The employees gain their position by being qualified, and they keep them by being helpful.

4. (past perfect) _____

   _____

5. (present perfect) _____

   _____

6. (future perfect) _____

   _____

- Your colleagues depend on you, and you deliver the reports on time.

7. (past perfect) _____

   _____

8. (present perfect) _____

   _____

9. (future perfect) _____

   _____

L07 Verbals

A **verbal** is formed from a verb but functions as a noun, an adjective, or an adverb. Each type of verbal—gerund, participle, and infinitive—can appear alone or can begin a **verbal phrase**.

▶ Gerund

A **gerund** is formed from a verb ending in *ing*, and it functions as a noun.

> Kayaking is a fun type of exercise. (subject)
>
> I love kayaking. (direct object)

A **gerund phrase** begins with a gerund and includes any objects and modifiers.

> Running rapids in a kayak is exhilarating. (subject)
>
> I enjoy paddling a kayak through white water. (direct object)

▶ Participle

A **participle** is formed from a verb ending in *ing* or *ed*, and it functions as an adjective.

> I was exhilarated by the experience. (adjective modifying *I*)
>
> That was an exhilarating ride! (adjective modifying *ride*)

A **participial phrase** begins with a participle and includes any objects and modifiers.

> Shocking my parents, I said I wanted to go again.

▶ Infinitive

An **infinitive** is formed from *to* and a present-tense verb, and it functions as a noun, an adjective, or an adverb.

> To kayak in rough waters is dangerous. (noun)
>
> I will schedule more time to kayak. (adjective)
>
> My whole family is eager to kayak. (adverb)

An **infinitive phrase** begins with an infinitive and includes any objects or modifiers.

> I want to kayak the Colorado River through the Grand Canyon.

Practice Identify each underlined verbal or verbal phrase by selecting the correct choice in parentheses (gerund, participle, infinitive).

1. <u>Rock climbing</u> is an extreme sport. (gerund, participle, infinitive)

2. I'd like <u>to climb El Capitan one day</u>. (gerund, participle, infinitive)

3. <u>Rappelling down a cliff in Arizona</u>, I almost slipped. (gerund, participle, infinitive)

4. <u>Catching myself</u>, I checked my lines and carabiners. (gerund, participle, infinitive)

5. <u>To fall while climbing</u> could be fatal. (gerund, participle, infinitive)

6. I keep my equipment in top shape <u>to avoid a mishap</u>. (gerund, participle, infinitive)

Practice Complete the following sentences by supplying the type of verbal (or verbal phrase) requested in parentheses.

1. My favorite exercise is _____ . (gerund)

2. _____ would get me into shape. (gerund)

3. _____ , I could stay in shape. (participle)

4. Perhaps I will also try _____ . (gerund)

5. When exercising, remember _____ . (infinitive)

6. _____ , I'll lose weight. (participle)

Practice For each verbal phrase, write a sentence that correctly uses it.

1. to work out _____

2. choosing a type of exercise _____

3. excited by the idea _____

---

verbal
a construction formed from a verb but functioning as a noun, an adjective, or an adverb

verbal phrase
phrase beginning with a gerund, a participle, or an infinitive

gerund
verbal ending in *ing* and functioning as a noun

gerund phrase
phrase beginning with a gerund and including objects and modifiers

participle
verbal ending in *ing* or *ed* and functioning as an adjective

participial phrase
phrase beginning with a participle and including objects and modifiers

infinitive
verbal beginning with *to* and functioning as a noun, an adjective, or an adverb

infinitive phrase
phrase beginning with an infinitive and including objects and modifiers

L08 Verbals as Objects

Though both infinitives and gerunds can function as direct objects, some verbs take infinitives but not gerunds, and others take gerunds but not infinitives.

► Gerunds as Objects

Verbs that tell something real or true use **gerunds** as direct objects. Table 19.7 lists verbs that are followed by gerunds.

Table 19.7 Verbs Followed by Gerunds				
admit	miss	discuss	regret	imagine
deny	recommend	finish	consider	recall
enjoy	avoid	quit	dislike	

I miss walking along the beach.

not I miss to walk along the beach.

I regret cutting our vacation short.

not I regret to cut our vacation short.

► Infinitives as Objects

Verbs that tell something you hope for or intend use **infinitives** as direct objects. Table 19.8 lists verbs that are followed by infinitives.

Table 19.8 Verbs Followed by Infinitives					
agree	volunteer	promise	need	fail	hesitate
demand	appear	want	refuse	offer	plan
hope	deserve	attempt	wish	seem	tend
prepare	intend	endeavor	consent	decide	

We plan to go back to the lake.

not We plan going back to the lake.

We intend to save money for the trip.

not We intend saving money for the trip.

► Gerunds or Infinitives as Objects

Some verbs use other gerunds or infinitives as direct objects. Table 19.9 lists verbs that can be followed by either gerunds or infinitives.

Table 19.9 Verbs Followed by Gerunds or Infinitives				
begin	love	stop	like	start
hate	remember	continue	prefer	try

I love walking by the ocean.

or I love to walk by the ocean.

Practice For the following sentences, select the appropriate verbal in parentheses.

1. I imagine (walking, to walk) along the Pacific Coast.

2. We want (seeing, to see) whales or dolphins when we are there.

3. I hope (getting, to get) some beautiful shots of the ocean.

4. We should avoid (getting, to get) sunburned when we are on the beach.

5. I enjoy (getting, to get) sand between my toes.

6. Maybe a surfer will offer (showing, to show) me how to surf.

7. We deserve (going, to go) on vacation more often.

8. Later, we will regret not (taking, to take) the time for ourselves.

9. I have never regretted (taking, to take) a vacation.

10. I wish (having, to have) a vacation right now.

Practice For the following verbs, write your own sentence using the verb followed by a gerund or an infinitive, as appropriate.

1. quit

_____

2. recall

_____

3. tend

_____

4. volunteer

_____

5. discuss

_____

6. decide

_____

gerund
verbal ending in *ing* and functioning as a noun

infinitive
verbal beginning with *to* and functioning as a noun,
an adjective, or an adverb

🌐 Real-World Application

Practice ▷ Rewrite the following paragraph, changing passive verbs to active verbs.

Bedford's school music program should be supported by Grohling Music Suppliers. Our instrument rentals and our sheet-music services have been used extensively by the school system. In these tough economic times, the school should be assisted by us.

_____

_____

_____

Practice ▷ In the following paragraph, change future-perfect verbs into past-perfect verbs.

We will have provided reduced-cost sheet music to the school system and will have added used and refurbished instrument rentals. In addition, we will have provided best-customer discounts to schools that will have rented and bought in volume.

Practice ▷ In the following paragraph, correct misused verbals.

I hope exploring these possibilities with you. We could recommend to make some of these changes the first year. I admit to have a soft spot for student performers. I recall to get my first flute as a student and to love music class after that.

Chapter

20

"When you catch an adjective, kill it. No, I don't mean utterly, but kill most of them—then the rest will be valuable."

—Mark Twain

Adjective and Adverb

The purpose of makeup is to accentuate the beauty that is already in your face. The focus should be on you, not on the mascara, lipstick, foundation, or blush you use.

In the same way, the real beauty of a sentence lies in the nouns and verbs. Adjectives and adverbs can modify those words, adding fine points to the message, but modifiers should never overwhelm a sentence. Use them sparingly to make your meaning clear. This chapter will show you how to get the most out of a few adjectives and adverbs.

Learning Outcomes

LO1 Adjective Basics
LO2 Adjective Order
LO3 Adverb Basics
LO4 Adverb Placement

What do you think?

What effect is created when lipstick overwhelms lips? What effect is created when adjectives overload nouns?

L01 Adjective Basics

An **adjective** is a word that modifies a noun or pronoun. Even **articles** such as *a, an,* and *the* are adjectives, indicating whether you mean a general or specific thing. Adjectives answer these basic questions: *which? what kind of? how many? how much?*

Adjectives often appear before the words they modify.

> I saw a beautiful gray tabby cat.

A **predicate adjective** appears after the noun it modifies and is linked to the word by a linking verb.

> The cat was beautiful and gray.

Proper adjectives are formed from proper nouns and are capitalized.

> I also saw a Persian cat.

▶ Forms of Adjectives

Adjectives have three forms: positive, comparative, and superlative.

- **Positive adjectives** describe a noun or pronoun without making a comparison.

  > Fred is a graceful cat.

- **Comparative adjectives** compare two nouns or pronouns.

  > Fred is more graceful than our dog, Barney.

- **Superlative adjectives** compare three or more nouns or pronouns.

  > He is the most graceful cat you will ever see.

NOTE: Create the comparative form of most one- or two-syllable words by adding *er*, and create the superlative form by adding *est*. For words of three syllables or more, use *more* (or *less*) to create comparatives and *most* (or *least*) to create superlatives. The adjectives *good* and *bad* have special comparative and superlative forms. Table 20.1 shows examples of the forms.

Table 20.1 Forms of Adjectives

Positive	Comparative	Superlative
big	bigger	biggest
happy	happier	happiest
wonderful	more wonderful	most wonderful

Positive	Comparative	Superlative
good	better	best
bad	worse	worst

Practice ▶ For the following sentences, identify the underlined adjectives as positive (P), comparative (C), or superlative (S).

1. The shelter had a <u>Siamese</u> cat with <u>crossed</u> eyes and <u>black</u> feet.

2. She was <u>more inquisitive</u> than the other cats.

3. Her eyes were the <u>bluest</u> I had ever seen in a cat.

4. Her <u>surprising</u> meow was <u>loud</u> and <u>insistent</u>.

5. But her name—Monkey—was the <u>most surprising</u> fact of all.

Practice ▶ Read the following paragraph and correct adjective errors. The first one has been done for you.

Some people say dogs are ~~more~~ tamer than cats, but cats have a more great place in some people's hearts. Cats were probably first attracted to human civilizations during the most early days of the agricultural revolution. The sudden surplus of grains attracted many mice, which in turn attracted cats. Cats that were the most best mousers were welcomed by humans. In time, more cute and more cuddly cats became pets. But cats have never given up their wildness. Even now, a barn cat that is not used to human touch can be feraler than a dog.

adjective
word that modifies a noun or pronoun

articles
the adjectives *a*, *an*, and *the*

predicate adjective
adjective that appears after a linking verb and describes the subject

positive adjective
adjective that modifies a noun or pronoun without making a comparison

comparative adjective
adjective that compares two nouns or pronouns

superlative adjective
adjective that compares three or more nouns or pronouns

L02 Adjective Order

Adjectives describe in different ways. Some adjectives refer to time; some refer to shape, size, color, and other features. English uses a specific order for adjectives when several of them appear before a noun. **Table 20.2** shows the correct order of different adjectives.

Table 20.2 Adjective Order

Begin with . . .

1.	articles	a, an, the
	demonstrative adjectives	that, this, these, those
	possessives	my, our, her, their, Kayla's

Then position adjectives that tell . . .

2.	time	first, second, next, last
3.	how many	three, few, some, many
4.	value	important, prized, fine
5.	size	giant, puny, hulking
6.	shape	spiky, blocky, square
7.	condition	clean, tattered, repaired
8.	age	old, new, classic
9.	color	blue, scarlet, salmon
10.	nationality	French, Chinese, Cuban
11.	religion	Baptist, Buddhist, Hindu
12.	material	cloth, stone, wood, bronze

Finally place . . .

13.	nouns used as adjectives	baby [seat], shoe [lace]

Example:

I visited that ruined ancient stone temple.

(1 + 7 + 8 + 12 + noun)

Insight Even though there is an accepted order for multiple adjectives, avoid stacking too many modifiers in front of a noun.

▶ ## Adjective Phrases and Clauses

There are many single-word adjectives to choose from when you write, but several kinds of phrases (prepositional, participial, infinitive) and adjective clauses also serve this purpose.

I enjoy the restaurant at the corner of 5th Avenue and Erie Street. (adjective phrase)

I'm impressed by chefs who take creative risks. (adjective clause)

Practice Rearrange each set of adjectives and articles so that they are in the correct order. Then insert them to create a complete sentence. The first one has been done for you.

1. blue   square   that

   I lost _____ that square blue _____ button.

2. my   Scottish   new

   A tailor made _____ kilt.

3. plastic   brand-new   few

   Go buy a _____ beads.

4. worthless   a   brass

   This is _____ tack.

5. classic   many   Kenyan

   The museum holds _____ masks.

6. aluminum   soda   Ted's

   Pick up _____ can.

7. key   silver   my

   Please fix _____ chain.

8. dilapidated   this   old

   Let's renovate _____ shack.

9. wool   her   woven

   Marie wore _____ cardigan.

10. identical   seven   music

    We'll need _____ stands.

11. young   the   bright

    Did you see _____ faces?

12. last   real   our

    Is that _____ option?

L03 Adverb Basics

An **adverb** modifies a verb (or **verbal**), an adjective, an adverb, or a whole sentence. An adverb answers these basic questions: *how? when? where? why? to what degree? how often? how long?*

> **Insight** Intensifying adverbs such as *very* and *really* should be used sparingly. Also, in academic writing, it is better to use a precise, vivid verb than to prop up an imprecise verb with an adverb.

Sheri leaped fearlessly.
(*Fearlessly* modifies the verb *leaped*.)

Sheri leaped quite readily.
(*Quite* modifies the adverb *readily*, which modifies the verb *leaped*.)

Obviously she wants to fly.
(*Obviously* modifies the whole sentence.)

NOTE: Most adverbs end in *ly*. Some can be written with or without the *ly*, but when in doubt, use the *ly* form.

loud ⟶ loudly   tight ⟶ tightly   deep ⟶ deeply

▶ Forms of Adverbs

Adverbs have three forms: positive, comparative, and superlative.

■ **Positive adverbs** describe without comparing.

Sheri leaped high and fearlessly.

■ **Comparative adverbs** (*-er, more,* or *less*) compare two actions.

She leaped higher and more fearlessly than I did.

■ **Superlative adverbs** (*-est, most,* or *least*) compare three or more actions.

She leaped highest and most fearlessly of any of us.

NOTE: Some adverbs have special comparative or superlative forms.

well ⟶ better ⟶ best   badly ⟶ worse ⟶ worst

Practice For the following sentences, provide the correct form of the adverb in parentheses—positive, comparative, or superlative.

1. My friend eats _____ (quickly).

2. She eats _____ (quickly) than I do.

3. She eats _____ (quickly) of all our friends.

4. My brother eats _____ (reluctantly).

5. He eats _____ (reluctantly) than a spoiled child.

6. Compared to his classmates, he eats _____ (reluctantly).

7. I eat _____ (slowly).

8. I eat _____ (slowly) than I used to.

9. Of all my family members, I eat _____ (slowly).

10. I suppose the three of us eat pretty _____ (oddly).

Practice For the following sentences, choose the correct adjective or adverb in parentheses. Then underline the word each adjective or adverb modifies.

1. My brother went to a (good, well) play.

2. He said the actors did (good, well) and that the plot was (good, well).

3. He even got a (good, well) deal on tickets for (good, well) seats.

4. He wanted (bad, badly) to see this play.

5. The problem was that one patron behaved (bad, badly).

6. He had a (bad, badly) attitude and even booed.

7. My brother told him to stop, but the guy took it (bad, badly).

8. The ushers did (good, well) when they asked the person to leave.

9. The audience even clapped for the ushers' (good, well) judgment.

10. My brother says the evening went (good, well).

---

adverb
word that modifies a verb, a verbal, an adjective, an adverb, or a whole sentence

verbal
word formed from a verb but functioning as a noun, an adjective, or an adverb

positive adverb
adverb that modifies without making a comparison

comparative adverb
adverb that compares two actions

superlative adverb
adverb that compares three or more actions

L04 Adverb Placement

Adverbs should be placed in a way that makes the meaning of the sentence plain.

- **How Adverbs:** These can appear in several places but not between a verb and a direct object.

  Steadily we hiked the trail.   We hiked the trail steadily.

  We steadily hiked the trail.   **not** We hiked steadily the trail.

- **When Adverbs:** Place these at the beginning or end of the sentence.

  We hiked to base camp yesterday. Today we'll reach the peak.

- **Where Adverbs:** Place these after the verb they modify but not between the verb and the direct object. (**NOTE:** Prepositional phrases often function as *where* adverbs.)

  The trail wound uphill and passed through rock-slide debris.

  We avoided falling rocks along the way.

  not We avoided along the way falling rocks.

- **Adverbs of *Degree*:** Place these right before the adverb or adjective they modify.

  I very definitely learned the value of good hiking boots. They were really helpful.

- **How Often Adverbs:** Place these right before an action verb (between the verb and its helping verb if it has one).

  I often remember that wonderful hike.

  I will never forget the sights I saw.

▶ Adverb Phrases and Clauses

There are many single-word adverbs to choose from when you write, but certain phrases (prepositional and infinitive) and adverb clauses also serve this purpose.

  Slowly and carefully, check each line of code. (adverb phrase)

  Before you submit the report, make certain to double-check your data. (adverb clause)

NOTE: Adverb clauses are dependent clauses, meaning they must connect to an independent clause to form a complete sentence.

Practice ▷ For the following sentences, insert the adverb (in parentheses) in the most appropriate position. The first one has been done for you.

1. In order to scare off bears, we *occasionally* made noise. (occasionally)

2. Bears avoid contact with human beings. (usually)

3. A bear surprised or cornered by people will turn to attack. (often)

4. A mother bear with cubs is likely to attack. (very)

5. If a bear approaches, playing dead may work. (sometimes)

6. Climbing a tree won't work. (usually)

7. Black bears climb trees. (often)

8. Grizzly bears knock the tree down. (usually)

9. Another defense is to open your coat to look large. (especially)

10. At the same time, try to make a loud noise. (very)

Practice ▷ In the following paragraph, move adverbs into their correct positions. The first one has been done for you.

We spot often wildlife on our hiking trips. Deer appear in fields occasionally and bears cross the path sometimes ahead of us. Porcupines, raccoons, and other small creatures into the underbrush scurry as we approach. Mountain lions are stealthy very and remain hidden. These big cats attack groups rarely and usually avoid human contact. However, no hikers should behind straggle.

🌐 Real-World Application

Practice In the following document, correct the use of adjectives and adverbs.

Clowning Around

1328 West Mound Road
Waukesha, Wi 53100
262-555-8180 ●

January 6, 2014

Mrs. Judy Bednar
38115 North Bayfield Drive
Waukesha, WI 53100

Dear Ms. Bednar:

It's time for a party birthday! You've thought of everything—balloons, decorations, cake. . . . But what about awesomely entertainment? How many kids are coming, and how much time do you have to keep them entertained?

Fear not. At Clowning Around, we specialize in making every birthday the memorablest it can be. For young kids, we offer balloon colorful animals, magic amazing tricks, and backyard goofy games. For older kids, we have water wild games and magic impressive illusions. And for kids of all ages, we have the most funny clowns, the most bravest superheroes, and the most amazingest impressionists.

That's right. You can throw a terrific very party for your loved one without worrying about the entertainment—and without paying a lot either. See the enclosed brochure for our services and rates. Then give us a call at Clowning Around, and we'll make your party next an event to remember.

Let's talk soon!

Dave Jenkins

Dave Jenkins
CEO, Clowning Around

Enclosure: Brochure

Chapter

21

"A family is a unit composed not only of children
but of men, women, an occasional animal, and
the common cold."

—Ogden Nash

Conjunction and Preposition

A family is a network of relationships. Some people have an equal relationship, like wives and husbands or brothers and sisters. Some people have unequal relationships, like mothers and daughters or fathers and sons. And the very young or very old are often dependent on middle-aged family members.

Ideas also have relationships, and conjunctions and prepositions show those relationships. When two ideas are equal, a coordinating conjunction connects them. When two ideas are not equal, a subordinating conjunction makes one idea depend on the other. And prepositions create special relationships between nouns and other words.

Conjunctions and prepositions help you connect ideas and build whole families of thought.

Learning Outcomes

LO1 Coordinating and Correlative Conjunctions
LO2 Subordinating Conjunctions
LO3 Common Prepositions
LO4 *By, At, On,* and *In*

What do you think?

What equal relationships do you have? What dependent relationships do you have?

L01 Coordinating and Correlative Conjunctions

A **conjunction** is a word or word group that joins parts of a sentence—words, phrases, or clauses.

► Coordinating Conjunctions

A **coordinating conjunction** joins grammatically equal parts—a word to a word, a phrase to a phrase, or a clause to a clause. A clause is a word group that has a subject and a predicate. Table 21.1 lists coordinating conjunctions.

Table 21.1 Coordinating Conjunctions						
and	but	or	nor	for	so	yet

- **Equal importance:** A coordinating conjunction shows that the two things joined are of equal importance.

    Rachel and Lydia enjoy arts and crafts.
    (*And* joins equal words.)

    They have knitted sweaters and pieced quilts.
    (*And* joins the phrases *knitted sweaters* and *pieced quilts*.)

    I tried to knit a sweater, but the thing unraveled.
    (*But* joins the two clauses, with a comma after the first.)

- **Items in a series:** A coordinating conjunction can join more than two equal parts.

    Rachel, Lydia, and I will take a class on making mosaics.
    (*And* joins *Rachel, Lydia,* and *I*, three parts of a compound subject. A comma follows each word except the last.)

    We will take the class, design a mosaic, and complete it together.
    (*And* joins three parts of a compound verb.)

► Correlative Conjunctions

Correlative conjunctions consist of a coordinating conjunction and another word or words. They connect related ideas that work together: word to word, phrase to phrase, or clause to clause. Table 21.2 lists correlative conjunctions.

Table 21.2 Correlative Conjunctions				
either/or	neither/nor	whether/or	both/and	not only/but also

- **Stressing equality:** Correlative conjunctions stress the equality of parts.

    Both Rachel and Lydia love crafts. They not only knit but also crochet.
    (*Both/and* stresses equal subjects; *not only/but also* stresses equal verbs.)

Practice For the following sentences, circle the best coordinating conjunction in parentheses.

1. I would like to learn knitting (but, for, or) crocheting.

2. Lydia, Rachel, (and, nor, yet) I enjoy making cloth with our hands.

3. We have different talents, (or, so, for) we teach each other what we know.

4. Lydia is best at knitting, (nor, but, for) I am best at tatting.

5. Rachel is our weaver, (but, yet, so) she is the loom master.

6. Each week, Lydia, Rachel, (and, but, or) I meet to share our work.

7. We want to broaden our skills, (and, or, yet) it's hard to learn something new.

8. I like yoga, Rachel likes pilates, (and, nor, so) Lydia likes spin cycling.

9. Come join us one day, (and, for, so) we love to teach beginners.

10. We'll show you our work, (but, nor, for) you'll decide what you want to learn.

Practice Write sentences of your own, using a coordinating conjunction (*and, but, or, nor, for, so, yet*) as requested.

1. join two words: _____

_____

2. join two phrases: _____

_____

3. create a series: _____

_____

4. join two clauses (place a comma after the first clause, before the conjunction):

_____

Practice Write a sentence that uses a pair of correlative conjunctions.

_____

_____

---

conjunction
a word or word group that joins words, phrases, or clauses

coordinating conjunction
a conjunction that joins grammatically equal parts

correlative conjunction
a conjunction pair that stresses the equality of the parts that are joined

L02 Subordinating Conjunctions

A **subordinating conjunction** is a word or word group that connects two clauses of different importance. A clause is a word group that has a subject and a predicate. Table 21.3 lists subordinating conjunctions.

Table 21.3 Subordinating Conjunctions

after	whenever	unless	that	since
as long as	although	where	until	though
if	because	as	whereas	when
so that	in order that	before	as if	while
till	than	provided that	even though	

- **Subordinate clause:** The subordinating conjunction comes at the beginning of the less-important subordinate clause, which does not form a complete thought. The **subordinate clause** can come before or after the more important clause (the **independent clause**).

    Summer is too hot to cook inside. I often barbecue.
    (two clauses)

    Because summer is too hot to cook inside, I often barbecue.
    (*Because* introduces the subordinate clause, which is followed by a comma.)

    I often barbecue because summer is too hot to cook inside.
    (If the subordinate clause comes second, a comma usually isn't needed.)

- **Special relationship:** A subordinating conjunction shows a special relationship between ideas. Table 21.4 shows the type of relationship that subordinating conjunctions indicate.

Table 21.4 Subordinating Conjunctions and Relationship

Time	after, as, before, since, till, until, when, whenever, while
Cause	as, as long as, because, if, in order that, provided that, since, so that, that
Contrast	although, as if, even though, though, unless, whereas, while

Whenever the temperature climbs, I cook on the grill. (time)

I grill because I don't want to heat up the house. (cause)

Even though it is hot outside, I feel cool in the shade as I cook. (contrast)

Practice In each sentence, provide an appropriate subordinating conjunction. Then choose the type of relationship it shows from the options in the parentheses.

1. _____ I marinated the chicken, I put it on the grill.
   (time, cause, contrast)

2. Grilling bratwurst is tough _____ the grease causes big flames.
   (time, cause, contrast)

3. _____ of trichinosis, pork should not be pink inside.
   (time, cause, contrast)

4. I like grilling chicken _____ my favorite food is steak.
   (time, cause, contrast)

5. I grill my steak rare _____ the FDA recommends well-done.
   (time, cause, contrast)

6. Some people use barbecue sauce, _____ I prefer marinades.
   (time, cause, contrast)

7. I use a gas grill _____ it is fast and convenient.
   (time, cause, contrast)

8. Purists use only charcoal _____ it creates a nice flavor.
   (time, cause, contrast)

9. _____ I was in Texas, I had great brisket.
   (time, cause, contrast)

Practice Create three of your own sentences using subordinating conjunctions, one for each type of relationship.

1. time: _____

   _____

2. cause: _____

   _____

3. contrast: _____

   _____

---

subordinating conjunction
a conjunction that connects clauses of different importance

subordinate clause
a word group that begins with a subordinating conjunction and has a subject and a predicate but does not express a complete thought

independent clause
a group of words with a subject and predicate that expresses a complete thought

L03 Common Prepositions

A **preposition** is a word or word group that creates a relationship between a noun or pronoun and another word. Table 21.5 shows common prepositions.

Table 21.5 Common Prepositions

aboard	back of	except for	near to	round
about	because of	excepting	notwithstanding	save
above	before	for	of	since
according to	behind	from	off	subsequent to
across	below	from among	on	through
across from	beneath	from between	on account of	throughout
after	beside	from under	on behalf of	'til *or* till
against	besides	in	onto	to
along	between	in addition to	on top of	together with
alongside	beyond	in behalf of	opposite	toward
alongside of	but	in front of	out	under
along with	by	in place of	out of	underneath
amid	by means of	in regard to	outside	until
among	concerning	inside	outside of	unto
apart from	considering	inside of	over	up
around	despite	in spite of	over to	upon
as far as	down	instead of	owing to	up to
aside from	down from	into	past	with
at	during	like	prior to	within
away from	except	near	regarding	without

▶ Prepositional Phrases

A **prepositional phrase** starts with a preposition and includes an object of the preposition (a noun or pronoun) and any modifiers. A prepositional phrase functions as an adjective or adverb.

> The Basset hound flopped on his side on the rug.
> (*On his side* and *on the rug* modify the verb *flopped.*)

> He slept on the rug in the middle of the hallway.
> (*On the rug* modifies *slept*; *in the middle* modifies *rug*; and *of the hallway* modifies *middle.*)

Insight A prepositional phrase can be used to break up a string of adjectives. Instead of writing "the old blue-awninged store," you can write "the old store with the blue awning."

Practice ▸ In the following sentences, underline the prepositional phrases and circle the word that each phrase modifies. The first one has been done for you.

1. Yesterday, I (ran) around the block and up the dirt road.

2. Another runner across the street waved at me.

3. I was so distracted that I tripped over a crack in the sidewalk.

4. Soon, though, I raced along my route again.

5. Birds chirped at me from tree branches.

6. Dogs barked from their backyards.

7. Clouds gathered in the sky.

8. Rain drops fell, making splotches on the road.

9. By the time I got home, the shower had stopped.

10. My shoes were soaked and caked with mud.

Practice ▸ Read each sentence that follows. Use each sentence as a model to write your own. Note how the writer uses prepositional phrases to create specific effects.

1. The coupe shot between the semis, around the limousine, down the tunnel, and up into bright sunlight.

   _____

2. I will look for you, but I also look to you.

   _____

3. Before the freedom of the road and the fun of the trip, I have finals.

   _____

4. Walk through the hallway, down the stairs, through the door, and into the pantry.

   _____

---

preposition
a word or word group that creates a relationship between a noun or pronoun and another word

prepositional phrase
a phrase that starts with a preposition, includes an object of the preposition (noun or pronoun) and any modifiers, and functions as an adjective or adverb

L04 *By, At, On,* and *In*

Prepositions often show the physical position of things—above, below, beside, around, and so on. Four specific prepositions not only show position but also have other uses in English.

I traveled
in a boat
on the Seine
by the roadway
in Paris
at dusk
on May 30.

Rostislav Glinsky, 2014 / Used under license from Shutterstock.com

▶ Uses for *By, At, On,* and *In*

■ **By** means "beside" or "up to" a certain place or time.

by the creek, by the garage

by noon, by August 16

■ **At** refers to a specific place or time.

at the edge, at the coffee shop

at 6:45 p.m., at midnight

■ **On** refers to a surface, a day or date, or an electronic medium.

on the table, on the T-shirt

on July 22, on Wednesday

on the computer, on the DVD

■ **In** refers to an enclosed space; a geographical location; a certain amount of time, a month, or a year; or a print medium.

in the hall, in the bathroom

in Madison, in France

in a minute, in December, in 2014

in the magazine, in the book

Say It   Team up with a partner. Take turns reading one of the following phrases or words, which the other person must use in a prepositional phrase beginning with *by, at, on,* or *in.* Together, discuss whether the prepositional phrase is correct and makes sense.

1. the den
2. June 23
3. 9:33 p.m.
4. the MP3 player
5. the corner

6. Pittsburgh
7. the counter
8. the diner
9. sunset
10. the newspaper

Practice For each sentence, circle the correct preposition in parentheses.

1. The guests arrived (by, on, in) 7:30 p.m., so we could eat (at, on, in) 8:00 p.m.

2. Put your suitcase (by, at, on, in) the trunk or (by, at, on) the rooftop luggage rack.

3. I looked for the new album in a music store, but could find it only (by, at, on, in) the Internet.

4. We waited (by, at, on, in) the lobby for a half-hour, but Jerry didn't show up or even call (by, at, on, in) his cell phone.

5. Three people standing (by, at, in) the corner saw a traffic accident (by, at, on) the intersection of 45th and Monroe.

6. Pranksters may post apocalypse hoaxes (by, at, on, in) the Internet.

7. Let's meet (by, at, in) the classroom.

8. Place your order form (by, at, on, in) the postage-paid envelope, write your return address (by, at, on, in) the envelope, and post it.

Practice Write three sentences. Include the prepositions given in parentheses.

1. (by, on) _____

_____

2. (in, at) _____

_____

3. (at, on, in) _____

_____

Real-World Application

Practice ▶ Correct the following email by inserting coordinating or subordinating conjunctions (see Tables 21.1 and 21.3) and replacing any incorrect prepositions with correct ones.

To: dkraitsman@delafordandco.com

Subject: Completed Photo Log

Attach: Photolog.doc

Dear Deirdra:

Attached, please find the photo log. The log shows all photos in the Web site. Some photos are from Getty Images. Others are from Shutterstock. A few are from Corbis. All photos have been downloaded. The downloads have the right resolution.

I hope you are pleased with the log. It includes permissions details. It also shows the resolution. I included a description of each photo. You can contact me in this email address if you have any comments about it.

I am available for more work starting in December 12. I could compile another photo log. I could also do the permissions work on these photos. I do writing and editing as well.

Please let me know in December 11 if you would like me to continue with this project.

Thanks,

Roger Haverson

Photo Editor

PART 7:

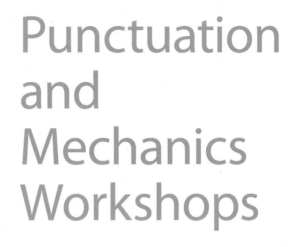

Punctuation and Mechanics Workshops

Part 7: Punctuation and Mechanics Workshops

Chapter

22

"Conventions are subject to the vagaries of time and fashion. . . . The writers of the Constitution capitalized words in the middle of sentences."

—Mitchell Ivers

Capitalization

Why is the word *mom* capitalized in "Did Mom call?" and not in "Did my mom call?" This is just one of the vagaries when it comes to proper capitalization in our language. As you review this chapter, you will find others.

One of the best ways to learn about the unexpected changes in capitalization is to become a reader and writer yourself. Combine regular reading and writing with the practice in this chapter and you will be well on your way to mastering correct capitalization. You can also use this chapter as a reference whenever you have questions about capitalization.

Learning Outcomes

LO1 Basic Capitalization
LO2 Advanced Capitalization
LO3 Other Capitalization Rules

What do you think?

Why do you suppose that we pay so much attention to the rules of capitalization? Why don't we capitalize common nouns in the middle of sentences?

L01 Basic Capitalization

► **First Words**

Capitalize the first word in every sentence and the first word in a direct quotation that is a full sentence.

> **P**rofessional sports has become far too important in the United States.

> Yvonne asked, "**W**hy do baseball players spit all of the time?"

► **Proper Nouns and Adjectives**

Capitalize all proper nouns (names of specific persons, places, things, and ideas) and all proper adjectives (adjectives derived from proper nouns). Table 22.1 lists examples.

Table 22.1 Proper Nouns and Adjectives

Days of the week	Saturday, Sunday, Tuesday
Months	March, August, December
Holidays, holy days	Christmas, Hanukkah, President's Day
Periods, events in history	the Renaissance, Middle Ages
Special events	Tate Memorial Dedication Ceremony
Political parties, organizations	Republican Party, Habitat for Humanity
Religions, Supreme Beings, holy books	Buddhism, Allah, the Holy Bible
Official documents	Bill of Rights
Trade names	Frisbee disc, Heinz ketchup
Formal epithets	Alexander the Great
Official titles	Vice President Al Gore, Senator Davis
Official state nicknames	the Garden State, the Beaver State
Planets, heavenly bodies	Earth, Mars, the Milky Way
Continents	Asia, Australia, Europe
Countries	France, Brazil, Japan, Pakistan
States, provinces	Montana, Nebraska, Alberta, Ontario
Cities, towns, villages	Portland, Brookfield, Broad Ripple
Streets, roads, highways	Rodeo Drive, Route 66, Interstate 55
Nationalities and ethnic groups	African, Navajo, Serbs
Sections of the U.S. and the world	the West Coast, the Middle East
Languages	Spanish, English, Hindi
Landforms and bodies of water	Appalachian Mountains, Lake Erie
Public areas	Central Park, Yosemite National Park

NOTE: Words that indicate sections of the country are proper nouns and should be capitalized; words that simply indicate directions are not proper nouns.

> I drove **southwest** on my way to the **M**idwest.

Practice In the following sentences, place capitalization marks (≡) under any letters that should be capitalized.

1. Musician louis armstrong helped make jazz popular to american and european audiences.

2. Armstrong grew up in new Orleans in a rough neighborhood called the "battleground."

3. he was sent to reform school because he fired a gun in the air on new year's eve.

4. Upon his release, he visited music halls like funky butt hall to hear king oliver play.

5. Oliver gave armstrong his first real cornet, and he played with oliver's band in storyville, a district in New orleans.

6. He also played with the allen brass band on the strekfus line of riverboats.

7. In 1919, Armstrong left New Orleans for Chicago and played with kid ory.

8. He really began to make a name for himself in the creole jazz band that played at Lincoln gardens in Chicago.

Practice Read the following paragraph. Place capitalization marks (≡) under any letters that should be capitalized in proper nouns, proper adjectives, or first words.

My great-grandfather Erv grew up in the midwest during the great depression. He lived in two different houses on villa street just south of the downtown area. Erv attended St. mary's Catholic School and Franklin school when he was a kid. His dad, my great-great-grandfather, came from Poland and started out by selling hot dogs at north beach. Because money was scarce, my great-grandfather's family sometimes had only corn on the cob for dinner. After high school, he enlisted in the U.S. navy but was turned down because of poor eyesight. He then joined the U.S. Army and fought in Europe during world war II. when Erv returned to the midwest, he went to work at massey harris, a company that made tractors.

L02 Advanced Capitalization

▶ Sentences in Parentheses

Capitalize the first word in a sentence that is enclosed in parentheses if that sentence is not within another complete sentence.

> I need to learn more about the health-care system in Canada. (**My** friend just married a guy from Toronto.)

NOTE: Do *not* capitalize a sentence that is enclosed in parentheses and is located in the middle of another sentence.

> Missy's husband (his name is Andre) works in a family business.

▶ Sentences Following Colons

Capitalize a complete sentence that follows a colon when that sentence is a formal statement, a quotation, or a sentence that you want to emphasize.

> Seldom have I heard such encouraging words: **The** economy is on the rebound.

▶ Words Used as Names

Capitalize words like *father, mother, uncle, senator,* and *professor* only when they are parts of titles that include a personal name or when they are substitutes for proper nouns (especially in direct address).

> Hello, **Representative** Baldwin. (*Representative* is part of the name.)
>
> It's good to meet you, **Representative**. (*Representative* is a substitute for the name.)
>
> Our **representative** is a member of two important committees.

> Who was the volleyball **coach** last year?
>
> We had **Coach Snyder** for two years.
>
> I met **Coach** in the athletic office.

To test whether a word is being substituted for a proper noun, simply read the sentence with a proper noun in place of the word. If the proper noun fits in the sentence, the word being tested should be capitalized. Usually the word is not capitalized if it follows a possessive, such as *my, his, our,* or *your.*

> Did **Mom** (Mary) pick up the dry cleaning? (*Mary* works in the sentence.)
>
> Did your **mom** (Mary) pick up the dry cleaning? (*Mary* does not work in the sentence; the word *mom* follows *your.*)

Practice In the following sentences, place capitalization marks (≡) under any letters that should be capitalized.

1. Golda Meir (the former prime minister of Israel) once said this about women: "whether women are better than men I cannot say—but I can say they are certainly no worse."

2. My dad is already planning for his retirement. (what will he do with so much free time?)

3. I chatted with coach after practice. He recommended that I meet with professor Thompson to discuss scheduling conflicts between class and away basketball games.

4. Every summer, pastor Bachman leads a group on a hike around Lake Geneva.

5. My mechanic made a bad day even worse: he told me that my car needed four new tires.

6. Whenever mom talks about politics, she eventually criticizes our local congressman.

7. At the celebration, my dad asked senator Ryan about health care.

Practice Read the following paragraph. Place capitalization marks (≡) under any letters that should be capitalized. Put a lowercase editing mark (/) through any letters that should not be capitalized.

From 1943-1954, the All American Girls Professional Baseball League brought women's baseball to the masses. The league was founded by Wrigley Chewing Gum president Philip K. Wrigley, who was also President of the Chicago Cubs at the time. Women's baseball filled an entertainment need created by World War II: many men, especially minor-leaguers, were serving overseas. The players wore dress uniforms with knee-high woolen socks. (they must have been careful about sliding.) Yet one thing was certain: the girls could play ball with the best of them. Years later the league inspired the movie *A League of Their Own*, which featured the famous quotation by the Manager of the Racine Belles: "there's no crying in baseball."

L03 Other Capitalization Rules

► Titles

Capitalize the first word of a title, the last word, and every word in between except articles (*a, an, the*), short prepositions, *to* in an infinitive, and coordinating conjunctions. Follow this rule for titles of books, newspapers, magazines, poems, plays, songs, articles, films, works of art, and stories.

The Dark Knight (movie)	*The Sound and the Fury* (novel)
"What a Wonderful World" (song)	"Death Penalty's False Promise" (essay)

► Titles of Courses

Words such as *history* and *science* are proper nouns when they are included in the titles of specific courses; they are common nouns when they name a field of study.

I'm glad **Introduction to Politics** fits my schedule. (title of a specific course)

Judy Kenner advises anyone interested in **politics**. (a field of study)

NOTE: Always capitalize *English*, even if it is used as a common noun.

► Organizations

Capitalize the name of an organization or a team and its members.

Habitat for Humanity	**Libertarian Party**
The Bill & Melinda Gates Foundation	**Chicago Cubs**

► Abbreviations

Capitalize abbreviations of titles and organizations.

MD	PhD	NAACP	CE	BCE	GPA

► Web Terms

The words *Internet* and *World Wide Web* are capitalized because they are considered proper nouns. When your writing includes a Web address (URL), capitalize any letters that the site's owner does (in print or on the site itself).

When doing research on the **Internet**, be sure to record each site's **Web** address (URL) and each contact's **email** address. One popular research site is **Google.com**.

Practice In the following sentences, place capitalization marks (≡) under any letters that should be capitalized.

1. To me, *a midsummer night's dream* is one of Shakespeare's best plays.

2. The San Francisco giants used to play in Candlestick park.

3. My night course, contemporary history 301, is always packed with students interested in history and current events.

4. The web is a treasure trove of information thanks to sites like google .

5. I participated in a fund-raising event for the American cancer society.

6. Our instructor had us bookmark grammar girl, a web site that provides grammar tips and practice.

7. Javier Lopez, an old friend from the neighborhood, earned a phd in history.

8. Perhaps the least known of the beatles is George Harrison; I love his song "here comes the sun."

9. Anna Quindlen's article "uncle sam and aunt samantha" first appeared in *newsweek*.

10. I'm interested in advanced statistics and data mining, so I might take the course introduction to statistical data processing.

Practice In the following paragraph, place capitalization marks (≡) under any letters that should be capitalized.

An article in last week's *standard press* promoted the event Market on the Square. The market, held every Thursday afternoon, is sponsored by the Brighton chamber of commerce. The vendors, who must reside within the local area, sell everything from fresh produce to tie-dyed T-shirts. In addition, organizations such as the american red cross and Brighton little league have informational booths at the market. A special feature is the live entertainment supplied by rainbow road, a local folk-rock band. They play a lot of Mumford and Sons, singing favorites like "I will wait."

🌐 Real-World Application

Practice In the following email, place capitalization marks (≡) under any letters that should be capitalized. Put a lowercase editing mark (/) through any letters that should not be capitalized.

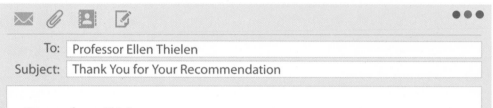

To: Professor Ellen Thielen

Subject: Thank You for Your Recommendation

Dear professor Thielen,

Thank you for recommending me for the internship at Cohill laboratories. During my interview last Monday, Dr. Keenan said that he had received your letter and had talked with you by phone. Apparently you said, "clearly Raul has demonstrated meticulous and thorough Lab techniques." I really appreciate this description of my work habits.

The outcome of the application and interviewing process could not have gone any better; this morning Dr. Keenan offered me the position. I will be working at Farwell science center, one of Cohill's newest Labs, helping various chemists with their work.

I am so glad that I had you for biochemistry III. You made that course interesting, and I learned so much. Dr. Keenan also was impressed that I had taken analytical chemistry I and II, taught by professor Williams.

Again, I can't thank you enough, professor, for your help. I know I will be busy next semester with the Internship, but I can't wait to get started. (you can expect to hear from me about my work.)

Sincerely,

Raul Samuelson

Pressmaster, 2014 / Used under license from Shutterstock.com

Pressmaster, 2014 / Used under license from Shutterstock.com

Chapter 23

"The writer who neglects punctuation, or mispunctuates, is liable to be misunderstood for the want of merely a comma."

—Edgar Allan Poe

Comma

When you speak, you communicate with much more than words. You pause, raise or lower your pitch, change your tone or volume, and use facial expressions and body language to get your point across.

When you write, you can forget about pitch or volume, facial expressions or body language. You're left with the tone of your words and with the pauses that you put in them. Commas give you one way to create soft pauses. They help to show which words belong together, which should be separated, and which line up in parallel. Commas are key to being understood.

In this chapter you will learn about the conventional use of commas. Understanding correct comma usage is an important step in becoming a college-level writer.

Learning Outcomes

LO1 In Compound Sentences and After Introductory Clauses

LO2 With Introductory Phrases and Equal Adjectives

LO3 Between Items in a Series and Other Uses

LO4 With Appositives and Other Word Groups

What do you think?

Imagine reading a book or newspaper without punctuation. What difficulties may you encounter? Explain.

L01   In Compound Sentences and After Introductory Clauses

The following principles will guide the use of commas in your writing.

▶ In Compound Sentences

Use a comma before the coordinating conjunction (*and, but, or, nor, for, yet, so*) in a compound sentence.

> Heath Ledger completed his brilliant portrayal as the Joker in *The Dark Knight,* **but** he died before the film was released.

NOTE: Do not confuse a compound verb with a compound sentence. Compound verbs should not be separated by commas.

> Ledger's Joker became instantly iconic and won him the Oscar for best supporting actor. *(compound verb)*
>
> His death resulted from the abuse of prescription drugs, but it was ruled an accident. *(compound sentence)*

▶ After Introductory Clauses

Use a comma after most introductory clauses.

> **Although Charlemagne was a great patron of learning,** he never learned to write properly. *(adverb dependent clause)*

When the adverb clause follows the independent clause and is not essential to the meaning of the sentence, use a comma. This comma use generally applies to clauses beginning with *even though, although, while,* or some other conjunction expressing a contrast.

> Charlemagne never learned to write properly, **even though he continued to practice.**

NOTE: A comma is not used if the adverb clause following the independent clause is needed for clarity.

> Charlemagne continued to practice **because he wanted to write well.**

Practice Read the following sentences. If the clause on each side of the coordinating conjunction could stand alone as a sentence, add a comma. Write "correct" for any sentence that should not contain a comma.

1. Catherine had questions about her class schedule so she set up an appointment with her academic adviser.   _____

2. I was going to play in the sand volleyball league but it conflicted with my work schedule.   _____

3. Trisha picked up some groceries and stopped by the bank.   _____

4. I normally don't listen to jazz music yet I love going to summer jazz concerts in the park.   _____

5. Should I finish my essay a day early or should I go to my friend's house party?   _____

6. Kevin has a job interview at the advertisement agency and he hopes he can make a good impression.   _____

7. Creativity is his best quality but leadership is not far behind.   _____

Practice In the following sentences, add a comma between the clauses if necessary. If no comma is needed, write "correct."

1. Even though digital books are the craze I prefer paperbacks.   _____

2. Although the crab dip appetizer was delicious my entrée left something to be desired.   _____

3. Because I'm starved for time online shopping is a convenient alternative to mall shopping.   _____

4. I toggled through radio stations as I waited at the tollbooth.   _____

5. Erin worried about giving her speech even though she had practiced for weeks.   _____

L02 With Introductory Phrases and Equal Adjectives

► After Introductory Phrases

Use a comma after introductory phrases.

> **In spite of his friend's prodding,** Jared decided to stay home and study.

A comma is usually omitted if the phrase follows an independent clause.

> Jared decided to stay home and study **in spite of his friend's prodding.**

You may omit a comma after a short (four or fewer words) introductory phrase unless it is needed to ensure clarity.

> **At 10:32 p.m.** he quit studying and went to sleep.

► To Separate Adjectives

Use commas to separate adjectives that equally modify the same noun. Notice in the following examples that no comma separates the last adjective from the noun.

> You should exercise regularly and follow a **sensible, healthful** diet.
> A good diet is one that includes lots of **high-protein, low-fat** foods.

► To Determine Equal Modifiers

To determine whether adjectives modify a noun equally, use these two tests.

1. Reverse the order of the adjectives; if the sentence is clear, the adjectives modify equally. (In the following example, *hot* and *crowded* can be switched, but *short* and *coffee* cannot.)

> Matt was tired of working in the **hot, crowded** lab and decided to take a **short coffee** break.

2. Insert *and* between the adjectives; if the sentence reads well, use a comma when *and* is omitted. (The word *and* can be inserted between *hot* and *crowded*, but *and* does not make sense between *short* and *coffee*.)

Practice ▶ In the following sentences, add commas after the introductory phrases as necessary. If no comma is needed, write "correct."

1. Before sending the email to Professor James make sure you reread it for errors.   _____

2. In accordance with the academic code plagiarism is deemed a major offense.   _____

3. After hitting the 10-mile jogging plateau Heather felt a great rush of adrenaline.   _____

4. Heather felt a great rush of adrenaline after hitting the 10-mile jogging plateau.   _____

5. Thankfully DeMarcus stopped the leak before it could do any real damage.   _____

6. Based on his past experience Wilson decided against going to the concert.   _____

7. To train for the triathlon Brent altered his diet.   _____

8. At the end of the day Erin recorded her favorite show.   _____

Practice ▶ In the following sentences, determine whether a comma is needed to separate the boldfaced adjectives. Add a comma if it is needed; write "correct" if a comma is not needed.

1. I'm expecting this to be a **rocking after** party.   _____

2. There's nothing like the **warm emerald** water off the Florida Gulf Coast.   _____

3. The exercise program included a **calorie-burning cardio** session.   _____

4. My **surly economics** professor is one of a kind.   _____

5. I'm in desperate need of a **relaxing summer** vacation.   _____

6. Marathon runners favor **light comfortable** shorts.   _____

L03   Between Items in a Series and Other Uses

▶ Between Items in a Series

Use commas to separate individual words, phrases, or clauses in a series. A series contains at least three items.

> Many college students must balance studying with **taking care of a family, working, getting exercise, and finding time to relax.**

Do not use commas when all the items are connected with *or, nor,* or *and.*

> Hmm . . . should I study **or** do laundry **or** go out?

▶ To Set Off Transitional Expressions

Use a comma to set off conjunctive adverbs and transitional phrases.

> Handwriting is not, **as a matter of fact,** easy to improve upon later in life; **however,** it can be done if you are determined enough.

If a transitional expression blends smoothly with the rest of the sentence, it does not need to be set off.

> If you are **in fact** coming, I'll see you there.

▶ To Set Off Dialogue

Use commas to set off the exact words of the speaker from the rest of the sentence.

> **"Never be afraid to ask for help,"** advised Ms. Kane.

> **"With the evidence that we now have,"** Professor Thom said, **"many scientists believe there could be life on Mars."**

Do not use a comma before an indirect quotation.

> Professor Thom said **that his astronomy class is full.**

▶ To Enclose Explanatory Words

Use commas to enclose an explanatory phrase that interrupts the flow of the sentence, providing extra information.

> Time management, **according to many professionals,** is an important skill that should be taught in college.

Practice ▷ Insert commas where needed in the following sentences.

1. I considered becoming a lawyer; however law school wasn't for me.

2. "Don't give up; don't ever give up" advised the late Jim Valvano.

3. Electronic beats, catchy lyrics and a pop-friendly sound characterize Calvin Harris's music.

4. Western Wisconsin as opposed to Illinois is relatively hilly.

5. In Boston I visited Fenway Park the U.S.S. *Constitution*, and Old North Church.

6. Thomas as you may have noticed is eager to share his vast knowledge of random facts.

7. In regard to public transportation, you may decide between the subway buses or taxicabs.

8. "While it certainly offers a convenient alternative to paper maps" said Emilie "my car's navigational system more often gets me lost."

9. Avocados the key ingredient of guacamole are a good source of fiber.

10. You need to determine if weather price or transportation will factor into your decision.

Practice ▷ Insert commas where needed in the following paragraph.

On an early summer morning in July I sat slumped in a terminal at Dulles Airport, reminiscing about my time in Washington, D.C. It had after all been a fun trip. I visited all the usual landmarks, including the Lincoln Memorial, Arlington National Cemetery and the Smithsonian Institute. However my favorite landmark was Mount Vernon the home and former estate of President George Washington. It's easy to see why Washington adored his home's location a beautiful tract of land on the banks of the Potomac. Besides Washington's plantation home, the estate included a distillery a blacksmith shop and acres of farmland. Mount Vernon according to my travel agent is a must-see for visitors to our nation's capital, and I agree.

L04 With Appositives and Other Word Groups

▶ To Set Off Some Appositives

Use commas to set off a specific kind of explanatory word or phrase called an **appositive**. An appositive identifies or renames a preceding noun or pronoun.

> Albert Einstein, **the famous mathematician and physicist,** developed the theory of relativity.

Do not use commas if the appositive is important to the basic meaning of the sentence.

> The famous physicist **Albert Einstein** developed the theory of relativity.

▶ With Some Clauses and Phrases

Use commas to enclose phrases or clauses that add information that is not necessary to the basic meaning of the sentence. For example, if the clause or phrase (in **boldface**) were left out of the following two examples, the meaning of the sentences would remain clear. Therefore, commas are used to set off the information.

> The locker rooms in Swain Hall, **which were painted and updated last summer,** give professors a place to shower. *(unnecessary clause)*
>
> Work-study programs, **offered on many campuses,** give students the opportunity to earn tuition money. *(unnecessary phrase)*

Do not use commas to set off necessary clauses and phrases, which add information that the reader needs to understand the sentence.

> Only the professors **who run at noon** use the locker rooms. *(necessary clause)*

▶ Using "That" or "Which"

Use *that* to introduce necessary clauses; use *which* to introduce unnecessary clauses.

> Campus jobs **that are funded by the university** are awarded to students only. *(necessary clause)*
>
> The cafeteria, **which is run by an independent contractor,** can hire non-students. *(unnecessary clause)*

Practice Indicate where commas are needed in the following sentences. If no commas are needed, write "correct."

1. The U.S.S. *Constitution* is a wooden-hulled three-masted ship that is still commissioned by the U.S. Navy.   _____

2. Gordon Ramsay the fiery chef and television star specializes in French, Italian, and British cuisines.   _____

3. Hall of Fame baseball player Roberto Clemente a notable philanthropist died in a plane crash while en route to Nicaragua to deliver aid to earthquake victims.   _____

4. The concert hall which is on the corner of Meridian Avenue and 1st Street is expected to revitalize the downtown district.   _____

5. Press passes that allow for backstage access are given out to special media members.   _____

6. John Quincy Adams who later became the sixth president of the United States authored the Monroe Doctrine in 1823.   _____

Practice Decide if the clause in bold type is necessary or unnecessary to the meaning of the following sentences. Then circle the correct conjunction in parentheses and supply commas if they are necessary. The first one has been done for you.

1. The flight *(which, that)* **our keynote speaker** is on has been delayed.

2. The Modesto Wind Farm *(which, that)* **was built last year** is scheduled to double in size by 2016.

3. Applications for scholarships *(which, that)* **are sponsored by the Kiwanis Club** are due next Tuesday.

4. Scholarship programs *(which, that)* **are funded by several different organizations** help many students pay for college.

5. The museum *(which, that)* **impressed Dad the most** was the Guggenheim.

---

appositive
a noun or noun phrase that renames the noun preceding it

🌐 Real-World Application

Practice ▶ Insert commas where they are needed in the following email message.

✉ 📎 📇 📝   ● ● ●

To: Michael_Green@shieldmarketing.com

Subject: Revised Agenda for Quarterly Update

Attach: Meeting Agenda 04-19-14.doc

Hi, Michael:

I've attached the agenda for the quarterly update with the marketing team. Daniel Gilchrest the senior marketing coordinator will moderate the meeting but I want you to familiarize yourself with the material. Here are some highlights of the new agenda:

1. The advertising allowance for Gillette, Hillsboro Farms and Justice Inc. has increased by 5 percent.

2. The penetrated market which accounts for actual users of products declined in the health-care sector.

3. We will shift the focus of marketing efforts to meet the digital and social media demands of today's market.

Please review the agenda by the end of the day.

Thanks,

Tru Sha

Marketing Associate

Luciano Mortula, 2014 / Used under license from Shutterstock.com

24

"Quotation marks and italics don't flash or blink,
but they do catch the reader's attention."

—Lois Krenzke

Quotation Marks and Italics

Broadway is plastered with billboards five stories high and jammed with marquees that flash in the night. They advertise plays and movies, books and magazines, albums and TV shows—all in spotlights or neon trying to make people take notice.

In writing, there are no spotlights. There is no neon. Instead of writing the names of plays, movies, books, short stories, or articles in giant, flashing letters, writers set them off with italics or quotation marks. This chapter will show you how to correctly punctuate titles as well as significant words, letters, and numbers.

Learning Outcomes

LO1 Quotation Marks

LO2 Italics

What do you think?

How are quotation marks and italics like flashing lights in writing? How are they different?

L01 Quotation Marks

► To Punctuate Titles of Smaller Works

Use quotation marks to enclose the titles of smaller works, including speeches, short stories, songs, poems, episodes of audio or video programs, chapters or sections of books, unpublished works, and articles from magazines, journals, newspapers, or encyclopedias.

Speech: "Ain't I a Woman?"

Song: "California Girls"

Short story: "The Tell-Tale Heart"

Magazine article: "Is Google Making Us Stupid?"

Chapter in a book: "The Second Eve"

Television episode: "The Empty Child"

Encyclopedia article: "Autobahn"

► Placement of Punctuation

When quoted words end in a period or comma, always place the period or comma inside the quotation marks.

"When you leave the kitchen," Tim said, "turn out the light."

When a quotation is followed by a semicolon or colon, always place the semicolon or colon outside the quotation marks.

I finally read "The Celebrated Jumping Frog of Calaveras County"; it is a hoot!

The student wrote, "This is what I learned"; then he stopped to think.

If an exclamation point or a question mark is part of the quotation, place it inside the quotation marks. Otherwise, place it outside.

Shawndra asked Mark, "Would you like to go to the movies?"

Did Mark actually say, "No thanks"?

▶ For Special Words

Quotation marks can be used (1) to show that a word is being referred to as the word itself; (2) to indicate that it is jargon, slang, or a coined term; (3) to show that it is used in an ironic or sarcastic sense; or for (4) quoting other people's words, such as a definition.

(1) & (4)   The word "chuffed" is British slang for "very excited."

(2)   I'm "chuffed" about my new computer.

(3)   I'm "chuffed" about my root canal.

Practice For the following sentences, insert quotation marks as needed.

1. Tim loves The Cask of Amontillado, a short story by Edgar Allan Poe.

2. Stephen King's short story The Body was made into a movie.

3. Fareed Zakaria wrote the article The Rise of Putinism.

4. Lisa told Jennie, Tonight is the pizza and pasta buffet.

5. Jennie asked, Isn't it buy one, get one free?

6. Was she thinking, That's a lot better than cooking?

7. Here is the main conflict of the story To Build a Fire: man versus nature.

8. I read an article entitled The Obese Fruit of Capitalism; it suggested that our modern obesity epidemic demonstrates the tremendous achievements of fast food and agribusiness.

9. What does the word hypertrophy mean?

10. I was thrilled to receive the unexpected bill.

11. Habeas Corpus is the title of the first part of the book *Fever* by Mary Beth Keane.

12. Everyone knows what being bummed out about something means, right?

Practice Write two sentences, each demonstrating your understanding of one or more rules for using quotation marks.

1. _____

_____

2. _____

_____

L02   Italics

► To Identify Titles of Larger Works

Use italics to indicate the titles of larger works, including newspapers, magazines, journals, pamphlets, books, plays, films, radio and television programs, movies, ballets, operas, long musical compositions, CDs, DVDs, software programs, and legal cases, as well as the names of ships, trains, aircraft, and spacecraft.

Magazine: *The Week*	**Newspaper:** *Chicago Tribune*
Play: *Cat on a Hot Tin Roof*	**Journal:** *Nature*
Film: *Casablanca*	**Software program:** *Final Draft*
Book: *Death's Disciples*	**Television program:** *Doctor Who*

► For a Word, Letter, or Number Referred to as Itself

Use italics or quotation marks (either is correct) to show that a word, letter, or number is being referred to as itself. If a definition follows a word used in this way, place that definition in quotation marks.

The word *courage* comes from the French word *cour*, which means "heart."

In the handwritten note, I couldn't distinguish an *N* from an *M*.

► For Foreign Words

Use italics to indicate a word that is being borrowed from a foreign language.

The phrase *et cetera* is a Latin phrase meaning "and so forth."

► For Technical Terms

Use italics to introduce a technical term for the first time in a piece of writing. After that, the term may be used without italics.

Particle physicists finally discerned the elusive *Higgs boson* particle in 2012. The Higgs boson is a subatomic particle thought to provide mass to all other particles.

If a technical term is being used within an organization or a field of study where it is common, it may be used without italics even the first time in a piece of writing.

Practice For the following sentences, write down or underline words that should be in italics.

1. One of my favorite novels is The Curious Incident of the Dog in the Night-Time by Mark Haddon.

2. Have you seen the amazing movie Memento?

3. The name of the dance paso doble comes from the Spanish words for "double step."

4. In 1945, the bomber called the Enola Gay dropped the first atomic bomb, a weapon predicted in 1914 in the H. G. Wells novel The World Set Free.

5. She always has a real joie de vivre.

6. To look at the PDF, you need Adobe Reader or Adobe Acrobat.

7. In this context, the words profane and profanity do not refer to swearing but simply to things that are not divine.

8. The television show Project Runway pits fashion designers against each other.

9. The password contains the letters z, v, and p.

10. The term hypertrophy refers to the enlargement of muscles through weight lifting.

Practice Write three sentences, each demonstrating your understanding of a rule for using italics. Underline any words that should be italicized.

1. _____

_____

_____

2. _____

_____

_____

3. _____

_____

_____

🌐 Real-World Application

Practice Insert any missing quotation marks and underline any words that should be italicized in the following email.

✉️ 📎 📇 🖊️   ● ● ●

To: Will McMartin

Subject: Metrameme Author Bio

Hi, Will:

Here is the author bio you requested from me to be published in my next book, War Child:

John Metrameme has published over a dozen novels, most recently the historical epic Sons of Thunder and the romp Daddy Zeus. He also has written articles for The Atlantic and The New Yorker, and his short story Me and the Mudman won the Rubel Prize. Metrameme is perhaps best known for his novel Darling Buds of May.

In his spare time, Metrameme enjoys volunteering at his community theater. He often leads the lessons during children's acting classes. Metrameme has also starred as Kit Gill in No Way to Treat a Lady and as Jonathan in Arsenic and Old Lace.

Will, please let me know if you need anything more from me.

Thanks,

John

Mila Supinskaya, 2014 / Used under license from Shutterstock.com

Chapter

25

"In writing, punctuation plays the role of body language. It helps readers hear the way you want to be heard."

—Russell Baker

Other Punctuation

Work is important, of course. Progress. Motion. Getting somewhere. Yet sometimes it's important to pause and take a breath. Breaks allow you to work even more effectively afterward.

Written materials need pauses and breaks, too. It doesn't have to be a full stop (a period); maybe something softer will do. Semicolons, colons, and dashes can give the reader just the right break to be refreshed and to set out again. This chapter covers these three punctuation marks as well as apostrophes and hyphens.

Learning Outcomes

LO1 Apostrophes for Contractions and Possessives

LO2 Semicolons and Colons

LO3 Hyphens

LO4 Dashes

What do you think?

How are punctuation and body language similar? What type of body language is the equivalent of a hyphen? What about a dash?

L01 Apostrophes for Contractions and Possessives

Apostrophes are used primarily to show that a letter or number has been left out or that a noun is possessive.

Contractions

Use an apostrophe to form a **contraction**. A contraction is a word formed by joining two words, leaving out one or more letters and using an apostrophe in their place.

do not—don't	he would—he'd	would have—would've
(*o* is left out)	(*woul* is left out)	(*ha* is left out)

► Missing Characters

Use an apostrophe to signal when one or more characters are left out.

class of '16	rock 'n' roll	good mornin'
(*20* is left out)	(*a* and *d* are left out)	(*g* is left out)

Possessives

Form possessives of singular nouns by adding an apostrophe and an *s*. The word before the apostrophe is the owner.

Sharla's pen	the man's coat	*The Pilgrim's Progress*

► Singular Noun Ending in *s* (One Syllable)

Form the possessive by adding an apostrophe and an s.

the boss's idea	the lass's purse	the bass's teeth

► Singular Noun Ending in *s* (Two or More Syllables)

Form the possessive by adding an apostrophe and an *s*—or by adding just an apostrophe.

Kansas's plains	*or*	Kansas' plains

► Plural Noun Ending in *s*

Form the possessive by adding just an apostrophe.

the bosses' idea	the Smiths' home	the girls' ball

► Plural Noun Not Ending in *s*

Form the possessive by adding an apostrophe and an *s*.

the children's toys	the women's room

> Insight Pronoun possessives *do not use* apostrophes: *its, whose, hers, his, ours.*

Practice For the following contractions, write the words that formed the contraction. For the following pairs of words, use an apostrophe to form the contraction.

1. you're _____

2. John is _____

3. would have _____

4. she'd _____

5. you would _____

6. shouldn't _____

7. it is _____

8. they are _____

Practice Rewrite the following sentences, replacing the "of" phrases with possessives using apostrophes.

1. I'm going to the house of Jeremy.

_____

2. The ice cream of the corner stand is amazing.

_____

3. The pace of the track star is impressive.

_____

4. I like the early work of the Rolling Stones.

_____

5. The persona of Texas is well represented in the slogan "Everything is bigger in Texas."

_____

6. The paintings of the artist were outstanding.

_____

7. I discovered the best pizza spot of Portland.

_____

8. She reviewed the notes of Kimbra.

_____

9. The contractor assessed the structure of the house.

_____

10. The position of the politician on health care remained firm.

_____

L02   Semicolons and Colons

Semicolon

A **semicolon** (;) can be called a soft period. Use the semicolon to join two sentences that are closely related.

> The mosquitoes have returned; it must be August in Wisconsin.

▶ Before a Conjunctive Adverb

Often, the second sentence will begin with a conjunctive adverb (*also, besides, however, instead, meanwhile, therefore*), which signals the relationship between the sentences. Place a semicolon before the conjunctive adverb, and place a comma after it.

> The outdoor mosquito treatment was rated for six weeks; however, it lasted only four.

▶ In a Series

Use a semicolon to separate items in a series if any of the items already include commas.

> Before the party, I'll cut the grass and treat the lawn; buy a bug zapper, citronella candles, and bug spray; and get ready to swat and scratch.

Colon

Use a **colon** (:) to introduce an example or a list.

> Here's one other mosquito treatment: napalm.
>
> I have one motto: No bug is going to use my blood to reproduce!

▶ After Salutations

In business documents, use a colon after a **salutation**, the formal greeting.

> Dear Ms. Alvarez: To: Tawnya Smith

▶ Times and Ratios

Use a colon to separate hours, minutes, and seconds. Also use a colon between the numbers in a ratio.

> 8:23 a.m.   4:15 p.m.   14:32:46   The mosquito-person ratio is 5:1.

Practice In the following sentences, add semicolons and commas as needed.

1. Mosquitoes here are a nuisance however in some places they are deadly.

2. Malaria kills many in Africa and South America it is carried by mosquitoes.

3. Each year, mosquito-borne illnesses affect 700 million victims many of them die.

4. Mosquitoes breed in stagnant water they need only a small amount.

5. Ponds would produce more mosquitoes however, many fish eat mosquito eggs and larva.

6. A female mosquito inserts her proboscis, injects an anti-clotting agent, and draws blood into her abdomen then she uses the blood proteins to create her eggs.

7. A mosquito bites you and gets away afterward she uses your blood to create more little horrors.

8. To prevent bites, you should purchase and use repellents stay indoors at dawn and dusk and avoid standing water.

Practice In the following sentences, add colons as needed.

1. Mosquitoes in Egypt can carry a deadly disease yellow fever.

2. Here's the real shame The mosquitoes don't catch the disease.

3. Thankfully, mosquitoes don't pass along this terrible disease AIDS.

4. A mosquito can, however, pass along another nasty payload parasites.

5. Millions die per year because of one critter the mosquito.

6. A world without mosquitoes would be utterly different for one species Homo sapiens.

---

semicolon
a punctuation mark (;) that connects sentences and separates items in some series

colon
a punctuation mark (:) that introduces an example or list and has other special uses

salutation
the formal greeting in a letter; the line starting with "Dear"

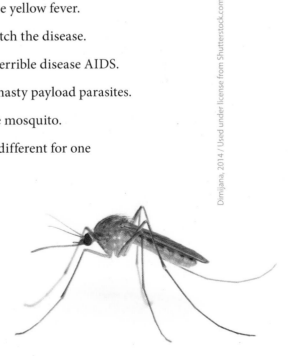

L03 Hyphens

A **hyphen** (-) joins words and letters to form various kinds of compounds.

▶ Compound Nouns

Use hyphens to create **compound nouns**.

city-state   fail-safe   fact-check   one-liner   mother-in-law

▶ Compound Adjectives

Use hyphens to create **compound adjectives** that appear before the noun. If the adjective appears after the noun, it usually is not hyphenated.

peer-reviewed article   an article that was peer reviewed

Don't hyphenate a compound made from an -ly adverb and an adjective or a compound that ends with a single letter.

newly acquired songs   grade B plywood

▶ Compound Numbers

Use hyphens in **compound numbers** from twenty-one to ninety-nine and in fractions.

twenty-two   fifty-fifty   three-quarters   seven thirty-seconds

▶ With Letters

Use a hyphen to join a letter to a word that follows it.

L-bracket   U-shaped   T-shirt   O-ring   G-rated   X-ray

▶ With Common Elements

Use hyphens to show that two or more words share a common element included in only the final term.

We offer low-, middle-, and high-coverage plans.

Practice Rewrite the following sentences, adding hyphens as needed.

1. I replaced the U bend and made a new P trap under the sink.

   _____

2. He guessed the board was three eighths inch thick.

   _____

3. Would you like to purchase low, medium, or high deductible insurance?

   _____

4. The double decker sandwich includes low fat ham and fat free mayonnaise.

   _____

5. The ham is low fat, and the mayonnaise is fat free.

   _____

6. In your graph, make sure to label the *x* and *y* axes.

   _____

7. The sales tax percentage is at an all time high.

   _____

8. My father in law is an attorney at law.

   _____

9. The T shirt showed the X ray of a rib cage.

   _____

---

hyphen
a short horizontal line (-) used to form compound words

compound noun
a noun made of two or more words, often hyphenated or spelled closed

compound adjective
an adjective made of two or more words, hyphenated before the noun but not afterward

compound numbers
two-word numbers from twenty-one to ninety-nine

L04 Dashes

Unlike the hyphen, the **dash** (—) does more to separate words than to join them. A dash is indicated by two hyphens with no spacing before or after. Most word-processing programs convert two hyphens into a dash.

▶ For Emphasis

Use a dash instead of a colon if you want to emphasize a word, phrase, clause, or series.

> Donuts—they're not just for cops anymore.
>
> There's only one thing better than a donut—two donuts.
>
> I like all kinds of donuts—fritters, crullers, and cake donuts.

▶ To Set Off a Series

Use a dash to set off a series of items.

> Elephant ears, Danish, funnel cakes—they just aren't as cool as donuts.
>
> They have many similarities—batter, frosting, and sugar—but where's the hole?

▶ With Nonessential Elements

Use a dash to set off explanations, examples, and definitions, especially when these elements already include commas.

> The hole—which is where the "dough nut" got its name originally—is a key component.

▶ To Show Interrupted Speech

Use a dash to show that a speaker has been interrupted or has started and stopped while speaking.

> "I'd like a—um—how about a fritter?"
>
> "You want an apple—"
>
> "Yes, an apple fritter. Well—make it two."

Insight In most academic writing, use dashes sparingly. If they are overused, they lose their effect.

Practice Add dashes where needed in the following sentences.

1. Which would you prefer a cruller, a glazed donut, or a long john?

2. I love a nice blintz basically like a crepe but from the Slavic region of Europe.

3. Donuts or do you prefer the spelling "doughnuts"? are yummy.

4. Could I have um what's on sale, anyway?

5. Today our sale is on wait, let me check yes, on donuts!

6. Batter, hot fat, frosting, sprinkles that's how you make a donut.

7. Making your own donuts is fun fattening, too!

8. A deep-fat fryer basically a deep pot filled with oil is needed to make donuts.

9. Let the donut cool before taking a bite extremely hot!

10. Decorate your donut with frosting, cinnamon, jelly whatever you want.

11. Don't eat too many donuts you'll end up with one around your middle.

Practice Write your own sentence, correctly using dashes for each of the situations indicated below:

1. For emphasis:

   _____

2. To set off a series:

   _____

3. With nonessential elements:

   _____

dash
long horizontal line that separates words, creating emphasis

🌐 Real-World Application

Practice ▶ The following letter sounds too informal because of the contractions. Cross out any contractions you find and use the words the contractions stand for instead. Also correct any apostrophe errors.

Redland State Bank

October 13, 2015

Phillip Jones
2398 10th Ave.
Westchester, NY 10959

Dear Mr. Jones:

This letter's a response to your inquiry about financing your housing project. I enjoyed discussing your project and appreciated your honesty about your current loan.

As of today, we've decided to make a commitment to your project. I've enclosed Redland State Banks' commitment letter. Please take time to read the terms of agreement.

If there's any part you don't understand, don't hesitate to call or email us. We'd be happy to answer any questions. As always's, we look forward to serving you.

Sincerely,

Melinda Erson

Melinda Erson
Loan Officer

Enclosure: Commitment Letter

Practice In the following email message, insert semicolons, colons, hyphens, and dashes where necessary.

To: All Staff

Subject: Parking During Parking-Lot Resurfacing

Hello, everyone

Fall is here, and we know what that means parking lot resurfacing. The east, west, and south lots will be resurfaced on separate days please follow this schedule

• Monday, September 20 Do not park in the east lot.

• Tuesday, September 21 Do not park in the west lot.

• Wednesday, September 22 Do not park in the south lot.

Spaces in the available lots may be tight please be considerate and take only one space. You can also park on the grass along the edges of the lot. Still, space will be tight. I have one suggestion car pool.

Thanks for your cooperation. Let's work together to achieve our goal resurfacing blacktop without ruining shoes.

Thanks,

Marissa Rogers

Practice ▶ In the following sentences, insert apostrophes, semicolons, colons, hyphens, and dashes where necessary.

1. The major pre WWI alliance was known as the Triple Entente, a pact between Russia, Great Britain, and France.

2. The Triple Ententes adversaries were two powerful states in Central Europe the Austro-Hungarian Empire and Germany.

3. The event that sparked World War I was the assassination of Austro Hungarian Archduke Franz Ferdinand however, tensions had been rising in Europe long before then.

4. Austria-Hungary's declaration of war on Serbia, Russia's declaration of war on Austria-Hungary, and Germany's attack on France and Belgium all these events spread the conflict.

5. Germany wanted to sack Paris and knock France out of the war before Russia could mobilize its large but low tech military.

6. To get to Paris, Germany needed to pass through Belgium. This action led to the first battle of WWI the attack on Liége.

7. Germany's war plan knock France out quickly so troops could be sent back east to fight Russia failed near the outskirts of Paris.

8. Americas involvement in WWI was spurred by German submarine warfare in the neutral waters of the North Atlantic and Mediterranean.

9. German U boats targeted and sank American ships in March 1917.

10. President Woodrow Wilson responded with a historic declaration war on Germany.

11. An influx of American troops, along with a blockade of food and resources to Germany, led to Germanys surrender.

12. The Treaty of Versailles set the official terms of the surrender the first World War was over.

PART 8:

Readings for Writers

Part 8: Readings for Writers

Chapter

26

Anthology

> "Imagine that you enter a parlor. . . . [O]thers have long preceded you, and they are engaged in a heated discussion. . . . You listen . . . until you decide that you have caught the tenor of the argument; then you put in your oar."
>
> —Kenneth Burke

In *The Philosophy of Literary Form*, Kenneth Burke describes all of history as an unending conversation. It is a conversation that has been going on long before anyone you know arrived, and one that will continue long after you are gone. But right now, you can listen until you get a sense of its direction and then add your own part to that conversation.

Your college career and education are also part of that unending conversation. With each new class you take, you arrive uncertain of exactly what will be said, listen for awhile, and then respond. Much of that "listening" will be in the form of reading. Much of your "speaking" will be in the form of writing.

The essays in this anthology provide another opportunity to listen to someone speak about a topic and then give your own response.

Readings

1 Conversational Ballgames

2 Stop Asking Me My Major

3 The Homeless Brother I Cannot Save

4 American Campuses Get Greener Than Ever

5 The Greatest Day in History

6 Phoebe Prince: Should School Bullying Be a Crime?

7 Undocumented Students Walk the "Trail of Dreams"

8 The Arab Spring's Cascading Effects

9 The Nomination of Judge Sonia Sotomayor to the United States Supreme Court

10 How is the American Dream Influenced by Social Stratification?

11 The Way I Work: Jennifer Hyman, Rent the Runway

12 Ex-Cons Relaunching Lives as Entrepreneurs

What do you think?

What is the purpose of the "unending conversation" Kenneth Burke describes? What part do you hope to play in that conversation?

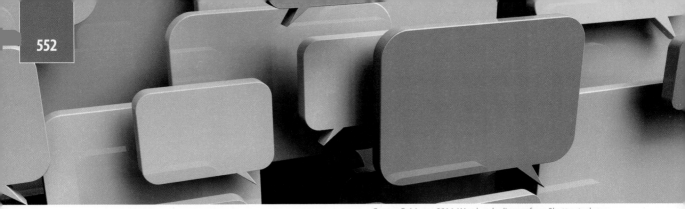

In this personal essay, author Nancy Sakamoto compares and contrasts American and Japanese conversation styles.

About the Author

Nancy Sakamoto is the author of the book *Polite Fiction: Why Japanese and Americans Seem Rude to Each Other*. Born in Los Angeles in 1931, she went on to marry a Japanese man and taught American studies in Japan from 1972 to 1982. She then returned to the U.S. and became a professor at Shitennoji Gakuen University in Honolulu.

Prereading

1. What do the title and first few paragraphs tell you about this selection?
2. What might be the intended purpose of this essay?
3. What, if anything, do you already know about this topic?
4. What do you expect to learn in your reading?

Conversational Ballgames

After I was married and had lived in Japan for a while, my Japanese gradually improved to the point where I could take part in simple conversations with my husband, his friends, and family. And I began to notice that often, when I joined in, the others would look startled, and the conversation would come to a halt. After this happened several times, it became clear to me that I was doing something wrong. But for a long time, I didn't know what it was. 1

Finally, after listening carefully to many Japanese conversations, I discovered what my problem was. Even though I was speaking Japanese, I was handling the conversation in a Western way. 2

Japanese-style conversations develop quite differently from Western-style 3 conversations. And the difference isn't only in the languages. I realized that just as I kept trying to hold Western-style conversations even when I was speaking Japanese, so were my English students trying to hold Japanese-style conversations even when they were speaking English. We were unconsciously playing entirely different conversational ballgames.

A Western-style conversation between two people is like a game of tennis. If   4
I introduce a topic, a conversational ball, I expect you to hit it back. If you agree with me, I don't expect you simply to agree and do nothing more. I expect you to add something—a reason for agreeing, another example, or a remark to carry the idea further. But I don't expect you always to agree. I am just as happy if you question me, or challenge me, or completely disagree with me. Whether you agree or disagree, your response will return the ball to me.

And then it is my turn again. I don't serve a new ball from my original   5
starting line. I hit your ball back again from where it has bounced. I carry your idea further, or answer your questions or objections, or challenge or question you. And so the ball goes back and forth.

If there are more than two people in the conversation, then it is like doubles   6
in tennis, or like volleyball. There's no waiting in line. Whoever is nearest and quickest hits the ball, and if you step back, someone else will hit it. No one stops the game to give you a turn. You're responsible for taking your own turn and no one person has the ball for very long.

A Japanese-style conversation, however, is not at all like tennis or volleyball,   7
it's like bowling. You wait for your turn, and you always know your place in line. It depends on such things as whether you are older or younger, a close friend or a relative stranger to the previous speaker, in a senior or junior position, and so on.

> A Japanese-style conversation, however, is not at all like tennis or volleyball, it's like bowling.

The first thing is to wait for your turn, patiently and politely. When your moment comes, you step up to the starting line   8
with your bowling ball, and carefully bowl it. Everyone else stands back, making sounds of polite encouragement. Everyone waits until your ball has reached the end of the lane, and watches to see if it knocks down all the pins, or only some of them, or none of them. Then there is a pause, while everyone registers your score.

Then, after everyone is sure that you are done, the next person in line steps up   9
to the same starting line, with a different ball. He doesn't return your ball. There

is no back and forth at all. And there is always a suitable pause between turns. There is no rush, no impatience.

No wonder everyone looked startled when I took part in Japanese conversations. I paid no attention to whose turn it was, and kept snatching the ball halfway down the alley and throwing it back at the bowler. Of course the conversation fell apart, I was playing the wrong game.   10

This explains why it can be so difficult to get a Western-style discussion going with Japanese students of English. Whenever I serve a volleyball, everyone just stands back and watches it fall. No one hits it back. Everyone waits until I call on someone to take a turn. And when that person speaks, he doesn't hit my ball back. He serves a new ball. Again, everyone just watches it fall. So I call on someone else. This person does not refer to what the previous speaker has said. He also serves a new ball. Everyone begins again from the same starting line, and all the balls run parallel. There is never any back and forth.   11

Now that you know about the difference in the conversational ballgames, you may think that all your troubles are over. But if you have been trained all your life to play one game, it is no simple matter to switch to another, even if you know the rules. Tennis, after all, is different from bowling.   12

Sakamoto, Nancy, "Conversational Ballgames." Originally appeared in *Polite Fictions*. Tokyo: Kinseido, Ltd., 1982. Reprinted by permission of the author.

Summarizing

Write a summary of "Conversational Ballgames." Remember that a summary presents the key points in a clear, concise form using your own words.

Reflecting

- What is the main idea or thesis of the selection?
- What pattern of organization does the writer primarily employ?
- How do the "ball games" help the writer develop her thesis?
- Does the writer employ an academic or personal voice? Explain.

Critical Thinking

- Business in today's economy is conducted globally. How does this selection apply to the global economy?
- What effect will technology have on conducting business and diplomacy? Explain.

This essay suggests that employability might not be the best reason for choosing a field of study. Pay careful attention to the author's reasons for this claim.

About the Author

Scott Keyes is a 2009 graduate of Stanford University. He majored in political science.

Prereading

1. What do the title, first two paragraphs, and first lines of other paragraphs tell you about the essay?
2. What do you think is the purpose of this selection?
3. Who might be the intended audience?

Stop Asking Me My Major

One of my best friends from high school, Andrew, changed majors during his first semester at college. He and I had been fascinated by politics for years, sharing every news story we could find and participating in the Internet activism that was exploding into a new political force. Even though he was still passionate about politics, that was no longer enough. "I have to get practical," he messaged me one day, "and think about getting a job after graduation. I mean, it's like my mom keeps asking me: What can you do with a degree in political science anyway?"

I heard the same question from my friend Jesse when students across campus were agonizing about which major was right for them. He wasn't quite sure what he wanted to study, but every time a field sparked his interest, his father would pepper him with questions about what jobs were available for people in that discipline. Before long, Jesse's dad had convinced him that the only way he could get a job and be successful after college was to major in pre-med.

My friends' experiences were not **atypical**.   3

Choosing a major is one of the most difficult things students face in college.   4
There are two main factors that most students consider when making this
decision. First is their desire to study what interests them. Second is the fear that
a particular major will render them penniless after graduation and result in that
dreaded postcollege possibility: moving back in with their parents.

All too often, the concern about a major's practical prospects are pushed   5
upon students by well-intentioned
parents. If our goal is to cultivate
students who are happy and successful,
both in college as well as in the job
market, I have this piece of advice for
parents: Stop asking, "What can you
do with a degree in (fill in the blank)?" You're doing your children no favors by
asking them to focus on the job prospects of different academic disciplines, rather
than studying what interests them.

> If our goal is to cultivate students who are happy and successful . . . [s]top asking, "What can you do with a degree in (fill in the blank)?"

It is my experience, both through picking a major myself and witnessing   6
many others enduring the process, that there are three reasons why parents
(and everyone else) should be encouraging students to focus on what they enjoy
studying most, rather than questioning what jobs are supposedly available for
different academic concentrations.

The first is psychological. For his first two years of college, Jesse followed   7
his dad's wishes and remained a pre-med student. The only problem was that he
hated it. With no passion for the subject, his grades slipped, hindering his chances
of getting into medical school. As a result his employability, the supposed reason
he was studying medicine in the first place, suffered.

The second reason to stop asking students what they can do with a major   8
is that it **perpetuates** the false notion that certain majors don't prepare students
for the workplace. The belief that technical majors such as computer science are
more likely to lead to a job than a major such as **sociology** or English is certainly
understandable. It's also questionable. "The problem," as my friend José explained
to me, "is that even as a computer-science major, what I learned in the classroom
was outdated by the time I hit the job market." He thought instead that the main
benefit of his education, rather than learning specific skills, was gaining a better

way of thinking about the challenges he faced. "What's more," he told me, "no amount of education could match the specific on-the-job training I've received working different positions."

Finally, it is **counterproductive** to demand that students justify their choice of study with potential job prospects because that ignores the lesson we were all taught in kindergarten (and shouldn't ignore the closer we get to employment): You can grow up to be whatever you want to be. The jobs people work at often fall within the realm of their studies, but they don't have to. One need look no further than some of the most prominent figures in our society to see illustrations. The TV chef Julia Child studied English in college. Author Michael Lewis, whose best sellers focus on sports and the financial industry, majored in art history. Matt Groening, creator of *The Simpsons*, got his degree in philosophy, as did the former Hewlett Packard chief executive Carly Fiorina. Jeff Immelt, chief executive of General Electric, focused on mathematics. Indeed, with the Department of Labor estimating that on average people switch careers (not just jobs) two or three times in their lives, relying on a college major as career preparation is misguided.

I'm not saying any applicant can get any job. Job seekers still need marketable skills if they hope to be hired. However, in a rapidly changing economy, which majors lead to what jobs is not so clear cut. Many employers look for applicants from a diverse background—including my friend who has a degree in biochemistry but was just hired at an investment consulting firm.

That doesn't mean that majors no longer matter. It is still an important decision, and students are right to seek outside counsel when figuring out what they want to study. But questioning how a particular major will affect their employability is not necessarily the best approach. Although parents' intentions may be pure—after all, who doesn't want to see their children succeed after graduation?—that question can hold tremendous power over **impressionable** freshmen. Far too many of my classmates let it steer them away from what they enjoyed studying to a major they believed would help them get a job after graduation.

One of those friends was Andrew. He opted against pursuing a degree in political science, choosing instead to study finance because "that's where the jobs are." Following graduation, Andrew landed at a consulting firm. I recently learned with little surprise that he hates his job and has no passion for the work. *12*

Jesse, on the other hand, realized that if he stayed on the pre-med track, he would burn out before ever getting his degree. During his junior year he changed tracks and began to study engineering. Not only did Jesse's grades improve markedly, but his enthusiasm for the subject recently earned him a **lucrative** job offer and admission to a top engineering master's program. *13*

Andrew and Jesse both got jobs. But who do you think feels more successful? *14*

atypical unusual	**counterproductive** to act against an aim or goal
perpetuate continue	**impressionable** easily influenced
sociology the study of social systems	**lucrative** producing profit

Summarizing

Write a summary of "Stop Asking Me My Major."

Reflecting

- What is the main idea of the essay? How far into the essay do you have to go before you can identify it?
- What three reasons does the author give to support his main idea?
- What will you remember from this essay?
- What questions do you still have about the topic?

Critical Thinking

- Do you agree with the author? Why or why not?
- What advice would you give a friend who is choosing a major? How would you justify this advice?
- How do you react to the claim that on-the-job training is more valuable than theories learned in the classroom?

In this first-person narrative, the author shares details about her relationship with her mentally ill brother. The article first appeared in *Salon* online magazine in March 2011.

About the Author

Ashley Womble is the author of *The Cahoots*, a memoir about loving a person suffering from mental illness.

Prereading

1. What do the title, first paragraph, and first lines of other paragraphs tell you about this narrative?
1. What do you already know about the topic?
2. What do you expect to learn from Ashley Womble's account?

The Homeless Brother I Cannot Save

Like any New Yorker, I was no stranger to homeless people. I passed by them on my way to the shiny glass tower where I worked for a glossy women's magazine: the older lady perched atop a milk crate in the subway station, the man curled up in a dirty sleeping bag and clutching a stuffed animal. They were unfortunate ornaments of the city, unlucky in ways I never really considered.

Until one hot summer day in 2009 when my little brother Jay left his key on the coffee table and walked out of his house in West Texas to live on the streets. In the days that followed, I spent hours on the phone with detectives, social workers, and even the FBI, frantically trying to track him down. A friend designed a "Missing" poster using the most recent picture I had of him; he was wearing a hoodie and a Modest Mouse T-shirt, a can of beer in his hand and a deer-in-headlights expression on his face. I created a Facebook group and contacted old acquaintances still living in our hometown of Lubbock, begging everyone I even remotely knew to help me find him. No luck. If it had been me, a pretty young white woman, chances are my face would have been all over the news—but the sudden disappearance of a 20-year-old guy with paranoid **schizophrenia** didn't exactly warrant an Amber Alert.

In the year and a half that mental illness had ravaged my brother's mind, I'd learned to lower my expectations of what his life would be like. The smart kid who followed politics in elementary school probably wouldn't become a lawyer after all. Instead of going to college after high school, Jay became obsessed with 9/11 conspiracy theories. What began as merely **eccentric** curdled into something **manic** and disturbing: He believed the planners of 9/11 were a group of people called "the **Cahoots**" who had created a 24-hour television network to monitor his actions and control his thoughts. Eventually, his story expanded until the Cahoots became one branch of the New World Order, a government whose purpose was to overturn Christianity, and he had been appointed by God to stop it.

> What began as merely eccentric curdled into something manic and disturbing.

This made it hard for him to act normal, even in public. He'd lost his job busing tables after yelling "Stop the filming and hand over the tapes" to everyone dining in the restaurant. Having friends or even a coherent conversation wouldn't be possible unless he took the **antipsychotic** medication he'd been prescribed while he was in the mental hospital. A legal adult, he was allowed to refuse treatment, and he did. Otherwise the Cahoots would win.

I counted each day he'd been missing until they became weeks, until the number was so high I wondered if he was even still alive. That number was about the only thing I continued to keep track of. Dirty clothes and dishes piled up at home, I missed deadlines at work, and I got out of bed only if it was absolutely necessary. I cried often, but especially during thunderstorms, a reminder that wherever my brother was, he was unprotected. Eventually it became clear that I was losing it, too. So I did what my brother wouldn't allow himself to do: I started taking a pill that helped usher away my anxiety and depression.

Weeks after Jay disappeared, police in Maryland found him talking to a spider and had him hospitalized. He stayed for 72 hours. Then he went missing again.

September 11, 2009, was one of those drizzling mornings when I thought of my brother. There was the usual undertone of **reverent** sadness in the city, but for me, the date was a reminder of all that had gone wrong inside Jay's mind. And on that day my phone finally rang.

"Hello." Jay's Southern drawl was unmistakable. I sat straight up in my desk   8
chair at work wondering what I should do. Record the call? Take notes?

"Where are you?" I asked, as images of him sitting in a jail cell or stranded   9
alone in an alley flashed in my head.

"Manhattan," he said. My heart filled with hope. Then he asked me if I'd gone   10
to the witchcraft celebration at the World Trade Center, where the Sorcerers had
ordered the wind and the rain to destroy the ceremony. Once again, I just felt like
a helpless stranger.

I asked nervously if I could buy him dinner. To my surprise, he agreed.   11
Twenty minutes later I met him near Penn Station; he was hunched under an
awning next to a big blue tarp that covered his backpack and the **paisley** duffel
he'd once borrowed. His pale skin had tanned and hair covered his face. He was
staring at people as they walked by, but he didn't see me until I said his name.
Standing face-to-face with him, I could see that he had lost a lot of weight.

His cheekbones jutted out from his once-full face. If I had seen his picture I   12
would have gasped. Instead, I just held out my arms.

Zagat has no recommendations for where to take your homeless brother to   13
dinner. We settled on the Mexican chain Chevys and sat in a booth near the back.
He told me about hitchhiking to New York and sleeping in Central Park until
the cops kicked him out. He grinned as he talked about sleeping on the steps of a
downtown school, his smile still as charming as it had been when he was 7.

"Do you consider yourself homeless?" I asked.   14

"Oh, yes!" he answered proudly.   15

I wondered if the constant motion of wandering from town to town helped   16
quiet the voices he heard. If it was his own kind of medication and, if so, could I
really tell him that was the wrong way to live?

Earlier in the year I'd bribed him with a trip to visit me on the condition that   17
he took his meds. Now he was sitting in front of me, and as much as I wanted to
let him stay in my apartment, I knew I couldn't let him (my therapist discouraged
it and my roommate rightly put her foot down). I approached the topic cautiously,
my voice shaking as I asked, "Do you know why you can't stay with me?" His
voice small and shamed, he answered, "Because I won't take my medication." He
had always denied that he had schizophrenia, but his admission gave me hope that

maybe some day that would change.

I tried to quiet my own inner voice, which told me Jay needed to be in the 18
hospital where a team of psychiatrists could experiment with medications that
would fix his mind. I could do some things for my brother: I could give him a
little money for cigarettes. I could buy him a new backpack, a sleeping bag, good
walking shoes. But the more I pushed him to get help, the more my own sanity
escaped me.

So I let him go. He went to New Jersey. Florida. Louisiana. To a place where 19
he told me from a pay phone he wouldn't call anymore because he didn't want me
to know his whereabouts. I can only imagine what he looks like after a year on
the streets: His hair must be long, skin tan and hardened, and his rail-thin body
caked in dirt. He probably doesn't look much different from the homeless people I
pass by on the streets of New York City. Seeing them makes my heart ache, makes
me think about those they may have left behind, people who long to dust them off
and put them on the right path but who know, in the end, it's not their choice.

This article first appeared in Salon.com, at http://www.Salon.com An online version remains in the *Salon* archives. Reprinted with
permission.

schizophrenia
a type of mental disorder that creates fragmentation
of thought, emotion, and perception

eccentric
irregular, odd

manic
deranged excitement

cahoots
conspiring together

antipsychotic
a medication for mental conditions that involve
perception of reality

reverent
deeply respectful

paisley
an intricately feathered design, originally based on a
pine-cone design from India

Zagat
a restaurant ranking service

Summarizing
Write a summary of "The Homeless Brother I Cannot Save."

Reflecting
- How is this selection as much about the author as it is about the brother? Explain.
- Does the writer use an academic or personal voice? Explain.
- What conclusion does the author come to?
- How has this essay affected your thinking about homelessness and mental illness?

Critical Thinking
- How is homelessness a personal problem? A social problem?
- How should city officials address homelessness?

holbox, 2014 / Used under license from Shutterstock.com

In this essay, the author describes how many college campuses in the United States are becoming more ecologically responsible.

About the Author

Anne Underwood is a reporter at *Newsweek*, where she writes about health and medicine. She lives in Hoboken, New Jersey.

Prereading

1. What do the title, first paragraph, and first lines of other paragraphs tell you about the selection?
2. What might be the purpose of this essay?
3. Who might be the intended audience?
4. What do you expect to learn?

American Campuses Get Greener Than Ever

If you attended this year's commencement at Williams College in western Massachusetts, you probably sampled the fresh cinnamon **gelato** made from locally produced, hormone-free milk. You might have tried the organic greens with edible chive blossoms (purple, of course, the Williams color) or sampled the fresh asparagus—all from nearby farms. These dishes not only tasted better than standard fare but also saved fossil fuels normally used to ship food long distances. Disposable plates and cutlery were nowhere to be found, reducing trash by 80 percent. And the rare disposable items were ecofriendly. "We used **compostable** paper napkins and biodegradable straws," says Stephanie Boyd, who helped organize the "green commencement" as part of her job as chair of Williams's climate-action committee.

It was not a stunt to impress parents. More and more colleges are getting serious about going green. In June, 284 university presidents representing some of the nation's most influential schools announced an agreement pledging to make their campuses "carbon neutral." The message was clear. "We're saying that **sustainability** is no longer an elective," says Cornell president David Skorton.

Their motivation wasn't merely to reduce energy consumption and waste. As a $315 billion sector of the economy—and one that will train future leaders— higher education has a special responsibility to encourage environmental **stewardship**. The university presidents hope that even students who don't pursue increasingly popular majors in environmental studies will learn simply from being on a green campus, living in green buildings, eating sustainable food and absorbing everyday messages of conservation. And who knows? Far- reaching environmental programs may create an air of excitement that attracts applicants. "In the long run, students will say, 'Why would I want to go to a school that doesn't care about this?'" says Michael Crow, president of Arizona State University, which has made a major commitment to sustainability.

At Harvard, going green starts before students even arrive on campus, when freshmen receive mailings urging them to buy only energy-efficient refrigerators for their dorm rooms and purchase compact fluorescent bulbs, which use an average of 18 watts apiece instead of 75. But some of the most effective lobbying comes from students themselves. Harvard pays 20 undergraduates to help get the green message out to fellow students in a fun way. That might mean whipping up a competition between residential houses to win the coveted Green Cup for the greatest energy reductions and biggest increases in recycling. Or it could be organizing trash-free dances or green movie nights (*Who Killed the Electric Car?*) with free ice cream for anyone who brings a recyclable bowl. One day a year, students collect trash from Harvard Yard and pile it into a single heap, dubbed "Mount Trashmore." The giant mound reminds students how much they are throwing away—and how much waste they could avoid by recycling. Students even compete to come up with the best eco-themed cartoons. This year's second-place winner showed Marilyn Monroe with her

> At Harvard, going green starts before students even arrive on campus, when freshmen receive mailings urging them to buy only energy-efficient refrigerators for their dorm rooms and purchase compact fluorescent bulbs. . . .

3

4

iconic billowing skirt under the caption "Wind does great things." The fun adds up to serious savings. "Energy use in the dorms has decreased 15 percent over the past few years, and recycling has risen 40 percent," says Leith Sharp, head of the Harvard Green Campus Initiative.

At many schools, the construction of a new building is another chance   5
to push green solutions. "What message does a conventional campus send?" asks David Orr, who teaches environmental studies at Oberlin. "It sends the message that energy is cheap and plentiful." At Oberlin and other colleges, administrators are seeking to reverse that message with energy-efficient buildings. The Lewis Center at Oberlin, opened in 2000, was one of the first. It's powered entirely by solar arrays, which produce 30 percent more energy than the building consumes—and this is in cloudy Ohio. Sensors throughout the building monitor energy use. And all wastewater is purified on site in a "living machine," an artificial wetland with carefully selected tropical plants and microorganisms that filter the water. Located in the building's lobby, the living machine looks like a greenhouse. "You'd have no clue it's a wastewater system," says Orr. It even includes an indoor waterfall, powered by the sun, with 600 gallons of water flowing across a rocky surface. As long as the sun is shining, the water flows. Orr credits the building with having helped to inspire hundreds of Oberlin students to choose professions in ecodesign, architecture and related fields—including Sadhu Johnston, class of 1998, who joined other students in brainstorming ideas for the new building and who now works as environment commissioner of Chicago.

If buildings can influence people, so can something as profound as the food   6
we eat. Melina Shannon-DiPietro of the Yale Sustainable Food Project says she tries to "seduce students into the sustainable-food movement" with tasty dishes. Favorites include grass-fed-beef burgers from a nearby **farmers' cooperative** and pizzas made with organic flour, heirloom tomatoes and organic basil. In all, 40 percent of the university's menu items now come from local organic farms. "Most food travels 1,500 miles before we eat it," she says. "It doesn't taste fresh, and transporting it long distances adds

> Melina Shannon-DiPietro of the Yale Sustainable Food Project . . . tries to "seduce students into the sustainable-food movement" with tasty dishes.

to the university's **carbon footprint**." Eating locally and organically solves those problems. And, as students learn from placards in the dining halls, the benefits don't stop there. "Connecticut loses farmland at the rate of 8,000 to 9,000 acres a year," says Shannon-DiPietro. "Supporting local farmers helps maintain a working agricultural landscape."

For those who want to go the extra carbon-neutral mile and formally study the environment, the possibilities are expanding. Sustainability has become a multidisciplinary field that goes beyond ecology and biodiversity to embrace architecture, engineering, urban planning, economics and public health. Arizona State has just opened an entire School of Sustainability that will start taking undergraduates in the fall of 2008, drawing faculty from 25 departments. "Sustainability is the **linchpin**," says Oberlin's Orr. "If you get it right, it reduces dependence on Middle East oil, cuts carbon emissions, takes care of pollution, reduces health-care costs associated with pollution, and creates jobs." ASU is now working on the employment aspect, setting up a high-tech business park to draw innovative, eco-oriented businesses from around the world—and to provide internships and, ultimately, employment for students. Early occupants include a Chinese water-purification company and a firm making lenses that focus more sunshine onto solar panels, generating added power for less money.

As vigorously as colleges are encouraging students to research environmental problems, students are prodding colleges to purchase renewable energy and set ambitious carbon targets. In part because of student lobbying, Middlebury College in Vermont adopted a goal of carbon neutrality by 2016, says Nan Jenks-Jay, dean of environmental affairs. "Students were telling us, 'You're not doing enough,'" she says. Undergrads at dozens of schools have gone so far as to vote for increases in their activities fees to help finance green initiatives. At St. Mary's College of Maryland, for example, 93 percent of students voted last spring for a $25 annual increase in fees, which will raise approximately $45,000 a year for the purchase of renewable energy.

There is, of course, room for improvement. "Not a single campus is even close to achieving sustainability at this point," says Richard Olson of Kentucky's Berea College, which aims to reduce its energy consumption to 45 percent below 2000 levels by 2015. "Colleges need to get out ahead and model truly sustainable behavior to society."

Many students are helping to do just that. This June, a group of 11 Dartmouth   *10*
students struck out across the country in a big green school bus fueled by waste
oil from fast-food restaurants. The bus itself contains the filters that make the
french-fry grease usable. Stopping at parks and music festivals, the vehicle became
"a science fair on wheels," says senior Brent Butler. But for sheer creativity, few
top Allison Rogers, Harvard class of 2004. After wrestling with her feminist
principles, she ran for and won the 2006 Miss Rhode Island title on a green
platform and spent the next year delivering a version of Al Gore's slide show to
schools and civic groups. It may be **an inconvenient truth**—but her post gave
Rogers a very convenient way to spread the word.

gelato
an Italian-style ice cream

compostable
able to be decayed for use in fertilizing soil

sustainability
involving methods that do not completely use up
natural resources

stewardship
the job of protecting and being responsible for
something

farmers' cooperative
an organization of farmers to sell products and
purchase equipment as a group effort

carbon footprint
the amount of carbon dioxide and similar compounds
a person or group releases into the environment

linchpin
a pin passed through a hole in the end of an axle, to
keep a wheel in place

an inconvenient truth
the name of a documentary about global warming

iconic
a long-standing or formal symbol

Summarizing

Write a summary of "American Campuses Get Greener Than Ever."

Reflecting

- What is the main idea of this selection?
- How is the selection organized—spatially, chronologically, or through examples?
- What does it mean to "go green"?
- Which of the green initiatives described in the essay appeals to you most? Which appeals to you least? Explain.

Critical Thinking

- If you were to create a different beginning or ending, what would it be?
- What is your own position on "going green"?

This narrative from author Nicholas Best's book entitled *The Greatest Day in History* describes the hours immediately following the conclusion of World War I. The fighting officially stopped at the eleventh hour on the eleventh day of the eleventh month. We celebrate Armistice Day, which coincides with Veterans Day, on November 11.

About the Author

Nicholas Best is an English author who grew up in Kenya. An alumnus of Trinity College, Dublin, he served in the Grenadier Guards and worked in London as a journalist before becoming a full-time author.

Prereading questions

1. What is the topic of this selection?
2. Who might be the intended audience?
3. What do you already know about WWI, and what do you expect to learn? Consider reading an encyclopedia article or online entry about the war before reading this narrative.

The Greatest Day in History

For most people at the front, the prevailing mood was one of distinct anticlimax as 11 o'clock passed and the firing died away all along the line. For as long as anyone could remember, there had always been firing somewhere within earshot, but now there wasn't any more. The quiet seemed unnatural after all the noise, almost a contradiction in terms. It took a great deal of getting used to.

Brigadier Richard Foot, an artilleryman supporting the Guards battalions at Maubeuge, had fired off the last of his surplus ammunition before 7 a.m. and then went to visit a couple of wounded soldiers at an advanced operating station. He spoke for millions as he returned later to his unit:

"It was a strange feeling to ride back to the battery in the quiet that followed

11 o'clock. One had got used to the background noise of shellfire, which could often be heard as far away as the south coast of England. Near the front, it seemed a continuous orchestration of deep and echoing sound, punctuated by the sharper rat-tat-tat of rifle or machine-gun fire. The landscape was different too; no observation balloons to be seen, no plumes of smoke from shell bursts or burning buildings, no aeroplanes glinting in the sky. After three and a half years of front-line service, broken only by short spells of leave or hospital, peace seemed a very strange and new experience."

Just outside Perquise, some German officers came forward in the silence to show the Royal Welch Fusiliers where the road was mined. They were followed by a hunchback with an accordion who played the "Marseillaise" in triumph as the Fusiliers marched into his village. The refugees were already beginning to return, wending their way home again now that there was no more shooting. Army chaplain Harry Blackburne watched some of them near Mons:

"The roads filled with civilians hurrying back to their homes which they had been forced to leave by the Germans, all of them struggling along the muddy roads, pushing their handcarts and barrows. It is like it was during the retreat from Mons: old women, pinched and ill, absolutely deadbeat. Our **lorries** pick up as many as they can, and our soldiers push along the wheelbarrows for the older ones who can hardly walk. More often than not, on arrival at their homes they find no home—it has been battered to pieces by shellfire: "It doesn't matter," they say, "we have tasted liberty."

In Mons itself, the inhabitants were determined to have a party for their liberators, even though many of the Canadians were so exhausted that they lay fast asleep in the street. The Canadians weren't due to make their official entry into the town until half past three, when they would march in with bands playing and colors flying, but the party had already begun and the inhabitants weren't about to stop now. The **reprisals** were beginning too. The Belgians wanted to get at the Germans captured in the fighting and take their revenge for four years of occupations. It needed all the Canadians' tact to stop the Belgians falling on their German prisoners and tearing them limb from limb.

Not far from Mons, men of the Royal Marine Light Infantry were lying in a line along a railway bank as the fighting came to an end. A battalion of the Manchester Regiment had lined up along the same bank during the retreat from Mons in 1914. After the shooting stopped, marine Hubert Trotman and a few others got up and strolled down to the wood in the nearby valley. They stumbled across some skeletons from 1914, men of the Manchesters still lying there from the beginning of the war. "Lying there with their boots on, very still, no helmets, no rusty rifles or equipment, just their boots." The sight was one that the marines never forget.

Everywhere, there was a feeling of disbelief that the war was actually over, a sense that it was all just a dream that wasn't really happening. US Private Arthur Jensen was one of many who said, "Don't worry, it'll soon start up again," when the firing stopped at eleven. British rifleman Aubrey Smith at Erquennes echoed his sentiments:

"To think there would be no more shells, no more bombs, no more **gas**, no more cold nights to be spent on **picket** through fear of lighting a fire. Of all the incredible announcements that had ever been made to us, this left us the most staggered. It must be only a dream! Surely we should hear the distant sound of guns in a minute or so, which would prove we had been deluded! We strained our ears for distant gunfire . . . Silence! Only the sound of church bells in other villages proclaiming the event. . . .

"Twice during the afternoon our hearts sank to our feet at the sound of a distant report like the firing of a big gun, but word came along presently that it was either blasting or else the exploding of some German mines under the roads! Everyone, troops and civilians, had knocked off work for the day, and we were welcomed into the cottages, where the good folks made cups of coffee out of the scanty supplies they had, and told us many tales of suffering and hardships. We palled up with a peasant and his family in a small cottage near our field, and we listened to stories which were a replica of those we had heard during the past week."

All along the line, French and Belgian civilians produced food that they had been hiding for this special day. The Germans had been through their houses so often that they had very little left beyond a bottle or two of wine buried in the garden and a few choice items that they had somehow managed to conceal. They happily produced what they had and thrust it on the soldiers, not realizing that the troops on the Allied side were perfectly well fed and had no need of anything to eat. It had been so long since civilians behind the German lines had eaten properly that they had forgotten what it was like to have a full stomach. Food was

8

9

10

11

their greatest gift, the most valuable present they had to offer to their liberators. They gave it willingly, delighted to do what they could to mark the occasion. At Maubeuge, one elderly Frenchman was so pleased at the day's events that he dressed up in his old uniform from the Franco-Prussian war in celebration.

Among the Americans, Harry Truman had been as glad as anyone to see an   12
end to the war. Like everyone else, however, he found it distinctly unsettling when the guns ceased to roar at eleven:

"It was so quiet it made me feel as if I'd been suddenly deprived of my ability   13
to hear. The men at the guns, the captain, the lieutenants, the sergeants and corporals looked at each other for some time and then a great cheer arose all along the line. We could hear the men in the infantry a thousand metres in front raising holy hell. The French battery behind our position were dancing, shouting and waving bottles of wine. . . ."

Truman's men promptly joined in, drinking all the red wine they could find   14
and more cognac than they could hold. The sun came out at midday and the party continued throughout the afternoon into the evening. Rockets were fired and **Very lights** soared as the men of the 129th Field Artillery celebrated the release from tension. Above them, Lieutenant Broaddus of Battery F watched unhappily from his balloon. He had been sent up earlier to direct the last of the artillery fire. The war had stopped while he was up there and everyone had forgotten about him in his excitement. It was two hours before they remembered him again and hauled him down.

Elsewhere, Americans wandered out into no-man's-land, looking for   15
souvenirs to take home now that the fighting was done. There was a market for souvenirs behind the lines, a brisk trade among base soldiers who had not themselves been anywhere near the action. Pistols, helmets, bayonets, anything good would fetch a price. Sometimes the souvenir hunters strayed too close to the Germans in the trenches opposite. Feldwebel Georg Bucher and his fellow lice-ridden scarecrows had emerged cautiously from their holes in the early afternoon, scarcely able to believe that their heads wouldn't be blown off as soon as they raised them above the **parapet**. They watched warily as the men they had machine-gunned that morning, who had dropped gas on them in return, now hunted for trophies a few yards away:

"We were squatting with **incredulous** eyes in front of the parapet. The   16
Americans were wandering around in no-man's land, but there wasn't much they

could find, for the shellfire had played havoc there. Some of them came within twenty yards of us. How angrily and contemptuously they looked at us! They didn't seem pleased that we still had hand grenades hanging from our belts and rifles in our hands. . . .

"Some of us tried to make friends with the enemy, but to no avail. The Americans were too bitter from the events of the previous day, which wasn't surprising. They had attacked three times and been beaten back with heavy losses. *17*

"It was indeed a strange sensation to be sitting openly in front of the trench. The reality was hard to believe; we were conscious of a vague fear that it might all turn out to be a dream." *18*

It was no dream. The war was really over and the fighting really had stopped. Whoever was in charge of the nightmare had finally come to their senses, and not a moment too soon. *19*

---

lorries
British word for trucks

reprisal
the act of retaliation

gas
in this case, mustard gas, a blistering agent that when breathed destroys the lungs

picket
a soldier or party of soldiers assigned a particular duty

Very lights
colored flares fired from a special pistol, for illumination at night or for signalling

parapet
a low protective wall

incredulous
not willing to believe

Summarizing

Write a summary of "The Greatest Day in History."

Reflecting

- What is the main idea of this selection?
- Why does the author quote soldiers from different sides of the war—British, American, and German?
- In paragraph 5, the civilians state they have "tasted liberty," so they were eager to get home. What does it mean to "taste liberty"?

Critical Thinking

- Some texts and films glorify war. Does this reading fit into this category? Why or why not?
- What is your own attitude about military service and war? How does it affect your feelings about this selection?

In this essay, which first appeared in *Newsweek*, journalist Jessica Bennett raises a number of difficult questions about bullying and how it should be addressed.

About the Author

Jessica Bennett lives in New York City, where she writes about women's issues, pop culture, and social issues and trends. She is a former senior editor at *Newsweek* and former executive editor for *Tumblr*.

Prereading

1. What do the title, first paragraph, and first lines of other paragraphs tell you about this selection?

2. What are your first thoughts about the author's purpose and audience?

3. What are your initial feelings about the topic?

Phoebe Prince: Should School Bullying Be a Crime?

It started with rumors, a love triangle, and a dirty look in a high-school bathroom. Soon jokes about an "Irish slut" cropped up on Facebook, and a girl's face was scribbled out of a class photo hanging up at school. One day, in the cafeteria, another girl marched in, pointed at her, and shouted "stay away from other people's men." A week later, as the girl walked home, a car full of students crept close. One kid hurled a crumpled soda can out the window, followed closely by shrieks of "whore!"

If your children had behaved like this, how would you want them punished? Certainly a proper grounding would be in order; computer privileges revoked. Detention, yes—maybe even suspension. Or what about 10 years in jail? Now what if we told you that the girl had gone home after the soda-can incident and killed herself—discovered by her little sister, hanging in a stairwell. Now which punishment fits the crime?

This is the **conundrum** of Phoebe Prince, the 15-year-old South Hadley, Mass., girl the media have already determined was "bullied to death"—her alleged "mean girl" tormentors charged with felony crimes. Bullied to death is the crime of the moment, the blanket explanation slapped on suicide cases from Texas to California, where two 13-year-olds recently killed themselves, bullied for being gay. The most twisted example yet came last week, when Tyler Clementi, an 18-year-old New Jersey college student, threw himself off the George Washington Bridge after his roommate and a friend allegedly streamed a Webcam video of his **tryst** with a man.

3

Cases like these are being invoked as potent symbols for why, in the digital age, schools need bullying policies and states need legislation. But do they? Is the notion of being bullied to death valid? No one would deny that Clementi's roommate did the unconscionable; the alleged crime is all the more disturbing because of the specter of antigay bias. Yet he couldn't have known how badly the stunt would end. (He and his friend now face up to five years in prison for privacy invasion; there is also talk of additional bias charges.) In the case of Prince, the answer of who's to blame might change if you knew that she had tried to kill herself before the **epithets**, was on medication for depression, and was struggling with her parents' separation. So where is the line now between behavior that's bad and behavior that's criminal? Does the definition of old-school bullying need to be rewritten for the new-media age?

4

> Is the notion of being bullied to death valid?
>
> Where is the line . . . between behavior that's bad and behavior that's criminal?

In effect, it already has been. Forty-five states now have anti-bullying laws; in Massachusetts, which has one of the strictest, anti-bullying programs are mandated in schools, and criminal punishment is outlined in the text for even the youngest offenders. It's a good-will effort, to be sure—prevention programs have been shown to reduce school bullying by as much as 50 percent. With 1 in 5 students bullied each year—and an appalling 9 in 10 gay and lesbian students— that's good news: kids who are bullied are five times more likely to be depressed, and nearly 160,000 of them skip school each day, fearful of their peers. Bullies themselves don't fare well, either: one study, of middle-school boys, found that 60 percent of those deemed "bullies" would be convicted of at least one crime by the time they reached 24.

5

But forget, for the moment, the dozens of articles that have called bullying 6 a "**pandemic**." Forget the talk-show specials, the headlines, the Florida dad who rushed onto a school bus to scare his 13-year-old daughter's bullies straight. School bullying can be devastating, but social scientists say it is no more extreme, nor more prevalent, than it was a half century ago. (And it's even gotten better over the past decade, says Dan Olweus, a leading bullying expert.) Today's world of cyberbullying is different, yes—far-reaching, more visually potent, and harder to wash away than comments scrawled on a bathroom wall. All of which can make it harder to combat. But it still happens a third less than traditional bullying. And those "mean girls" we keep hearing about? Turns out, boys are still twice as likely to bully as girls.

The reality may be that while the incidence of bullying has remained 7 relatively the same, it's our reaction to it that's changed: the helicopter parents who want to protect their kids from every stick and stone, the cable-news commentators who whip them into a frenzy, the insta-**vigilantism** of the Internet. When it comes down to it, bullying is not just a social ill; it's a "**cottage industry**," says Suffolk Law School's David Yamada—complete with commentators and prevention experts and a new breed of legal scholars, all preparing to take on an enemy that's always been there. None of this is to say that bullying is not a serious problem (it is), or that tackling it is not important. But like a stereo with the volume turned too high, all the noise distorts the facts, making it nearly impossible to judge when a case is somehow criminal, or merely cruel.

> When it comes down to it, bullying is not just a social ill; it's a "cottage industry," says Suffolk Law School's David Yamada.

In Phoebe Prince's case, it's hard to make sense of the punishment without 8 first understanding the crime. Court records indicate that Phoebe's problems at South Hadley High School began around November of last year, when the freshman became involved with two senior boys—Austin Renaud and Sean Mulveyhill, the school's star football player—both of whom had girlfriends. According to their **indict**ments, the boys, their girlfriends, and students Ashley Longe and Sharon Velasquez engaged in what the DA described as a "nearly three-month campaign" of verbal assault and physical threats against Phoebe. What appear to be the worst of their crimes involves repeated taunts of "whore" and

"Irish slut"; threats to "beat Phoebe up"; and, on the day of her death, the soda-can incident, which left Phoebe in tears. When Phoebe got home that afternoon, she texted a friend: "I can't do it anymore." At 4:30 pm, her sister found her body, hanging from the scarf she'd given her for Christmas.

> At 4:30 pm, her sister found her body, hanging from the scarf she'd given her for Christmas.

Phoebe's death, understandably, sent normally quiet South Hadley into a spiral of shame and blame. The school principal opened an internal investigation, but allowed the then-unidentified bullies to remain in class. A community member sympathetic to Phoebe's story went to *The Boston Globe*, which published a column chastising school officials for allowing the "untouchable mean girls" to remain in school, "defiant, unscathed." A Facebook group with the headline "Expel the three girls who caused Phoebe Prince to commit suicide" suddenly had thousands of fans. School officials took to the press—defending how they could have let the bullying go on, asserting they had only learned of the problem the week before Phoebe's death. "I'm not naive [enough] to think we'll have zero bullying . . . but this was a complex tragedy," the principal of South Hadley High School, Dan Smith, tells *Newsweek*.

Enter District Attorney Elizabeth Scheibel, whose profile on the National District Attorneys Association Web site, until recently, detailed how, as a child, she beat up a schoolyard bully who was picking on her brother. On March 29, Scheibel released the names of the six students she would indict on felony charges, whose "relentless activity," she said, was "designed to humiliate [Phoebe] and make it impossible for her to remain at school." Since there is no law in Massachusetts explicitly making bullying a crime, Scheibel charged two of them with stalking, two with criminal harassment, and five with civil-rights violations resulting in bodily injury, alleging that Phoebe's ability to get an education had been made impossible. She also charged both of the boys with **statutory rape**, for allegedly having sex with Phoebe while she was underage—an offense punishable by up to three years in jail. The civil-rights violation carries a maximum of 10 years. (All six defendants have pleaded not guilty.)

The law (and the media) may assess the world in black or white, but the players in the case don't fall into neat categories. Quiet and pretty, Phoebe had moved only recently from Ireland to South Hadley, a working-class town full of wood-paneled homes, manicured lawns and a vibrant Irish-American community where Phoebe's family fit right in. She would ultimately suffer a terrible tragedy, but court filings, uncovered by Emily Bazelon, of *Slate Magazine*, have since revealed that Phoebe had her own demons, too. She struggled with depression, self-mutilation, had been prescribed Seroquel (a medication used to treat bipolar disorder, among other psychiatric conditions), and had attempted suicide once before. Bazelon also reported that Phoebe—like nearly a third of kids who are victimized by bullies, studies show—had also played the role of bully, calling another girl a "paki whore" while she was still in Ireland, enrolled in a private school. By the same token, each of the students charged with bullying Phoebe were in good academic standing, says South Hadley's superintendent, Gus Sayer.

Does that in any way excuse their behavior? Not at all—and each has been out of school since March, suspended, indefinitely, until their case is resolved in court. (Their trials are expected early next year.) But it goes to show there's more to this story than the headlines might imply. "These are not the troubled kids we sometimes deal with," Sayer tells *Newsweek*. "These are nice kids, regular kids. They come from nice families. They were headed to college. And now, in addition to losing Phoebe, we're losing [them] too."

Phoebe's father, Jeremy Prince, has said he would ask the court for leniency   *12* if the teens confess and apologize. Yet even if they are acquitted, it's clear their lives are forever altered—their names and faces now international symbols of teen callousness. None completed school last year; Mulveyhill has already lost a football scholarship to college. Angeles Chanon, the mother of Sharon Velasquez, says her daughter is studying for her GED, but heartbroken that she can't return to class—and since there aren't any other public high schools in South Hadley (and schools in Massachusetts can deny entrance based on a felony charge) her

> Phoebe—like nearly a third of kids who are victimized by bullies, studies show—had also played the role of bully.

options are slim. In the meantime, Sharon is haunted by the tragedy of Phoebe's death. It's hard for her to turn on the television without seeing Phoebe's smiling face (or her own) staring back at her; reporters camp out in the parking lot outside her mother's housing complex, peering into windows at all hours. Sharon sits at home most days, reading, listening to music—but scared to leave the house alone. Her family has received death threats, prank calls, and a rock thrown through a second-story window—along with a stream of nasty unsigned letters delivered to their door. Some call for Sharon to be "raped and killed"; others hurl insults and racial slurs. "I don't know if I can even describe what my family has been through," says Sharon's mother, who agreed to speak exclusively to *Newsweek*, in the presence of her lawyer. "The cameras in our faces, the harassment, the letters—I'd come home and people would be in the parking lot waiting for me."

The irony, of course, is that it all sounds a bit like the kind of torment Phoebe   *13* allegedly endured—particularly when it comes to the anonymous vigilantes who've taken to the Web to chastise the teens, publishing their phone numbers and addresses to the public, along with violent rape imagery and calls for their deaths. "It's painful to watch what [these kids] have had to go through," says Colin Keefe, the attorney for Velasquez. Indeed, if these students are bullies, according to the law, what does that make the rest of us? Massachusetts's anti-bullying statute defines bullying as repeated behavior that, among other things, "causes emotional harm" or "creates a hostile environment" at school. If it were applied to the real world, wouldn't most of us be bullies? It's easy to see how the blossoming field of bullying law could ultimately criminalize the kind of behavior we engage in every day—not just in schoolyards, but in workplaces, in politics, at home. And what do you do when the bullies get bullied? "You're not going to prevent a lot of this stuff," says former New York prosecutor Sam Goldberg, a Boston criminal attorney. "It may seem harsh, but to some degree, you're going to have to tell your kid, 'Sometimes people say mean things.'"

What most bullying experts and legal scholars agree on is that prosecution—   *14* in the Prince case, anyway—may be the worst possible scenario. There is longstanding research to show that law is not a deterrent to kids who respond emotionally to their surroundings; ultimately, labeling a group of raucous teens as "criminals" will only make it harder for them to engage with society when they return. Certainly, there is behavior that should be treated as a crime—the story of Clementi, the young Rutgers student who jumped off the bridge, is particularly hard to stomach. But many kids "just mess up," says Sameer Hinduja, a criminologist at Florida Atlantic University, and the codirector of the Cyberbullying Research Center. "They react emotionally, and most of them express a lot of remorse. I think most kids deserve another chance."

conundrum
a difficult, puzzling question

cottage industry
a business based in the home

epithet
an adjective describing an innate quality, often a negative one

indict
to formally charge with a crime

pandemic
a disease that has spread across a nation, a region, or the entire world

statutory rape
for an adult to have sexual intercourse with a minor

tryst
a private, romantic meeting of lovers

vigilantism
when individuals take the law into their own hands, typically for vengeance

Summarizing

Write a summary of "Phoebe Prince: Should School Bullying Be a Crime?"

Reflecting

- What is the main idea of the essay? Is this idea directly stated or implied?
- What pattern of organization is employed—chronological, spatial, or logical?
- What is the topic and main point of paragraph 7?
- In paragraph 12 you learn about Sharon Velasquez. What is significant about her experience?
- What is the main point of paragraph 14? Do you agree with the conclusion? Explain.

Critical Thinking

- Why was Phoebe's case a "complex tragedy"? Give two reasons.
- Who and/or what is to blame for school bullying?
- In your opinion, what should or should not be done to prevent bullying in school?

In this article, Cindy Long discusses the challenges facing undocumented students on their path to higher education.

About the Author

Cindy Long is a writer and editor for the National Education Association.

Prereading

1. What do the title and first few paragraphs tell you about this selection?
2. What do you already know about the topic?
3. What questions about the topic would you like answered in your reading?
4. How might the author's position affect her approach to the topic?

Undocumented Students Walk the "Trail of Dreams"

Felipe Matos, 24, teaches English to young students in Miami. When he asked his class one day who had been told that they would never make it to college, every hand went up. The students were only in first grade, and Matos was appalled that they were already so discouraged about their futures, but he wasn't surprised. The students were also mostly **undocumented** immigrants, brought to the United States by their parents. 1

Matos understands their circumstances. He's also undocumented. 2

Born to a single mother in the slums of Brazil, he was sent to the United States at age 14 so that he could have a chance at a better life. He worked hard, and graduated fourth in his high school class of 500. With dreams of becoming a teacher, he was accepted at top universities, but was **barred** from receiving financial aid and couldn't afford to go. 3

Instead, he attends Miami Dade Community College, where he studies economics and is ranked one of the top 20 college students in the United States 4 for academic excellence. Still, he's unable to enter the classroom because of his immigration status.

"My dream is to become a teacher in an inner city high school, so that I can   5
tell students going through the same thing that they can succeed in life, that they are not worthless, but that they are worth a million," he says. "We can't keep denying young people their dreams."

> "We can't keep denying young people their dreams."

It was for the dreams of the estimated 65,000 undocumented immigrants who   6
graduate from high school each year, but are unable to go to college, that Matos walked 1,500 miles from Miami to Washington, D.C.

He's one of four college students, including Gaby Pacheco, Carlos Roa, and   7
Juan Rodríguez, who left Miami on January 1 in a march they call the **"Trail of Dreams."**

Brought here as children, the United States is the only country they call   8
home. Even though they have the same dreams as other American children, and have excelled in school, they live in the shadows of society, unable to work and put their years of schooling to use.

Gaby Pacheco, 25, came to the United States from Ecuador when she was   9
seven, and was considered a "gifted student" by her American teachers. She now has three education degrees from Miami Dade College, and dreams of one day becoming a special education teacher, using music therapy as a communication tool to teach autistic children and adults.

She says she marched 1,500 miles from Florida to Washington so she could   10
say to President Obama, "We just want a chance."

Just days after Arizona passed a law allowing the police to stop suspected   11
illegal immigrants and demand proof of citizenship, hundreds of immigrant rights **advocates** joined the four Miami students—as well as five other immigrant students who marched 250 miles from New York City—at the White House on May 1 for the "March for America" rally, asking President Obama to live up to his campaign promise of passing comprehensive immigration reform.

Waving American flags and signs that said "We are ALL Arizona" and   12
"Education, Not Deportation," participants in the rally heard the Trail of Dreamers speak about the importance of the DREAM Act—a bill now before Congress that would help immigrants brought here as children, and who have

grown up in the United States, gain permanent status after six years by going to college or joining the military.

Students from around the country joined in the rally, including a busload of DREAM Act supporters from Harrisonburg, Virginia, organized in their hometown by special education teacher Sandy Mercer.   13

Mercer collaborates in English classes, focusing on reading and writing, often with ELL students. The stories written by her undocumented students convinced her that they deserve a chance to earn legal residency in the country they call home.   14

"I support the DREAM Act because as an educator for over 30 years, I understand what happens when students lose hope," Mercer says. "I am not willing to stand by and do nothing and allow the spark I see in these students to fade."   15

Many of her undocumented students have trusted her with their stories, and she has worked tirelessly to help them pursue their educations, including a young man whose parents fled with him and his brother from Guatemala after a gang "tagged" their house, a signal that they planned to kill the two brothers for not agreeing to join the gang.   16

Now an Honors Society Student, this young man hopes to study astronomy and one day work at NASA, but he never thought it was possible for him to attend college.   17

"These students have more courage in their little fingers than I will ever have. It takes courage to keep working when one sees little hope for a future," Mercer says. "These are bilingual, talented, motivated, hard-working, family-loving young people in whom our schools and communities have invested so much."   18

> "These students have more courage in their little fingers than I will ever have. It takes courage to keep working when one sees little hope for a future. . . ."

Mercer has told her students about the few scholarships that don't have **residency** requirements, and that they can attend the local community college, although they must pay out-of-state tuition. She's networked with other Virginia teachers who've helped their students go on to college, and has worked with local financial aid officers to brainstorm ways for students to get money for tuition   19 since they're not eligible for federal loans or grants.

She and her colleagues also continually try to raise funds through members   *20*
of the community willing to sponsor the students' education. But she's most
committed to working for passage of the DREAM Act.

"Anyone who works with students recognizes this legislation needs to be   *21*
passed now," she says.

Long, Cindy, "Undocumented Students Walk the Trail of Dreams." Published at nea.org. May 2010. Copyright National Education Association.

---

undocumented
not having the official documents needed to live or
work in a country legally

barred
denied

"Trail of Dreams"
a play on the "Trails of Tears," the forced march of
Native Americans from eastern states such as Georgia
and Florida to the Oklahoma Territory

advocates
people arguing for or supporting a cause

residency
in this case, being a resident of a state

Summarizing

Write a summary of "Undocumented Students Walk the 'Trail of Dreams.'"

Reflecting

- What is the main idea of this article? Is this idea directly stated or implied?
- Paragraph 3 includes background details about Felipe Matos. What pattern is used to organize the details?
- Paragraph 12 identifies the DREAM Act. What is the goal of this act?
- In paragraph 18, one teacher describes these students as "courageous." Why are they courageous?

Critical Thinking

- How has this article confirmed or changed your attitude about undocumented students?
- Why is helping undocumented students considered a controversial topic?
- Why is immigration in general a common theme in the United States, past and present?

In this essay, the author addresses the connection between digital media and the widespread social uprisings in the Middle East occurring in 2010 that became known as the Arab Spring.

About the Author

Philip N. Howard is a professor of communication, information, and international studies at the University of Washington. He has authored numerous books, including *Democracy's Fourth Wave? Digital Media and the Arab Spring*.

Prereading

1. What do the title, the first few paragraphs, and the headings tell you about this essay?
2. What do you already know about this topic?
3. How might the author's background qualify him to discuss this topic?

The Arab Spring's Cascading Effects

Over the last few months, social unrest has cascaded across the major urban centers of North Africa and the Middle East. Journalists and communications media are often part of such moments of upheaval. Yet this recent wave of unrest is unlike other discrete periods of rapid political change. Through digital media, the stories of success in Tunisia and Egypt have spread over social networks to many other authoritarian regimes. Digital media has not only caused a cascade of civil disobedience to spread among populations living under the most unflappable dictators, it has made for unique new means of civic organizing.

During the heady days of protests in Cairo, one activist succinctly tweeted about why digital media was so important to the organization of political unrest. "We use Facebook to schedule the protests, Twitter to coordinate, and YouTube to tell the world," she said. The protesters openly acknowledge the role of digital media as a fundamental infrastructure for their work. Moammar Gadhafi's former aides have advised him to submit his resignation through Twitter.

    Yet digital media didn't oust Hosni Mubarak. The committed Egyptians   3
occupying the streets of Cairo did that. As Barack Obama put it, mobile phones
and the Internet were the media by which soulful calls for freedom have cascaded
across North Africa and the Middle East. Just as the fall of Suharto in Indonesia
is a story that involves the creative use of mobile phones by student activists, the
falls of Zine El Abidine Ben Ali in Tunisia and Mubarak in Egypt will be recorded
as a process of Internet-enabled social mobilization.

    It is difficult to know when the Arab Spring will end, but we can already say   4
something about the political casualties and long-term regional consequences of
digitally enabled political protest.

Understanding the Cascading Effects

    Newsweek called it Egypt's "Facebook Revolt"; *Fast Company* argued   5
"Massive Egyptian Protests Powered by YouTube, Twitter, Facebook, Twitpic"; and
American U.N. Ambassador Susan Rice has said, "The power of this technology,
the power of social networking to channel and champion public sentiment, has
been more evident in the past few weeks than ever before."

    However, overemphasizing the role of information technology diminishes   6
the personal risks that individual protesters took in heading out onto the streets
to face tear gas and rubber bullets. While it is true that the dynamics of collective
action are different in a digital world, we need to move beyond **punditry** about
digital media, simple claims that technology is good or bad for democracy, and a
few favored examples of how this can be so. Pundits often miss three things about
why digital media is important for understanding contemporary social change.

    First, digital media are social networks. It matters not whether social   7
mobilization occurs face to face over a lunch counter or through a short text
message sent by mobile phones. It has become a false **dichotomy** to describe
strong ties as being face to face communications and weak ties as being short
text messages. The personal decision to face rubber bullets and tear gas is only
ever taken when appeals for solidarity come through social networks. Images of
friends and family being beaten by security services draw people into the streets.
Increasingly, those appeals come digitally, as wall posts, tweets and pixilated
YouTube videos hastily recorded by mobile phones.

    Second, the significant structural change in how political life is organized   8 is not so much about new connections between the West and the Arab Street, but about connections between Arab Streets. The digital storytelling by average Tunisians is what spread across North Africa and the Middle East. Protesters in Tunisia and Egypt used social media to link up. Telling stories about their shared grievances and sense of desperation became much of the content flowing over these networks.

Eventually, such content spilled over the social networks that transcended national boundaries. The cascade effect, however, wasn't simply that shared grievances spread from Tunis to Cairo. Instead, it was the inspiring story of success—overthrowing Ben Ali—that spilled over networks of family and friends that stretch from Morocco to Jordan.

In a sense, there is an important parallel between Obama's success and Mubarak's failure. An important part of Obama's successful 2008 presidential bid was the ability of his campaign to use digital media to connect his supporters to each other.

Traditional political campaigns work hard to connect potential voters to a block captain, who is connected to a neighborhood captain, who is connected to a regional director, who is connected to a state's campaign representative. In contrast, Obama's campaign treated the links between supporters as important as the connections to the party organization. By facilitating the creation of social networks within the context of his campaign organization, Obama built an agile and responsive organization.

Third, the content that seems to have the biggest cascading effect over digital media is personal, not **ideological**. In most previous social upheavals and political revolutions, there is an ideologically driven opposition that topples a dictator from another part of the political spectrum. Radical socialists, left-leaning union leaders or a Marxist army from the countryside would lead a popular revolt. Or religious conservatives or right-wing generals would lead a coup. But most of the reports from the ground suggest that these rebellions are largely leaderless and without traditional ideological labels. The political parties—and religious fundamentalists—are bit players.

Digital Media and the Modern Recipe for Democratization

Let's begin with the catalogue of political casualties since a desperate Tunisian shopkeeper set himself on fire, activating a transnational network of citizens exhausted by authoritarian rule. Within weeks, digitally enabled protesters in Tunisia tossed out their dictator.

Social media spread both discontent and inspiring stories of success from Tunisia across North Africa and into the Middle East. The protests in Egypt have drawn the largest crowds in 50 years, and the crisis is not over. The discontent has spread through networks of family and friends to Algeria, Jordan, Lebanon and Yemen. Autocrats have had to dismiss their cabinets, sometimes several times, to placate frustrated citizens. Algerians had to lift a 19-year "state of emergency" and are gearing for demonstrations over the weekend. Even Libyan dictator Moammar Gadhafi had to make **concessions** to activists brave enough to raise street protests against government housing policy, although he's fighting violently against the final step in the program—his removal.   *14*

But perhaps the most important casualty in terms of global politics is the U.S. preference for stability over democracy in North Africa and the Middle East. This preference, expressed in different foreign policies, seems untenable when groundswells of public opinion mobilize for democracy.   *15*

Research suggests that since 1995, the most consistent causal features of democratization include a wired civil society that uses digital media to undermine authoritarian rule in the course of national and global public opinion. Over the last decade, information and communication technologies have had consistent roles in the narrative for social mobilization: *16*

- Coordinating and publicizing massive mobilizations and nonviolent resistance tactics against pseudo-democratic regimes after stolen elections
- Allowing foreign governments and **diaspora** communities to support local democratic movements through information, electronic financial transfers, off-shore logistics and moral encouragement
- Organizing radical student movements to use unconventional protest tactics at sensitive moments for regimes, particularly during (rigged) elections, elite power struggles or diplomatic visits to undermine the appearance of regime popularity
- Uniting opposition movements through social-networking applications, shared media portals for creating and distributing digital content, and online forums for debating political strategy and public policy options
- Attracting international news media attention and diplomatic pressure

through digital content such as photos taken "on the ground" by citizens, leaking videos and documents to foreign journalists, or by diplomats raising flags over human rights abuses, environmental disasters, electoral fraud, and political corruption

- Transporting mobilization strategies from one country to another, sharing stories of success and failure, and building a sense of transnational grievance with national solutions

There certainly are other causal recipes. The classic understanding of social   17
mobilization is that it depends on the appearance of collective identities, shared motivations and grievances, and ultimately a change in the opportunity structure for collective action.

cascading
in this case, a process that occurs in steps, producing an overall effect

civil disobedience
refusal to obey certain laws or government demands

unflappable
not easily upset

punditry
a source of opinion, a critic

dichotomy
a difference between two opposite things

ideological
relating to ideas or a set of beliefs that form a system

concessions
admitting of a point, yielding a point

diaspora
people who live outside the area in which they had lived for a long time

Summarizing

Write a summary of "The Arab Spring's Cascading Effects."

Reflecting

- What is the main idea of the essay?
- What is the overall pattern of organization for this essay—spatial, chronological, or cause-effect?
- What important point is made in paragraph 6?
- In paragraph 12, what do you learn about the "biggest cascading effect" of digital media?
- The bulleted list in paragraph 16 reviews the role that digital media has played in ground mobilization in the Arab uprisings. How would you explain points 2 and 5 using your own words?

Critical Thinking

- How has digital media been used to initiate change in the United States?
- Has the use of digital media in the Middle East continued to be important, or has it run its course? Explain.

Gary Blakeley, 2014 / Used under license from Shutterstock.com

In the first part of this transcript from May 26, 2009, President Barack Obama announces his nomination of Judge Sonia Sotomayor to the United States Supreme Court. In the second part, Judge Sotomayor accepts the nomination. Sotomayor became the first Supreme Court justice with Hispanic roots.

About the Authors

Barack Obama is the 44th president of the United States. **Sonia Sotomayor** is an associate justice of the Supreme Court of the United States.

Prereading

1. What do the title and the two bold headings tell you about the topic of this selection?
2. What do you already know about Judge Sotomayor?
3. What would you like to learn about her?

The Nomination of Judge Sonia Sotomayor to the United States Supreme Court

President Barack Obama: Of the many responsibilities granted to a President by our Constitution, few are more serious or more **consequential** than selecting a Supreme Court justice. The members of our highest court are granted life **tenure**, often serving long after the Presidents who appointed them. And they are charged with the vital task of applying principles put to paper more than 20 [sic] centuries ago to some of the most difficult questions of our time.

1

So I don't take this decision lightly. I've made it only after deep reflection and careful deliberation. And while there are many qualities that I admire in judges across the spectrum of judicial philosophy, and that I seek in my own nominee, there are few that stand out that I just want to mention.

2

First and foremost is a **rigorous** intellect, a mastery of the law, an ability to hone in on the key issues and provide clear answers to complex legal questions.

3

Second is a recognition of the limits of the judicial role, an understanding that a judge's job is to interpret, not make law, to approach decisions without any particular ideology or agenda, but rather a commitment to **impartial** justice, a respect for **precedent**, and a determination to faithfully apply the law to the facts at hand.

These two qualities are essential, I believe, for anyone who would sit on our nation's highest court. And yet, these qualities alone are insufficient. We need something more. Supreme Court Justice Oliver Wendell Holmes once said that the life of the law has not been logic; it has been experience; experience being tested by obstacles and barriers, by hardship and misfortune; experience insisting, persisting, and ultimately overcoming those barriers. It is experience that can give a person a common touch and a sense of **compassion**, an understanding of how the world works and how ordinary people live. And that is why it is a necessary ingredient in the kind of justice we need on the Supreme Court. . . .

> "The life of the law has not been logic; it has been experience."

4

After completing the exhaustive nominating process, I've decided to nominate an inspiring woman who I believe will make a great justice, Judge Sonia Sotomayor of the great state of New York. . . .

5

Over a distinguished career that spans three decades, Judge Sotomayor has worked at almost every level of our judicial system, providing her with a depth of experience and a breadth of perspective that will be invaluable as a Supreme Court justice.

6

Sonia's parents came to New York from Puerto Rico during the Second World War. Her mother is part of the Women's Army Corps. . . . Sonia's father was a factory worker with a third-grade education who didn't speak English. But like Sonia's mother, he had a willingness to work hard, a strong sense of family, and a belief in the American Dream. . . .

7

Along the way, Judge Sotomayor faced down barriers, overcame the odds, and lived out the American Dream that brought her parents here so long ago. And even as she has accomplished so much in her life, she has never forgotten where she began, never lost touch with the community that supported her. . . .

8

Judge Sonia Sotomayor: Thank you, Mr. President, for the most humbling honor of my life. You have nominated me to serve on the country's highest court,

9

and I am deeply moved. . . . Although I grew up in very modest and challenging circumstances, I consider my life to be immeasurably rich. I was raised in a Bronx public housing project, but studied at two of the nation's finest universities. I did work as an assistant district attorney, prosecuting violent crimes that devastate our communities. But then I joined a private law firm and worked with international corporations doing business in the United States. I have had the privilege of serving as a Federal District trial judge, and am now serving as a Federal Appellate Circuit Court judge.

The wealth of experience, personal and professional, have helped me appreciate the variety of perspectives that present themselves in every case that I hear. It has helped me to understand, respect and respond to the concerns and arguments of all **litigants** who appear before me, as well as to the views of my colleagues on the bench.   *10*

It is a **daunting** feeling to be here. Eleven years ago, during my confirmation process for appointment to the Second Circuit, I was given a private tour of the White House. It was an overwhelming experience for a kid from the South Bronx. Yet never in my wildest childhood imaginings did I ever envision that moment, let alone did I ever dream that I would live this moment.   From WhiteHouse.gov.   *11*

---

consequential having importance	**rigorous** strict and demanding	**compassion** feeling of deep sympathy
tenure states indicating that a position or employment is permanent	**impartial** fair, just	**litigant** person involved in lawsuit
	precedent an act or instance that may be used as an example	**daunting** difficult to do or deal with

Summarizing

Write a summary of "The Nomination of Judge Sonia Sotomayor to the United States Supreme Court."

Reflecting

- President Obama identifies three qualities needed to be a Supreme Court Justice. What are they?
- What is the purpose of Judge Sotomayor's response?

Critical Thinking

- How might Judge Sotomayor offer a unique voice to the Supreme Court?
- Why might Judge Sotomayor "appreciate the variety of perspectives that present themselves in every case"?

linked to the specific economic and social structure of a society and to a nation's position in the system of global stratification.

Systems of Stratification

Around the globe, one of the most important characteristics of systems of stratification is their degree of flexibility. Sociologists distinguish among such systems based on the extent to which they are open or closed. In an *open system*, the boundaries between levels in the hierarchies are more flexible and may be influenced (positively or negatively) by people's achieved statuses. Open systems are assumed to have some degree of social mobility. . . .   6

In a *closed system*, the boundaries between levels in the hierarchies of social stratification are rigid, and people's positions are set by **ascribed** status. Open and closed systems are ideal-type constructs; no actual stratification system is completely open or closed. Three key systems of stratification—slavery, caste, and class—are characterized by different hierarchal structures and varying degrees of mobility.   7

From Kendall, *Sociology in Our Times* 9E. © 2013 Cengage Learning.

culminated ended or arrived at a final stage	**hierarchical** ranking one above the other	**affluent** wealthy
stratification state of being divided into social classes	**ideologies** beliefs that guide individuals	**ascribed** credited to or assigned

Summarizing

Write a summary of "How Is the American Dream Influenced by Social Stratification?"

Reflecting

- Does the author employ an academic or personal voice? Explain.
- What is the main topic of paragraph 2? How is that topic defined?
- What caution is offered in paragraph 3?
- Open and closed systems are part of the discussion in paragraphs 6–7. Explain the two terms.

Critical Thinking

- Do you think the dream of attainment discussed in the first part of this essay is unique to this country? Explain.
- How would you answer the question posed in the title: "How Is the American Dream Influenced by Social Stratification?"

In this narrative essay, fashion **entrepreneur** Jennifer Hyman describes how her interests, work, and life intertwine.

About the Author

Issie Lapowsky is a staff writer at *Inc.* magazine. She has also written for *New York Daily News, BlackBook* magazine and *The Brooklyn Rail.* She resides in Manhattan.

Prereading

1. What is your opinion about the fashion industry?
2. In the first sentence, the subject is described as a "self-diagnosed shopaholic." What might this say about the voice and purpose of the essay?
3. What do the first sentence of other paragraphs tell you about this selection?

The Way I Work: Jennifer Hyman, Rent the Runway

Jennifer Hyman is a self-diagnosed shopaholic, but it takes more than a keen eye for fashion to run Rent the Runway. The New York City-based company, which Hyman cofounded in late 2009 with her friend and fellow Harvard Business School graduate Jenny Fleiss, rents out designer dresses by the likes of Vera Wang and Versace. The company charges $50 to $400 to rent a gown for a few days. 1

A little more than two years after its founding, Rent the Runway has 62 employees, 1.5 million customers, and a wide selection of dresses from 150 designers as well as accessories and handbags. Along the way, Hyman, who held management positions at Starwood Hotels, WeddingChannel, and IMG before earning her M.B.A. (and is still just 31), has had to learn a lot about fashion, Web design, logistics, jewelry repair, and dry cleaning. On a typical day, she might spend her time combing through customer data, conferring with one of her many mentors, or meeting with some of the biggest names in fashion. 2

The first thing I do in the morning is look at my iPhone calendar, so I can   *3*
figure out how to dress. If I have meetings with employees in the office, I can wear
my Lululemon comfy clothes. If I'm meeting with a clothing designer, I might put
on a Moschino dress and Louboutins. I usually end up running around the city
like a crazy person in 4-inch heels. I frequently wear dresses from our inventory,
but Rent the Runway has totally changed the way I shop. Now I invest in key
pieces that I'll have forever.

I walk to work, which is one of the perks of convincing my boyfriend, Peter   *4*
[Mack], to move to the West Village. I get to the
office around 8:30. It feels a bit like a newsroom.
It's a big open space—no cubicle walls or offices.
I sit at the end of a long desk with eight members
of our marketing team. My sister Becky, who
handles marketing to college students, sits a few

> [The office] feels a bit like
> a newsroom. It's a big
> open space—no cubicle
> walls or offices.

seats away from me. That's one of the great joys of coming to work every day. Even
though she's my younger sister, Becky's definitely a role model in my life. She's
the most genuinely positive person I've ever met. I've tried to create the company
culture in her image. I want this to be a place where we are always looking on the
bright side and believing the best in people.

My Mondays and Tuesdays are pretty packed with staff meetings. I like to   *5*
schedule them early in the week, so I can influence the agenda. I'll meet with
each of our teams, including senior management, marketing, fashion, and tech. I
change gears a lot, but that's my favorite part of the job. If I were just working on
one part of the business, I'd be totally bored.

We have a fashion meeting every Tuesday. That's when we look at what's   *6*
working and what isn't. We spend millions of dollars on inventory, so we need to
buy dresses based on data. We look at how often the dresses get rented, and which
dresses are popular with different age groups and in different geographic areas.
For example, dresses from designers like Lela Rose, Milly, and Shoshanna, which
are more feminine and conservative, tend to be more popular in the South. And
boho-chic styles tend to be more popular on the West Coast.

Last year, we got a lace Nicole Miller dress that was very popular across   *7*
all **demographics**. That was our first indication that lace was going to be big.
Recently, a good percentage of our holiday inventory was lace. We were able to
take that kind of risk because of our research.

Of course, there's an art to buying, too. Each season, our five buyers and I   8
go into designers' studios, meet the heads of sales, look at the collections, and
make our selections. Sometimes we see a piece that has nothing to do with our
analytics, and we're just like, "We need to have this!" There was a dress from
Opening Ceremony we saw that we just couldn't say no to. It had a cutout on the
front, which was very different, as well as a long length and textured fabric that
made it look sophisticated. It's now one of our most popular dresses. The numbers
ground you, but you have to leave something to passion, whimsy, and fun.

We haven't had any serious flops, but over time we have figured out which   9
dresses work best for our business. For instance, dresses with very delicate
beading do not do well, because they typically can't be dry-cleaned over and over.
Our buyers have become experts on fabrics and styles that are both fabulous and
durable. I still have some influence in the buying process, but I think being a good
CEO is about trusting and empowering your team.

On Tuesdays, I also meet with Jonathan Betz, our senior vice president of   10
engineering. His team has been working on redesigning our Web site, adding
features like a photo-sharing function that allows women to upload photos or
videos of themselves in their Rent the Runway dresses. I do what I can to help
him by identifying customer experience issues that we've had. For instance, if I'm
searching dresses by size, everything that shows up should be available in my size.
For a long time, we didn't have a technology leader. We outsourced development—
my cofounder, Jenny Fleiss, and I didn't do any coding ourselves. But I've gone to
tech meetups, talked to engineers all over the city, and read books and blogs. I'm
constantly amazed at how much I've learned over the past two years, but also how
much I still have to learn.

I talk with Jenny, who is the company's president, throughout the day. I love   11
the people-managing side of the business, but Jenny's the best person I know at
getting stuff done. Jenny's very quick. She doesn't want to sit and discuss things
for hours on end. When I work with her, I try to make the conversation as efficient
as possible. I lay out a game plan and let her execute. That's different from how I
work with Ashley Seidman, our creative director. Ashley oversees the look of our
Web site, emails, and other areas of design. Taking one idea and thinking about
it from 10 different angles is what gets her creative juices flowing. There are very
different personalities at this company, and all of them approach work in different
ways. I try to work with people the way they prefer.

The rest of my week varies, and I'm usually in and out of the office. A couple   *12*
of times a month, I'll visit our warehouse in New Jersey. It's a breathtaking
40,000-square-foot space with 25,000
dresses, 4,000 accessories, a full dry cleaner,
and a jewelry repair shop. When I'm there,
I meet with our head of operations to talk
about dry cleaning, shipping issues, tailoring,
and technology in the warehouse. What
some people don't realize is that we're a
logistics company. We're sending out tens
of thousands of units of inventory over and
over. We need to make sure that inventory looks absolutely brand new before we
send it to every customer.

> There are very different personalities at this company, and all of them approach work in different ways. I try to work with people the way they prefer.

I also have meetings with fashion designers at least once a week. I typically   *13*
meet with every designer we work with several times a year. I try to do a lot more
listening than talking. When we were starting out, it took time to get designers
to understand what we were doing. They were afraid of retail cannibalization
and brand dilution. But 98 percent of our customers rent brands they've never
bought before. That just doesn't happen in e-commerce. Typically, when people
shop online, they buy brands they're already familiar with. But if you can rent
that Helmut Lang dress first, and then realize, "Oh, my God, I love this designer,"
maybe you'll go out and buy the Helmut Lang leather leggings.

We try to be brand ambassadors for the designers. One way we're doing that   *14*
now is by creating landing pages for each designer with videos, photos, and bios to
educate women about individual brands. Our goal is to teach young women who
were brought up on H&M and Forever 21 that designer clothes are expensive for a
reason. They're works of art.

I talk with my investors several times a week. They're incredible mentors. I   *15*
have a lot of other mentors in my life, too, including Carley Roney, who founded
TheKnot.com, and Dan Rosensweig, the CEO of Chegg.com. Carley's a genius
marketer, and Dan's exactly the kind of leader I aspire to be. This company is the
largest team I've ever managed, and my mentors have been especially helpful in
teaching me how to lead and inspire a team.

I usually leave the office around 8 p.m. I like to call my parents on the walk   *16*
home. I come from a very close family. Rent the Runway takes up a lot of hours

of my day, but I'm not willing to sacrifice relationships with my family and friends. When I call my parents, I'll rehash the most important parts of my day. Sometimes I'll talk about what's going on at Rent the Runway. Or maybe I'll talk about Peter or my friends, the new coat I want to buy, or upcoming plans. My parents have always encouraged me to follow my passions.

At least once a week, I'll meet friends for dinner. I grew up in New Rochelle, 17 New York, and I often get together with my friends from elementary school. Other nights, I come home, cook dinner, and watch TV with Peter. If a show has singing and dancing in it, I'm the No. 1 consumer. I love *Glee*. I wish I were on that show. I grew up doing theater, and my personal goal for this year is to start singing in a cover band. I also love *American Idol* and *So You Think You Can Dance*. Basically, if a 12-year-old is watching it, then so am I.

I'm not one of those people who have their iPhones out at the dinner table 18 and are working like crazy all night. Then again, I never really unplug from Rent the Runway completely, because the people I work with have become some of my closest friends. It doesn't feel like a job to go in to work, because I'm surrounded by incredible people—people I love and am inspired by, people who make me better.

Republished with permission of Mansueto Ventures LLC. From *Inc: The Magazine for Growing Companies*. From Issie Lapowsky, January 24, 2012; permission conveyed through Copyright Clearance Center, Inc.

---

entrepreneur
a person who creates, organizes, and manages a business or enterprise

demographics
statistical data related to groups of people

boho-chic
influenced by bohemian and hippy movements

logistics
detailed coordination of an organization or resources

analytics
systematic calculation and evaluation of data

Summarizing

- Write a summary of "The Way I Work: Jennifer Hyman, Rent the Runway."

Reflection

- What is the main idea of this selection? How is the text organized?
- Does the writer use a personal or academic voice? Explain.

Critical Thinking

- How does this selection illustrate that for some fortunate individuals there is a fine line between work and play?
- Hyman says "Rent the Runway takes up a lot of hours of my day, but I'm not willing to sacrifice relationships with my family and friends." Why is it important to balance work and personal relationships? How can you maintain such a balance?

In this essay, journalist Kris Frieswick reveals surprising links between an entrepreneurial director of a rehabilitation program and the ex-convicts being rehabilitated.

About the Author

An award-winning journalist, **Kris Frieswick** is senior editor at *Inc.* She has also been published in *The Wall Street Journal*, the *Economist*, *The Boston Globe Magazine*, *Departures*, and *Hemispheres*.

Prereading

1. What do the terms "ex-cons" and "entrepreneurs" together lead you to expect from the essay?
2. What do the first four paragraphs tell you about the text?
3. What do you expect to learn?

Ex-Cons Relaunching Lives as Entrepreneurs

Catherine Rohr stands at the front of a drab, fluorescent-lit classroom in Midtown Manhattan. Her 27 students, who sit crammed into chair-desks, are ex-cons whose crimes include narcotics trafficking and murder. Rohr, 35, is dressed conservatively in long black pants, a button-down white shirt, fitted jacket, and high heels. Beneath her razor-straight bangs, Rohr's kohl-rimmed eyes zero in on a man in the back of the room, leaning against the wall.

"Are you sleeping back there?" she barks.

"No," says the man. "I'm just not feeling that well."

"From now on, no one in the back row can rest their heads against the wall," she orders. "It looks like you're not paying attention."

These men are the inaugural class of Defy Ventures, a yearlong, M.B.A.-style program that Rohr created to teach former inmates how to start their own companies. For months, they have been meeting here for 14 to 16 hours a week to learn about things such as cash flow, balance sheets, intellectual property, accounting, and taxes. There are workshops on how to behave in professional settings, how to speak in public, and how to be a better parent. These men are also learning how to create business plans. In June, they will compete in a business-plan competition. The winners will split $100,000 in **seed funding**.

Rohr has an interesting theory about criminals. She says that many of the   6
qualities that made these men good at being bad guys (until they got caught, of course) are the same qualities that make effective entrepreneurs. Some of the men in this class had up to 40 employees under management. Though their merchandise was illegal

> She says that many of the qualities that made these men good at being bad guys . . . are the same qualities that make effective entrepreneurs.

narcotics and not, say, office supplies, these men developed certain business skills—the ability to motivate a team, identify new markets, manage risk, and inspire loyalty and hard work. Rohr's goal is to help these students apply their abilities to legal endeavors.

Rohr continues today's lesson, evaluating the company names proposed by   7
each student. "What's the name of your business?" she asks, pointing to one of the students.

"Mine's is . . . "   8

"What did you say?" Rohr pounces. She's a stickler for proper speech. He   9
stops and takes a deep breath.

"Mine is . . . " he carefully enunciates. Rohr smiles slightly as the man   10
continues.

In this room of former criminals, Rohr may be the most intimidating figure.   11
She runs the show. It's not just because these men respect her, though they clearly do, but because part of the deal of being in this room is doing what Rohr tells them to do. In exchange, they get a once-in-a-lifetime opportunity. And for that, they are willing to sit up straight, put their personal lives on hold, and study hard.

This program is the type of second chance that none of these men ever   12
thought they would get. It's also a second chance for Rohr, who not very long ago had her own—very public—fall from grace.

At age 25, Rohr found God. She and her husband, Steve, a lawyer, began   13
attending a church in the Bay Area. She worked as an associate at Summit

Partners, a venture capital firm in Palo Alto. At church, Rohr was introduced to the concept of tithing, giving away 10 percent of her income to the church or charity. Donating felt really good. So good that she resolved to make $1 million a year by age 30, just so she could give away 95 percent of it.

> [S]he resolved to make $1 million a year by age 30, just so she could give away 95 percent of it.

A couple of years later, after landing a job in New York City at American Securities Capital Partners, a private equity firm, Rohr took a trip to several prisons in Texas as part of a Christian outreach program. It was there that Rohr first made the connection between criminals and entrepreneurs. These men exhibited many of the same qualities she looked for when she met with founders as an investor.   14

In 2004, Rohr launched the Prison Entrepreneurship Program, or PEP, in Houston to teach inmates basic business skills. After several months of running the program remotely, Rohr left her job and moved to Texas to focus all her efforts on PEP. She and her husband spent nearly every penny they had, including her entire **401(k)**, on the program. She and volunteer executives taught classes about marketing, finance, and how to act professionally. And it was all topped with a thick frosting of religion—both because it fueled Rohr's passion and because religion is an unspoken requirement for any prison rehabilitation program in Texas.   15

Rohr believed God had called her to this ministry. And what she was able to accomplish in a short time struck many as miraculous. In five years, about 500 students graduated from the program. About 60 of them started businesses when they left prison. More important, the **recidivism** rate of graduates—at the time, around 10 percent—was much lower than the US average of 40 percent. Rohr and her program received several honors for public service, including awards from Texas Governor Rick Perry and President George W. Bush.   16

But everything came crashing down in 2009, when Rohr admitted to her staff of volunteers that she had had inappropriate relationships with four graduates of her prison program. "I felt like I'd been punched in the gut," says Bert Smith, one of those volunteers. After someone sent an anonymous letter to the Texas Department of Criminal Justice, which has strict policies against volunteers becoming personally involved with inmates, the department launched   17 an investigation. Rohr says that none of the relationships started until after the prisoners were out of jail. But the department barred her from ever entering the Texas prison system again, citing security concerns. It also threatened to kick PEP out of the prison system if Rohr was involved in the program in any way. Devastated, she resigned.

The troubles, says Rohr, started a year earlier, when her husband asked for a divorce after nine years of marriage. In retrospect, the divorce wasn't so unexpected, she says. As the program grew, Rohr traveled frequently, visiting prisons and raising money for the program. She slept four hours a night and was rarely home. "I didn't have good boundaries in terms of working a certain number of hours and then I'll be home and be a wife," says Rohr. "I wasn't living sustainably." 18

After the divorce, she felt ashamed. "Instead of reaching out for help, I chose to be on my own," Rohr says. "And in that aloneness, I didn't make the best decisions." Rohr won't discuss specifics but claims that not all four relationships were "what people thought." 19

The media, which had frequently celebrated Rohr's efforts to reform prisoners, pounced on the story of her downfall. The scandal became news as far away as China. "Prisons Ban Founder for 'Improper Relationships,'" read the headline in the *Austin American-Statesman*. That particular story attracted more than 60 online comments, most of them negative. "Let me guess, the greater the crime committed by the ex-convict, the dirtier the sex?" wrote one commenter. Others claimed to have knowledge of more than four affairs. "I was just bawling my eyes out," says Rohr. "They wrote untrue things—all sorts of uninformed comments. I didn't want to live anymore. I thought that I would live my whole life covered in shame." 20

> "What would it be like if you were known for the worst thing that you ever did in your life?" Now, she was in that very situation.

Before the scandal, Rohr often spoke at churches and conferences about the prison program. She would always ask the crowd, "What would it be like if you were known for the worst thing that you ever did in your life?" Now, she was in that very situation. 21

At the lowest point of her life, something unexpected happened that helped Rohr pick herself back up. "I got over a thousand emails from people of love and 22

support," she says, still looking surprised by it nearly three years later. "They were saying, 'What are you doing next?' and 'Thank you for your honesty.' Some came back with confessions of their own."

It was far too soon, the pain still too fresh, for her to realize what these messages were telling her about the way this failure would transform her life. But those notes of encouragement gave her the strength to reach out to friends for support. With their help, she put the contents of her apartment in storage and got out of Texas. She traveled for six months, staying with friends. "I went through a period of questioning my calling, or that I could be worth anything or do anything good for the world ever again," she says. "But at the same time, I had this sense that I was born to lead. I needed to get my crap together so I could be an effective leader." 23

Rohr decided she had had enough sitting around. She dyed her auburn hair back to its naturally darker shade and moved back to New York City, hoping that the city's energy would help jolt her back to life. She entertained a job offer from a **VC firm** before finally giving in to what her heart was telling her to create: a new nonprofit. She would create a version of PEP that operated outside the prison system. (PEP is still going strong in Texas. "We came very close to having the doors locked," says Bert Smith, who is now CEO of the program. "There were a number of people who were convinced that without Catherine Rohr, PEP would fail. I'm happy to say that it didn't.") 24

Defy Ventures has raised more than $1.5 million in donations and pledges from VC firms, **hedge fund**s, businesses, and private foundations. Last fall, Rohr began accepting applications for the first class. After requesting referrals from the New York parole and probation departments and about 25 prisoner rehabilitation programs, Defy received more than 180 applications from former inmates interested in the free classes. Rohr looked for candidates who had high school diplomas or GEDs, who owned up to their crimes, and who were motivated to change their lives. 25

Today, when Rohr stands before a classroom of ex-cons and future   *26*
entrepreneurs, everyone understands that the group shares a common story of
failure—separated by degrees, of course. A few weeks after the program began,
she told them all about what happened in Texas. "I was very hesitant to step foot
in the classroom again," says Rohr. "I was concerned about how would these guys
look at me. But I've never felt that. They are so respectful. I think that I'm able to
be a better leader now that, in a way, we have a shared experience. I know what it
feels like to let people down."

Here in the classroom, student Marlon Llin, who served 10 years for   *27*
conspiracy to sell narcotics, stands at the blackboard. Llin, 37, is trying to figure
out how much he should charge for the various services he provides through his
new company, Mylo's Repairs. Kene Turner, an instructor from the Network for
Teaching Entrepreneurship and one of
Defy's course leaders, is teaching the men
about pricing. Turner asks Llin what he
charges to remodel a bathroom. Llin says
$150 to $200, and the customer pays for
the materials. As the class watches, Turner

> They had been used to thinking like men living paycheck to paycheck. . . . Now they are seeing what it means to think like entrepreneurs.

shows Llin all the things he will have to pay for out of that fee, including insurance,
gas for his truck, office supplies, and taxes. As it turns out, Llin isn't making nearly
as much as he thought he was. "You're undercharging," says Turner.

Llin—and every other man in the room—has a visible "aha" moment. "I   *28*
never thought about it that way before," says Llin. "I get it," adds another man in
the back. They had been used to thinking like men living paycheck to paycheck,
worried only about how much they needed to make per hour to survive and feed
their families. Now they are seeing what it means to think like entrepreneurs.

At its core, the true purpose of Defy is to change the way these men think   *29*
about themselves and their lives, says Rohr. One of her techniques is something
she calls the Ten Bear Hugs. Every class starts with group hugs. It's a strange
sight, watching these men, many of whom have done decades of hard time,
warmly embrace one another and everyone else in the room. "Initially, we didn't
like it," says Jeff Ewell, who was incarcerated for a little less than a year for
conspiracy to sell firearms. He is creating an online music exchange that would

let artists buy instrumental tracks directly from producers. "But now we have to get told, 'Sit down, stop hugging each other; we've got to get stuff done.'" Rohr's goal is to break down the walls these men have had up around themselves for much of their lives.

Fabian Ruiz spent more than half his life with corrections officers who, he says, "don't even look at inmates as people." At 16, Ruiz killed the man who shot his older brother. While awaiting trial on Rikers Island in New York City, he attempted to escape and was recaptured. He was tried as an adult and sentenced to 20 years to life. He spent the next 21 years in a series of maximum-security prisons in New York State. He was released about a year ago at the age of 37.   30

Ruiz learned about Defy from a friend. His brown eyes dance when he talks about his start-up, Infor-Nation. It will sell printouts of Web pages to inmates of New York's prison system, who are blocked from using the Internet. Ruiz thinks his business has huge market potential. He really wants to win the business-plan competition—all the students do. The winners not only get the prize money, but they will also get to participate in Defy's six-month incubator program, helped by a team of entrepreneurs-in-residence and volunteer accountants, lawyers, and other mentors.   31

> To succeed, these men must learn to reject failure, which isn't always easy. Failure can have its own comforts, says Rohr.

But the benefits of this program go well beyond prize money, says Ewell. Defy has helped him open up to other people, he says. "I've always been the type of person to attack everything alone," says Ewell. "The one thing we never learned to do was trust in another individual." But he developed a powerful bond with his fellow classmates. "We kind of became a brotherhood," he says.   32

To succeed, these men must learn to reject failure, which isn't always easy. Failure can have its own comforts, says Rohr. "When Jesus would go up to a leper or a blind person and ask, 'Do you want to be healed?' it always seemed to me such an idiotic question," she says. "Of course you want to be healed. But a leper was taken care of. If you're not a leper anymore, you have to provide for yourself. You have all these different expectations if you're no longer the blind man. That's how it is with our guys, too. And not all of them want to see."   33

In fact, almost half the class has quit—Rohr started with 50 students. Some   *34*
left because they got jobs they couldn't pass up. Others just couldn't hack the
workload. Those who have stayed hope that maybe they won't be known for the
worst thing they ever did. Maybe they will be known for building something
great. The same goes for Rohr, who hopes to eventually expand Defy Ventures to
other cities around the country. "I've spent my whole life talking about grace and
second chances," she says, "and I have now been the recipient of it."

401(k)
a type of employee savings plan for retirement

hedge fund
a high-risk, high-returns partnership of investors

kohl
a black powder used for eye makeup, especially
popular in Eastern countries

recidivism
a pattern of repeat criminal behavior

seed funding
an early investment in a new company

VC firm
a business that invests "venture capital" (VC) money
into a business with a potential for long-term growth

Summarizing

Write a summary of "Ex-Cons Relaunching Lives as Entrepreneurs."

Reflecting

- What is the main idea of this essay? (**Hint:** Focus on paragraph 6.)
- What is the purpose of this essay—to inform, to persuade, to entertain? Who is the
  intended audience?
- Why does this essay contain a story within a story?
- What is the purpose of the "Ten Bear Hugs" described in paragraph 29?
- How does the revelation of Rohr's "fall from grace" relate to the situation of the ex-
  cons she teaches?

Critical Thinking

- React to this comment by Rohr: "The qualities that made these men good at being
  bad guys are the same qualities that make effective entrepreneurs." What types of
  qualities is she talking about? Is she correct?
- Consider the names of the two programs Rohr started: PEP (Prisoner
  Entrepreneurship Program) and Defy Ventures. Why do you think she chose those
  names? What expectations do the names create for the participants? For potential
  investors? For Rohr and her staff?

Appendix **A**
A Guide to Strong Writing

Figure A.1 serves as a guide to strong writing. Your writing will be clear and effective when it can "pass" each point. This checklist is especially helpful during revising, when you are deciding how to improve your writing.

Figure A.1 A Guide to Strong Writing

Ideas

_____ 1. Does an interesting and relevant topic serve as a starting point for the writing?

_____ 2. Is the writing focused, addressing a specific feeling about or a specific part of the topic? (Check the thesis statement.)

_____ 3. Are there enough specific ideas, details, and examples to support the thesis?

_____ 4. Overall, is the writing interesting and informative?

Organization

_____ 5. Does the writing form a meaningful whole—with opening, middle, and closing parts?

_____ 6. Does the writing follow a logical pattern of organization?

_____ 7. Do transitions connect ideas and help the writing flow?

Voice

_____ 8. Does the writer sound informed about and interested in the topic?

_____ 9. Does the writer sound sincere and genuine?

Word Choice

_____ 10. Does the word choice clearly fit the purpose and the audience?

_____ 11. Does the writing include specific nouns and verbs?

Sentence Fluency

_____ 12. Are the sentences clear, and do they flow smoothly?

_____ 13. Are the sentences varied in their beginnings and length?

Conventions

_____ 14. Does your writing follow the rules of the language?

Appendix B

Using an Editing Checklist

Figure B.1 serves as a guide to editing writing. This checklist is helpful for checking your writing for style, grammar, punctuation, and spelling errors.

Figure B.1 Editing Checklist

Words

_____ 1. Have I used specific nouns and verbs?

_____ 2. Have I used more action verbs than "be" verbs?

Sentences

_____ 3. Have I avoided improper shifts in sentences?

_____ 4. Have I avoided fragments, run-ons, and rambling sentences?

Conventions

_____ 5. Do I use correct verb forms (*he saw*, not *he seen*)?

_____ 6. Do my subjects and verbs agree (*she speaks*, not *she speak*)?

_____ 7. Have I used the right words (*their, there, they're*)?

_____ 8. Have I capitalized first words and proper nouns and adjectives?

_____ 9. Have I used commas after long introductory word groups and to separate items in a series?

_____ 10. Have I used commas correctly in compound sentences?

_____ 11. Have I used apostrophes correctly in contractions and to show possession?

Appendix C
Using Standard English

Standard English (**SE**) is English that is considered appropriate for school, business, and government. You have been learning **SE** throughout your years in school. Table C.1 shows the basic differences between non-Standard English (**NS**) and **SE**.

Table C.1 Using Standard English

Differences in . . .	NS	SE
1. Expressing plurals after numbers	10 mile	10 miles
2. Expressing habitual action	He always be early.	He always is early.
3. Expressing ownership	My friend car . . .	My friend's car . . .
4. Expressing the third-person singular verb	The customer ask . . .	The customer asks . . .
5. Expressing negatives	She doesn't never . . .	She doesn't ever . . .
6. Using reflexive pronouns	He sees hisself . . .	He sees himself . . .
7. Using demonstrative adjectives	Them reports are . . .	Those reports are . . .
8. Using forms of *do*	He done it.	He did it.
9. Avoiding double subjects	My manager he . . .	My manager . . .
10. Using *a* or *an*	I need new laptop. She had angry caller.	I need a new laptop. She had an angry caller.
11. Using the past tense of verbs	Carl finish his . . .	Carl finished his . . .
12. Using *isn't* or *aren't* versus *ain't*	The company ain't . . .	The company isn't . . .

Appendix D
Understanding the Word Parts

The information that follows shows common prefixes, suffixes, and roots. Many of our words are made up of combinations of these word parts.

Prefixes

Prefixes are word parts that come *before* the root words (*pre* = before). Depending upon its meaning, a prefix changes the intent, or sense, of the base word. As a skilled reader, you will want to know the meanings of the most common prefixes, including numerical prefixes (see Table D.1), and then watch for them when you read.

a, an [not, without] amoral (without a sense of moral responsibility), atypical, atom (not cuttable), apathy (without feeling), anesthesia (without sensation)

ab, abs, a [from, away] abnormal, abduct, absent, avert (turn away)

acro [high] acropolis (high city), acrobat, acronym, acrophobia (fear of height)

ambi, amb [both, around] ambidextrous (skilled with both hands), ambiguous, amble

amphi [both] amphibious (living on both land and water), amphitheater

ante [before] antedate, anteroom, antebellum, antecedent (happening before)

anti, ant [against] anticommunist, antidote, anticlimax, antacid

be [on, away] bedeck, belabor, bequest, bestow, beloved

bene, bon [well] benefit, benefactor, benevolent, benediction, bonanza, bonus

bi, bis, bin [both, double, twice] bicycle, biweekly, bilateral, biscuit, binoculars

by [side, close, near] bypass, bystander, by-product, bylaw, byline

cata [down, against] catalog, catapult, catastrophe, cataclysm

cerebro [brain] cerebral, cerebrum, cerebellum

circum, circ [around] circumference, circumnavigate, circumspect, circular

co, con, col, com [together, with] copilot, conspire, collect, compose

coni [dust] coniosis (disease that comes from inhaling dust)

contra, counter [against] controversy, contradict, counterpart

de [from, down] demote, depress, degrade, deject, deprive

deca [ten] decade, decathlon, decapod (10 feet)

di [two, twice] divide, dilemma, dilute, dioxide, dipole, ditto

dia [through, between] diameter, diagonal, diagram, dialogue (speech between people)

dis, dif [apart, away, reverse] dismiss, distort, distinguish, diffuse

dys [badly, ill] dyspepsia (digesting badly), dystrophy, dysentery

em, en [in, into] embrace, enslave

epi [upon] epidermis (upon the skin, outer layer of skin), epitaph, epithet

eu [well] eulogize (speak well of, praise), euphony, euphemism, euphoria

ex, e, ec, ef [out] expel (drive out), ex-mayor, exorcism, eject, eccentric (out of the center position), efflux, effluent

extra, extro [beyond, outside] extraordinary (beyond the ordinary), extrovert, extracurricular

for [away or off] forswear (to renounce an oath)

fore [before in time] forecast, foretell (to tell beforehand), foreshadow

hemi, demi, semi [half] hemisphere, demitasse, semicircle (half of a circle)

hex [six] hexameter, hexagon

homo [man] Homo sapiens, homicide (killing man)

hyper [over, above] hypersensitive (overly sensitive), hyperactive

hypo [under] hypodermic (under the skin), hypothesis

il, ir, in, im [not] illegal, irregular, incorrect, immoral

in, il, im [into] inject, inside, illuminate, illustrate, impose, implant, imprison

infra [beneath] infrared, infrasonic

inter [between] intercollegiate, interfere, intervene, interrupt (break between)

intra [within] intramural, intravenous (within the veins)

intro [into, inward] introduce, introvert (turn inward)

macro [large, excessive] macrodent (having large teeth), macrocosm

mal [badly, poorly] maladjusted, malady, malnutrition, malfunction

meta [beyond, after, with] metaphor, metamorphosis, metaphysical

mis [incorrect, bad] misuse, misprint

miso [hate] misanthrope, misogynist

mono [one] monoplane, monotone, monochrome, monocle

multi [many] multiply, multiform

neo [new] neopaganism, neoclassic, neophyte, neonatal

non [not] nontaxable (not taxed), nontoxic, nonexistent, nonsense

ob, of, op, oc [toward, against] obstruct, offend, oppose, occur

oct [eight] octagon, octameter, octave, octopus

paleo [ancient] paleoanthropology (pertaining to ancient humans), paleontology (study of ancient life-forms)

para [beside, almost] parasite (one who eats beside or at the table of another), paraphrase, paramedic, parallel, paradox

penta [five] pentagon (figure or building having five angles or sides), pentameter, pentathlon

per [throughout, completely] pervert (completely turn wrong, corrupt), perfect, perceive, permanent, persuade

peri [around] perimeter (measurement around an area), periphery, periscope, pericardium, period

poly [many] polygon (figure having many angles or sides), polygamy, polyglot, polychrome

post [after] postpone, postwar, postscript, posterity

pre [before] prewar, preview, precede, prevent, premonition

pro [forward, in favor of] project (throw forward), progress, promote, prohibition

pseudo [false] pseudonym (false or assumed name), pseudopodia

quad [four] quadruple (four times as much), quadriplegic, quadratic, quadrant

quint [five] quintuplet, quintuple, quintet, quintile

re [back, again] reclaim, revive, revoke, rejuvenate, retard, reject, return

retro [backward] retrospective (looking backward), retroactive, retrorocket

se [aside] seduce (lead aside), secede, secrete, segregate

self [by oneself] self-determination, self-employed, self-service, selfish

sesqui [one and a half] sesquicentennial (one and one-half centuries)

sex, sest [six] sexagenarian (sixty years old), sexennial, sextant, sextuplet, sestet

sub [under] submerge (put under), submarine, substitute, subsoil

suf, sug, sup, sus [from under] sufficient, suffer, suggest, support, suspend

super, supr [above, over, more] supervise, superman, supernatural, supreme

syn, sym, sys, syl [with, together] system, synthesis, synchronize (time together), synonym, sympathy, symphony, syllable

trans, tra [across, beyond] transoceanic, transmit (send across), transfusion, tradition

tri [three] tricycle, triangle, tripod, tristate

ultra [beyond, exceedingly] ultramodern, ultraviolet, ultraconservative

un [not, release] unfair, unnatural, unknown

under [beneath] underground, underlying

uni [one] unicycle, uniform, unify, universe, unique (one of a kind)

vice [in place of] vice president, viceroy, vice admiral

Table D.1 Numerical Prefixes

Numerical Prefixes

Prefix	Symbol	Multiples and Submultiples	Equivalent	Prefix	Symbol	Multiples and Submultiples	Equivalent
tera	T	10^{12}	trillionfold	centi	c	10^{-2}	hundredth part
giga	G	10^{9}	billionfold	milli	m	10^{-3}	thousandth part
mega	M	10^{6}	millionfold	micro	u	10^{-6}	millionth part
kilo	k	10^{3}	thousandfold	nano	n	10^{-9}	billionth part
hecto	h	10^{2}	hundredfold	pico	p	10^{-12}	trillionth part
deka	da	10	tenfold	femto	f	10^{-15}	quadrillionth part
deci	d	10^{-1}	tenth part	atto	a	10^{-18}	quintillionth part

Suffixes

Suffixes come at the end of a word. Very often a suffix will tell you what kind of word it is part of (noun, adverb, adjective). For example, words ending in *-ly* are usually adverbs.

able, ible [able, can do] capable, agreeable, edible, visible (can be seen)

ade [result of action] blockade (the result of a blocking action), lemonade

age [act of, state of, collection of] salvage (act of saving), storage, forage

al [relating to] sensual, gradual, manual, natural (relating to nature)

algia [pain] neuralgia (nerve pain)

an, ian [native of, relating to] African, Canadian, Floridian

ance, ancy [action, process, state] assistance, allowance, defiance, truancy

ant [performing, agent] assistant, servant

ary, ery, ory [relating to, quality, place where] dictionary, bravery, dormitory

ate [cause, make] liquidate, segregate (cause a group to be set aside)

cian [having a certain skill or art] musician, beautician, magician, physician

cule, ling [very small] molecule, ridicule, duckling (very small duck), sapling

cy [action, function] hesitancy, prophecy, normalcy (function in a normal way)

dom [quality, realm, office] freedom, kingdom, wisdom (quality of being wise)

ee [one who receives the action] employee, nominee (one who is nominated), refugee

en [made of, make] silken, frozen, oaken (made of oak), wooden, lighten

ence, ency [action, state of, quality] difference, conference, urgency

er, or [one who, that which] baker, miller, teacher, racer, amplifier, doctor

escent [in the process of] adolescent (in the process of becoming an adult), obsolescent, convalescent

ese [a native of, the language of] Japanese, Vietnamese, Portuguese

esis, osis [action, process, condition] genesis, hypnosis, neurosis, osmosis

ess [female] actress, goddess, lioness

et, ette [a small one, group] midget, octet, baronet, majorette

fic [making, causing] scientific, specific

ful [full of] frightful, careful, helpful

fy [make] fortify (make strong), simplify, amplify

hood [order, condition, quality] manhood, womanhood, brotherhood

ic [nature of, like] metallic (of the nature of metal), heroic, poetic, acidic

ice [condition, state, quality] justice, malice

id, ide [a thing connected with or belonging to] fluid, fluoride

ile [relating to, suited for, capable of] missile, juvenile, senile (related to being old)

ine [nature of] feminine, genuine, medicine

ion, sion, tion [act of, state of, result of] contagion, aversion, infection (state of being infected)

ish [origin, nature, resembling] foolish, Irish, clownish (resembling a clown)

ism [system, manner, condition, characteristic] heroism, alcoholism, Communism

ist [one who, that which] artist, dentist

ite [nature of, quality of, mineral product] Israelite, dynamite, graphite, sulfite

ity, ty [state of, quality] captivity, clarity

ive [causing, making] abusive (causing abuse), exhaustive

ize [make] emphasize, publicize, idolize

less [without] baseless, careless (without care), artless, fearless, helpless

ly [like, manner of] carelessly, quickly, forcefully, lovingly

ment [act of, state of, result] contentment, amendment (state of amending)

ness [state of] carelessness, kindness

oid [resembling] asteroid, spheroid, tabloid, anthropoid

ology [study, science, theory] biology, anthropology, geology, neurology

ous [full of, having] gracious, nervous, spacious, vivacious (full of life)

ship [office, state, quality, skill] friendship, authorship, dictatorship

some [like, apt, tending to] lonesome, threesome, gruesome

tude [state of, condition of] gratitude, multitude (condition of being many), aptitude

ure [state of, act, process, rank] culture, literature, rupture (state of being broken)

ward [in the direction of] eastward, forward, backward

y [inclined to, tend to] cheery, crafty, faulty

Roots

A *root* is a base upon which other words are built (see Table D.2). Knowing the root of a difficult word can go a long way toward helping you figure out its meaning. For that reason, learning the following roots will be very valuable in all your classes.

acer, acid, acri [bitter, sour, sharp] acrid, acerbic, acidity (sourness), acrimony

acu [sharp] acute, acupuncture

ag, agi, ig, act [do, move, go] agent (doer), agenda (things to do), agitate, navigate (move by sea), ambiguous (going both ways), action

ali, allo, alter [other] alias (a person's other name), alibi, alien (from another place), alloy, alter (change to another form)

alt [high, deep] altimeter (a device for measuring heights), altitude

am, amor [love, liking] amiable, amorous, enamored

anni, annu, enni [year] anniversary, annually (yearly), centennial (occurring once in 100 years)

anthrop [man] anthropology (study of mankind), philanthropy (love of mankind), misanthrope (hater of mankind)

anti [old] antique, antiquated, antiquity

arch [chief, first, rule] archangel (chief angel), architect (chief worker), archaic (first, very early), monarchy (rule by one person), matriarchy (rule by the mother)

aster, astr [star] aster (star flower), asterisk, asteroid, astronomy (star law), astronaut (star traveler, space traveler)

aud, aus [hear, listen] audible (can be heard), auditorium, audio, audition, auditory, audience, ausculate

aug, auc [increase] augur, augment (add to; increase), auction

auto, aut [self] autograph (self-writing), automobile (self-moving vehicle), author, automatic (self-acting), autobiography

belli [war] rebellion, belligerent (warlike or hostile)

bibl [book] Bible, bibliography (list of books), bibliomania (craze for books), bibliophile (book lover)

bio [life] biology (study of life), biography, biopsy (cut living tissue for examination)

brev [short] abbreviate, brevity, brief

cad, cas [to fall] cadaver, cadence, caducous (falling off), cascade

calor [heat] calorie (a unit of heat), calorify (to make hot), caloric

cap, cip, cept [take] capable, capacity, capture, reciprocate, accept, except, concept

capit, capt [head] decapitate (to remove the head from), capital, captain, caption

carn [flesh] carnivorous (flesh eating), incarnate, reincarnation

caus, caut [burn, heat] caustic, cauterize (to make hot, to burn)

cause, cuse, cus [cause, motive] because, excuse (to attempt to remove the blame or cause), accusation

ced, ceed, cede, cess [move, yield, go, surrender] procedure, secede (move aside from), proceed (move forward), cede (yield), concede, intercede, precede, recede, success

centri [center] concentric, centrifugal, centripetal, eccentric (out of center)

chrom [color] chrome, chromosome (color body in genetics), chromosphere, monochrome (one color), polychrome

chron [time] chronological (in order of time), chronometer (time measured), chronicle (record of events in time), synchronize (make time with, set time together)

cide, cise [cut down, kill] suicide (killing of self), homicide (human killer), pesticide (pest killer), germicide (germ killer), insecticide, precise (cut exactly right), incision, scissors

cit [to call, start] incite, citation, cite

civ [citizen] civic (relating to a citizen), civil, civilian, civilization

clam, claim [cry out] exclamation, clamor, proclamation, reclamation, acclaim

clud, clus, claus [shut] include (to take in), conclude, claustrophobia (abnormal fear of being shut up, confined), recluse (one who shuts himself away from others)

cognosc, gnosi [know] recognize (to know again), incognito (not known), prognosis (forward knowing), diagnosis

cord, cor, cardi [heart] cordial (hearty, heartfelt), concord, discord, courage, encourage (put heart into), discourage (take heart out of), core, coronary, cardiac

corp [body] corporation (a legal body), corpse, corpulent

cosm [universe, world] cosmic, cosmos (the universe), cosmopolitan (world citizen), cosmonaut, microcosm, macrocosm

crat, cracy [rule, strength] democratic, autocracy

crea [create] creature (anything created), recreation, creation, creator

cred [believe] creed (statement of beliefs), credo (a creed), credence (belief), credit (belief, trust), credulous (believing too readily, easily deceived), incredible

cresc, cret, crease, cru [rise, grow] crescendo (growing in loudness or intensity), concrete (grown together, solidified), increase, decrease, accrue (to grow)

crit [separate, choose] critical, criterion (that which is used in choosing), hypocrite

cur, curs [run] concurrent, current (running or flowing), concur (run together, agree), incur (run into), recur, occur, precursor (forerunner), cursive

cura [care] curator, curative, manicure (caring for the hands)

cycl, cyclo [wheel, circular] Cyclops (a mythical giant with one eye in the middle of his forehead), unicycle, bicycle, cyclone (a wind blowing circularly, a tornado)

deca [ten] decade, decalogue, decathlon

dem [people] democracy (people-rule), demography (vital statistics of the people: deaths, births, and so on), epidemic (on or among the people)

dent, dont [tooth] dental (relating to teeth), denture, dentifrice, orthodontist

derm [skin] hypodermic (injected under the skin), dermatology (skin study), epidermis (outer layer of skin), taxidermy (arranging skin; mounting animals)

dict [say, speak] diction (how one speaks, what one says), dictionary, dictate, dictator, dictaphone, dictatorial, edict, predict, verdict, contradict, benediction

doc [teach] indoctrinate, document, doctrine

domin [master] dominate, dominion, predominant, domain

don [give] donate, condone

dorm [sleep] dormant, dormitory

dox [opinion, praise] doxy (belief, creed, or opinion), orthodox (having the correct, commonly accepted opinion), heterodox (differing opinion), paradox (contradictory)

drome [run, step] syndrome (run-together symptoms), hippodrome (a place where horses run)

duc, duct [lead] produce, induce (lead into, persuade), seduce (lead aside), reduce, aqueduct (water leader or channel), viaduct, conduct

dura [hard, lasting] durable, duration, endurance

dynam [power] dynamo (power producer), dynamic, dynamite, hydrodynamics

endo [within] endoral (within the mouth), endocardial (within the heart), endoskeletal

equi [equal] equinox, equilibrium

erg [work] energy, erg (unit of work), allergy, ergophobia (morbid fear of work), ergometer, ergonomic

fac, fact, fic, fect [do, make] factory (place where workers make goods of various kinds), fact (a thing done), manufacture, amplification, confection

fall, fals [deceive] fallacy, falsify

fer [bear, carry] ferry (carry by water), coniferous (bearing cones, as a pine tree), fertile (bearing richly), defer, infer, refer

fid, fide, feder [faith, trust] confidant, Fido, fidelity, confident, infidelity, infidel, federal, confederacy

fila, fili [thread] filament (a single thread or threadlike object), filibuster, filigree

fin [end, ended, finished] final, finite, finish, confine, fine, refine, define, finale

fix [attach] fix, fixation (the state of being attached), fixture, affix, prefix, suffix

flex, flect [bend] flex, reflex (bending back), flexible, flexor (muscle for bending), inflexibility, reflect, deflect

flu, fluc, fluv [flowing] influence (to flow in), fluid, flue, flush, fluently, fluctuate (to wave in an unsteady motion)

form [form, shape] form, uniform, conform, deform, reform, perform, formative, formation, formal, formula

fort, forc [strong] fort, fortress (a strong place), fortify (make strong), forte (one's strong point), fortitude, enforce

fract, frag [break] fracture (a break), infraction, fragile (easy to break), fraction (result of breaking a whole into equal parts), refract (to break or bend)

gam [marriage] bigamy (two marriages), monogamy, polygamy (many spouses or marriages)

gastr(o) [stomach] gastric, gastronomic, gastritis (inflammation of the stomach)

gen [birth, race, produce] genesis (birth, beginning), genetics (study of heredity), eugenics (well born), genealogy (lineage by race, stock), generate, genetic

geo [earth] geometry (earth measurement), geography (earth writing), geocentric (earth centered), geology

germ [vital part] germination (to grow), germ (seed; living substance, as the germ of an idea), germane

gest [carry, bear] congest (bear together, clog), congestive (causing clogging), gestation

gloss, glot [tongue] glossary, polyglot (many tongues), epiglottis

glu, glo [lump, bond, glue] glue, agglutinate (make to hold in a bond), conglomerate (bond together)

grad, gress [step, go] grade (step, degree), gradual (step-by-step), graduate (make all the steps, finish a course), graduated (in steps or degrees), progress

graph, gram [write, written] graph, graphic (written, vivid), autograph (self-writing, signature), graphite (carbon used for writing), photography (light writing), phonograph (sound writing), diagram, bibliography, telegram

grat [pleasing] gratuity (mark of favor, a tip), congratulate (express pleasure over success), grateful, ingrate (not thankful)

grav [heavy, weighty] grave, gravity, aggravate, gravitate

greg [herd, group, crowd] gregarian (belonging to a herd), congregation (a group functioning together), segregate (tending to group aside or apart)

helio [sun] heliograph (an instrument for using the sun's rays to send signals), heliotrope (a plant that turns to the sun)

hema, hemo [blood] hemorrhage (an outpouring or flowing of blood), hemoglobin, hemophilia

here, hes [stick] adhere, cohere, cohesion

hetero [different] heterogeneous (different in birth), heterosexual (with interest in the opposite sex)

homo [same] homogeneous (of same birth or kind), homonym (word with same pronunciation as another), homogenize

hum, human [earth, ground, man] humus, exhume (to take out of the ground), humane (compassion for other humans)

hydr, hydra, hydro [water] dehydrate, hydrant, hydraulic, hydraulics, hydrogen, hydrophobia (fear of water)

hypn [sleep] hypnosis, Hypnos (god of sleep), hypnotherapy (treatment of disease by hypnosis)

ignis [fire] ignite, igneous, ignition

ject [throw] deject, inject, project (throw forward), eject, object

join, junct [join] adjoining, enjoin (to lay an order upon, to command), juncture, conjunction, injunction

juven [young] juvenile, rejuvenate (to make young again)

lau, lav, lot, lut [wash] launder, lavatory, lotion, ablution (a washing away), dilute (to make a liquid thinner and weaker)

leg [law] legal (lawful; according to law), legislate (to enact a law), legislature, legitimize (make legal)

levi [light] alleviate (lighten a load), levitate, levity (light conversation; humor)

liber, liver [free] liberty (freedom), liberal, liberalize (to make more free), deliverance

liter [letters] literary (concerned with books and writing), literature, literal, alliteration, obliterate

loc, loco [place] locality, locale, location, allocate (to assign, to place), relocate (to put back into place), locomotion (act of moving from place to place)

log, logo, ogue, ology [word, study, speech] catalog, prologue, dialogue, logogram (a symbol representing a word), zoology (animal study), psychology (mind study)

loqu, locut [talk, speak] eloquent (speaking well and forcefully), soliloquy, locution, loquacious (talkative), colloquial (talking together; conversational or informal)

luc, lum, lus, lun [light] translucent (letting light come through), lumen (a unit of light), luminary (a heavenly body; someone who shines in his or her profession), luster (sparkle, shine), Luna (the moon goddess)

magn [great] magnify (make great, enlarge), magnificent, magnanimous (great of mind or spirit), magnate, magnitude, magnum

man [hand] manual, manage, manufacture, manacle, manicure, manifest, maneuver, emancipate

mand [command] mandatory (commanded), remand (order back), mandate

mania [madness] mania (insanity, craze), monomania (mania on one idea), kleptomania, pyromania (insane tendency to set fires), maniac

mar, mari, mer [sea, pool] marine (a soldier serving on a ship), marsh (wetland, swamp), maritime (relating to the sea and navigation), mermaid (fabled sea creature: half fish, half woman)

matri [mother] maternal (relating to the mother), matrimony, matriarchate (rulership of women), matron

medi [half, middle, between, halfway] mediate (come between, intervene), medieval (pertaining to the Middle Ages), Mediterranean (lying between lands), mediocre, medium

mega [great, million] megaphone (great sound), megalopolis (great city; an extensive urban area including a number of cities), megacycle (a million cycles), megaton

mem [remember] memo (a reminder), commemoration (the act of remembering by a memorial or ceremony), memento, memoir, memorable

meter [measure] meter (a metric measure), voltameter (instrument to measure volts), barometer, thermometer

micro [small] microscope, microfilm, microcard, microwave, micrometer (device for measuring small distances), omicron, micron (a millionth of a meter), microbe (small living thing)

migra [wander] migrate (to wander), emigrate (one who leaves a country), immigrate (to come into the land)

mit, miss [send] emit (send out, give off), remit (send back, as money due), submit, admit, commit, permit, transmit (send across), omit, intermittent (sending between, at intervals), mission, missile

mob, mot, mov [move] mobile (capable of moving), motionless (without motion), motor, emotional (moved strongly by feelings), motivate, promotion, demote, movement

mon [warn, remind] monument (a reminder or memorial of a person or an event), admonish (warn), monitor, premonition (forewarning)

mor, mort [mortal, death] mortal (causing death or destined for death), immortal (not subject to death), mortality (rate of death), mortician (one who prepares the dead for burial), mortuary (place for the dead, a morgue)

morph [form] amorphous (with no form, shapeless), metamorphosis (a change of form, as a caterpillar into a butterfly), morphology

multi [many, much] multifold (folded many times), multilinguist (one who speaks many languages), multiped (an organism with many feet), multiply nat, nasc [to be born, to spring forth] innate (inborn), natal, native, nativity, renascence (a rebirth, a revival)

neur [nerve] neuritis (inflammation of a nerve), neurology (study of nervous systems), neurologist (one who practices neurology), neural, neurosis, neurotic

nom [law, order] autonomy (self-law, self-government), astronomy, gastronomy (art or science of good eating), economy

nomen, nomin [name] nomenclature, nominate (name someone for an office)

nov [new] novel (new, strange, not formerly known), renovate (to make like new again), novice, nova, innovate

nox, noc [night] nocturnal, equinox (equal nights), noctilucent (shining by night)

numer [number] numeral (a figure expressing a number), numeration (act of counting), enumerate (count out, one by one), innumerable

omni [all, every] omnipotent (all-powerful), omniscient (all-knowing), omnipresent (present everywhere), omnivorous

onym [name] anonymous (without name), synonym, pseudonym (false name), antonym (name of opposite meaning)

oper [work] operate (to labor, function), cooperate (work together)

ortho [straight, correct] orthodox (of the correct or accepted opinion), orthodontist (tooth straightener), orthopedic (originally pertaining to straightening a child), unorthodox

pac [peace] pacifist (one for peace only; opposed to war), pacify (make peace, quiet), Pacific Ocean (peaceful ocean)

pan [all] panacea (cure-all), pandemonium (place of all the demons, wild disorder), pantheon (place of all the gods in mythology)

pater, patr [father] paternity (fatherhood, responsibility), patriarch (head of the tribe, family), patriot, patron (a wealthy person who supports as would a father)

path, pathy [feeling, suffering] pathos (feeling of pity, sorrow), sympathy, antipathy (feeling against), apathy (without feeling), empathy (feeling or identifying with another), telepathy (far feeling; thought transference)

ped, pod [foot] pedal (lever for a foot), impede (get the feet in a trap, hinder), pedestal (foot or base of a statue), pedestrian (foot traveler), centipede, tripod (three-footed support), podiatry (care of the feet), antipodes (opposite feet)

pedo [child] orthopedic, pedagogue (child leader; teacher), pediatrics (medical care of children)

pel, puls [drive, urge] compel, dispel, expel, repel, propel, pulse, impulse, pulsate, compulsory, expulsion, repulsive

pend, pens, pond [hang, weigh] pendant pendulum, suspend, appendage, pensive (weighing thought), ponderous

phil [love] philosophy (love of wisdom), philanthropy, philharmonic, bibliophile, Philadelphia (city of brotherly love)

phobia [fear] claustrophobia (fear of closed spaces), acrophobia (fear of high places), hydrophobia (fear of water)

phon [sound] phonograph, phonetic (pertaining to sound), symphony (sounds with or together)

photo [light] photograph (light-writing), photoelectric, photogenic (artistically suitable for being photographed), photosynthesis (action of light on chlorophyll to make carbohydrates)

plac [please] placid (calm, peaceful), placebo, placate, complacent

plu, plur, plus [more] plural (more than one), pluralist (a person who holds more than one office), plus (indicating that something more is to be added)

pneuma, pneumon [breath] pneumatic (pertaining to air, wind, or other gases), pneumonia (disease of the lungs)

pod (see ped)

poli [city] metropolis (mother city), police, politics, Indianapolis, Acropolis (high city, upper part of Athens), megalopolis

pon, pos, pound [place, put] postpone (put afterward), component, opponent (one put against), proponent, expose, impose, deposit, posture (how one places oneself), position, expound, impound

pop [people] population, populous (full of people), popular

port [carry] porter (one who carries), portable, transport (carry across), report, export, import, support, transportation

portion [part, share] portion (a part; a share, as a portion of pie), proportion (the relation of one share to others)

prehend [seize] comprehend (seize with the mind), apprehend (seize a criminal), comprehensive (seizing much, extensive)

prim, prime [first] primacy (state of being first in rank), prima donna (the first lady of opera), primitive (from the earliest or first time), primary, primal, primeval

proto [first] prototype (the first model made), protocol, protagonist, protozoan

psych [mind, soul] psyche (soul, mind), psychiatry (healing of the mind), psychology, psychosis (serious mental disorder), psychotherapy (mind treatment), psychic

punct [point, dot] punctual (being exactly on time), punctuation, puncture, acupuncture

reg, recti [straighten] regiment, regular, regulate, rectify (make straight), correct, direction ri, ridi, risi [laughter] deride (mock, jeer at), ridicule (laughter at the expense of another, mockery), ridiculous, derision

rog, roga [ask] prerogative (privilege; asking before), interrogation (questioning; the act of questioning), derogatory

rupt [break] rupture (break), interrupt (break into), abrupt (broken off), disrupt (break apart), erupt (break out), incorruptible (unable to be broken down)

sacr, sanc, secr [sacred] sacred, sanction, sacrosanct, consecrate, desecrate

salv, salu [safe, healthy] salvation (act of being saved), salvage, salutation

sat, satis [enough] saturate, satisfy (to give as much as is needed)

sci [know] science (knowledge), conscious (knowing, aware), omniscient (knowing everything)

scope [see, watch] telescope, microscope, kaleidoscope (instrument for seeing beautiful forms), periscope, stethoscope

scrib, script [write] scribe (a writer), scribble, manuscript (written by hand), inscribe, describe, subscribe, prescribe

sed, sess, sid [sit] sediment (that which sits or settles out of a liquid), session (a sitting), obsession (an idea that sits stubbornly in the mind), possess, preside (sit before), president, reside, subside

sen [old] senior, senator, senile (old; showing the weakness of old age)

sent, sens [feel] sentiment (feeling), consent, resent, dissent, sentimental (having strong feeling or emotion), sense, sensation, sensitive, sensory, dissension

sequ, secu, sue [follow] sequence (following of one thing after another), sequel, consequence, subsequent, prosecute, consecutive (following in order), second (following "first"), ensue, pursue

serv [save, serve] servant, service, preserve, subservient, servitude, conserve, reservation, deserve, conservation

sign, signi [sign, mark, seal] signal (a gesture or sign to call attention), signature (the mark of a person written in his or her own handwriting), design, insignia (distinguishing marks)

simil, simul [like, resembling] similar (resembling in many respects), assimilate (to make similar to), simile, simulate (pretend; put on an act to make a certain impression)

sist, sta, stit [stand] persist (stand firmly; unyielding; continue), assist (to stand by with help), circumstance, stamina (power to withstand, to endure), status (standing), state, static, stable, stationary, substitute (to stand in for another)

solus [alone] soliloquy, solitaire, solitude, solo

solv, solu [loosen] solvent (a loosener, a dissolver), solve, absolve (loosen from, free from), resolve, soluble, solution, resolution, resolute, dissolute (loosened morally)

somnus [sleep] insomnia (not being able to sleep), somnambulist (a sleepwalker)

soph [wise] sophomore (wise fool), philosophy (love of wisdom), sophisticated

spec, spect, spic [look] specimen (an example to look at, study), specific, aspect, spectator (one who looks), spectacle, speculate, inspect, respect, prospect, retrospective (looking backward), introspective, expect, conspicuous

sphere [ball, sphere] stratosphere (the upper portion of the atmosphere), hemisphere (half of the earth), spheroid

spir [breath] spirit (breath), conspire (breathe together; plot), inspire (breathe into), aspire (breathe toward), expire (breathe out; die), perspire, respiration

string, strict [draw tight] stringent (drawn tight; rigid), strict, restrict, constrict (draw tightly together), boa constrictor (snake that constricts its prey)

stru, struct [build] construe (build in the mind, interpret), structure, construct, instruct, obstruct, destruction, destroy

sume, sump [take, use, waste] consume (to use up), assume (to take; to use), sump pump (a pump that takes up water), presumption (to take or use before knowing all the facts)

tact, tang, tag, tig, ting [touch] contact, tactile, intangible (not able to be touched), intact (untouched, uninjured), tangible, contingency, contagious (able to transmit disease by touching), contiguous

tele [far] telephone (far sound), telegraph (far writing), television (far seeing), telephoto (far photography), telecast

tempo [time] tempo (rate of speed), temporary, extemporaneously, contemporary (those who live at the same time), pro tem (for the time being)

ten, tin, tain [hold] tenacious (holding fast), tenant, tenure, untenable, detention, content, pertinent, continent, obstinate, abstain, pertain, detain

tend, tent, tens [stretch, strain] tendency (a stretching; leaning), extend, intend, contend, pretend, superintend, tender, extent, tension (a stretching, strain), pretense

terra [earth] terrain, terrarium, territory, terrestrial

test [to bear witness] testament (a will; bearing witness to someone's wishes), detest, attest (bear witness to), testimony

the, theo [God, a god] monotheism (belief in one god), polytheism (belief in many gods), atheism, theology

therm [heat] thermometer, therm (heat unit), thermal, thermostat, thermos, hypothermia (subnormal temperature)

thesis, thet [place, put] antithesis (place against), hypothesis (place under), synthesis (put together), epithet tom [cut] atom (not cuttable; smallest particle of matter), appendectomy (cutting out an appendix), tonsillectomy, dichotomy (cutting in two; a division), anatomy (cutting, dissecting to study structure)

tort, tors [twist] torture (twisting to inflict pain), retort (twist back, reply sharply), extort (twist out), distort (twist out of shape), contort, torsion (act of twisting, as a torsion bar)

tox [poison] toxic (poisonous), intoxicate, antitoxin

tract, tra [draw, pull] tractor, attract, subtract, tractable (can be handled), abstract (to draw away), subtrahend (the number to be drawn away from another)

trib [pay, bestow] tribute (to pay honor to), contribute (to give money to a cause), attribute, retribution, tributary

turbo [disturb] turbulent, disturb, turbid, turmoil

typ [print] type, prototype (first print; model), typical, typography, typewriter, typology (study of types, symbols), typify

ultima [last] ultimate, ultimatum (the final or last offer that can be made)

uni [one] unicorn (a legendary creature with one horn), unify (make into one), university, unanimous, universal

vac [empty] vacate (to make empty), vacuum (a space entirely devoid of matter), evacuate (to remove troops or people), vacation, vacant

vale, vali, valu [strength, worth] valiant, equivalent (of equal worth), validity (truth; legal strength), evaluate (find out the value), value, valor (value; worth)

ven, vent [come] convene (come together, assemble), intervene (come between), venue, convenient, avenue, circumvent (come or go around), invent, prevent

ver, veri [true] very, aver (say to be true, affirm), verdict, verity (truth), verify (show to be true), verisimilitude

vert, vers [turn] avert (turn away), divert (turn aside, amuse), invert (turn over), introvert (turn inward), convertible, reverse (turn back), controversy (a turning against; a dispute), versatile (turning easily from one skill to another)

vic, vicis [change, substitute] vicarious, vicar, vicissitude

vict, vinc [conquer] victor (conqueror, winner), evict (conquer out, expel), convict (prove guilty), convince (conquer mentally, persuade), invincible (not conquerable)

vid, vis [see] video, television, evident, provide, providence, visible, revise, supervise (oversee), vista, visit, vision

viv, vita, vivi [alive, life] revive (make live again), survive (live beyond, outlive), vivid, vivacious (full of life), vitality

voc [call] vocation (a calling), avocation (occupation not one's calling), convocation (a calling together), invocation, vocal

vol [will] malevolent, benevolent (one of goodwill), volunteer, volition

volcan, vulcan [fire] volcano (a mountain erupting fiery lava), volcanize (to undergo volcanic heat), Vulcan (Roman god of fire)

volvo [turn about, roll] revolve, voluminous (winding), voluble (easily turned about or around), convolution (a twisting)

vor [eat greedily] voracious, carnivorous (flesh eating), herbivorous (plant eating), omnivorous (eating everything), devour

zo [animal] zoo (short for zoological garden), zoology (study of animal life), zodiac (circle of animal constellations), zoomorphism (being in the form of an animal), protozoa (one-celled animals)

Table D.2 The Human Body

The Human Body

capit	head	gastro	stomach	osteo	bone
card	heart	glos	tongue	ped	foot
corp	body	hema	blood	pneuma	breathe
dent	tooth	man	hand	psych	mind
derm	skin	neur	nerve	spir	breath